SOHO ON SCREEN

SOHO ON SCREEN

CINEMATIC SPACES OF BOHEMIA AND COSMOPOLITANISM, 1948–1963

Jingan Young

berghahn
NEW YORK • OXFORD
www.berghahnbooks.com

First published in 2022 by
Berghahn Books
www.berghahnbooks.com

© 2022, 2025 Jingan Young
First paperback edition published in 2025

All rights reserved. Except for the quotation of short passages for the purposes of criticism and review, no part of this book may be reproduced in any form or by any means, electronic or mechanical, including photocopying, recording, or any information storage and retrieval system now known or to be invented, without written permission of the publisher.

Library of Congress Cataloging-in-Publication Data
A C.I.P. cataloging record is available from the Library of Congress
Library of Congress Cataloging in Publication Control Number: 2021052781

British Library Cataloguing in Publication Data
A catalogue record for this book is available from the British Library

ISBN 978-1-80073-477-7 hardback
ISBN 978-1-80539-729-8 paperback
ISBN 978-1-80539-931-5 epub
ISBN 978-1-80073-478-4 web pdf

https://doi.org/10.3167/9781800734777

Contents

List of Figures	vii
Foreword Peter Bradshaw	ix
Acknowledgements	xi
Introduction. Soho, 'The Forbidden City'	1
1 Tracking Shot: Soho Square to Wardour Street, London's 'Film Row'	9
2 Soho's Bohemian-Cosmopolitans and Postwar British Cinema	25
3 'God Is Everywhere!': Engineering the Immigrant Landscape of *Miracle in Soho* (1957)	46
4 Soho-Hollywood: The Birth of the Soho 'B' Film	70
5 Old Perils, New Pleasures: *West End Jungle* (1961) and the Birth of Commercial Vice	88
6 'An' I Fort Jews Were Supposed to Be Lucky!': Jewish Wide Boys, Johnny Jackson and Sammy Lee	102
7 Soho Melodrama: Cinematic Spaces of Sexual Blackmail, *The Flesh Is Weak* (1957) and *The Shakedown* (1960)	122
8 Subversive Female Sexualities and the Soho Coffee Bar: *Beat Girl* (1960) and *Rag Doll* (1961)	143
9 Soho Strip Clubs (Part One): The Windmill Theatre and Its Cinematic Legacy	164

10 Soho Strip Clubs (Part Two): The Stage and the Dressing Room   181

Conclusion. 'Warm-Hearted Tarts' and the Year 'Old Soho' Died:
    Campaigns, Rebirth and *The World Ten Times Over* (1963)   194

Filmography   211

Bibliography   215

Index   245

Figures

0.1.	Map of Soho, 1720	xii
1.1.	Jim's late-night ramble in Soho. Still from *Spin a Dark Web/Soho Incident*	12
2.1a.	Berwick Street Market from above. Still from *Sunshine in Soho*	26
2.1b.	Young dancers from the Italia Conti School perform in Soho Square. Still from *Sunshine in Soho*	28
3.1a.	Opening tracking shot across Soho from *Miracle in Soho*	47
3.1b.	Meeting Mr Bishop (Cyril Cusack). Still from the opening of *Miracle in Soho*	47
3.1c.	Marking the boundaries of St Anthony's Lane. Still from the opening of *Miracle in Soho*	48
3.1d.	A Chinese family observe the disturbance. Still from the opening of *Miracle in Soho*	48
3.1e.	The road gang close the lane. Still from the opening of *Miracle in Soho*	49
3.2a.	Mr Swoboda's Bakery. Still from *Miracle in Soho*	55
3.2b.	The Anacapri Restaurant. Still from *Miracle in Soho*	55
3.2c.	The Pig and Pot Pub. Still from *Miracle in Soho*	56
3.2d.	Mrs Coleman's pet shop. Still from *Miracle in Soho*	56
3.2e.	St Anthony's Church. Still from *Miracle in Soho*	57
4.1.	Linda (Carole Landis) prepares to take down Sugiani with the help of her fiancé, a local boxing club and the London Metropolitan Police. Still from *Noose*	75
5.1.	Director Arnold L. Miller 're-creates' sex work on the streets of London. Still from *West End Jungle*	95
6.1.	Johnny swindles Leon whilst grabbing 'the worst salt beef sandwiches in Soho' at his coffee bar. Still, *Expresso Bongo*	103
6.2.	Sammy as MC of the Peep Show Club. Still, *The Small World of Sammy Lee*	112

7.1. The clip-joint where Marissa receives her first payment from a client for entertaining him all evening. Still from *The Flesh Is Weak*   133
8.1. Jennifer dances with an uncredited Oliver Reed in the underground club at the Off-Beat Café. Still from *Beat Girl*   144
8.2. Carol (Christina Gregg) arrives in Soho. Still, *Rag Doll*   153
10.1. Maisie (Sylvia Syms) performs at the In-Time Theatre. Still from *Expresso Bongo*   183

Foreword
Peter Bradshaw

When I met Jingan Young to talk about Jules Dassin's movie *Night and the City* for her Soho and film podcast, it was at the Curzon Soho Cinema on Shaftesbury Avenue, a road that slopes down like London's Broadway to Piccadilly. The cinema is just over the road from Chinatown, and down from Cambridge Circus. Our conversation took place in a Soho that Jules Dassin would probably have recognised, and that Gerald Kersh, author of the original book, would also have recognised. Bounded (roughly) by Shaftesbury Avenue to the south, Regent Street to the west, Tottenham Court Road to the east and the Oxford Street to the north, Soho is a dense area of media activity, daytime drinking, clubbing and bohemianism, and until recently it was the epicentre of the sleaze industry and bought sex trade, which for decades was more or less comanaged by the corrupt officers of the Met's Obscene Publications Squad – the 'dirty squad'.

It has been cleaned up a lot recently – garish sex clubs and furtive spielers are now Pret-A-Mangers. A sex cinema that was shamelessly right on Piccadilly Circus is now a gleamingly gigantic Gap. I'm incidentally not at all sentimental and romantic about Soho's nasty, seedy past, which was all about the exploitation of women. But I have a certain connection with a part of London that has been my place of work for almost twenty years: I go to press screenings in little private cinemas that are worryingly like the smut cinemas of old. Just down from where Jingan and I had our chat is the Queen's Theatre, showing *Les Miserables*, where I was listlessly propositioned by a woman in the middle of the morning. That was a while ago, in the pre-hookup-app, pre-internet age.

I remember hanging around nervously, with a bunch of other people in Brewer Street, near the bizarrely bulbous NCP car park building, while an extremely dodgy bloke did the three-card monte on an upturned cardboard box: Find the Lady, an ace, a queen and an ace, asking you to have a go without betting, at first: 'No money, mate, no money, no money, just for fun, just for fun. Which one do you think it is?' This is while his extremely dodgy mates crowded round the back of you, making it unsubtly harder for you to leave. And another dodgy mate would have the job of pretending to see a copper coming along when it suited the card sharp to take your money and pack up for the day.

It was nearby, in Greek Street, that I had an epic lunch with the late Christopher Hitchens in the now defunct restaurant The Gay Hussar, surely the last place in Soho, or anywhere in the English-speaking world, that still used the word 'gay' in its old nonhomosexual sense. I remember staggering out into Soho Square at about 4 PM drunker than I would be on a Saturday night. But Christopher was unaffected.

I've been drinking at Black's and in the Groucho (both in Dean Street), at the Coach and Horses when it was the site of the Private Eye lunches, and in the Colony Room Club in the era of Ian Board and Muriel Belcher, though sadly never setting eyes on Francis Bacon. And relatively recently, I took a lairy minicab home after a rousing evening at Soho House in Greek Street and the driver tried to sell me a gun.

The strangely sinister anti-glamour of Soho is still there in real life, and yet it's also preserved in the movies that Jingan writes about so well. I experience it in both senses, and that's why I'm glad that Jingan has written this book.

Peter Bradshaw has been chief film critic of *The Guardian* since 1999 and has recently published *The Films That Made Me*, an edited selection of his essays and reviews. He has also published three novels, of which the most recent is *Night of Triumph*.

Acknowledgements

First, I must thank Peter Bradshaw for his beautiful Foreword and ongoing support. Thank you to Charles Drazin for providing access to the archive of Film Finances, the collection teams at the British Film Institute's National Archive, Jacob Smith from the British Board of Film Classification, Matthew Garbutt for lending me his 'Films and Filming' archive, Sarah Cronin-Stanley of Talking Pictures Television, the Soho community for welcoming me with open arms, Leslie Hardcastle and Clare Lynch of the Soho Society, and Tony Shrimplin of the Museum of Soho. Thank you to those scholars, critics and producers who assisted me in both my research and engaging with the wider community through my podcasts and interviews: Henry Miller, Melanie Williams, John Hill and Dom Delargy. Finally, thank you to my doctoral supervisors from King's College London, Lawrence Napper and Mark Shiel. I must also thank the team at Photo Fest and of course, my editors at Berghahn Books, Amanda Horn, Sulaiman Ahmad and Caroline Kuhtz.

The pursuit of this research has proved to be one of the most rewarding experiences of my life. For over half a decade, I wholly immersed myself in the fabric of Soho's past, present and future. In 2009, when I moved to London from Hong Kong, once a cosmopolitan locus in its own right, it was through the passageway of Soho that a young émigré fell in love with a city.

This book is dedicated to my husband Slane and my mother Kerrie for their love, encouragement, support, and advice. I also dedicate this book to my son Ydra and lastly, to Soho.

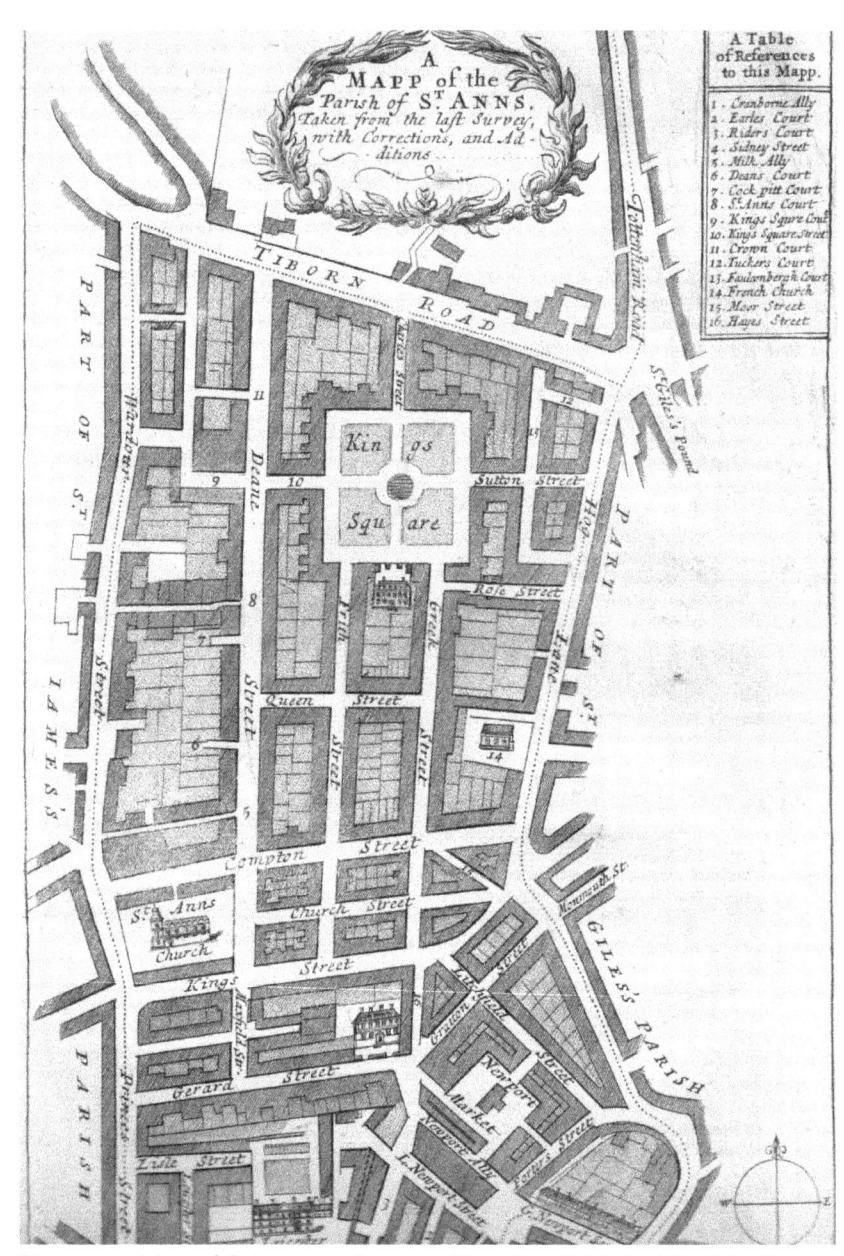

Figure 0.1. Map of Soho, 1720. Survey of London. Published by John Strype from a plate originally published by John Stow. Author's own

INTRODUCTION
Soho, 'The Forbidden City'

Soho is a film.

—Colin MacInnes, 1959

Soho is like 'The Forbidden City'.

—Leslie Hardcastle (OBE), 2015

Soho Histories

London's Soho is no longer considered the *demi-monde* of the metropolis. Like an urban village, its rapid gentrification has led to the sanitisation of its bohemian and cosmopolitan past. Since the turn of the twenty-first century, public campaigns, concerned with its preservation as a site of subcultures, have admirably sought to protect its reputation in the public imagination as a melting pot of desire, subversion and transgression. After the Second World War, Soho's reputation as a permissive space for hedonists, beatniks, impresarios, restauranteurs, striptease artists and spivs was cemented in the public imagination by bohemian writers and filmmakers. This constructed identity was deeply rooted in its historical function as a refuge for immigrants and its early modern development as a centre of consumption. The birth of this bifurcated identity transpired during the commercial renaissance to the area following the devastation of the war, dictated by local entrepreneurs, in consonance with the popular press, who promoted their diverse businesses, from coffee shops to strip clubs, to the nation and the world as inherently cosmopolitan with a strong undercurrent of bohemian sensibility. Furthermore, they explicitly linked themselves to the area's blossoming commercial vice industries in order to cater to a new audience that included a postwar generation who no longer felt bound by prewar conservative attitudes towards public displays of nudity.

How did Soho garner such a multifarious reputation in the public imagination? In 1925, Reverend Wilson, then-rector of St Anne's Church, illuminated readers of his book *The Story of Soho* with the etymology of Soho's unusual name. Pronounced 'So-Hoe!, the name was 'originally a hunting cry … applied to this district as early as 1632, when it occurs in the Rate books of St. Martins-in-the-Fields, the Mother Parish'.[1] One article published in 1897 stated: 'Some have considered that the neighbourhood owes its name to the cry with which footpads (highwaymen operating on foot) used to greet their victims when money was often sacrificed for the sake of life.'[2] There is often confusion with the famed district called 'SoHo' in Manhattan, New York, which refers to the area located south of Houston Street. There is also a suggestion that the origins of Soho's name could similarly refer to its location south of the area of Holborn in London. However, this explanation is largely disputed. Soho is also one of London's youngest districts. In *Capital Affairs London and the Making of the Permissive Society* (2010), Frank Mort has described the early modern development of Soho after 1820 whereby 'four major thoroughfares … either constructed or substantially remodelled … came to form Soho's material and symbolic outer limits. Oxford Street to the north, Coventry Street to the south, Charing Cross Road to the east, and Regent Street to the west functioned as Soho's boundary line, enclosing the area in a great 'rectangle' or what was more precisely a skewed parallelogram'.[3] Judith Summers similarly described the area in her celebrated history, *Soho: A History of London's Most Colourful Neighbourhood* (1989) as 'a small island land-locked in London's West End, where for 300 years it has held away … half a square mile in size, it is cut off from the metropolis … Soho is a place to linger in'[4] (see Figure 0.1).

The Biographical City

As an immigrant in London who was born in Hong Kong, before the former British colony was handed back to the People's Republic of China in 1997, my engagement with London and Soho began long before my arrival. Historically, Hong Kong has held a similar role to Soho as both a commercial centre and refuge for immigrants. Soho's multifarious identity continues to be defined by its function as a commercial centre, as well as its role as a place of refuge, cultural tourism, and lucrative opportunities for investment and trade.[5] Working on this project has been an unadulterated joy, notwithstanding the fact I too discovered the city of London through the gateway of Soho, due to its proximity to my university campus, alongside my innate desire to seek out the comforts of home in Chinatown. This area, although it is much younger than Soho (it was confirmed officially as London's Chinatown only in the mid-1980s by the local Westminster Council), remains one of the main draws for tourists visiting the area today.

Therefore, despite Soho's rich cultural history, prior, celebrated function as the locus for the British film industry and the growth in literature examining the relationship between cinema and the city in the last twenty years, it is peculiar that there remains an absence of scholarship on the cinematic representation of this urban space. Until recently, the city of London has 'not been among those privileged cinematic cites' such as Berlin, New York, Paris and Los Angeles.[6] Charlotte Brunsdon was one of the first scholars to publish a dedicated and extensive examination on London in film. My interest in pursuing Soho as a research subject was greatly influenced by Brunsdon, who argued the iconography of London is a 'complex imbrication of narratives' that existed long before the age of cinema.[7] In her own analysis of Soho, she describes it as an 'an alluring place which promises an escape from the everyday, the ordinary and local. This was a geography of pleasure for all classes of people'.[8] I believe too that Soho is a temporal space, 'not directionally or geographically coherent ... it is also a gendered cinematic space of sensation and attractions'.[9] She has also briefly remarked upon the fact that 'Soho [in British films and television] deserves a book of its own'.[10] This book attempts to address this absence, tracing Soho's screen identity amidst shifting debates around British national identity, London's immigrant history, youth culture, sex and commercialism, as well as the British film industry's relationship with Hollywood, before looking ahead to Soho's gentrification and the rebranding of contemporary Soho.

The Cinematic City

My decision to embark on an investigation of cinematic Soho was greatly encouraged by Brunsdon's focus on the ways in which London is *read* for the modern city is 'relational [and] each particular location in a film is rendered meaningful by its relation to the other locations'.[11] Although films that claim London as their setting 'must engage with the hegemonic discourse of location', there are further complications because of London's role in relation to the rest of

Britain.[12] The capital city must be understood cinematically in the same way as it is understood historically, 'between the West and East Ends, north and south of the river, and the West End, city and the suburbs'.[13] However, besides the city's connection to the nation historically (the British Empire) and politically (Whitehall), London can also be understood from the 'point of view of a life lived in it'.[14]

This book takes a step further by drawing on the work of urban scholars in order to 'illuminate the live spaces of the city and urban societies ... in the context of global capitalism'.[15] The legacy of urban theorists from the 1920s and 1930s such as Georg Simmel, Walter Benjamin, and Louis Wirth are interwoven into the very fabric of cinema's negotiation with the irrationalities of metropolitan life that Simmel identified as the 'intensification of nervous stimulation which results from the swift and uninterrupted change of outer and inner stimuli'.[16] The mechanism of cinema similarly produces a cascade of 'onrushing impressions'.[17] Postwar urban studies by Jurgen Habermas and Siegfried Kracauer impacted scholarship of city and cinema through the practice of examining space and spatialisation.[18] By delving deeper into the way in which a city film is spatially organised, we may uncover new and significantly intense meanings behind the engagement between spectator and space.

British cinema has a long tradition of structuring the cinematic city within specific iconographic markers, and as responses to rapid social and historical changes within a post-imperial world. David Robinson has argued that: 'Every sustained period of success of the British film has seemed to be based in a realist approach to contemporary life'.[19] For Soho films, 'realism' is largely isolated to its representation of sexuality and cosmopolitanism. As John Hill has argued, British films 'do more than just "reflect"; they also actively explain and interpret the way in which the world is to be perceived and understood'.[20] Postwar Soho films also reveal more complex representations of the area's development, reflecting the wider changes in London society. Primarily low-budget productions, these films unabashedly exploited debates of the period such as mass commercialisation and the growing sex industry. This included a critique for the driving force behind them.

Soho Filmography

During the compilation of my Soho filmography, which involved watching over one hundred films, I began my research by charting the area's frequency as a film location from the 1900s onwards. I then developed an initial framework for defining a Soho film. First, films on this list should cinematically represent the real topography of Soho, either by shooting on location or by constructing the area artificially on a set (the mode that was most preferred by lower budget films in this period). I then isolated the search to include films that featured Soho's more well-known commercial and subcultural spaces such as the coffee bar, the strip club and other night life businesses. This proved fruitful for streamlining my Soho filmography, as it swiftly became clear that Soho featured as a prominent locus in films released after the Second World War up until 1963, a watershed year that featured intense innovations in cinema technology, urban reconstruction and growing permissive attitudes, aspects that I will expand upon later, for they dramatically shaped modern Britain and contribute towards our current understanding of modern Soho and its representation on screen.

Cinematic Soho has emerged as a space that cannot not be separated from several thematic consistencies that include a fascination for migrant displacement, sexual difference and generational fracture. These films also have a tendency to spotlight social and cultural transformations of the area and the capital city, such as the impact of the Street Offences Act (1959), which banned street prostitution and inadvertently created new forms of commercial nightlife, as well as the emerging youthquake and alleged moral panic for premarital sex through a bohemian and cosmopolitan lens. Soho filmmakers (all male) exploited the growing permissive attitudes in a decade where cinema would soon be eclipsed by commercial television, particularly in films on the dangers of the city and premarital sex like in *The Flesh is Weak* (1957) and *Rag Doll* (1961). In the 1920s and 1930s, Soho appeared in a handful of films like *Piccadilly* (E.A. Dupont, 1920) and the musical romantic comedy *Greek Street/Latin Love* (Sinclair Hill, 1930). However, although I briefly look to these films in Chapter 2 on immigrant communities, for the purposes of this introductory study of Soho in cinema, I prioritised films that contributed towards Soho's postwar development beginning in 1948. The crime film *Noose* (Edmond T. Gréville, 1948) forms a bridge between the interwar and postwar years, and provides vital historical and social context for my later examination of Soho, as well as anticipating those chief themes mentioned in subsequent 1950s and 1960s low-budget Soho films such as *Street of Shadows* (Richard Vernon, 1953), *Soho Incident* (Vernon Sewell, 1956), *The Flesh is Weak* (Don Chaffey, 1957), *The Shakedown* (John Lemont, 1960), *Beat Girl* (Edmond T. Gréville, 1960), *Rag Doll* (Lance Comfort, 1961), *Too Hot to Handle* (Terence Young, 1960) and *The Small World of Sammy Lee* (Ken Hughes, 1963). Larger budget films including the Rank Studio/Emeric Pressburger passion project *Miracle in Soho* (Julian Amyes, 1957) and the comedy *Expresso Bongo* (Val Guest, 1960), based on a successful stage musical, assisted in cementing Soho's positioning at the national/global level as a space of commercial vice, bohemian youth and thriving cosmopolitanism. I conclude my examination of Soho films in 1963 because the desire for filmmakers to examine those previously outlined debates within cinema (and Soho) all but disappeared until the mid-1980s, where we see a return to examining Soho's postwar past in films such as *Absolute Beginners* (Julien Temple, 1986) and the more recent *The Look of Love* (Michael Winterbottom, 2013) and *Adrift in Soho* (Pablo Behrens, 2019). In Chapters 9 and 10, I highlight the ways in which these films were produced as responses to the legacy of leading bohemian figures in the area such as the striptease entrepreneur Paul Raymond, who, due to the deployment of fierce marketing strategies, evolved into a leading contributor to the shifting arrangement of Soho's sex industry into a more commercial, isolated product, reflecting the growth in permissive attitudes from the late 1950s onwards.

Realism and Spectacle

In this book I have taken a wholly interdisciplinary approach, drawing upon historical, cultural and urban studies to support my critical discussion and close analysis of twelve unique, primarily low-budget British films. My decision to look specifically at low-budget filmmaking resulted in some critical losses, particularly regarding the diversity of films and filmmakers that will be discussed. However, I do address the absence of Chinatown and other migrant communities in Chapter 2 on Soho's bohemian-cosmopolitan spaces. It is clear that these films privilege particular representations of Soho over others. Nevertheless, in each of the ten following chapters, which are arranged largely chronologically but also, to some extent, thematically, I reappraise these majority 'B' films more rigorously and consider them in the unique context of Soho. I have taken a bolder approach to structuring the book, and it is arguably full of intersecting tangents that, in many ways, imitate the labyrinth-like geography of Soho. Through case studies of these Soho-set films, I aim to discover the area's links to London, which were more often treated by filmmakers as two conflicting, ambiguous modes of insiders versus outsiders.

This book introduces the area of Soho as a significant and relevant locus for cinema scholarship and appreciation. Melding realism with myth, produced under great technological and financial constraints, these films offer us new understandings of the postwar period and British filmmaking through the lens of Soho, a place with a historically mutable heritage. These distinct films also function as visual artefacts, with numerous sequences shot on location in the area (signalling changes in the film industry at large to favour realism over spectacle). I have strived to interrogate these films and the 'views of the world which they promoted', which 'may well have obscured as much as they enlightened and obstructed as much as they initiated to the potential for social change and reconstruction'.[21] Although these films privileged a particular representation of Soho, it is clear their shared cinematic language, which was unmistakably connected to Soho's double signifier, a mode which I have defined in this book as the 'cosmopolitan-bohemian' identity.

Notes

1. G.C. Wilson, *The Story of Soho* (Gloucester: British Publishing, 1925), 1.
2. Anon, 'Past Days in Soho', *Chambers' Journal of Popular Literature, Science and Arts*, 19 June 1897, 399.
3. Frank Mort, *Capital Affairs: London and the Making of the Permissive Society* (New Haven: Yale University Press, 2010), 204.
4. Judith Summers, *Soho: A History of London's Most Colourful Neighbourhood* (London: Bloomsbury, 1991), 1.
5. Charlie Q.L. Xue's *Hong Kong Architecture 1945–2015: From Colonial to Global* (2016) details this transformation further. Following the destructive Japanese occupation during the Second World War and the Chinese Civil War, refugees flooded the city which meant that: 'By the end of 1946, the population had grown from 600,000 to 1.6 million people.' The British Labour government's plans to rebuild Hong Kong to support this ongoing flux of immigrants instigated the Colonial Development and Welfare Act in 1945, which invested $500,000 out of a total of £1 million allocated to support a ten-year welfare plan for the city. Led by Sir Patrick Abercrombie, the world-renowned Professor of Town Planning at University College London, who was also partly responsible for the *Greater London Plan* and the *County of London*

Plan, proposals for the redevelopment for the heavily bombed capital (Hong Kong was also bombed exponentially by Allied forces), visited Hong Kong in 1947 for thirty-seven days. After his visit, he then compiled a preliminary planning report that outlined a blueprint for the city: 'Abercrombie had good ideas that included the establishment of a garden city, satellite towns and organic dispersion. These ideas had proved effective in his Greater London plan ... and he looked forward to applying them to the Far East.' Although the plan was ultimately 'shelved' due to the outbreak of the Korean War in the early 1950s, his proposals influenced later policies that were ultimately realised. See Charlie Q.L. Xue's *Hong Kong Architecture 1945–2015: From Colonial to Global* (Springer Nature: Singapore, 2016), 4.
6. See 'Introduction' in Pam Hirsch and Chris O'Rourke (eds), *London on Film: Screening Spaces* (London: Palgrave Macmillan, 2017), 4.
7. See Charlotte Brunsdon, 'The Poignancy of Place: London and the Cinema', *Visual Culture in Britain*, 5(1) (2004), 59.
8. Charlotte Brunsdon, *London in Cinema: The Cinematic City since 1945* (London: BFI, 2007), 90.
9. Ibid., 110.
10. Ibid., 122.
11. Ibid., 12.
12. Ibid., 23, 10.
13. Ibid., 12.
14. Ibid.
15. Mark Shiel and Tony Fitzmaurice, *Cinema and the City Film and Urban Societies in a Global Context* (Chichester: John Wiley & Sons, 2008), 6.
16. Georg Simmel, 'The Metropolis and Mental Life' (1903), in Georg Simmel, *The Sociology of Georg Simmel*, edited and translated by K.H. Wolff (New York: Free Press, 1950); Louis Wirth, 'Urbanism as a Way of Life', *American Journal of Sociology* 44(1) (1938): 1–24; Walter Benjamin, 'The Work of Art in the Age of Mechanical Reproduction' (1935), in *Illuminations: Essays and Reflections,* translated by Harry Zohn (New York: Schocken Books, 2007 [1955]), 217–52.
17. Ibid., 410.
18. See Jurgen Habermas, *The Structural Transformation of the Public Sphere: An Inquiry into a Category of Bourgeois Society* (1962), translated by Thomas Burger, with the assistance of Frederick Lawrence (Cambridge, MA: MIT Press, 1991); Michel de Certeau, *The Practice of Everyday Life*, translated by Steven Rendall (Berkeley: University of California Press, 1988); and Siegfried Kracauer, 'The Hotel Lobby', *Postcolonial Studies* 2(3) (1999): 289–97.
19. David Robinson, 'United Kingdom', in Alan Lovell (ed.), *Art of the Cinema in Ten European Countries* (Strasbourg: Council for Cultural Co-operation of the Council of Europe, 1967).
20. Raymond Durgnat, *A Mirror for England: British Movies from Austerity to Affluence*, 2nd edn (London: BFI, 2011).
21. Ibid., 3.

CHAPTER 1
Tracking Shot
Soho Square to Wardour Street, London's 'Film Row'

Hear them down in Soho Square, Dropping 'h's' everywhere.
—Lerner and Loewe, *My Fair Lady* (1956)

Man, you don't advertise, you ain't easy to find!
—*Soho Incident* (Vernon Sewell, 1956)

Soho Square and the Surrounding Streets

In 1878, one author named Walter Thornbury proclaimed the geographical boundaries of Soho 'impossible to define accurately'.[1] Thornbury was neither the first nor the last author to emphasise Soho's transforming borders. In his third volume for *Old and New London*, he described Soho's geographical distribution in the period as 'roughly ... lying between St. Martin's and St. Giles-in-the-Fields, Leicester Square and Oxford Street, but its limits on the western side are very vague'.[2] Soho's development, of course, would undergo 'imaginative remapping ... in the nineteenth century ... as a parallelogram bounded by the heavily commercialised West End thoroughfares of Oxford Street to the north, Regent Street to the west, Charing Cross Road to the east, and Coventry Street and Leicester Square to the south'.[3] But wedged neatly in-between Soho's narrow, interlocking streets, there are pockets of bucolic respite to be found for the tourist, worker or wanderer. Located northeast of the centre of this parallelogram, below the shopping mecca of Oxford Street, and on the eastern border of Charing Cross Road is a popular garden called Soho Square, first built in 1681. The square was previously known as 'King's Square', built in memory of the Duke of Monmouth, the illegitimate son of King Charles II whose statue by Cauis Gabriel Cibber remains on dutiful watch in the square, placed in front of a mock-Tudor gardener's hut that was constructed to conceal an electricity substation and used during the Second World War as an air-raid shelter.[4] The largest green area in Soho, besides Golden Square and St Anne's Churchyard to the south, the square acts as a threshold to the southern part of Soho, Greek Street 'the worst street in London' and Frith Street, home to the historic coffee shop Bar Italia and Ronnie Scott's Jazz Club. The square also provided an accessible walking route north to Oxford Street via Soho Street. It became widely known as a 'fashionable' area for aristocratic families in the seventeenth and eighteenth centuries. According to Mort, Soho Square also housed places of sexual entertainment for the upper class in the period, like the 'Temple of Festivity' at Carlisle House on the west side, 'a fashionable venue for balls and masquerades, involving 'indecency and mocking of solemn feelings and principles'.[5] However, like the rest of Soho, it endured extensive redevelopment for various commercial purposes in the nineteenth century and beyond.[6] In the nineteenth and twentieth centuries, the square was immortalised in literature, as a location in Charles Dickens' *A Tale of Two Cities* (1859) and as an ironic critique of working-class pronunciation in the lyrics of the satirical song 'Why Can't the English?' in Lerner and Loewe's stage musical *My Fair Lady* (1956).

In the early part of the twentieth century, Soho Square and the surrounding area became a popular address for creative industries. Wardour Street was even famously known as London's 'Film Row' from the 1930s onwards for it housed several film production offices and editing studios. Soho Square continues to function as the site for several notable enterprises, such as the headquarters for the British censors, the British Board of Film Classification (BBFC), the Hollywood film studio Twentieth Century Fox, St Patrick's Catholic Church, the French Protestant Church of London and the House of St Barnabas, a members-only club and arts charity.

In the immediate postwar period, Soho Square was also the locus for the strategic rebranding of Soho through a staged summer festival that first took place in 1955. It was first planned around the time of the Festival of Britain in 1951 and Queen Elizabeth's coronation in 1953, driven no doubt by the dubious media spotlight that was placed on the more disreputable areas of the metropole like Soho and the West End, highlighting an increase in crime and prostitution. Although Soho was aligned with a boisterous and celebrated diversity, it was simultaneously and rather notoriously known as an area rife with street prostitution, particularly during and after the war. The most notable visitor to remark upon the overt display of sexual transactions on the streets of London was the American sexologist Alfred Kinsey. Accompanied by his wife Clara and an 'assistant keeper of the British Library', Kinsey toured the capital in 1955, 'tracking across the dense network of narrow streets and cross routes that led north from Piccadilly Circus and Leicester Square into Soho'.[7] Kinsey was 'astounded by the sheer amount of sexual activity' particularly in the 'red-light district of Soho'.[8] When interviewed by Wolfenden's committee, he declared he had never seen so much 'prostitution ... except in Havana'.[9]

According to Stefan Slater, although 'prostitution in Soho was reputedly as old as the area itself', the popular press exploited the sex industry in a 'sensational vein, regardless of empirical truth, in order to sell papers'.[10] This resulted in a campaign directed by Soho's commercial leaders that aimed to transform the area's moral character, which, by this period, was cemented in the public imagination as one of transgression and vice. In many ways, as Mort states, this 'cultural experiment' diluted Soho's foreign character into one that was more 'consumer-led' lines in an effort to promote the area as a concentrated locus of consumption – a district that would offer an unthreatening network of shopping, eating and family entertainment within a densely packed square mile.[11]

In cinema, the square, surrounding streets and its topographical features are, unsurprisingly, a ubiquitous presence in postwar Soho films. Soho's dense network of streets featured in most if not all films, although sections of the area were primarily reconstructed on studio lots, as in the case of *Noose* (1948), *Street of Shadows* (1953), *The Flesh Is Weak* (1957), *Beat Girl* (1960), *Expresso Bongo* (1960), *The Shakedown* (1960), *Rag Doll* (1961) and *The Small World of Sammy Lee* (1963). However, there was a real attempt made to balance the artificial reproductions of Soho by filming on location and later compositing the two types of shooting together in the final edit. Montage was also frequently used as a device to juxtapose the cosmopolitan aspects of Soho with the more lewd, bohemian nightlife economy, bombarding us with neon signage, imbibing patrons and other acts of hedonism in cubist-style arrangements. Regarding Soho Square specifically, in the opening sequence of *Noose* (1948), an anonymous priest is framed pinning a letter to a noticeboard that reveals Soho as its address before panning out to reveal the actual exterior of the House of St Barnabas. In the low-budget noir film *Soho Incident* (1956), the protagonist, Jim, a Canadian ex-soldier (Lee Patterson), goes in search of his army buddy in Soho. He swiftly becomes lost in the throng crowds spilling out of shops and bars in night-time Soho, looping around Greek

Figure 1.1. Jim's late-night ramble in Soho. Still from *Spin a Dark Web/Soho Incident* (Vernon Sewell, 1956). DVD, Sony Pictures Choice Collection, 2012

Street and Frith Street, before eventually finding his way north to a dilapidated building at '44 Soho Square' (a fictional address) where a prostitute is soliciting customers outside.

St Patrick's Church was unmistakably used as a model for the design of the fictional Roman Catholic church of St Anthony's in *Miracle in Soho* (1957), which even deployed cross-promotion with the Soho fair (releasing the film in the same month as the 1957 event) in order for its studio, the Rank Organisation, to capitalise upon the film's positive attitudes towards migration and ethnic diversity in the nation. This wholesome film also subtly suggests that street prostitution exists in the otherwise parochial neighbourhood of the film through the unnamed character of an independent young woman who lives alone and keeps night-time hours.

One of my main arguments in this book is that postwar filmmakers created a specific Soho iconography through the frequent inclusion of real-life locations such as Soho Square and the surrounding streets, particularly Wardour Street, which was once considered to be the headquarters of the British film industry. This setting, combined with specific technical flourishes like tracking shots or montage, attempted to imitate the titillation and excitement of nightlife culture, and succeeded in reproducing what the tabloids of the period purported as a disreputable, sin-ridden area. However, the unfixed nature of Soho's function(s), particularly regarding its cosmopolitan past as a refuge for immigrants, makes this distinction more ambiguous, for above and adjacent to the seedy underbelly was a richly diverse community. Nevertheless, it would be the showcasing of the corruptible nature of Soho that became and has continued to be the predominant choice for filmmakers, who clearly believed that this biased expression of the area was the more commercially profitable due to its sensationalist nature.

This chapter is divided into three sections. The first section provides an overview of Soho's historical significance within the film industry and the implication of its placement amongst other commercial avenues as a source of the archetypal depictions of 'seedy' or 'low-life' Soho. In the second section, I discuss the use of what I argue is the ubiquitous Soho tracking shot in greater detail, tracing its antecedents within literature, particularly travel guidebooks, which, in rare instances, also strived to depict Soho's heterogeneity. In the third section, through film's integration of Soho's historical association with cultural tourism and its later alignment with the vice industries, we can clearly track the emergence of Soho's future, on screen identity.

Wardour Street: An 'Unreal' Space?

Marking the boundary between St Anne's and St James' parishes respectively, Wardour Street, previously known as Coleman Hedge Lane, evolved into one of the most popular commercial roads in Soho during the latter half of the seventeenth century. Situated in the centre of the square mile, it runs directly from Oxford Street in the north, London's shopping locus, down south to Coventry Street, past the West End, London's theatre district, just west of Leicester Square. The Survey of London notes that 'in the last quarter of the 17th century it was the northern half of this lane' that became known as 'Old Soho' and there was 'evidence that hunting took place over the lands to the west of Wardour Street'.[12] By the 1680s, it was renamed Wardour Street after Edward Wardour, a landowner, though the southern section retained its name Princes Street, referring to the parallel Rupert Street to the west of Wardour Street, which was named after Prince Rupert. By 1878, Wardour was extended to include Princes Street and the entire length of the lane from Oxford Street became 'known by its present name'.[13] In the late nineteenth century, as Judith Summer points out, the street had a 'healthy trade in second-hand books and fake antiques … the name Wardour Street has become synonymous with things unreal'.[14] In 1988, Harold Myers, former London bureau chief of *Variety*, recalled his time working in and around the area as an entertainment reporter in the 1950s:

> Remember Wardour Street? Between the two world wars it really was London's film row, home to virtually every major distribution and exhibition company … It is a different story today, with only a couple of majors and a handful of independents … An overworked gag at the time had it that Wardour Street was the only one that was shady on both sides.[15]

In 1927, the street had become the primary location for the headquarters of film production, postproduction facilities and film distribution companies.[16] But the reasons behind its evolution to becoming the centre of London film production have rarely been discussed independently of individual histories of leading members within the British film industry. The most prominent figure to emerge during Wardour Street's early transformation was American filmmaker Charles Urban. Ohio-born Urban was the 'most important producer of films in Britain in the pre-1914 period [whose] greatest triumph came with the two-colour (red-green) Kinemacolor system, the world's first natural colour film system in 1906'.[17] Shortly after emigrating to Britain in 1897, he worked as a manager to Edison concessionaries Maguire & Baucus. After building a reputable position as a producer and distributor of films in Britain, he established his own company in 1903 called 'The Charles Urban Trading Company'. He was the first member of the film industry to relocate his business to Soho in 1908 to a building located at 89–91 Wardour Street. He renamed the building 'Urbanora House', and it has retained the name, although today it houses the 'Las Vegas Casino and Arcade'.[18]

Geoffrey Macnab has provided wonderful anecdotes about film impresarios working in Soho during the 1940s and 1950s in his biography of J. Arthur Rank, where renowned filmmaker David Lean wrote of 'nerve-racking afternoons spent in Wardour Street viewing rooms' and the 'doyen of distributors' C.M. Woolf once guiding his protégé Arthur J. Rank 'through the dark vale of Wardour Street where there were rumoured to be "shadows on both sides"'.[19] In 2017, British Pathé produced a short film entitled *8 Things Made Inside 103 Wardour Street* for its online community. The film explored eight functions of the Pathé Building, located at

103 Wardour Street. The Pathé building was opened in 1910 and used for multitude of production purposes until 1970. This included the production of newsreels, film, television, music and radio. Despite retaining its original name, the building now houses luxury apartments.

Myers' description of Wardour Street as once being 'shady on both sides' could easily be interpreted as a reference to street prostitution. However, as Richard Tames has suggested, it could also form part of a critique of the questionable ethics of the entertainment industry.[20] During this period, Soho was also confirmed as the home to the headquarters of the British music industry. The world-renowned music publishers Novello & Co. built its headquarters Novello House at 152–160 Wardour Street in 1906. Today, Novello House remains in use for the music business as a retail branch for Yamaha Music. Additionally, Soho played host to a variety of night-time economies that sprang up during the mid-1920s and continued to flourish after the Second World War.[21] In 1925, G.C. Wilson declared Soho a 'mecca for the pleasure seeker'.[22] In the decades that followed, 'Soho's bohemian character was changing under the impact of music-based cultures with their emphasis on youth … jazz and blues musicians and their audiences'.[23] The notorious underground jazz clubs and private drinking dens that lined the street from the mid-1950s to the 1960s, such as the Flamingo Club at 33–37 Wardour Street and the Marquee Club at 90 Wardour Street, preserved Soho's 'reputation for transgressive nightlife [that] vastly expanded from restaurants and cafés to a handful of illicit bohemian dance clubs located in underground basements'.[24] The Harvard business economist Michael Porter established the term 'clustering' in his seminal publication *The Competitive Advantage of Nations* (1990), for which he is perhaps most well-known. In 1998, Porter expanded upon his definition of clustering as a 'geographically proximate group of interconnected companies and associated institutions in a particular field'.[25] It is wholly unsurprising that the geographical clustering of film, music, television and other commercial night-time leisure/retail industries would exist and thrive in Soho.

The welcomed and unwelcomed presence of Hollywood marked the final elucidation of the Wardour Street 'shady' gag. Unlike nearby Dean Street, Wardour Street survived the London Blitz (1940 –41), but Film Row had been fighting its own economic war since the mid-1920s, which saw quota regulations forced upon British exhibitors as a result of Hollywood domination at the box office.[26] This battle with Hollywood generated the production of a series of low-budget films that became known as the British 'B' or second feature film, the most prevalent and popular genre for Soho-set features.

Soho Films and Soho Filmmakers

It will come as no surprise to learn that in this period, Soho films were being churned out by Soho-based filmmakers. In 1951, *Sight and Sound* published a list of British and Hollywood companies and studios in active production. The listing identified over twenty-seven British film production companies, British subsidiaries of major Hollywood studios and documentary/short film production companies with headquarters located on Wardour Street and the surrounding Soho district.[27] There were also multiple animation studios located within Soho. This included Halas & Batchelor, whose offices were located at 10a Soho Square (a short walk from the offices of the British censors) in 1962, and Bob Godfrey's studio 'Biographic Cartoons'. Godfrey, the Academy-Award winning animator and 'godfather' of British animation, operated at a Dean Street location from 1960.[28]

British film production companies with offices located on Wardour Street and the square mile produced and distributed several Soho-set films released in the immediate postwar period. Angel Productions, which produced British director Val Guest's second Soho-set thriller preceding the adaptation of the West End musical *Expresso Bongo* (1960), was located at Nascreno House at 27 Soho Square and Guest's crime thriller entitled *Murder at the Windmill/Mystery at the Burlesque* (1949), a whodunnit that is set entirely in the Windmill Theatre. Émigré writer/director Emeric Pressburger's *Miracle in Soho* (1957) was produced by the Rank Organisation, whose distribution company General Film Distributors was located at 127 Wardour Street. Butcher's Film Service, which distributed the Soho exploitation crime drama *Rag Doll* (1961), Renown Pictures Corporation, which released youth-in-revolt film *Beat Girl* (1960), and Columbia British Pictures, which distributed *Soho Incident* (1956), all chose Film Row for their place of business with offices located at 175, 111 and 139 Wardour Street respectively.

Soho's Creative Clusters

Wardour Street and the surrounding area is no longer regarded as the locus of power for the British film industry. Today, many film production and distribution companies choose to locate their offices on the periphery of Soho and in other central areas of the city such as Covent Garden, Clerkenwell, Old Street and Fitzrovia, the area north of Soho. However, Wardour Street and Soho retain a diverse array of leisure and commercial businesses, and principally houses independent postproduction, sound and digital effects studios. The contemporary film community of Wardour Street has been discussed more recently in a wide range of scholarly research such as Andy C. Pratt's worth on microclustering of the media industries in major cities, for: 'Historically, the footprint of [British] film has been bifurcated: one foot in Soho, Wardour Street to be precise, and the other in outer North and West London studios (for example, Pinewood and Shepperton).'[29] Andy C. Pratt's work on creative clusters in London is part of a number of studies in this century, published by Pratt with Galina Gornostaeva in 2009 and S. Bahar Durmaz in 2015, which contribute to extending current knowledge of contemporary Soho's role in the ongoing development, organisation and innovation of London's film industry.

Durmaz has defined creative and/or media clusters as 'geographic concentrations of interconnected companies and institutions in a particular field'.[30] The analysis of the sociospatial qualities of a place that 'attract and retain creatives' may be applied to Soho and Wardour Street, which continue to house digital effects, postproduction and distribution companies. Pratt begins his study of creativity and innovation in the film industry by spotlighting the establishment of 'Sohonet' in 1995. Sohonet is responsible for creating a digital network that allows massive data transfer between film studios and postproduction houses from Soho to Hollywood production companies. Pratt also attributed the 'booming digital effects economy [that] projected London to the forefront of digital effects production in the world' in the late 1990s as one key example of the ways in which London competes on a global scale with regard to reinvestment in 'skill and technology ... perhaps London's greatest asset in the media industries cluster'.[31] This may also be applied to our understanding of the clustering of the film industry in Soho.

Pratt and Gornostaeva have identified Soho's diverse array of food and leisure industries as responsible for providing the 'critical service' for filmmakers, enabling the exchange of knowledge through 'serendipitous interactions 'on the street' and 'in the restaurant' confirming Soho as a vital geographical locus for creative production in the twenty-first century.[32] Although Charles Urban is often credited as the figure who began the trend for film industries to cluster in Soho, Durmaz has suggested that it is the combination of businesses, like food, music and other forms of entertainment, positioned in close proximity that led to 'economic prosperity through providing a competitive advantage'.[33] Today, Wardour Street does contain some connection to the film industry whilst simultaneously catering to particular appetites in most every respect (food, clothes and music). Its survival as a commercial locus remains reliant upon its ability to exploit its multifarious roots, although primarily through mass redevelopment, which includes the demolition of existing buildings and the construction of luxury property in their place.

The Soho Tracking Shot

Charlotte Brunsdon holds the view that the pervasive use of 'Landmark London' sequences in British film 'is the shorthand iconography of location … For the paradox of landmark imagery is that it must be already familiar in order to elicit recognition, and "already familiar" is often, already, overfamiliar'.[34] These urban gestures, shots or sequences that contain British imperial or national landmarks are repurposed in Soho films as expressive tracking shots and rapid montage sequences to establish their urban setting(s) and characters' inner psychology and sexual difference. Tracking shots may be defined as 'when the camera moves parallel to the ground … moves physically through space … in a very smooth and precise fashion. More often, cameras were – and still are – mounted on wheels, or dollies, thus enabling them to move freely in a variety of directions'.[35] Luis Fernando Morantes describes montage, a technique developed during the early years of silent cinema, as, while still only holding 'diverse' and 'unsatisfactory' definitions, essentially 'the principal tool for constructing audio-visual narratives and activating emotional responses in viewers … the term *montage* comes from engineering and theatre and means, in its literal sense, the process of construction of machines and vessels'.[36] Montage refers simply to the way in which a film is assembled – the selection and joining of footage – during the editing process. Rapid montage is used to disrupt the linear chronology of film in order to condense the passing of time. Soho films share a motivation to situate their audiences within Soho as both a tourist and consumer.

Although rooted in silent cinema, these methods of visual storytelling were also used in response to early British cinema from 1896 to 1910, which 'employed trick events within a context of re-staged events'.[37] Ian Aitken notes the most prolific producer of these films in the early twentieth century was Charles Urban. However, Soho's isolated geography was perhaps more suited to the organic, improvised style of the British Documentary Film Movement of the 1930s and 1940s, led by John Grierson and later, in the 1950s by the Free Cinema Movement led by directors Lindsay Anderson, Karel Reisz and Tony Richardson.[38] As with other film genres, we may chart a clear move away from the theatrical, 'staged' depictions of Soho in prewar and interwar crime films like *Murder in Soho* (Norman Lee, 1939), which was shot entirely on a set with zero specific markers to place, to the more fluid, on-location shooting of postwar Soho films we will be discussing here.

Commercial and Sexual Mapping: A Shared Soho Language?

Films such as *Soho Incident, Expresso Bongo, West End Jungle, The Small World of Sammy Lee* and *The World Ten Times Over* execute both tracking shots and montage particularly well, deploying handheld cameras following behind or in front of their (largely male) actors, attaching the camera to a dolly or moving vehicle whilst zooming horizontally, from one frame to the next, passing commercial businesses like theatres, cinemas, restaurants and strip clubs. Low-budget crime-noirs *Soho Incident* and *The Small World of Sammy Lee* are both extremely successful in utilising the urban space of Soho as a metaphor to introduce their protagonists' state of mind. *Soho Incident* uses a tracking sequence through evening Soho that is thrilling and technically complex. In this sequence, Jim is in search of his old army buddy who now works for the Francesi gang, whose offices are located in Soho Square. Sewell uses a handheld camera to follow Jim as he loops around Shaftesbury Avenue, Dean Street, Firth Street and Old Compton Street. Like Limpy, he moves past throngs of patrons, tourists and glittering Soho frontages that include Bar Italia on Frith Street and Quo Vadis on Dean Street. Jim's later induction into the world of gambling and Sammy's gambling addiction suggest more parallels between the film's depiction of the protagonist's state of mind.

In *The Small World of Sammy Lee,* Ken Hughes constructed Soho as a monochromatic racetrack, suggesting that the Jewish protagonist Sammy (Anthony Newley) and Soho are temporal spaces, 'not directionally or geographically coherent'.[39] The temporality of Soho is reinforced by the melancholic opening sequence, which follows a dustbin lorry whilst it travels, in no particular sequential order, through the city, weaving in and out of the labyrinth-like, filth-ridden streets of Soho.[40] This 'world that is waking with the traders on Berwick Street market and simultaneously crawling to bed as the spielers kick out their night's trade onto Old Compton Street' is not the vibrant, titillating pleasure centre of the West End at night depicted and advertised by *Expresso Bongo*.[41] The opening sequence functions as a visual representation of Sammy's physical and spiritual transformation. It also acts as a pseudo-metaphor for the gradual, commercial sanitisation of Soho and the development of the permissive society in Great Britain. I will discuss the importance of both *Expresso Bongo* and *The Small World of Sammy Lee* in greater detail in Chapters 6, 8 and 9.

Soho: A Dangerous Space for Women?

There are, of course, restrictive limitations regarding the depictions of male and female characters' engagement with Soho. In films that specifically follow the experiences of young women in Soho, like *The Flesh Is Weak*, *Beat Girl* and *Rag Doll*, the camera is undisguised in the way it represents the voyeuristic behaviour of predatory men or sexual innocence. Instead of swiftly moving the camera along a track, the camera remains either tentative to follow or static. In *Beat Girl*, sixteen-year-old Jennifer (Gillian Hills) walks rather defiantly from the coffee bar to the strip club in order to prove a point to her 'Beatnik' friends whilst she is shot from a slightly low angle. Her innocence is brought to the fore here, seemingly oblivious to any impending sexual or physically violent advances that the film immediately fulfils, as she is harassed by a male customer exiting the club who asks if she'd 'like a go'. In *Beat Girl* and *Rag Doll*, there are two parallel scenes where the female protagonists move through crowds down Berwick Street's once-bustling food market to suggest a kind of domestic freedom. However, although Soho does offer social mobility through commerce, female characters are inevitably cursed to remain within the confines of their future predicament(s) in the film's plot, which is indicated by mirroring of their naivety to the city's subcultures. It is particularly overt in *The Flesh Is Weak*, which follows a young Italian woman Marissa (Milly Vitale) who is groomed into prostitution by the young, attractive leader of a sex trafficking ring called Tony (John Derek). Although we are exposed to a montage of Marissa's seduction by Tony in the guise of moving through London and its landmarks on their various romantic dates, the slow manner in which the frames dissolve into one another creates a stark sense of apprehension and warning for Marissa's future of being sexual blackmailed. In the pseudo-documentary *West End Jungle* (1961), we observe the destabilisation of these male/female interactions through the 'staged' scenarios of sexual transactions in the city.

Montage as a form of commercial mapping and sexual difference is greatly highlighted by *Street of Shadows* (1953), where it clarifies the juxtaposition between the suburban life of the upper-class female character Barbara (Kay Kendall) and her attempts to escape through decadent consumption. In one early sequence, she drinks her way through seedy nightclubs in order to forget about her marriage troubles. It is signalled to us through the rapid cutting between neon signage and superimposed champagne bottles over imbibing and partially obscured figures of patrons. However, Barbara is framed only sitting down during the sequence and interacts very little with her drinking party. This suggests that although she actively seeks out a world that is dangerous and thrilling, she remains trapped within a domesticated enclosure controlled by her upper middle-class identity.

Conclusion

The deployment of tracking shots and montage in postwar Soho films emulated tourist guides in visual form. They demonstrated technical advancement, but also, through specifically framing Soho's diverse commercial industries within the same locality (for instance, editing footage to include the same group of streets repeatedly in one sequence), suggest they hold a privileged awareness for the film industry and its personnel in Soho. This produces a partly universal, albeit isolated cinematic iconography for Soho that becomes instantly recognisable, even to those who have never been there. During this period, the combination of industry (insiders) versus audiences (outsiders) meant that cinematic Soho was encoded with its own language, one that attempted to embrace viewers through a shared understanding of its past and present cultural history.

Notes

1. Judith Walkowitz, *Nights out: Life in Cosmopolitan London* (New Haven: Yale University Press, 2012), 13.
2. Ibid.
3. Ibid., 2–3.
4. Jonathan Prynn, 'Bomb Shelter under Soho Square Could Be London's Next Top Restaurant Venue', *Evening Standard*, 20 January 2015. Retrieved 8 October 2021 from https://www.standard.co.uk/news/london/bomb-shelter-under-soho-square-could-be-londons-next-top-restaurant-venue-9989241.html.
5. In the 1760s and 1770s, Teresa Cornelys, friend of Casanova and mother to his child, hosted 'elaborated costumed and masked semi nudity' performances at Carlisle House. The house was demolished in 1791. See Frank Mort, *Capital Affairs: London and the Making of the Permissive Society* (New Haven: Yale University Press, 2010), 249.
6. Walter Thornbury, 'Soho', in *Old and New London: Volume 3* (London, 1878), 173–84.
7. Mort, *Capital Affairs*, 2.
8. Ibid., 2.
9. See 'Alfred Kinsey to Departmental Committee on Homosexual Offences and Prostitution Notes of a Meeting', 29 October 1955, PRO HO 345/8, 12–13.
10. See Stefan Anthony Slater, 'Containment-Managing Street Prostitution in London, 1918–1959', *Journal of British Studies* 49 (2010), 332.
11. Mort, *Capital Affairs*, 214.
12. 'Wardour Street Area: Pulteney Estate', in F.H.W. Sheppard (ed.), *Survey of London: Volumes 33 and 34, St Anne Soho* (London: London County Council, 1966), 288–96.
13. Ibid.
14. Judith Summers, *Soho: A History of London's Most Colourful Neighbourhood* (London: Bloomsbury, 1991), 133.
15. Harold Myers, 'Wardour St. Back When', *Variety*, 20 January 1988, 126.
16. Summers, *Soho*, 180.
17. Luke McKernan, 'Charles Urban (1867–1942)', *BFI Screenonline*. Retrieved 8 October 2021 from http://www.screenonline.org.uk/people/id/514893.
18. Born in Ohio, Charles Urban managed a Kinetoscope and phonograph parlour in Detroit during the late nineteenth century, 'The bioscope projector was developed for him and with this notable asset, he was taken on by *Edison* concessionaries *Maguire & Baucus*.' He was sent to Britain as a manager for the American firm before producing his own films and marketing the bioscope. He then set up his own company the Charles Urban Trading Company. Urban's move to Soho may have been for financial reasons, but it may also have been the draw of stage theatre. See ibid.
19. Geoffrey Macnab, *J. Arthur Rank and the British Film Industry* (New York: Routledge, 1993), 22–23.
20. Richard Tames, *London: A Cultural History* (Oxford: Oxford University Press, 2006), 215.
21. Andrew Spicer, *Typical Men: The Representations of Masculinity in Popular British Culture* (London: I.B. Tauris, 2001), 126.
22. G.C. Wilton, *The Story of Soho* (Gloucester: British Publishing, 1925), 38.
23. Mort, *Capital Affairs*, 227–28.

24. Walkowitz, *Nights out*, 215.
25. Historians Frank Mort and Judith Walkowitz both highlight the ways in which Soho 'networks' operate, but do not explicitly use the term 'clustering' to define the ways in which creative industries 'cluster' in close spatial proximity. S. Bahar Durmaz is one of the few scholars who have published extensive literature examining contemporary Soho's role in clustering; see S. Bahar Durmaz, 'Analyzing the Quality of Place: Creative Clusters in Soho and Beyoğlu', *Journal of Urban Design* 20(1) (2015), 93–124. See also a recent examination of the United Kingdom's creative industries by Nicola J. Thomas, Harriet Hawkins and David C. Harvey, 'The Geographies of the Creative Industries: Scale, Clusters and Connectivity', *Geography* 95(1) (2010), 14–21.
26. In 1926, thirty-six films were British-made, but only 5% were shown in British cinemas. A total of 620 American films were released in the same year and comprised 84% of releases. See Mark Glancy, 'Hollywood and Britain: MGM and the British "Quota" Legislation', in Jeffrey Richards (ed.), *The Unknown 1930s: An Alternative History of British Cinema, 1929–1939* (London: I.B. Tauris, 2000), 59.
27. See 'Film Companies and Studios', *Sight and Sound* 19(10) (1 March 1951), 69.
28. Nick Smurthwaite, 'One Man and His Wobbly Dog', *The Guardian*, 20 April 2001. Retrieved 8 October 2021 from https://www.theguardian.com/film/2001/apr/20/culture.features2.
29. See Andy C. Pratt, 'Microclustering of the Media Industries in London', in Charlie Karlsson and Robert G. Picard (eds), *Media Clusters: Spatial Agglomeration and Content Capabilities* (Cheltenham: Edward Elgar, 2011), 130.
30. See Durmaz, 'Analyzing the Quality of Place', 94. For primary scholarship on clustering, a field of interest that grew in the 1990s, and coined by the American economist Michael Porter, please see *The Competitive Advantage of Nations* (New York: Free Press, 1990) (republished with a new introduction in 1998) and *On Competition* (Cambridge: MA, Harvard Business School Press, 1998), 199. See also research by the California School led by Allen J. Scott and Michael Storper, which emphasised the clustering of key industry districts in Los Angeles: Allen J. Scott, *New Industrial Spaces* (London: Pion, 1988), Allen J. Scott, *Technopolis: High-Technology Industry and Regional Development in Southern California* (Berkeley: University of California Press, 1993), and Michael Storper, *Keys to the City: How Economics, Institutions, Social Interaction, and Politics Shape Development* (Princeton University Press, Princeton, USA, 2013).
31. Pratt, 'Microclustering', 130.
32. Ibid.
33. S. Bahar Durmaz provides a comparative study of the clustering in Soho and Beyoğlu in Istanbul in 'Analyzing the Quality of Place: Creative Clusters in Soho and Beyoğlu', *Journal of Urban Design* 20(1) (2015), 93. See also Michael Porter, 'Clusters and the New Economics of Competition', *Harvard Business Review* (November–December 1998), 77–90.
34. Charlotte Brunsdon, *London in Cinema: The Cinematic City since 1945* (London: BFI, 2007), 21.
35. Ed Sikov, *Film Studies: An Introduction* (New York: Columbia University Press, 2010), 26.
36. Luís Fernando Morales Morante, *Editing and Montage in International Film and Video: Theory and Technique* (New York: Taylor & Francis, 2017), 1–2.
37. See Ian Aitken, 'Documentary', *BFI Screenonline*, Retrieved 8 October 2021 from http://www.screenonline.org.uk/film/id/446186/index.html.
38. Ibid.
39. See Brunsdon, *London in Cinema*, 122.

40. Cathi Unsworth emphasises the film's imagining of Soho in her 'retro' review from 2014: 'Hitch a time tunnel ride on the back of a dustbin lorry through the Soho of 1963 … Watch mesmerised.' See Cathi Unsworth, 'Saturday Night at the Movies', *3am Magazine*, 27 June 2009.
41. Ibid.

CHAPTER 2
Soho's Bohemian-Cosmopolitans and Postwar British Cinema

Soho is a good place which can do fine things.
—Manchester Guardian, 10 July 1955

The Rebirth of Cosmopolitan Soho

At 3.50 PM on 10 July 1955, the Mayor of Westminster relaunched cosmopolitan Soho to the world by officiating the opening ceremony of the inaugural Soho Fair. The summer festival was primarily centred around Soho Square and its peripheries, and was co-organised by the Soho Association and the proprietor of the York Minster pub (today known as The French House) Gaston Berlemont conveyed to a reporter from *The Spectator* that he got the idea for the fair at the deconsecration service at St Anne's, Soho's parish church: 'Now there was no church ... there should be a fair in her honour.'[1] Drawing on Soho's reputation for cultural and ethnic diversity, the organisers of the Soho Fair were able to 'create an idiosyncratic mood of celebration that could be marketed to local and national audiences via the media and entertainment industries'.[2] The fair offered a week of spectacles such as a float parade, live performances, a waiter's race and other competitions involving the area's diverse industries.

Historically, this marked a rare moment where Soho's bifurcated character joined together to produce a hybrid, cosmopolitan-bohemian artefact. The Soho Fair ambitiously plotted to celebrate and exploit Soho's identities to promote itself on the postwar, global stage. From its successful debut, the Fair became an annual, televised event organised by Soho's local entrepreneurs that was largely an attempt to rebrand the area nationally due to the sensationalised reports made by the popular press alleging that the increase in prostitution and crime in the West

Figure 2.1a. Berwick Street Market from above. Still from *Sunshine in Soho* (Burt Hyams, 1956). BFI Player. Free documentary

End and Soho had subsequently fostered a 'climate of disgust over the state of the metropolis'.[3] This occurred during the run-up to the Festival of Britain in 1951 and the coronation of Queen Elizabeth II that took place in 1953 and was the first televised coronation in history. It involved '[l]avishly illustrated press supplements … together with the Pathé newsreel footage [and] depicted London as a site of glamorous international and imperial spectacle'.[4] This form of 'imperial spectacle' filtered into the distinctly continental forms of entertainment offered by Soho's entrepreneurs for the inaugural fair of 1955.

Documenting the Soho Fair

Fortunately for film and Soho historians, the first Soho Fair was chronicled on film by Burt Hyams, written by Edward Eve and produced by George Cunliffe Foster (his only professional credit as a producer), and distributed by British-Columbia Pictures. The half-hour documentary *Sunshine in Soho* (1956) mimics the style of a pseudo-travelogue that transports us to a gloriously sunny square mile filled with parades and fairgrounds, projecting localised spaces where traders, restaurateurs, dancers and jazz musicians congregate together in celebration of their 'cosmopolitan' roots. From tours of Italian coffeehouses to lavish float parades through Soho's streets, the film presents a kaleidoscopic, though controlled, view of Soho's commercial industries. Interestingly, the film's director had already directed a number of documentaries during the immediate postwar period, which included a recording of a children's music and dance revue called *Kiddies on Parade* (1935); *Rainbow Round the Corner* (1944), a showcase of a boxing tournament at a London casino; and the International Horse Show at White City aptly titled *Jumping for Joy* (1950).[5] Shot in Eastmancolor, the film chronicled several events of the inaugural Soho Fair of 1955. Hyams also included an extended sequence that depicted a day in the life of local businesses such as cafés, restaurants, bakeries, bars and jazz nightclubs. Narrated by Howard Marion-Crawford, it features a joyful, fairground-inspired soundtrack composed by Frank Phillip, which was performed by the Soho Serenaders. The film persistently uses rapid montage to bombard the viewer with shop windows, street signs and denizens with rare moments for development besides a somewhat overextended sequence depicting the young dance students from the Italia Conti School who perform routines called 'The Impression of Paris' and 'The Dance of the Big Top' to a large crowd in Soho's Golden Square. This results in the extreme commodification of Soho. By creating a false perception of the area's density through editing, the film actively reorganises Soho into 'narrative geographies where urban fragments are collaged into spatial episodes'.[6]

The opening sequence of *Sunshine in Soho* highlights this feeling of disjointedness by using a reverse long shot that tracks down several streets in Soho, accompanied by the film's title song, 'Soho Waltz', a fairground-inspired theme tune. This is followed by the voice of the unseen narrator (Crawford) who welcomes us to 'the most fabulous square mile in the world [this] labyrinth of narrow streets and gas-lit corners'.[7] In this way, the film draws upon a guidebook type filmmaking used by media outlets such as British Pathé News. David Gilbert and Fiona Henderson, who discuss 'London and the Tourist Imagination' in their book *Imagined Londons,* suggest that the 'complicated negotiation between the changing city and the cultural expectations of insiders and outsiders' intensifies 'the significance of the lowly tourist guidebook in cultural contact and exchange within the city'.[8] Hyams uses his lens to act as the outsider's gaze in order to

Figure 2.1b. Young dancers from the Italia Conti School perform in Soho Square. Still from *Sunshine in Soho* (Burt Hyams, 1956). BFI Player. Free documentary

reconstruct a Soho topography that reinforces its function as an entertainment and leisure centre with continental roots. Soho has historically existed as a fascinating subject for travel writers wishing to capture the essence of its foreignness. At the turn of the twentieth century, writers weaved a fictional Soho fabric full of romance, confusion and foreigners:

> A sharp turn out of Wardour Street and the frontier is passed. A moment ago, our eyes rested only on English names, and only English words fell upon our ears. Now the names over the shops are all foreign… all mixed up in the brouhaha of chatter that mingles day and night.[9]

Besides documenting performances and events, the film also provides us with a fascinating odyssey through the area's diverse range of food industries. As we rapidly move through food markets, cafés and delicatessens, Crawford declares: 'Yes, the epicure in his element in Soho. Every kind of sausage … the rarest food the world produces … every kind of shop has its own display of tempting things from foreign lands. Soho is like a big open door for all our continental friends.'[10] We then swiftly cut to sequences featuring pubs and restaurants offering French, Swiss, Hong Kong, Italian and Turkish drink and cuisine.

For fiction film, *Miracle in Soho* (1957), written and produced by the auteur filmmaker Emeric Pressburger, remains the only onscreen, big-budget representation of Soho's migrant community through an overwhelmingly positive, if not naïve lens. The production also collaborated with the Soho Fair during the week of its release, with the aim to boost public engagement with the film, a romance that chronicles the relationship between a local Italian girl (Belinda Lee) and an Irish womaniser (John Gregson).

The week-long Soho Fair was also recorded by Pathé News in the form of short black-and-white films like *Soho Goes Gay!* (British Pathé, 1955), which were screened in British cinemas throughout the summer. The popular press expressed their bemusement at the Fair: 'The idea that Soho is a romantic little "Continental Quarter" in the heart of innocent England – a myth – almost became reality yesterday afternoon.'[11] The *New Statesman* was horrified: 'There used to be – I daresay there still is – an admirable honesty about Soho. It does not pretend to be something: it just *was*. But the bell is tolling. Soho is having a Fair ... Someone has had the idea of producing Soho to the world so that it is not only to *be* Soho, but also to pretend to be.'[12] In the same hyperbolic vein, *The Spectator* magazine reported the Fair to be filled with absurdities:

> There are many absurdities at the Soho Fair ... A garish Dutch organ plays in Golden Square, painted with Elizabethan musicians and Victorian odalisques: a band of West Indians pours out Latin-American rhythms ... Bohemian young Frenchman ... a dark, Celtic Lady plies a spinning-wheel in Shaftesbury Avenue.[13]

Further 'absurdities' included a competition for the best float participating in the street parade, the eponymous waiter's race, and various dramatic and dance performances staged throughout the day.[14] The fair's carnivalesque atmosphere and continental ambience underpinned the shifts in 'Soho's hierarchies of social leadership', which were moving 'away from traditional gentry patronage and towards the dominance of family-based businesses'.[15] However, this was largely rejected by Soho's bohemians such as Daniel Farson, a journalist, photographer, biographer of Francis Bacon and author of *Soho in the Fifties*, first published in

1987, who, according to Frank Mort 'insisted that in the dash for respectability Soho needed to retain its reputation for sexual and cultural nonconformity'.[16]

British Cinema, Postwar London and the Soho Fair

As a feature film, *Miracle in Soho* held great ambitions to produce an authentic rendering of the Soho locality with cinematic spectacle that were akin to the Soho Fair's overarching aim for commercial reinvention. This was directly aligned with postwar reconstruction for the metropolis and 'schemes for the beautification of the central area' in the 'interests of national and imperial renewal'.[17] The first and most prominent of those plans was the *County of London Plan* commissioned by the London County Council (LCC) due to the extent of the bombing during the war. The plans were led by John Forshaw, chief architect for the LCC, and Patrick Abercrombie, the LCC's planning consultant and Professor of Town Planning at University College London. The plan reimagined London after the war through a comprehensive series of diagrams, maps, plates and illustrations that 'dealt heavily in the business of image making and forms of representation'.[18] The launch of the plans in 1943 took the shape of a large-scale exhibition at County Hall located on the South Bank on the River Thames. The exhibition was 'visited by Royalty, Government ministers and many thousands of Londoners' and were then published in a 'lavishly illustrated' large-format book that, 'despite wartime paper shortages', became a bestseller.[19] A documentary film detailing the plans was also produced to accompany and promote the launch entitled *The Proud City* (1945), which was screened in British cinemas.

Mort has detailed the ways in which the plans of Forshaw and Abercrombie 'insisted on a comprehensive reordering of the West End ... Acknowledging that currently the West End was 'one of the worst planned and architecturally designed areas of London', which in parts was now nothing more than 'a central slum'.[20] He stresses that a move away from consensus planning occurred from the early 1950s onwards and highlighted the collapse of interest in the collective consciousness and a shift towards one of commercial interest, a 'familiar facet of urban growth'.[21] In many ways, these various social and commercial interests to London's development converge at the Soho Fair, which, like the rebuilding of the metropole in this period, was directed by 'an alliance of financiers, property developers and architects'.[22] The 'self-consciously progressivist' LCC envisaged London as a 'modern imperial metropole' and in conjunction with the Soho Association, the LCC's new approach to the urban regeneration of Soho meant that the Fair could take the form of counter publicity, which was supported by a deeply transitional period at the time of the coronation.[23]

Insiders (Cosmopolitans) versus Outsiders (Bohemians)

As early as the seventeenth century, although Soho was classified as a 'fashionable but mixed neighbourhood', it also became known as the 'refuge for the rejected of Europe', and in the nineteenth century it was deemed a 'haven for political dissidents'.[24] During this period, the rapid development of the West End and, in particular, Regent Street led to further bifurcation: 'Nineteenth-century thoroughfares ripped through the central rookeries of Old London ... providing a parade ground and shopping street for a fashionable neighbourhood.'[25] The expansion of the West End area then continued at a vigorous pace. However, these metropolitan improvements soon resulted in the 'eviction of thousands of poor inhabitants ... intensifying the problem of overcrowding'.[26] Despite the limited number of housing estates that were built for the displaced inhabitants, the city planners were far more concerned with the economy, 'streets and vistas that carefully hewed to pre-existing roads', numerous music halls, theatres and an array of department stores were erected almost simultaneously. The completion of the Selfridges department store on Oxford Street in 1909 ultimately enclosed Soho and the West End within 'commercial peripheries'.[27] However, although these new borders effectively promoted entertainment, they existed within conflicting zones of slums and poverty.[28]

By 1906, the swell in the population of immigrants led to an increase in crime and prostitution that provided the media with an opportunity to denounce Soho as a place of sin and vice (foreign in origin) to the British public.[29] However, if the early Soho inhabitants, 'aristocrats, foreign ambassadors, and Huguenot Protestant artisans', had not made room for poverty-stricken immigrants, anarchists, bohemians and the 'demi-monde' that filled its four borders two centuries later, Soho would not have obtained its status as the pleasure centre of London. Daniel Farson, journalist, raconteur and author of *Soho in the Fifties*, arrived in London 'fresh from Cambridge University in 1951 [and] insisted that the area was as much a "state of mind" as it was the "only area in London where the rules did not apply'".[30] Of course, Farson was very much referring to its bohemian character, for Soho has always played an important role in the development of homosexual culture in London. Published articles, guides and books about the area published throughout the 1920s onwards reinforced Soho's 'sexual unorthodoxy among young educated men ... being bohemian also involved regular visits to Soho's queer pubs and clubs, which [Francis] Bacon referred to as his "sexual gymnasium of the city"'.[31] According to Mort: 'In the years before 1914, Soho and its environs were a focal point for the capital's expanding homosexual culture.'[32] Before the First World War, Soho businesses 'contained almost every type of homosexual customer' and 'sexualised spaces in Soho were open to double meanings whereby homosexual sex was advertised as an open secret to the initiated'.[33] Much like New York's Greenwich Village or the Pigalle quarter in Paris, Soho's 'markets for commercial sex overlapped with or lay adjacent to the area's bohemian culture'.[34]

Soho's reputation for cosmopolitanism was produced by waves of immigration and foreign entrepreneurs who were chief directors of the development of its commercial geography and cultural diversity. The production of Soho's bohemia relied upon the consumption of the area's cosmopolitan atmosphere and sexual economies by bohemians that consisted of flâneurs, novelists, poets, artists and journalists who constructed and cemented a subjective Soho identity. John Eade, who has detailed the area's transformation further in his book *Placing London*, argues that: 'In the context of the West End and London ... Soho serves to sustain an ethnic boundary between insiders (the English/British majority) and outsiders (a varied minority of foreign, predominantly Continental, exotics.'[35] Although the promotion of 'otherness' in the public imagination helped to establish Soho as a distinctly cosmopolitan quarter and its commercial businesses were promoted by its bohemian tourists, it largely failed to attract mainstream British and International filmmakers to use Soho as a title setting for their films. As Eade has shown: 'During the twentieth century the link between London and the nation was crucially altered by the collapse of the world's most extensive empire. London's prestige as the epicentre of empire and nation was diminished between the 1950s and 1970s.'[36] The wave of immigrants after the Second World War marked this transition with 'racialised boundaries between insiders and outsiders'.[37] Similar transformations played out in Soho, a space that flourished because of its historical function as an immigrant locus. However, its role in the promotion of a commercially focused global Britain in the immediate postwar period directly contradicted its reputation as a seedy underbelly, which had been cemented during the 1920s. These binary functions challenge any one singular recognition of Soho and therefore confirm its rich, multifarious, though unfixed identity.

Soho Cosmopolitans and British Cinema

From the 1930s onwards, British films did attempt to explore these 'transformations' of national versus global Britain. However, as Ann Ogidi states, Black actors in British films of this period were often depicted as 'token representation(s) of black communities in England'.[38] British cinema in the 1960s gradually opened up to the possibilities of more complex stories with films like *Sapphire* (1959) and *Flame in the Streets* (1961). According to Ogidi: 'This was also the decade when Black film pioneers Lionel Ngakane (*Jemima + Johnny*, 1966), Lloyd Reckord (*Ten Bob in Winter*, 1963) and Frankie Dymon (*Death May Be Your Santa Claus*, 1969) were making their first films about the experiences of Black people in the UK.'[39] Similarly, there are only a handful of films depicting the lives of Soho's cosmopolitan and largely European community. The musical film *Greek Street* (1930, retitled *Latin Love* for US release), directed by Sinclair Hill, follows a traditional love story between an Italian émigré Rikki (William Freshman), a café owner who falls in love (perhaps to the point of obsession) with a rising English singer Anna (Sari Maritza) who lives upstairs from him. She is then groomed into stardom by a vicious impresario (Martin Lewis). This forgotten film remains unavailable for general release, but is available to view on request at the BFI National Archive in London. Val Guest's satirical comedy *Give Us the Moon* (1944), which is based on the novel *The Elephant is White* by Caryl Brahms and S.J. Simon, follows a group of immigrants (their origins remain unspecified). Their members-only club is in the backroom of a restaurant called *The Silver Samovar* located in Soho. The group is led by Russian immigrant Nina (Margaret Lockwood) who are part of the 'Society of the White Elephants' where one's unemployment is the *only* requirement for membership. *Soho Conspiracy* (1950), which was directed by Cecil H. Williamson, partly drew inspiration from and incorporated footage from Mario Costa's musical film *Mad about Opera* (1948), and follows the daughter of an Italian restaurant owner and her fiancée as they attempt to organise a concert to restore a Soho church damaged during the Blitz.

Jewish Soho

Another notable migrant population group in Soho included the Jewish community who made dramatic impacts upon the development of Soho's commercial boundaries from the late nineteenth century. Jewish Soho begins on the peripheries of Soho in London's East End. Gerry Black has identified the ways in which the East End functioned as the primary entry point for Jewish immigrants towards the end of the seventeenth century, with large numbers of Russian and Polish immigrants arriving between 1880 and 1910.[40] In Whitechapel, both Jewish and Italian immigrants 'staffed the sweatshops which made poor-quality garments for the lower end of the tailoring industry'.[41] According to Black, 15,000 Jews resided in the East End by the 1820s, and this number swiftly rose to 18,000 by 1830. The East End held 'three primary requisites for Jewish communal life – synagogues, Jewish schools and kosher butchers'.[42] Following the Whitechapel tailors' strike of 1891, Jewish families chose to re-locate to Soho and the West End, where they found 'cleaner air, larger and more magnificent houses, fashionable districts, and distinguished residents'.[43] According to Judith Summers, Soho and the West End became the Jewish immigrant community's alternative 'starting-off' place and 'the streets around Berwick Street market had become predominantly Yiddish-speaking, with kosher butchers, fishmongers, bakeries and restaurants opening up around D'Arblay Street, Wardour Street, Berwick Street and Noel Street … Before long, Soho had several small Synagogues'.[44]

By the end of the nineteenth century, the total population of Soho residents numbered 13,000. Local surveys estimated that 60% of the population of Soho were foreign-born.[45] By 1900, the total Jewish population of the West End was 15,000 and Soho 'always accounted for less than half of these numbers'.[46] During this period, several Jewish schools opened in the West End, Soho and Fitzrovia. By 1911, 25% of the pupils attending St Anne's on Dean Street were Jewish.[47] Jewish émigrés and Anglo Jews proved their strength in innovation and entrepreneurialism in the early twentieth century, particularly in the food and leisure industries. Judith Walkowitz states that London's Jewish population 'mentally transformed the commercial West End boulevards from a *space* created by finance capital and state rationalities into quotidian and democratic *place* where they could present themselves as competent moderns'.[48] The attraction of the commercial West End for Jewish residents and entrepreneurs also included spaces of entertainment: '[In the early 1930s] Jews had monopolized the "flashy side of life". They dominated cinema queues for first-run movies in the West End, [and] they transformed Wardour Street into a "glossy ghetto".'[49] In 1920, 57% of shops on Soho's Berwick Street were owned by Jews, which rose to 71% in 1930. This included the famed J. Lyons food empire, founded in 1887, whose 'fungus-like growth' during the 1890s and until 1945 cemented this department store and other Jewish operated shops as one of the most popular social/leisure spaces in London located on the peripheries of Soho: Coventry Street (1909), the Strand (1915), and the corner of Oxford Street and Tottenham Court Road (1929) providing Londoners and tourists with 'music, inexpensive food and a taste of luxury for common folk'.[50] They were also the largest employers of freelance musicians, most of them 'Jews from the East End or Soho'.[51] Although the numbers of Jews in Soho would never be as substantial as those residing and working in the East End, 'variations between East and West neighbourhoods were minor. Their Jewish identity was a more powerful influence on them than the particular area of London in which they lived'.[52]

Chinatown

Regarding the depiction of nonwhite European immigrants, the silent film *Piccadilly* (E.A. Dupont, 1929) remains the most widely recognised British film that featured Chinese actors as active characters and is noteworthy for its setting in London's West End. It famously starred the Hollywood star Anna May Wong as a nightclub dancer Shosho who becomes embroiled in a ménage à trois and is ultimately murdered. However, the film's critical and commercial success, along with Wong's sexually fluid performance remains, to this day a crucial moment for East Asian representation on British screens. The critic and historian Matthew Sweet writes: 'Now it is recognised as a masterpiece whose power is derived, in part, from Wong's skilful manipulation of familiar oriental clichés. "I danced once before in Limehouse", reads one tantalising intertitle. "But there was trouble, men, knives".'[53] Soho's Chinatown and its community appear only in two films, both released in the 1980s: *Ping Pong* (Po-Chih Leong, 1986) and *Soursweet* (Mike Newell, 1988). Other feature films set outside London on the British Chinese diaspora are the relatively unknown *Peggy Su!* (Frances-Anne Solomon, 1988), a romantic comedy set in Liverpool, and perhaps the only film to date set in twenty-first-century London, *She, a Chinese* (Xiaolu Guo, 2009), which follows a young

Chinese women's journey from China to Britain. These films were released a decade after the establishment of the Chinatown enclave below Shaftesbury Avenue in the 1970s. Although 'Chinese migration to Britain dates back to the 19th century ... the first "Chinese quarter" of London in Limehouse – hosting at least 30 Chinese-owned businesses in 1914, primarily laundries and restaurants – disappeared after the area's intense bombing during the war-time Blitz'.[54] In the 1960s, with mass immigration from both China during the revolution and the former British colony Hong Kong, which was 'financed through informal loans collectively arranged on family and community grounds, the first Chinese restaurants started to appear on Gerrard Street, at the Southern edge of Soho, then a run-down, and therefore cheap, part of London's West End'.[55] Westminster Council formally recognised the area as London's Chinatown during the boom in trade during the mid-1980s, during which Britain saw its Chinese population diversify and grow.

Chinatown has also been fighting its own battle against mass development in recent years, almost a decade before the 'Save Soho' campaign was launched in 2014. In 2003, a property developer purchased the lease to a building located 'to the east side' of Chinatown with the aim 'to turn it into a mall aimed at attracting high street brand names. In April 2004, local Chinese businesses including restaurants, grocery shops, a fishmonger, a newsagent ... some of whom had been there for more than 20 years, were given notice to quit their tenancy'.[56] This prompted the 'Save Chinatown' campaign by local activists, targeting both the 'developer and Westminster Council, who had sold the lease without consultation'.[57] Unfortunately, 'it failed to gain council support and the development plan was implemented, leading to 20 evictions by March 2005'.[58]

Set in and around Chinatown, *Ping Pong* follows British-born Chinese lawyer Elaine Choi (Lucy Sheen) who is hired to consult on the will of the recently deceased patriarch of a wealthy family, duly becoming embroiled in a web of family secrets, whilst also falling in love with the youngest son Mike (David Yip). Pak Lin-Wan writes that: 'The film is filled with quirky scenarios and surreal imagery depicting the East-West cultural clash.'[59] The similarities to *Miracle in Soho* are remarkable in the film's allusions to myth, but also in its dedication to realism. Released two years later, and perhaps unsurprisingly a film that also spotlights a British Chinese family was *Soursweet*, which was adapted from the novel by British-Chinese Timothy Mo. The screenplay was written by novelist Ian McEwan and the film was directed by Mike Newell, known for *Four Weddings and a Funeral* (1994) and one of the Harry Potter films. It is a comedy drama about an immigrant family from Hong Kong who must acclimatise to their new London life. *Variety* reviewed the film as follows: 'It's the small details that are most significant … the way traditional Chinese customs give way in the face of British culture and lifestyle.'[60] This handful of films, which have been all but forgotten by audiences and are rarely promoted in the public domain, are unfortunately the only British films to depict the British Chinese experience in London's Chinatown, which is perhaps one of the capital's biggest attractions, representing the 'success of multicultural London … and a significant resource for a highly diverse community'.[61] Chinatown continues to undergo dramatic development, largely due to substantial and aggressive investment from Mainland China. The 'British Chinatown' brand continues to evolve, along with what is considered 'Chinese'. In 2016, the pagoda that stood at the entrance to Newport Place for almost three decades was demolished and a new structure that was said to be reinstalled has never materialised.[62] The discussion surrounding the severe lack of films depicting the British Chinese community in general is complex and deserves a substantial reconsideration in future.

Soho Bohemians and British Cinema

According to various literary sources, bohemia blossomed in Soho before the First World War. However, one could argue this reputation was confirmed in the national and global imagination during the 1950s. Mort states that 'the area's reputation for cultural difference [was] embedded in its extremely localized public spaces, its complex history and its unique customers and characters'.[63] In *Capital Affairs*, Mort has extensively mapped the transformation of sexual attitudes in Britain from Queen Elizabeth II's coronation in 1953 to the Profumo sex scandal in 1963. He magnifies Soho and the West End as the urban prism that highlights the importance of the acceleration of mass commercial industries in the redefining of sexual attitudes. In cinematic renderings of postwar Soho, there is a tendency to similarly map the capital of London's pleasure industries: prostitution, homosexuality, race, pathology, crime and consumerism. This book, like Mort, maps 'sex in the capital as a story of difference, dissidence and power [highlighting] sexuality as a contested terrain, shot through with the divisions that marked contemporary England'.[64]

Since the early twentieth century, Soho has played an important role in the development of homosexual culture in London. According to Mort: 'In the years before 1914, Soho and its environs were a focal point for the capital's expanding homosexual culture.'[65] Before the First World War, Soho businesses 'contained almost every type of homosexual customer' and 'sexualised spaces in Soho were open to double meanings whereby homosexual sex was advertised as an open secret to the initiated'.[66] However, despite this rich relationship, the examination of queer urban culture was elusive in Soho-set films until after 1963 for 'the 1960s industry was mainly concerned with the regulation of heterosexual freedom, and the challenges posed by contraception and female emancipation'.[67] Sue Harper has identified several films that provide minor debates about lesbianism such as *The L-Shaped Room* (Bryan Forbes, 1962) and *The World Ten Times Over* (Wolf Rilla, 1963). The latter film I will examine in greater detail in my conclusion. The film stars Sylvia Syms as a lesbian hostess named Billa who works at the fictional 'Ecstasy Club' in Soho. As Chris O'Rourke has shown, cinematic depictions of male homosexuality began to emerge during the mid-1950s and 1960s during 'scandals involving high-profile figures', which in turn meant a 'new interest in the city's sexual subcultures'.[68] The British realist film *Victim* (Basil Dearden, 1961) is arguably one of British cinema's most powerful responses to the Wolfenden Report. As Christine Geraghty states, the film is the 'most explicit contribution to the discussion' on homosexuality in the 1950s.[69]

Since the 1990s, we have seen a growth in literature that has examined the gay and lesbian experience in London and other metropolitan areas during the interwar period. London historian Peter Ackroyd has published numerous London histories on the City, Clerkenwell, the Thames and more recently *Gay London*, in which he pinpointed Soho's coffee bars as the 'harbingers for the gay occupation of that neighbourhood' in postwar London.[70] Matt Houlbrook's *Queer London: Perils and Pleasures in the Sexual Metropolis, 1918–1957* (2006) and Richard Hornsey's *The Spiv and the Architect: Unruly Life Is Postwar London* (2010) both examine metropolitan queer life. According to Hornsey, since the late 1950s, 'London's queer men were developing a productive mode of self-making intimately rooted in consumerist practices and modes of urban display'.[71] Houlbrook similarly explores 'the historical production of diverse modes of sexual difference … the relationship between "being queer" and the city', whilst he simultaneously scrutinises 'the competing understandings of masculinity, sexuality and character that shaped men's participation in queer urban culture and relate these to differences of class, race, age, and place'.[72] Until 1967, male homosexuality in Britain was illegal, so its depiction on screen was rare. In 1975, Quentin Crisp, 'the outrageously effeminate young quean' whose 'choice of Soho location was in part a deliberate attempt to identify with the world of bohemian squalor', was brought to television screens in the critically acclaimed *The Naked Civil Servant* (Jack Gold, 1975, starring John Hurt as Crisp).[73] Soho's queer history, which the press linked to prostitution, imprinted itself on the very fabric of Soho's sexual geography and subcultures. In 2018, the topic re-emerged and was depicted in the independent film *Postcards from London* (Steve McLean, 2018). The film explored gay prostitution and closed the BFI Flare: London LGBT Film Festival in 2018.

Bohemian-Cosmopolitan Figures

Although there are clear distinctions between Soho's cosmopolitan and bohemian identities, we do see the convergence of these two modes embodied by various archetypal figures like the Soho 'wide boy' or 'spiv', slang for petty criminals who rose to prominence in literature and film during the autumn of 1945. Mark Roodhouse describes him as a 'Janus-faced figure ... a penny capitalist flogging goods of unknown origin to a public hungry for controlled goods'.[74] He was a black-market racketeer, specialising in off-ration and under-the-counter sales of regulated goods during the Second World War and in the postwar years of austerity. The popular press capitalised on the pervasive presence of the wide boy in the news, engineering an affiliation with the American gangster, as depicted by interwar American crime fiction, in order to boost circulation figures.[75] This underground figure dressed 'flashily ... The style of dress came from the more fashion-conscious of the racing gangsters of the thirties'.[76] The press cemented the wide boy's origins as Irish, Italian or Jewish. Roodhouse suggests that linking foreigners to organised crime seemed both 'natural and inevitable'.[77] However, due to their overrepresentation in trades that were subject to intense regulation, a disproportionate number of Jewish traders were prosecuted for black-market offences during the war. For the popular press, the Jewish trader 'proved a more promising folk devil ... Both the black marketeer and the Jew were seen as exerting a baleful and hidden influence on society'.[78] The popular press continued to align London's Jewish community with the black market throughout the immediate postwar period, positioning their stories which suggested a type of 'Jewish invasion' of the city, in Soho and Whitechapel. Their imagining of Soho, the demi-monde of London, was a sinister labyrinth filled with elusive spivs and black-market racketeers. They in turn fixed Whitechapel, one of London's chief Jewish centres, as a notorious locus of crime and poverty.[79]

This image of Jewish wide boys operating within the black market permeates a series of postwar British films known as the 'spiv cycle' that flourished between 1945 and 1950.[80] In his seminal examination of the cycle, Robert Murphy identifies Lou Hyams (John Slater) and Morry Hyams (Sydney Tafler) as Jewish wide boys in the film *It Always Rains on Sunday* (Robert Hamer, UK, 1947), which is set in London's East End and was based on Arthur Le Bern's novel of the same name published in 1945. In this period, Bethnal Green was 'something of a ghetto, with its Jewish community, small-time criminals, and church missions packed tight within a railway line'.[81] The film stars British-Jewish actor Sydney Tafler, who would later star in *Wide Boy* (1952) directed by Ken Hughes.

Yiddish actor Meier Tzelniker, who plays music record executive Mr Mayer in *Expresso Bongo* (1960), made his film debut in *It Always Rains on a Sunday* as an 'an old immigrant newspaper seller, [who] despairs at the shady activities of his son, the owner of an entertainment arcade, who fixed boxing matches and gives his winnings to the local Christian-run youth club'.[82] The film also features actress Googie Withers as Rose Sandigate who would go on to play Helen Nosseross, wife of the corrupt Soho nightclub owner Phil Nosseross (Francis L. Sullivan) in Julian Dassin's *Night and the City* (1950), which stars American actor Richard Widmark as Harry Fabian, one of British cinema's most infamous spivs. Chief film critic for *The Guardian* Peter Bradshaw called Harry a 'genius of self-invention' in discussions on his experience of Soho.[83] Numerous other scholars, including Steve Chibnall, Richard Hornsey, Andrew Spicer, Sarah Street and Peter Wollen, have discussed the wide boy/spiv cycle in rich and engaging detail; however, there remains a peculiar absence of scholarship on the historical 'congruence between Jewish stereotypes and the figure of the black-market racketeer' in Soho and its effect on British cinema's portrayal of Jews.[84] In Chapter 6, I argue that there are nuanced (though rare in number) portrayals to be found in this figure of the Jewish wide boy in cinema, particularly when located in Soho. These depictions hold an intrinsic relationship to Soho's evolving migrant communities and, more importantly, represent a convergence of the bohemian with the cosmopolitan, forming a new hybrid identity emerging in an increasingly commercialised postwar world.

Bohemian-Cosmopolitan Spaces

After the Second World War, Soho and the rest of central London was fiercely promoted by entrepreneurs, journalists, artists and filmmakers, who constructed their Soho through the spaces (lens) in which they operated, from coffee bars to underground jazz clubs. Soho's dense geography meant that these spaces were located within proximity to one another. Inevitably, the geographical authenticity of Soho's industries was treated histrionically by cinema and, due to the absence of British and Asian stories, was largely ignored the entrepreneurs or workers who operated them. In Edmond T. Gréville's cult film *Beat Girl* (1960) and Lance Comfort's crime melodrama *Rag Doll* (1961), the white female (outsider) protagonists begin their Soho journeys within the familiar, safe enclosure of the coffee bar, a space proclaimed to be the birthplace of teenage culture and rock 'n' roll. The coffee bar is frequently constructed directly across from or above the underground and/or adjacent strip club, a space these characters become ultimately trapped within. These films are particularly explicit in their mission statement that Soho functions as a gateway to hedonism. Regarding the entrepreneurs who operated these spaces, since the Second World War, British cinema predominantly painted them as disreputable foreign gangsters who commit heinous offences against women and their local community, as seen in films such as *Noose* (1948) and *The Flesh is Weak* (1957), where their Italian or other European villains operated black-market and sex-trafficking rings. As we will discover, from the 1960s onwards, there is clear shift from the 'foreign devil' image into a more sympathetic, though still apathetic, and amoral character of the Jewish Soho wide boy (or swindler) such as part-conman, part-music manager Johnny Jackson (Laurence Harvey) in *Expresso Bongo* and strip club compere/toxic gambler Sammy Lee (Anthony Newley) in *The Small World of Sammy Lee* (1963).

Notes

1. See 'There Are Many Absurdities at the Soho Fair', *The Spectator*, 15 July 1955, 85.
2. Ibid., 198.
3. Stefan Anthony Slater states that although 'prostitution in Soho was reputedly as old as the area itself', the popular press exploited the sex industry in a 'sensational vein', regardless of empirical truth, to sell papers. See Slater, 'Containment-Managing Street Prostitution in

London, 1918–1959', *Journal of British Studies* 49 (2010), 332. See also Frank Mort, *Capital Affairs: London and the Making of the Permissive Society* (New Haven: Yale University Press, 2010), 214. See also the full Wolfenden report: John Wolfenden and Great Britain, Scottish Home Department, *Report of the Committee on Homosexual Offences and Prostitution*, Cmnd. 247 (London: HMSO, 1957).

4. See Frank Mort, 'Scandalous Events: Metropolitan Culture and Moral Change in Post-Second World War London', *Representations* 93 (2006), 122.
5. Burt Hyams documented many revues and recreation/sporting events during his career after the war. See Denis Gifford's *The British Film Catalogue: Volume 1. Fiction Film, 1895–1994*, 3rd edn (London: Routledge, 2001), 640.
6. François Penz and Andong Lu, *Urban Cinematics: Understanding Urban Phenomena through the Moving Image* (Bristol: Intellect, 2011), 14.
7. See the documentary *Sunshine in Soho* (Burt Hyams, 1956), which is available free on the BFI Player.
8. Pamela K. Gilbert, Ed, *Imagined Londons* (Albany: State University of New York Press, 2002), 124.
9. George R. Sims describes the 'turn' into the foreign unknown during his journey through Soho in 'Trips about Town', *Strand Magazine: An Illustrated Monthly* 29 (1905), 275.
10. Narration from *Sunshine in Soho* (Burt Hyams, 1956).
11. See 'A Fair Week's Run for the Real Soho', 10.
12. See Burt Hyams, 'Pretending to Be Soho', *The New Statesman and Nation*, 16 July 1955, 65–66.
13. Part of *The Spectator's* Notebook, this amusing short piece gives a first-hand look at the origins of the Soho Fair. See 'There Are Many Absurdities at the Soho Fair', *The Spectator*, 15 July 1955, 86.
14. The waiter's race consists of waiters from local establishments who must complete a running course whilst balancing a bottle of Champagne on a tray. This continues today – a much smaller more localised version of the Soho Fair called the 'Soho Village Fete' has run for forty years every summer in the gardens of St Anne's Church. See 'Soho Summer Fete', *This Is Soho*. Retrieved 13 October 2021 from https://www.thisissoho.co.uk/news/soho-village-fete.
15. Mort, *Capital Affairs*, 230.
16. Daniel Farson's *Soho in the Fifties* is part-memoir, part-ethnographic study of the Soho bohemians of the 1950s, including Francis Bacon and Muriel Belcher, the landlady of The Colony Room drinking club. See Mort, *Capital Affairs*, 230.
17. Ibid., 96–97.
18. Ibid., 96.
19. See 'The County of London Plan', *London Metropolitan Archives*. Retrieved 13 October 2021 from https://www.cityoflondon.gov.uk/things-to-do/london-metropolitan-archives/the-collections/Pages/county-of-london-plan.aspx.
20. Mort, *Capital Affairs*, 99–100.
21. Seeking a broader perspective, Peter J. Larkham and David Adams note that although the *County of London Plan* indeed 'shaped the history of planning and contemporary approaches', there existed a 'hierarchy of plans and range of planners' throughout the 1940s and 1950s. See Peter J. Larkham and David Adams, 'The Post-war Reconstruction of Planning of London: A Wider Perspective', *Centre for Environment and Society Research Working Paper Series No. 8* (Birmingham: Birmingham City University, 2011), 1 – 3.

22. Mort states that: 'The lifting of building controls by the Conservative Government in November 1954 opened the way for a property boom that continued unabated until 1964.' This fuelled the rise of home building and duly gave rise to the 'property tycoon', foreshadowing the arrival of Paul Raymond. See Mort, *Capital Affairs*, 92–93.
23. Ibid., 91.
24. Judith Walkowitz, *Nights out: Life in Cosmopolitan London* (New Haven: Yale University Press, 2012), 18. See also Gerry Black's history, *Living up West: Jewish Life in London's West End* (London: London Museum of Jewish Life, 1994), 24.
25. Walkowitz, *Nights out*, 19.
26. Ibid.
27. Ibid., 20, 182.
28. Ibid., 21.
29. One local police officer proclaimed Greek Street 'the worst street in the West End', which duly made newspaper headlines the following day. See ibid., 23.
30. Mort, *Capital Affairs*, 201.
31. Ibid.
32. Ibid., 213.
33. Ibid., 214.
34. Ibid., 216.
35. John Eade, *Placing London: From Imperial Capital to Global City* (Oxford: Berghahn Books, 2000), 61.
36. Ibid., 1.
37. Ibid., 11.
38. Ann Ogidi, 'Black British Film', *BFI Screenonline*. Retrieved 13 October 2021 from http://www.screenonline.org.uk/film/id/1144245/index.html.
39. Ibid.
40. Black, *Living up West*, 13–16.
41. Judith Summers, *Soho: A History of London's Most Colourful Neighbourhood* (London: Bloomsbury, 1991), 162.
42. Black, *Living up West*, 14.
43. Jewish tradesmen found 'better work as high-class outside workers, sewing, pressing and finishing men's suits for the nearby, very posh Savile Row tailors'. Ibid., 15.
44. Ibid.
45. See Mort, *Capital Affairs*, 210.
46. Black, *Living up West*, 21.
47. Summers, *Soho*, 164.
48. Walkowitz, *Nights out*, 182.
49. Ibid., 202.
50. See Roy Porter. *London: A Social History* (Cambridge, MA: Harvard University Press, 1994), 325; Black, *Living up West*, 269, 291 and Walkowitz, *Nights out*, 195.
51. Walkowitz. *Nights out*, 198.
52. Ibid., 26.
53. Matthew Sweet, 'Snakes, Slaves and Seduction', *The Guardian*, 6 February 2008. Retrieved 13 October 2021 from https://www.theguardian.com/film/2008/feb/06/china.world.

54. Panos Hatziprokopiou and Nicola Montagna. 'Contested Chinatown: Chinese Migrants' Incorporation and the Urban Space in London and Milan', *Ethnicities* 12(6) (2012), 712.
55. Ibid., 713.
56. Ibid., 707.
57. Ibid.
58. Ibid.
59. Pak Ling-Wan, 'Ping Pong (1986)', *BFI Screenonline*. Retrieved 13 October 2021 from http://www.screenonline.org.uk/film/id/475922/index.html.
60. 'Soursweet', *Variety*, 31 December 1988. Retrieved 13 October 2021 from https://variety.com/1988/film/reviews/soursweet-1200427837.
61. 'At the heart of the city, Chinatown today represents an image of the success of multicultural London, an established urban feature celebrated in its successful Olympic bid. In 2006, the Lord Mayor of London launched the "China in London" celebrations in recognition of the area's business potential and as one of the capital's most visited attractions, containing over 80 restaurants frequented by Londoners and tourists.' See Hatziprokopiou and Montagna, 'Contested Chinatown', 713.
62. 'Chinatown Pagoda Is Demolished as Part of Regeneration Scheme', *West End Extra*, 28 November 2016. Retrieved 13 October 2021 from http://westendextra.com/article/chinatown-pagoda-is-demolished-as-part-of-regeneration-scheme.
63. Mort, *Capital Affairs*, 201.
64. Ibid., 351.
65. Ibid., 213.
66. Ibid., 214.
67. See Sue Harper, *Women in British Cinema: Mad, Bad and Dangerous to Know* (London: Continuum, 2000), 124.
68. Chris O'Rourke, 'Queer London on Film: *Victim* (1961), *The Killing of Sister George* (1968), and *Nighthawks* (1978)', in Pam Hirsch and Chris O'Rourke (eds), *London on Film* (London: Palgrave Macmillan, 2017), 117.
69. Christine Geraghty, *British Cinema in the Fifties: Gender, Genre and the 'New Look'* (London: Routledge, 2000), 177.
70. See Peter Ackroyd, *Queer City: Gay London from the Romans to the Present Day* (London: Chatto & Windus, 2017), 1.
71. Richard Hornsey, *The Spiv and the Architect Unruly Life in Postwar London* (Minneapolis: University of Minnesota Press, 2010), 261.
72. Matt Houlbrook, *Queer London: Perils and Pleasures in the Sexual Metropolis, 1918–1957* (Chicago: University of Chicago Press, 2006), 8.
73. Ibid.
74. Both 'wide boy' and 'spiv' are often used interchangeably to describe a male hustler or black-market racketeer. However, the word 'spiv' displaced the term 'wide boy' by the end of 1946. 'The word has a meteoric linguistic career, moving from criminal cant to low slang to popular slang.' See Mark Roodhouse, *Black Market Britain: 1939–1955* (Oxford: Oxford University Press, 2013), 243.
75. Ibid., 228.
76. Robert Murphy, *Realism and Tinsel: Cinema and Society in Britain 1939–48* (New York: Routledge, 1992), 50.

77. Roodhouse, *Black Market Britain*, 232.
78. Roodhouse states that: 'Of the four national papers studied, the Daily Telegraph and the Daily Express presented the most distorted view of Jewish involvement in evasion. The committee estimated that 11% of prosecutions for black market offences involved Jews during the study period but reports in the Telegraph and Express gave the impression that the proportion was 25% and 29% respectively.' See Ibid., 233–35.
79. The East End 'seemed a world apart from the rest of London. Suicides were commonplace in the East End. In Shoreditch, for four shillings and sixpence return, you could escape the poverty for a day at the Newmarket races. It was into this chaotic and dangerous world that Jack Spot [the gangster] was born'. See Clarkson Wensley, *Hit 'Em Hard: Jack Spot – King of the Underworld* (London: HarperCollins, 2002), 1–3. See also press representations of the East End, Jack the Ripper and the Whitechapel murders of the late nineteenth century in L. Perry Curtis Jr., *Jack the Ripper and the London Press* (New Haven: Yale University Press, 2001).
80. Murphy, *Realism and Tinsel*, 151.
81. Kevin Gough-Yates, 'Jews and Exiles in British Cinema', *Leo Baeck Institute Yearbook* 37(1) (1992), 539.
82. Ibid., 549.
83. Peter Bradshaw, 'Soho and *Night and the City* (1950)'. Interview by Jingan Young, *Soho Bites Podcast*. Retrieved 13 October 2021 from https://itunes.apple.com/au/podcast/sohoonscreen/id1444212180.
84. Roodhouse, *Black Market Britain*, 233.

CHAPTER 3

'God Is Everywhere!'
Engineering the Immigrant Landscape of *Miracle in Soho* (1957)

> *In front of the church kneels Julia. Sam stops near the entrance. He wouldn't disturb her prayers for anything in the world. Nobody else is in the church except the old man and the young girl, and silence, and mystery, and faith.*
>
> *Art Dept. Please Note: This set mainly consists of the 'Pig & Pot' Pub at one end & Church at other.*
>
> —Production script, *Miracle in Soho*, Emeric Pressburger, n.d.

Anglo-Italian Julia Gozzi (Belinda Lee) is kneeling at the altar of St Anthony of Padua, the patron saint of lost things.[1] She is praying for a miracle. We move to a close-up of her determined face, brilliantly lit by a golden candelabra as she urgently pleads for the return of Michael Morgan (John Gregson), an Irish road labourer and incorrigible breaker of hearts, including her own. Shortly thereafter, her prayers are answered. Outside St Anthony's Church, the water mains beneath asphalt that have been newly laid by Morgan and his road gang burst open, flooding the lane. 'Yes, yes, God *is* everywhere!' proclaims Salvationist postman Sam Bishop (Cyril Cusack) as the locals lament the unforeseen damage to their beloved street. The following morning, Michael returns with the road gang to repair the street and the lovers are reconciled.[2]

This sequence marked the conclusion to *Miracle in Soho*, which was directed by Julian Amyes and released in the summer of 1957. The film was executive produced by Earl St John for the J. Arthur Rank Organisation and co-produced and written by Emeric Pressburger, whose original version of the script was written in 1934 under the title *The Miracle in St. Anthony's Lane*. The final film charts its narrative over a week in the life of a fictional Soho street called St Anthony's Lane. Upon its release, the film was a failure both critically and at the box office.

Figure 3.1a. Opening tracking shot across Soho from *Miracle in Soho* (Julian Amyes, 1957). DVD, Strawberry Media, 2014

Figure 3.1b. Meeting Mr Bishop (Cyril Cusack). Still from the opening of *Miracle in Soho* (Julian Amyes, 1957). DVD, Strawberry Media, 2014

48 · SOHO ON SCREEN

Figure 3.1c. Marking the boundaries of St Anthony's Lane. Still from the opening of *Miracle in Soho* (Julian Amyes, 1957). DVD, Strawberry Media, 2014

Figure 3.1d. A Chinese family observe the disturbance. Still from the opening of *Miracle in Soho* (Julian Amyes, 1957). DVD, Strawberry Media, 2014

Figure 3.1e. The road gang close the lane. Still from the opening of *Miracle in Soho* (Julian Amyes, 1957). DVD, Strawberry Media, 2014

Commentators seemed unanimous in their disappointment with the cinematically engineered Soho set designed by Carmen Dillon, who had won an Academy Award for her work on *Hamlet* (Laurence Olivier, 1948). The self-contained, artificially constructed spaces of St Anthony's Lane, where commercial spaces of the pub, restaurant and church are erected side by side, adds a bygone theatricality to the film. Soho is cinematically mapped as a cosmopolitan quarter, where the area's commercial and moral spaces are two conflicting and artificially constructed mechanisms.

Despite its negative reception, this forgotten film is a rare big-budget treatment of London's Soho and a significant example of the British film industry's attempt to combat the British public's increased consumption of commercial television through the implementation of cross-marketing and other strategies aimed to appeal to the global marketplace. It was also a film that deliberately linked itself to Soho. The studio behind the film, the Rank Organisation released the film during the week-long Soho Fair of 1957, going so far as to stage promotional one-offs, such as frivolous competitions where members of the principal cast such as Belinda Lee attended as guests. Pressburger, like most filmmakers, regularly visited

Soho, once the physical locus of British film industry headquarters from the 1930s until the end of the century and felt inclined to capture the area's cultural diversity on film.[3] How did Pressburger's identity as an émigré filmmaker inform the film's reconstruction of the area? By this period, the Hungarian-Jewish filmmaker had been living in Great Britain for over two decades, having emigrated as a refugee in 1935 before gaining full British citizenship in 1946. The topographical specificity found within Pressburger's final screenplay does suggest a fundamental and instinctive understanding of the urban arrangement of Soho's commercial economies. As a space of 'cultural difference [along with] extremely localised public spaces, complex history, unique customs and characters', Soho makes the ideal transitional site for exploring the immigrant and native interaction on screen.[4] However, the film's chief love story between the hedonist native Michael and the moral immigrant Julia conflicts with the film's underlying critique of urban life and the historical significance of Soho's entrepreneurs, largely immigrants, who provided the 'commercial blueprint for the area's renewal'.[5]

This chapter will discuss the film's reconstruction of Soho's immigrant landscape in the context of postwar commercial development and British cinema's treatment of cosmopolitanism, whilst also providing one of the first extensive looks at its production history, its relationship with the area's development, and Pressburger's forgotten unproduced screenplays. I will argue that this is a unique and important film, both as a contribution to migrant portraits on screen and also as an admirable attempt to depict Soho's diversity. It is also worthy of reconsideration as a film that has an intrinsic relationship with Soho's renewal as a cosmopolitan-bohemian centre on the national and global stage.

The Making of an Englishman: Immigration and Exile

In the biography of Pressburger written by his grandson, the acclaimed Scottish director Kevin Macdonald, we learn of the 'peculiar twists of fate' that prevented the original *Miracle in Soho* script, first written in 1934, from going into full production: 'There did indeed seem to be a touch of divine intervention in the fortunes of *The Miracle in St. Anthony's Lane* ... It was forever being bought or optioned.'[6] Macdonald also directed and produced a television documentary on his grandfather's life called *The Making of an Englishman*, which first aired on Channel 4 in the United Kingdom in 1995. The film documents Pressburger's journey to England and further underscores the importance of his identity as an exile-filmmaker in England. Both of Macdonald's biographies of Pressburger further contribute towards our understanding of his grandfather's films, for 'like so many other European refugees from Hitler', he became 'more Anglophile than the English'.[7]

The chief protagonists of *Miracle in Soho* emulate and assimilate Englishness. This echoes Pressburger's own story of exile. Born in Hungary as Imre József Pressburger in 1902, his migrant childhood led him to living in Prague, Stuttgart and Budapest following the outbreak of the First World War. After arriving in Berlin in the 1920s, he found employment with the German UFA studios and worked on scripts in their dramaturgy department before leaving for France (Paris) in 1933 when working conditions for Jews became more difficult. He arrived in London two years later, becoming a protégé of the fellow exile, producer Alexander Korda of London Films, who would later introduce him to the director Michael Powell. Pressburger's successful working partnership with Michael Powell had come to an end the year before the release of *Miracle in Soho*. Together, the pair had produced thirteen films between 1943 and 1955 under the alias of 'The Archers', the majority of which 'expressed a deep fascination with and affection for Britishness'.[8] Following their separation, Powell's second project was the psychological crime thriller *Peeping Tom* (1960), which utilises Newman Passage in London's Fitzrovia (or North Soho) for its opening sequence in which a young filmmaker Mark Lewis (Carl Boehm) brutally murders a prostitute whilst simultaneously recording the violent act on his camera. Pressburger's second project, following a lost film entitled *Men Against Britannia* (Marcel Hellman, 1957), was *Miracle in Soho*, which he also co-produced.

Kevin Gough-Yates proclaims Pressburger 'one of only two exile script-writers who shaped significant careers in Britain', for he is 'unique in that the sense of emptiness and dejection that he experienced as an exile'.[9] Interestingly, Pressburger's original script for the film told the story of German exiles in Paris and sought to explore the notion of the miracle as not so much a physical act, but one of imagination:

> A few years earlier he had slept rough in a famous Berlin synagogue, planning to creep out just before morning service. Too late, he heard the congregation chanting, and crept down, only to be welcomed as a member of the quorum; the service had not started, and the sounds he had heard has been in his imagination.

'Surely', he claimed, 'a miracle.' A René Chair-like idea, full of character, with a number of interlocking stories, Miracle in St. Anthony's Lane *was another story of exile.*[10]

Alternate versions of Pressburger's script provide more expansive detail into the Gozzi family's process of emigration and initially plotted their journey to New York instead of Canada. The Rank Organisation's other top promoted films released in 1957 included the Dirk Bogarde vehicle *Campbell's Kingdom* (Ralph Thomas), a 'large-scale adventure story set in Canada', and *Hell Drivers* (C. Baker Endfield), 'a tough tale about short-haul lorry drivers' starring Stanley Baker as an ex-con and Herbert Lom as an Italian driver called Gino Rossi.[11] In one of Pressburger's later draft versions of the script reset in London, he devotes an entire scene to detailing the Gozzi family's visit to the American Embassy in Grosvenor Square, which he describes as: 'A small, new, clean, efficient room, divided by a counter [where] Notices inform you that you are on American soil.'[12] Although I have found no clear explanation for this change from the Gozzi's emigration to Canada instead of the United States, this change may have been due to Canada's Commonwealth status and would sit reasonably well within the Rank Organisation's reprioritisation of promotion of its products and stars both nationally and throughout Europe.[13]

However, it would be several decades before the film impresario J. Arthur Rank would put into motion Pressburger's new version of his portrayal of a cosmopolitan village and its habitués, 'reset among the Italian community in London's Soho', which opens with the sudden and unwelcome invasion of a road gang to replace the asphalt of the fictitious St Anthony's Lane, described by Pressburger as a 'tiny haven in the heart of Cosmopolitan Soho' where 'quietness reigns'.[14] The finalised story for the film is that of the redemption of the self-serving philanderer Michael Morgan through the love of a good woman (and Soho local) Julia Gozzi, an Italian immigrant who works at the local pet shop. A potential love affair is interrupted by her family's decision to emigrate to Canada. Michael's redemption is manifested through Julia's prayer for a miracle to stop him leaving Soho after finishing work on the lane, which ultimately results in the water mains flooding the street, causing him to return. Yet, the doubts vehemently expressed by Julia Gozzi's siblings Mafalda (Rosalie Crutchley) and Fillipo (Ian Bannen) on emigrating abroad are never fully developed, and their expressed desire to cultivate their own commercial businesses is abruptly dropped by the film. The siblings' overarching desire is to remain part of the Soho fabric as opposed to remaining in the family unit with Mama Gozzi (Marie Burke) and Papa Gozzi (Peter Illing). This choice reflects the work of Louis Wirth, of the Chicago School, who argued the social heterogeneity found within cities reinforces the tendency of the individual to pursue their own interests, leading to a loss of community ties, traditions and the increase in social disorganisation.[15]

Italians in Soho and the Soho Fair

Pressburger's decision to spotlight an Italian family living in Soho was wholly unsurprising. As Britain's allies in the First World War, the population of Italians in London 'peaked in 1911, at 12,000 but these fell by only a couple of hundred by 1921'.[16] The largest Italian colony in Britain was originally located in London, around the area known as Saffron Hill in Clerkenwell. There, Italian immigrants 'cultivated their own industries … catering for their own needs with cafés, delicatessen, restaurants, clubs, a theatre and dance hall'.[17] The 'brilliantly coloured' procession known as 'Our Lady of Mount Carmel', which occurred every July from St Peter's Church located on 136 Clerkenwell Rd, was one of several public spectacles organised by the community each summer in London between the wars.[18] Elisabetta Girelli, who has partly examined the representation of the Italian family in *Miracle in Soho*, notes that by the 1920s, 'Italian catering continued to thrive … Italians in London were entering the exclusive hotel and restaurant industry'.[19] After the First World War, the population of Italians in that area moved westwards, largely to Soho. By 1934, according to Jerry White, Soho became known as 'London's Italian quarter'.[20] The area's close proximity to the entertainment centres of Piccadilly Circus and the West End rendered it a dining hub and Italian restaurants prospered. They were run by prewar immigrants who 'had made their way up the catering trade' and were 'skilled in the demands of display, décor and performance', providing the English public with continental food and taste.[21]

According to Judith Walkowitz, Italian restaurants in Soho were places of hard work and strict regimentation for the immigrants employed there. The Gozzi family's work ethic and value for the Soho community is emphasised by both the community's support of their emigration and their hierarchical positions within various commercial businesses located in the area and on the lane. The eldest Gozzi daughter Mafalda (Rosalie Crutchley) manages the Anacapri Restaurant, her brother Filippo comanages Ferrari's Wine Store and youngest daughter Julia is a shop assistant at Mrs Coleman's pet shop. The Anacapri Restaurant is the film's second most-used location after St Anthony's Church. Interwar and postwar Soho's catering establishments 'provided stage sets for English fantasies of travel and escape'[22] and the interiors of the Anacapri restaurant are plastered with aspirational travel posters depicting illustrations of Sardinian coastlines.

Walkowitz has also highlighted how Italian restaurants were stages for political drama, for 'Fascists used the portable food culture of Italy as a vehicle to solidify fiercely nationalistic patriotism at home and abroad. Beginning in 1921, they especially targeted the West End and Soho catering industry as the focal point for Fascist takeover of the "Italian colony"'.[23] Conflicts between fascists and anti-fascists community of Italians in Soho existed, but the outbreak of the Second World War and Mussolini's subsequent declaration of war on Britain and its allies in 1940 further intensified racial hostility towards Italian émigrés. Anti-Italian demonstrates took place throughout the country. In Soho, there was an anti-fascist riot prompted by Mussolini's speech in the summer of 1940, which saw the smashing of windows of local Italian businesses and was later labelled by the press as 'The Battle of Soho'.[24] Although *Miracle in Soho* does contain stereotypical representations of émigrés (for example, the Gozzi family regularly use exaggerated hand gestures during tense exchanges), it is still a sympathetic portrayal (perhaps even acting as a type of anti-fascist protest) of the hardworking Italian family who are respected members of the Soho community. The other commercial/trade spaces are owned and run by the immigrant community: Ferrari's Wine Shop and Mr Swoboda's Continental Bakery. The bakery shop window, which is deliberately kept in shot during the arrival of the road gang to the street in the opening sequence, contains a sign that assures us that this shop is *entirely* British. This may refer to the end of food rationing in Britain in 1954. However, when Michael defends his skirt-chasing habits to the postman Sam Bishop, he pointedly responds that women *aren't* on the ration, suggesting the film takes place in the years of derationing.

The Soho Fair does not explicitly feature in *Miracle in Soho.* However, the film has a reciprocal relationship with it. The film was released during the week of the third Soho Fair in July 1957. Events scheduled during the Soho Fair to complement the film's release listed in the weekly London magazine *What's on in London* include the '*Miracle in Soho* Window Dressing Competition' and the 'Belinda Lee Challenge Cup', which took place at Lysbeth Hall in Soho Square.[25] The inhabitants of St Anthony's Lane might also have been drawn explicitly from the local

Figure 3.2a. Mr Swoboda's Bakery. Still from *Miracle in Soho* (Julian Amyes, 1957). DVD, Strawberry Media, 2014

Figure 3.2b. The Anacapri Restaurant. Still from *Miracle in Soho* (Julian Amyes, 1957). DVD, Strawberry Media, 2014

Figure 3.2c. The Pig and Pot Pub. Still from *Miracle in Soho* (Julian Amyes, 1957). DVD, Strawberry Media, 2014

Figure 3.2d. Mrs Coleman's pet shop. Still from *Miracle in Soho* (Julian Amyes, 1957). DVD, Strawberry Media, 2014

Figure 3.2e. St Anthony's Church. Still from *Miracle in Soho* (Julian Amyes, 1957). DVD, Strawberry Media, 2014

entrepreneurs, chefs, waiters, dancers and jazz musicians who feature in Burt Hyams' 1956 whimsical documentary *Sunshine in Soho*, which chronicles the first Soho Fair. The documentary's influence on the film is most evident in the opening sequence, where the camera sweeps across grey and brown weather-beaten rooftops with the addition of a voiceover from an unseen (uncredited) male narrator who declares:

> There is an island in the great city of London, a little foreign island called Soho … Italians live there and Greeks, French, Spaniards and Germans, Czechs and Hungarians, Maltese, Cypriots, Hindus and Muhammads. There's probably an Eskimo or two, certainly a few Scotsman.[26]

The narrator emphatically underscores the fact that Italians live in Soho, which precedes his listing of other communities. This not only emphasises the film's focus on the Gozzi family, but also suggests the popular association of Italians and Italian culture in Soho during the period. Voiceover narration and the use of montage and tracking shots through Soho markets appear throughout Hyams' documentary. They are almost parallel to those camera movements used by director Amyes to sweep across fictional St Anthony's Lane storefronts and apartment windows during the opening sequence. According to Pressburger's screenplay these windows belong to: 'Negros, Chinese, Spanish Woman, Mrs. Mop, Swoboda, Mrs. Belucci, Buddy Brown.'[27] This personalised engagement of geographical and cultural difference visually suggests a commodification of the experience of the modern world. Both films view Soho as a continental gateway and major thoroughfare to the tourist city (London), serving as an intercultural/contact zone between national and global identities. The use of voiceover and tracking shots, a regular Soho device, mimics the transcultural text of the guidebook and acts as a mediation between cultural differences. Although the film makes an admirable attempt to 'gaze' briefly at the lives of the Soho minority during the opening, it functions on a rather superficial level, adding a splash of exoticism. This is in contrast to *Sunshine in Soho*, where we are provided with, though still somewhat one-dimensional depictions, greater access to these communities and their livelihoods. Nevertheless, the emphasis on the 'otherness' of Soho's migrant communities within these films remains starkly apparent.

Miracle in Soho and 1950s Britain

There is a peculiar irony to the ultimate cinematic realisation of Pressburger's script in mid-1950s Britain. Christopher Booker, one of the founding members of *Private Eye* (1961–63) and resident scriptwriter for the satirical television series *That Was the Week That Was* (1962–63), has described in enigmatic detail the 'Never had it so good' prosperity of mid-1950s Britain, where: 'Increasing personal incomes and homeownership caused a boom in consumer goods, American-style supermarkets and strip-tease clubs swiftly spread throughout Soho and the cities of the North. Commercial television entered a golden age.'[28] The income boom in 1950s Britain created novel forms of popular leisure, and the increase in television ownership inevitably led to the decline of cinema-going. In 1957, cinema attendance was down from 17 per cent on the previous year.[29] In the same year, the Rank Organisation, one of the most dominant forces in UK film production in the period, and the production company behind *Miracle in Soho*, was forced to amalgamate its Gaumont and Odeon cinema circuits, resulting in eighty of the Rank Organisation's cinemas closing over the next three years. Concurrently,

Rank and other British studios were struggling to option films that would appeal to younger audiences, who comprised nearly half of their cinemas' regular weekly audience. But this did not deter its founding head J. Arthur Rank whose ferocious promotional strategies for its stars and films in this period, which, as Steve Chibnall has highlighted, included 'a drive to popularise its contract artists on a scale never before attempted.' These strategies included Rank's expansion of 'contract artists' during the 1950s, which was 'met with a cautious welcome by a press that was suspicious of publicist hype'.[30]

The film's director Julian Amyes began his feature film career with a 'competent, if unadventurous, Korean war-story' and joined the BBC in 1951 as a producer.[31] His engagement as director on *Miracle in Soho* was most likely a strategic move on behalf of the studio to employ a technically competent and knowledgeable individual who saw the potential of strengthening the relationship between cinema and television. According to an article published in *Sight and Sound* (1958), Amyes was 'one of the most accomplished directors working in British television', which certainly appears to be in accordance with the Rank Organisation's measured initiatives to collaborate with television. Interestingly, Amyes would only work as a director with the Rank Organisation on *Miracle in Soho*, a film 'less realistic in style and perhaps for that reason less successful'.[32]

The film was shot in Eastmancolor on a mammoth studio set located at Pinewood Studios in Buckinghamshire. The film's director of photography was Christopher Challis, a British cinematographer with a career spanning over seventy British feature films. He was also a long-time collaborator of Pressburger and Powell on films such as *The Small Back Room* (1949), *The Tales of Hoffman* (1951) and *Ill Met by Moonlight* (1957), the latter being the final Powell and Pressburger 'The Archers' film. One black-and-white photograph found within the Moviestore Collection taken during production displays the complexity of art director Carmen Dillon's design and reconstruction of this neighbourhood (albeit fictional) of Soho. In the photograph, we see Challis, cameramen, supporting actors and lighting rigs positioned within close proximity to one another.[33] The façades of the diverse array of shops, schools, flats and restaurants operated by residents of the street that are specifically dictated by Pressburger's screenplay highlight the imagined-authentic sphere of commercial Soho, but also one that is utilised by guidebook-style filmmaking.[34]

The film is also an important artefact in our examination of technological transformations in the British film industry. Sarah Street has briefly discussed the film in relation to the history of Eastmancolor, a 'relatively cheap widely available film stock' that revolutionised British film from the end of the 1950s onwards. In the article, she examines the ways in which colour films from the period such as *Miracle in Soho* and Mankowitz's *A Kid for Two Farthings* (1955) 'provided an opportunity for greater realism'.[35] Whilst both films were more 'magical realist than hard-hitting social realist films, their vibrant, multicultural settings invested them with a quasi-documentary imperative to deliver "authenticity" at a time when colour was still a relative novelty'.[36] Street states that for *Miracle in Soho*, Dillon created a particularly 'muted' palette for the film in her re-creation of the cosmopolitan locus. The only visibly vibrant or bright colours used in the film is for the scarlet-coloured road closure sign used by the road gang, for 'Chris Challis's cinematography was designed to convey a gritty, realist palette that was supported by art director Carmen Dillon's "'restrained' vision", she later said, "We decided that all the colours should be as muted as possible, with no strong blacks, whites or primaries. The only patch of sky to be seen was through a narrow alley".'[37] This choice to evoke a muted realism was undoubtedly employed to assist in the dilution of the film's magical realist elements, as embodied by Julia's miracles.

Critical Reception: An 'Inauthentic' Soho?

Following the film's release, critics were disappointed with what they saw as an artificially rendered Soho. *Monthly Film Bulletin* declared: 'This depressing production, with its synthetic Soho setting, has characters conceived strictly within the less happy conventions of British comedy.' *Variety* said 'A rather slow-moving sentimental yarn' and the movie fan magazine *Picturegoer* condemned its 'wispy plot, set in a studio-built Soho street', though the magazine suggests the film provided a hopeful premise in its introduction to a 'peaceful mixture of people, far removed from the gangsters and floozies that usually people the screen Soho'.[38] Critics in recent years have taken a similar view. The British Film Institute's Fiction Curator Dylan Cave said: 'The huge sets [which although they] complemented Pressburger's view of the magic that appears in everyday life … in a climate increasingly dominated by social realism … looked stilted and fake.'[39] The announcement for the film's premiere in London was splashed on the front page of *What's on in London* in 1957. The film was described as a 'sentimental little fairy story' that failed in its cinematic representation of Soho. However, it also jokingly added in its review: 'Of course, this isn't really Soho at all, but I don't suppose that's going to worry anyone except a few fussy Sohoians.'[40]

According to Steve Chibnall, during this period, J. Arthur Rank had 'supped with the devil' in extending his efforts promoting films by advertising on new platforms, including purchasing advertising slots in commercial television and popular women's magazines. For the film's publicity, Rank even produced a 20-minute film entitled *Full Screen Ahead*, which was screened in Rank's cinemas in April 1957, several months before the film was released in cinemas.[41] The film takes its audience on a day out at Pinewood Studios led by the actress Belinda Lee with a visit to the set of *Miracle in Soho*. In the year of the film's release, Lee endorsed cosmetics such as Vitapointe of Paris in the *Daily Express*. Marketing for the product even managed to incorporate Pressburger's film, for the tagline reads: 'I want to tell the world! I've found a hair dressing cream that works miracles!'[42] Simultaneously, *Picturegoer* ran several profiles of Lee in a partial attempt to reinvent her public persona from pin-up to 'serious' actress.[43] This emphasises the painstaking efforts by studios in this period, including the Rank Organisation's big idea of 1955–57, which involved forging the American film market for Europe: 'When Rank had a star such as Belinda Lee, who they believed would appeal to the Italian market, they used the most talented of Studio Favalli's illustrators to promote her films … Cesselon depicted her as an Anglo-Italian girl in *Miracle in Soho*.'[44]

On paper, the film was seemingly the perfect vehicle for Lee's rise to stardom and Rank's move to colonise the European marketplace. Unfortunately, their respective efforts did little to increase the film's appeal at home or abroad.[45] I believe that the negative position of critics on the superficial 'authenticity' of the film's Soho could not have been wholly satisfied due to the technological constraints of the period, alongside the filmmakers' and the Rank studio's desire for control, as opposed to the potential risks and great costs of on-location shooting. However, the particular reconstruction of Soho and its community was no doubt driven by Pressburger's imagining of Soho as an area of romantic mysticism and religious faith. His representation succeeds only partially, specifically in the depiction of the convergence of cultural diversity in Soho, but the film's refusal to delve deeper into the area's history, legacy and development, alongside failing to acknowledge the more salacious and criminal aspects of Soho, produces an arguably one-dimensional product.

Further changes could also have accounted for *Miracle in Soho*'s negative reception. In one version of the film written in 1937, Pressburger paints a new incarnation of the character of Sam Bishop as a more pivotal figure, who he names Mr Brewer. He opens the film and initially protests to the local council against repairs scheduled to be made on St Anthony's Lane. This idea was developed later in a script sent to Michael Powell. The opening scene of this version conveys the ignorance of London magistrates and city planners for the isolated St Anthony community in Soho and parodies political bureaucracy. In the scene, Mr Brewer, a Soho district officer, comes to plead for the road to be repaired, which is met with bemused silence:

> Mr. Brewer was called to give evidence on road repairs in St Anthony's Lane.
> SPEAKER: Where's that, sir? Never heard of it.
> MR. BREWER: Tiny little street, sir.
> SPEAKER: But where is it?!
> CHAIRMAN: West 3 – Soho – London – England.
> SPEAKER: Thank you, sir.
> CHAIRMAN: Pleasure.
> SPEAKER: I thought we finished with the Soho repairs, Mr. Chairman.[46]

This sequence was not simply reflective of the bureaucracy of British government, but also retrospectively predicted Soho's renewal after the war. By reinventing the role of Mr Brewer and diluting Mr Bishop's purpose, replacing him instead with the Irish protagonist of Michael Morgan, who is alien to the cosmopolitan culture of Soho, Pressburger strengthens the reciprocity of perspective, but at the expense of the migrant characters. Michael explores a world outside of his own culture as not only a passive observer but an active participant. His involvement with the Gozzi family and cosmopolitanism grows more intense after he acts as mediator with the rest of the Gozzi family after Filippo announces he will forgo Canada to stay in Soho to marry Gwladys, a voluptuous barmaid at the Pig and Pot who, only the night before, had almost committed adultery with Michael. Later scenes depict Michael's true circumstances, living in a poorly maintained, shared flat with his father (Wilfrid Lawson), a London cabbie. This sequence, the only one to take place outside Soho, is vital to our understanding of Michael's aspirations to involve himself with the close-knit Gozzi family. Listening to a concert at the Royal Albert Hall on the radio, we learn that Michael is restricted in terms of pursuing the cultivated world he desires outside Soho's peripheries. It is most certainly one of the film's more poignant moments, for through music, another world is created, an aspirational world of civilisation and beauty.

St Anthony's Lane

In many respects, Soho can be likened to a cultural experiment where large-scale movements of capital and culture are played out in intensely local settings.[47] The localised spaces of the pub and church located on opposite ends of St Anthony's Lane act as a metaphor for the conflicting lives of immigrants and natives. This is demonstrated by the Pig and Pot pub, a working-class space that is patronised by predominantly English labourers and tradesmen. In the film, this space is not frequented by the lane's migrant populations; even the pub's landlord Old Bill (Douglas Ives) warns Michael to beware foreigners who 'carry knives' (perhaps another signalling of racial discrimination against Italians in the period). The film also plays on existing archetypal representations of Britishness. Charlotte Brunsdon's identification of the pub as a 'low-life landmark' rings true in the case of *Miracle in Soho*. The Pig and Pot's dark and smoky interior 'permit[s] chance interactions and can easily be produced in the studio' and makes the distinction between public and private spaces.[48] This designation aligns with other British films of the period, providing familiar markers for national audiences.

Two miracles, in fact, take place within St Anthony's Church. The first is a scene which takes place shortly after Filippo's discovery of Morgan and Gwladys' secret liaison, which causes him to renounce his family forever. The Gozzi family then attend Sunday mass with other members of the migrant community. Whilst the congregation prays, Julia stands and lights a candle. The camera closes in on her face and we hear her internal thoughts. She prays for her brother to 'do the right thing' by her father. Her prayers are soon answered when Filippo enters the church and joins his family who are singing the hymn, 'Praise, My Soul, the King of Heaven' acting as a visual representation of reconciliation.[49]

Kevin Gough-Yates has suggested that Julia's answered 'miracles' are in fact a reflection of the changes Pressburger made in his scripts from the 1930s and 1940s; 'The question is less whether the "miracle" is actually a miracle, conjured up by a prayer in the church, but more whether it exists in the imagination of a lovesick girl.'[50] This may relate to Michael Powell's pass on directing the film.

Gough-Yates suggests that the filmmaker believed the script lacked substance and recognised it as too close to their 1946 film *A Matter of Life and Death* and didn't want to tread old ground.[51] The film arguably draws upon the 'rich and strange' magical realism that Raymond Durgnat claims pervades Powell and Pressburger's films released during and shortly after the Second World War.[52] In addition, Powell and Pressburger's films have an equal fascination for the cinematic relationship between character and place. Durgnat states: 'The impact of place on character is explored, [by Powell and Pressburger] as landscapes imprint their effect on protagonists, or as concrete places become externally projected renditions of subjective states. These new worlds are given a sense of magic – sometimes utopian, sometimes threatening, sometimes surreal'.[53]

As one body, St Anthony's Lane is a device employed by Pressburger to emphasise his predominant themes of 'community under threat' and 'faith in doubt'. These themes wholly manifest themselves during the climactic moments of the film when Julia proves her moral fortitude embodied by her final prayer to St Anthony. The concluding sequence is not simply a demonstration of the magical; it is also a selfless act of redemption. Julia, the daughter of Italian immigrants, has sacrificed the promise of a new life with her family in Canada for Michael, a self-proclaimed lothario who does little to prove he is worthy of her love. We can reapply Wirth's argument to Julia's journey, for: 'The city is the product of growth rather than of instantaneous creation ... [the] great expansion of the modern city must acknowledge its rural origins for our social life bears the imprint of an earlier folk society.'[54] Julia's longstanding devotion for her adopted home of St Anthony's Lane and her belief in a man she has barely known a week represent her unconscious desire for romantic and urban entanglement. She returns to Soho against the demands of her family in order to fulfil her potential. Julia's miracles echo the critical reception of the film's 'peaceful' objective to paint Soho as a surreal place, where dreams come true against the odds. But this relegates the perhaps more interesting and relevant story of a family's immigration and replaces it with the conventional trope of fairytale romance. The miracles, which are proposed as a result of Julia's self-sacrifice (forgoing immigrating to Canada for the uncertain life in Soho), become obstructed within the film's negotiation of an alleged utopian, cosmopolitan landscape.

Conclusion

Miracle in Soho provides an underlying criticism for the disorganisation of urban life, but through the prism of an isolated locality and its engagement with the city. It is also a highly commercial product, competing within a marketplace that saw the dramatic decline of cinema-going and the rapidly growing popularity of commercial television in a decade described by Sue Harper and Vincent Porter as a 'largely unknown country, regarded by critics as dull'.[55] The film was a lost opportunity to convey the real-life evolving migrant ethnography and the tensions found within late 1950s Soho. Perhaps the potentially more powerful transformative story was obstructed by Pressburger's love for magical realism, embodied by the symbolic existence of the damaged St Anthony's Lane and the Gozzi family, who represented his own voyage to Britain. Along with the aggressive commercial strategies for the film employed by producer J. Arthur Rank, it would appear the filmmakers involved in the production failed to successfully negotiate their own imagined Soho.

Regardless of its limitations, the film remains a welcome addition to a postwar world massively riven by discord and is a great contribution to a filmography of postwar Soho films that contains an exhaustive array of narratives involving strippers, pornographers and prostitutes. This film provides a rare cinematic representation of Soho as a moral space for the native Englishman. Michael is the sinner who learns the errors of his ways as a result of immigrant Julia's love, personified by her loyalty, devotion and imagination. Like so many of Pressburger's films with Powell, this is a fairytale that explores the morality of the native and immigrant, positioned within the localised urban and cosmopolitan centre of Soho.

Notes

1. For Italian immigrants in post-Second World War Toronto, St Anthony of Padua held special meaning. The story of the saint's shipwrecked arrival in Sicily resonated with thousands finding their way from the docks of Halifax to Toronto's Little Italy. The film's religious themes further contribute to producer J. Arthur Rank's 'big idea' of the 1950s for films to appeal to the predominantly Catholic, Italian marketplace. See Jordan Stranger-Ross, *Staying Italian: Urban Change and Ethnic Life in Postwar Toronto and Philadelphia* (Chicago: University of Chicago Press, 2009), 76. For more on Rank's 'big ideas', see Steve Chibnall, 'Banging the Gong: The Promotional Strategies of Britain's J. Arthur Rank Organisation in the 1950s', *Historical Journal of Film, Radio and Television* 37 (2016), 1–30.

2. In his script, Emeric Pressburger gives his character Michael Morgan a motto for living: 'Never go back ... there will be another street, another set of women to woo.' See Emeric Pressburger, 'Miracle in Soho Post-production Script', (Domestic Version), 27 June 1957. J. Arthur Rank Productions Ltd. Donated by BAFTA (London: BFI National Archive), 1.
3. Wardour Street in Soho was once referred to as 'film row'. In 1927, the street had become the primary location for the headquarters of film production, postproduction facilities and film distribution companies. See more in Judith Summers, *Soho: A History of London's Most Colourful Neighbourhood* (London: Bloomsbury, 1991), 180.
4. See Frank Mort, *Capital Affairs: London and the Making of the Permissive Society* (New Haven: Yale University Press, 2010), 201.
5. Ibid., 230.
6. Kevin Macdonald's published biography of his grandfather describes the various obstacles for the production of *Miracle in Soho* before the Second World War. See Kevin Macdonald, *Emeric Pressburger: Life and Death of a Screenwriter* (London: Faber & Faber, 1996), 107. See also Raymond Durgnat, who further describes the ironies of the Powell–Pressburger relationship in terms of national and foreign identity in 'The Powell and Pressburger Mystery', *Cineaste* 23(2) (1997), 16–19.
7. See Macdonald, *Emeric Pressburger* 122.
8. Pressburger is often miscredited as working solely as writer/producer, with Powell as director/producer, though in recent decades this simplification of his role has been rectified by figures such as Kevin Gough-Yates and Ian Christie, who argue that Pressburger played a far more complex role in their filmmaking partnership. Ian Christie states that Pressburger was 'far more than the scenarist whose work Powell rewrote [and] created most of their stories, was responsible for most of the producing, collaborated (but never on the floor) in the directing, and worked patiently in the editing room'. Pressburger and Powell parted ways following the release of *Ill Met by Moonlight* in 1956. See Ian Christie, 'Alienation Effects: Emeric Pressburger and British Cinema', *Monthly Film Bulletin* 51(600) (1984), 318. Kevin Gough-Yates reviews Macdonald's biography of his grandfather shedding light on Powell's other half in 'Pressburger: England and Exile', *Sight and Sound* 15(12) (1995), 30.
9. The other writer was the German-born Wolfgang Wilhelm, who emigrated to Britain after the Nazis rose to power. He cowrote several films in different genres, such as *Farewell Again* (Tim Whelan, 1937) and the spy-comedy *I See A Dark Stranger* (Frank Launder, 1946) starring Deborah Kerr and Trevor Howard. He also cowrote some of 'The Saint' film series with RKO and wrote the Powell/Pressburger-produced *The End of the River* (Derek Twist, 1947). See Andrew Moor, *Powell & Pressburger: A Cinema of Magic Spaces* (London: I.B. Tauris/ Palgrave Macmillan, 2005), 2. See also Gough-Yates, 'Pressburger: England and Exile', 31–32.
10. Gough-Yates, 'Pressburger: England and Exile', 35.
11. See Emeric Pressburger, *Miracle in St. Anthony's Lane*. An original story by Emeric Pressburger. Script written by Emeric Pressburger in collaboration with Michael Powell, n.d. (with special permission by the Michael Powell Estate, London), 37. For Pinewood's twenty-first birthday, it ran a series of promotional 'guides' for cinema audiences, including in fan magazine *Picturegoer* regular 'Stepping out Tonight?' written by Margaret Hinxman. *Miracle in Soho* stands out as the only romance film. See Margaret Hinxman, 'Stepping out Tonight?', *Picturegoer*, 28 September 1957, 5.
12. See Pressburger, *Miracle in St. Anthony's Lane*, 44.

13. See Chibnall, 'Banging the Gong', 25.
14. Pressburger, 'Miracle in Soho Post-production Script', 1.
15. The Chicago School developed their research during an era of extreme and rapid social change as the 'influx of millions of immigrants at the turn of the century' settled primarily in urban areas. Comparably, Britain in the 1950s was extremely crowded in comparison to its neighbours in Europe and was easily the 'most urbanised country in Europe. In 1956, the United Kingdom of Great Britain and Northern Ireland was home to just over fifty million people.' The urban sociologists of the Chicago School 'reinvented modern sociology by using the city of Chicago as a "living laboratory"'. For a more comprehensive overview of the Chicago School, see Earl Smith, 'Louis Wirth and the Chicago School of Urban Sociology: An Assessment and Critique', *Humanity and Society* 9 (1985), 1.
16. Jerry White, *London in the Twentieth Century: A City and Its People* (London: Vintage Books, 2008), 107.
17. For a fuller history of Italians in London, see James Strang, 'The Italian Colony in London', *Good Words* 40 (1899), 119–25; and White, *London in the Twentieth Century*, 107.
18. White, *London in the Twentieth Century*, 108.
19. In her commentary on the film's 'open racism', Elisabetta Girelli explores the film's use of Italian stereotypes and rightly claims that the character of Julia is more of a 'sketch' than a character. See Elisabetta Girelli, *Beauty and the Beast: Italianness in British Cinema* (Bristol: Intellect Books, 2009), 110.
20. Ibid.
21. Judith Walkowitz, *Nights out: Life in Cosmopolitan London* (New Haven: Yale University Press, 2012), 94.
22. Ibid.
23. Ibid.
24. Ibid., 132.
25. 'Miracle in Soho', *What's on in London*, 12 July 1957, n.p. Pamphlet scan courtesy of Steve Crook.
26. See Emeric Pressburger, '*Miracle in Soho* Post-production Script, Domestic Version', 27 June 1957, 1–2.
27. Ibid., 1–3.
28. The phrase 'Never had it so good' first appeared in a speech made by the British Prime Minister Harold Macmillan in 1957. According to Booker, the phrase has 'never been so damagingly distorted'. Macmillan's actual words were: 'Let's be frank about it; some of our people had never had it so good.' See Christopher Booker, *The Neophiliacs: Revolution in English Life in the Fifties and Sixties*, 2nd edn (London: Pimlico, 1992), 132–35. See also Historian Dominic Sandbrook's *Never Had It So Good: A History of Britain from Suez to The Beatles* (London: Abacus, 2005) which provides a wonderfully engaging and thorough history of postwar Britain; see 'Britain in 1956', 31–66.
29. In 1956, the total cinema attendance was 1,101 millions, having declined from an attendance of 1, 635, 000 million a decade earlier in 1946. See Chibnall, 'Banging the Gong', 265.
30. In 1957, the J. Arthur Rank Organisation was forced to amalgamate its Gaumont and Odeon cinema circuits, which resulted in 300 workers being made redundant alongside the postponement of four productions at Pinewood Studios. See ibid., 253.
31. See 'British Feature Directors: An Index to Their Work', *Sight and Sound*, Fall (1958), 289.

32. Born Cambridge in 1917, Amyes produced and acted in repertory before the war and after Army service joined the Stratford Memorial Theatre company. He joined the BBC as a television producer in 1951 and was responsible for such TV productions as *Dial M for Murder*. See ibid.
33. There are several uncredited photographs that are currently owned by the British-based Moviestore Collection, including on-set photographs taken during the filming of *Miracle in Soho*. See Moviestore Collection, by appointment only, http://www.moviestorecollection.com.
34. See Jingan Young, 'Belinda Lee and the Soho Fair', International Association for Media and History, *IAmHist blog*, 3 October 2017. http://iamhist.net/tag/cosmopolitanism.
35. Sarah Street's article is part of the seminal research she is leading on the 'Eastmancolor Revolution and British Cinema 1955–85'. See Sarah Street, 'The Colour of Social Realism', *Journal of British Cinema and Television* 15(4) (2018), 470.
36. Ibid.
37. Ibid., 473–74. See also Carmen Dillon, 'Building Soho at Pinewood', *Kinematograph Weekly*, 28 March 1957, ix.
38. Films released that year include the Oscar-winning David Lean's epic prisoner-of-war film *The Bridge on the River Kwai*. See Clem, 'Review: Miracle in Soho', *Variety*, 24 July 1957, 26. See also 'Review: Miracle in Soho', *Monthly Film Bulletin* 24(276) (1957), 104; and 'Miracle in Soho', *Picturegoer*, 3 August 1957, 14.
39. See Dylan Cave, 'Miracle in Soho (1957)', *BFI Screenonline*. Retrieved 13 October 2021 from http://www.screenonline.org.uk/film/id/712912.
40. 'Miracle in Soho', What's On in London, 12 July 1957, courtesy of Steve Crook, The Powell & Pressburger Pages Online, http://www.powellpressburger/reviews/57_Miracle/Whatson.html.
41. The documentary also featured 'scenes from *Across the Bridge* and *Doctor at Large*; and interviews with Peggy Cummins about *Hell Drivers*, and with Flora Robson about *High Tide at Noon*'. In the following January, the Rank Organisation divided the UK provincial press into six regions and appointed corresponding press officers to work from branch offices in Manchester, Birmingham, Glasgow, Leeds, Cardiff and London. They provided a service to 'provincial editors, news, art and feature editors, film and gossip columnists, women's writers and special writers'. See Chibnall, 'Banging the Gong', 253.
42. The black-and-white advertisement uses a large photograph of Lee to promote Vitapointe of Paris with a tagline below that reads: 'Just 1-minute brushing – and my hair is shining! By Belinda Lee.' See *Daily Express*, 26 September 1957, 13.
43. These profile articles were written by journalist Derek Walker for *Picturegoer* on the actress entitled 'Belinda Lee Covers up Her Past'. In part two of the series, we are provided with the 'exclusive' story of how Lee landed the role of Julia Gozzi. The story goes that Pressburger saw her photograph outside of his offices at Pinewood and then and there decided '*that* is just what I want for *Miracle in Soho*'. Derek Walker's profile is accompanied by several images of Lee as a 'pin-up' who wished to change her image into a more dramatic actress. See 'Belinda Lee Covers up Her Past', *Picturegoer*, 16 March 1967, 5.
44. See Chibnall, 'Banging the Gong', 12.
45. After Rank signed Lee, she told reporter Tom Hutchinson: 'I don't suppose I am going to learn all that much about acting with the Rank Organisation, but I am going to learn about being a personality'. See Tom Hutchinson, *Screen Goddesses* (London: Deans International, 1984), 147.
46. In Pressburger's 1937 original handwritten notes in pencil on the script sent to Powell, he described Mr Bishop as 'a little queer, maintains he must tell the truth about the calamity

regarding road repairs in St. Anthony's Lane. He is removed by force'. See Emeric Pressburger's original hand-written notes in pencil', BFI: London, 1937 and his Handwritten Treatment of *Miracle in Soho*. Special permission The Michael Powell Collection, n.d., 48.

47. Frank Mort, 'Cityscapes: Consumption, Masculinities and the Mapping of London since 1950', *Urban Studies* 35(5/6) (1998), 894.
48. See Charlotte Brunsdon, *London in Cinema: The Cinematic City since 1945* (London: BFI, 2007), 43–45.
49. 'Praise, My Soul, the King of Heaven' was written by Henry Francis Lyte in 1834, set to the tune LAUDA ANIMA by John Goss in 1869 in various languages. It is a paraphrase of Psalm 103. It appeared in the Spirit of the Psalms, published in 1834. See Malcolm C. Doubles, *The Seduction of the Church: How the Concern to Create Gender-Neutral Language in Bible and Song Is Being Misused to Betray Members' Faith* (Eugene, OR: Wipf & Stock, 2010), 125.
50. See Gough-Yates, 'Pressburger: England and Exile', 35.
51. Ibid., 30–32.
52. See 'The Powell and Pressburger Mystery', *Cineaste* 23(2) (1997), 16.
53. See Andrew Moor, *Powell & Pressburger: A Cinema of Magic Spaces* (New York: I.B. Tauris, 2005), 3.
54. Ibid.
55. See Sue Harper and Vincent Porter, *British Cinema of the 1950s: The Decline of Deference* (Oxford: Oxford University Press, 2003), 1.

CHAPTER 4

Soho-Hollywood
The Birth of the Soho 'B' Film

I didn't bring you all this way across the Atlantic to write stories about gangsters. We don't have any over here.

—*Noose* (Edmond T. Gréville, 1948)

Britain's mood at the beginning of the 1950s could 'scarcely have been bleaker … By 1951, the cost of living was rising by 1 per cent a month … The Labour Government [was] hanging by a thread'.[1] Despite the new wave of optimism created by the Labour government, which had been elected to power five years earlier and prompted the 'prospect of a bright horizon of peace and prosperity', the bitter winter of 1946–47 in Britain that saw 'power cuts, coal rationing, dark and frozen nights and days' became a metaphor for the state of the nation where 'the momentum of radical legislation had faltered … economic difficulties … actually worsened'.[2] Restrictions placed upon the nation's consumption of food, clothing and goods during the war were maintained to achieve 'anti-inflationary and dollar economy policy objectives', which were part of the Labour government's commitment to 'economic planning and fair shares'.[3] Christopher Booker has described the postwar landscape as a place where 'spivs and snoek and government snoopers were still the staple fare of cartoonists and comedians [and] rationing and shortages were almost as bad as ever'.[4] Meanwhile, in Britain's Commonwealth: 'Murderous wars and civil wars sprang up over the settlements of empire in India and the Middle East. By the end of 1949, the brave dream of 1945 had been extinguished.'[5]

Despite the harsh, wartime restrictions pressed upon the British film industry, film studios expanded, cinemas reopened and the success of British films at the domestic and international levels saw an increase in cinema attendance.[6] The decade also saw the meteoric rise of British producer J. Arthur Rank and the Rank

Organisation, whose lavish and globally minded films would dominate the interwar and postwar years.[7] However, the unrelenting wave of film legislation, first implemented in 1927 under the first Films Act in order to ward off Hollywood's dominance over the British box office, would continue to impact the nation's film industry in immeasurable and complex ways, particularly regarding the production of low-budget features films, also known as the British 'B' film.[8]

Media-circulated reports in the boom in crime and the increase in underground economies such as the black market that flourished during the first two years of the war permeated the narratives of low-budget British films. The imagining of the metropolis as a sinister labyrinth filled with crooked deals and sadistic spivs was also heavily influenced by prewar American crime fiction. According to Mark Roodhouse: 'Britons were not alone in making this mental link, and Americans and Canadians imagined their black markets in similar fashion.'[9] By the 1950s, the crime genre had formed an 'essentially stabilizing ingredient of the British film industry'.[10] These films are strong examples of the growing popularity of the crime film, a genre that was 'comfortably the dominant ... representing, on average, around 30 per cent of the total output of feature films, peaking in 1957 at 39.5 per cent'.[11] Their setting of Soho as a transgressive space allowed filmmakers to position their stories of corruption, exploitation and greed in the heart of the nation's capital, which was deemed acceptable for national audiences. The Soho films *Noose* (Edmond T. Gréville, 1948), *Street of Shadows* (Richard Vernon, 1953) and *Soho Incident* (Vernon Sewell, 1955) are examples of films that placed strong importance upon the black market as their locus. They positioned their shared criminal-on-the-run narratives within a permissive space where their tormented protagonist may engage with violent and/or erotic encounters, in turn reinforcing the area of Soho's mythic identity and its prewar reputation as a locale of vice. Furthermore, all three films imported Hollywood actors for their leading roles and partially relied upon American investment and distribution, reflecting the wartime presence of American GIs and other servicemen in London and their impact on commercial development.[12] Like all postwar Soho films, they were shot primarily within studios with some exterior sequences filmed on location in Soho.

This chapter does not wish to add to the expansive scholarship of film legislation and censorship in British cinema. It focuses instead on the birth of the Soho 'B' film, the impact of Hollywood and the performance of its American stars. The films *Noose*, *Street of Shadows* and *Soho Incident*, which were released uncut and certified 'A' (suitable for adults) by the British censors, are key films in the canon, due to their inherent understanding of the commercial developments undergoing postwar cinema and Soho's cosmopolitan past. They drew inspiration from foreign cinemas such as American and European film noir in order to cinematically render the area of Soho as a transatlantic space, reinforced by their decision to cast American actors in an effort to bolster their appeal in the global film marketplace. These films foreshadow the ways in which Soho's entrepreneurs directed the reorganisation of the area on 'more contemporary, consumer-led lines'.[13] The sheer number of these Soho/London crime films released in this period marked the beginning of an inextricable relationship, one that, despite mass commercial gentrification to Soho and the alleged sanitisation of its lewd past in recent years, has survived and continues as a popular trope today (for instance, contemporary director Edgar Wright's Soho-set thriller *Last Night in Soho*).

Hollywood Stars in Soho

British independent studios, Anglo-American film companies and British subsidiaries of Hollywood studios exhaustively imported Hollywood actors in order to bolster their appeal for British audiences at the box office and to secure overseas distribution deals. The Italian villain Edouardo Sugiani of Richard Llewellyn's *Noose* was played by Maltese-born American actor Joseph Calleja. Jim Bankley, the American wide boy protagonist of *Soho Incident*, was played by Canadian-born Lee Patterson. Supporting roles also went to American actors. Jim's ex-army mate-turned-racketeer Buddy was played by Robert Arden and the Soho femme fatale Bella Francesi was played by Faith Domergue. The film was distributed by the British subsidiary of Columbia Pictures. In *Street of Shadows*, New York-born Cesar Romero was cast as Luigi, the owner of a pintable saloon, bar and casino in Soho who is framed for murdering his ex-girlfriend.[14] It was distributed by US production company Lipper Productions.

Films produced before and at the onset of the Second World War similarly imported Hollywood stars for their Soho gangsters. New York native Jack La Rue played American gangster Steve Marco in Norman Lee's *Murder in Soho* (1939), ten years before he would take the role of the sociopathic gangster Slim Grisson in the British-made, New York-set *No Orchids for Miss Blandish* (St John Legh Clowes, 1949). It was based on the novel by British author James Hadley Chase, the film was produced by Sidney Box. Upon its release, the film was denounced by critics and politicians for its brutal and sadistic portrayal of sex and violence. *Monthly Film Bulletin* called it the 'most-sickening exhibition of brutality, perversion and sadism ever to be shown on a cinema screen'.[15] No other Soho crime film experienced such similar controversy during this period.[16]

Soho-Hollywood Spaces

For Walkowitz, Soho's reputation as a 'racy cosmopolis' intensified during the First World War where French, Belgian, Serbian, American, Canadian and African troops sought refuge in Soho's nightclubs and pubs. These establishments prospered as a result, for it was their 'transatlantic flavour', extracted and adopted from American prohibition-era speakeasies.[17] The neon-flickering signs of the cavernous clubs and the candy-coloured awnings of the French and Italian cafés and night clubs that populated Wardour Street and Soho were duly appropriated for Soho crime films. There is also a clear influence of the urban modernism as depicted by the architecture of films released during Hollywood films from the 1930s. For example, Marco's Cotton Club in *Murder in Soho* (Norman Lee, 1939) and the Blue Parrot nightclub in *The Blue Parrot* (John Harlow, 1953) greatly resembled the Art Deco-style architecture and costume seen in Fred Astaire and Ginger Rogers musicals directed by Mark Sandrich such as *The Gay Divorcee* (1934) and *Top Hat* (1935).

The speakeasies and jazz clubs of these two Soho films were the British equivalent of the nightclubs depicted in Hollywood gangster films such as *Scarface* (Howard Hawks, 1932) and *The Thin Man* (W.S. van Dyke, 1934). But postwar design influences also pervaded 'B' films from the mid-1950s. The American expat Luigi in *Street of Shadows* owns a pin-table saloon and casino that is reminiscent of the funhouse hall of mirrors in *The Lady from Shanghai* (Orson Welles, 1947). According to Nick Browne, the 'modern art deco nightclub exists as an idyllic capitalist … concrete and "clubby" space of socially lavish and lavishly social display'.[18] The nightclub, cocktail lounge and salon are 'spaces where 'ideas' and 'passions' of the characters are revealed in the 'dialogue' that the salon allows.'[19] In *Noose*, the Blue Moon nightclub sits opposite the fictional St Giuseppe Church on a fictional Redmayne Street and evokes the commercialised exoticism of the Buenos Aires casino featured in the film noir *Gilda* (Charles Vidor, 1946). However, the ostentatious design of the Blue Moon Club also confirms the inherent desire for its proprietor, the black-market racketeer Edouardo Sugiani (Joseph Calleia), to acquire respectability within London high society.

The themes, spaces and mise-en-scène of these Soho crime films explicitly reference Hollywood and European film noir. Ginette Vincendeau has challenged the widely held belief that French film noir evolved solely from Hollywood: 'French writers showed a strong attraction to the underbelly of society, the "*bas-fonds*" ("lower depths"), from the early modern period onwards and in particular in the 18th-century *roman noir*.'[20] These films also relied on a 'wide range of cinematic precedents' used by the intellectual neorealist filmmakers who admired Hollywood for both their 'realist and epic ... cinematic visions'.[21] Italian neorealist filmmakers relied upon French films from directors such as Jean Renoir and Marcel Carné as they formulated their 'culture of resistance to fascism'.[22] This partially suggests that Soho crime films are similarly a hybrid of Hollywood-European cinemas. They display an international approach to filmmaking that reflected the attempt by filmmakers to capture Soho's cosmopolitan history such as Emeric Pressburger's reimagining of its habitués in *Miracle in Soho* (1957).[23]

Noose

Before turning his lens to the expresso bars and strip clubs of 1960s Soho in *Beat Girl* (1960), Gréville placed his discerning eye on the British black market in *Noose*, retitled *The Silk Noose* for its US release in 1948. The story follows an American fashion journalist, Linda Medbury (Carole Landis), who, with the help of her fiancé Jumbo Hoyle (Derek Farr), an ex-commando, attempts to destroy a notorious Italian black-market racketeer, Edouardo 'Knucksie' Sugiani, after Linda discovers he has strangled his girlfriend Milly Sharp (and later several other female victims) whose body is retrieved from the River Thames by Inspector Rendall of Scotland Yard (Stanley Holloway).

The film's screenplay was written by the novelist Richard Llewellyn and was adapted from his own stage play *The Noose*, which was produced in the spring of 1947 at the Saville Theatre, located on the borders of Soho at 135–49 Shaftesbury Avenue. Llewellyn is perhaps best known for his critically acclaimed bestselling novel *How Green Was My Valley* (1939), which was adapted for the screen in 1941. The film was directed by John Ford and won five Academy Awards, including Best Picture, in 1942. Reporter Diack Hunter called Llewellyn's play an 'amusing story

Figure 4.1. Linda (Carole Landis) prepares to take down Sugiani with the help of her fiancé, a local boxing club and the London Metropolitan Police. Still from *Noose* (Edmond T. Gréville, 1948). DVD, 2009, Renown Productions Ltd.

with enough action to keep it going, and produced at a pace which covers up the flatness of dialogue'.[24] However, he was swift to note the implausibility of Llewellyn's creation of Soho gangland: 'The cast in general did not appear to believe in [Soho] at all, and they can hardly be blamed for that.'[25] Robert Murphy states that Llewellyn had submitted an earlier version of *Noose* entitled 'Murder in Soho' to the British censors in 1937. This is often confused with Norman Lee's film of the same name written by American screenwriter F. McGrew Willis, which starred the Hollywood actor Jack La Rue. Llewellyn's script was initially rejected by the British Board of Film Classification (BBFC) for its arguably more truthful portrayal of vice-ridden, postwar Soho but was ultimately passed after its more violent aspects were toned down.[26]

Critics of the original stage play praised it overall, including Nigel Patrick's performance of the character Bar Gorman, a role he reprised in the film. However, the screen version received lukewarm reviews. *Variety* described the film as 'a nice subject to help fill the quota bill at home but isn't likely to go too big in the export market, despite American names in leads'.[27] However, in recent decades, the film has been celebrated for its aesthetic 'sophistication' by Tim Pulleine and described as a master work of cinema by Peter Wollen.[28] According to Vincent Porter in his discussions of French émigré directors in Britain during and following the Second World War, the film 'boasts a formal intricacy held together by stunning camera movements ... symbolic and allegorical ... and ends in a riot of surreal images'.[29] Wollen, expanding upon the work of Murphy, firmly positions the film within the British spiv cycle, a genre of British cinema 'where melodrama decisively triumphs over realism, where British cinema unashamedly enters the eerie and fascinating realm of noir, the world of violence, darkness and death which Hollywood exploited so memorably at the very same time'.[30] *Noose* has grown popular amongst audiences following its restoration and release on DVD by British independent film distributors Renown Pictures in 2009. According to Bertrand Tavernier, the filmmaker's friend and biographer, *Noose* was one of Gréville's favourite films.[31]

I agree with Pulleine's sentiments that *Noose* is filled with paradoxical images.[32] This reflects Gréville's dual Anglo-French heritage. Born in Nice, France, to a schoolteacher and an evangelist, Gréville began his career as a poet and a writer before turning to filmmaking. After his emigration to Britain, he worked as an assistant to the German émigré director E.A. Dupont on *Piccadilly* (1929). According to Ian Christie, this celebrated silent film starring American-Chinese actress Anna May Wong 'aimed to reveal the drama potential of London itself'.[33] According to Tavernier, Gréville was the 'bard of desire and sexual obsessions' whose efforts 'bring to mind those of Michael Powell'.[34] He argues the director held an 'attraction to twilight moods and murky zones ... the same determination to cast off the yoke of realism and visualize everything, including feelings and passions – to favour the cosmic in their cinema'.[35] These 'attractions' are on full display in *Noose*, though they are arguably not so prevalent in his later Soho offering, *Beat Girl*. Echoing this, the film's cinematographer Hone Glendinning had worked on several British crime-melodramas during the Second World War, such as George King's film *The Case of the Frightened Lady* (1940), which was based on a play by Edgar Wallace. In *Noose*, the climactic finale that intercuts between Sugiani's apartment, the Blue Moon Club and St Giuseppe Church confirms his deft skill in creating threatening, melodramatic, and imaginary spaces. Pulleine has praised Glendinning's masterful use of lighting and framing throughout the film.[36]

European Noir Spaces

The film was shot primarily at Warner Brothers First National Studios in Teddington except for the opening sequence, which features a panoramic aerial shot of Wardour Street and the exterior of the House of St Barnabas. Located at 1 Greek Street, the chapel of the House of St Barnabas functioned as the fictional St Giuseppe Church, which establishes the film's Soho location. Today, the House of St Barnabas operates, in its own words, as a 'social enterprise' and members-only club.[37] However, it once operated as the House of Charity, a charity for the relief of destitute and houseless poor in the capital that moved to St Barnabas in 1862. During this period, an architect named Joseph Clarke ambitiously planned to construct a refectory, chapel, cloisters and dormitories behind the building. However, 'only that for the chapel was ever realised ... ready for use in 1864'.[38] The chapel's design drew from 'mid-eighteenth-century English Rococo style', adopted from the original French.

Art director Bernard Robinson constructed an entirely original interior to stand in for the St Giuseppe Church. The church is used during the climactic sequence of *Noose* following Linda's failed attempt to trap Sugiani inside his apartment so that she can achieve retribution for the murder of his ex-girlfriend Annie Foss by his assassin, the unnamed 'barber' (Hay Petrie). Sugiani flees to take refuge inside the church, where he is strangled by his own employee. The film strives to enhance feelings of isolation, anxiety and fear that stemmed from 'the loss of self in the modern world, and the parallel [that] runs steady along the social and psychological dislocations of a demoralized Germany twenty years earlier' in the First World War.[39] These filmmakers developed cinematic concepts such as '*stimmung* (the aura or shimmer of mood resonating from an object filmed) and the *umwelt* (the uniting and protective rays of light generating a recognition of objects and characters clustered in their discreetly intimate environment'.[40] These techniques are greatly evident in the film's denouement in order to express postwar anxieties generated by the conflicting modes of urban vice and pleasure, 'ignominy and corruption ... a moral conundrum'.[41]

Besides its association with earlier Hollywood crime films of the 1930s like *The Thin Man*, partly embodied by the spiv character of Bar Gorman, *Noose* may also be treated as an attempt to assimilate the French film noir of the années noires, a term used to describe films produced during the German occupation of France during the war. According to Vincendeau, the 'dominant genres of the 220 films of the period were "escapist": costume films, musicals and comedies ... substantial *policier* production was predominantly recast as light comedy'.[42] Vincendeau identifies one 'startling' example of the canon, *120 rue de la gare* (Jacques Daniel-Norman, 1946), a film adapted from a crime novel by Léo Malet. According to Vincendeau: 'The film rewrites [Malet's] double noir material into a comedy, in large part because of wartime censorship ... tone and casting pull in the opposite direction.'[43] Undoubtedly, Gréville's own Anglo-French identity and strong fascination for the urban village and its criminal underbelly means that Soho is largely articulated on screen as a space of contradictions, a pastiche rendering of a foreign-in-origin violent world.

Street of Shadows (Richard Vernon, 1953)

Street of Shadows marked the first Anglo-American co-production of Anglo-Amalgamated Productions led by producers Nat Cohen and Stuart Levy. Anglo-Amalgamated began its operation as a distribution company that primarily packaged British-made featurettes with American 'A' movies. They would later form a film production company with Merton Park producer Julian Wintle.[44] According to Chibnall and McFarlane, *Street of Shadows* was aimed at the first feature market.[45] In 1952, *Variety* reported the film was part of a deal for six co-productions between Anglo-Amalgamated Film Distributors and William Nassour Pictures.[46] Like *Noose*, the film continues to attract a wider audience after its remastered release on DVD in 2016 by StudioCanal.[47]

The film received a lukewarm reception from critics. *Picturegoer* praised Romero's performance, deeming it 'immaculate ... in this routine crime melodrama'.[48] American trade paper *Boxoffice* was one of the few publications that recognised its underlying intention to conquer the American market.[49] Before *Street of Shadows*, Romero was cast in one other British-made film entitled *Lady in the Fog/Scotland Yard Inspector* (Sam Newfield, 1952) as an American detective in London. The film was based upon the BBC serial by Lester Powell with a screenplay by Orville Hampton and was produced by Hammer/Exclusive Films. *Lady in the Fog* opens in a similarly dramatic fashion to *Street of Shadows* with the body of a dead man framed lying beneath a lamppost on a foggy London street. Like Calleia, Romero also expressed a desire to appear on the London stage during the production of *Noose*.

John Hill has suggested that the key to understanding Britain in the 1950s is '"affluence", of a nation moving inexorably forward from postwar austerity and rationing to "Macmillan's soap-flake Arcadia"'.[50] *Street of Shadows* partly resists modernity by locating Luigi within traditional forms of variety entertainment and depicting him as the owner of a pin-table saloon. However, Luigi's desire to advance within London society by pursuing upper-class Barbara romantically is also indicative of the values promoted by consumer culture. This is confirmed during a scene where he reveals his émigré background to the love interest, a common trope of Soho-set films including *Noose*, in which Sugiani gives a laborious monologue to Linda that details his emigration to Britain. In *Street of Shadows*, Luigi invites Barbara to his Soho flat for a home-cooked meal. Barbara discovers a photograph of his deceased father, who Luigi describes as a 'Professor of the Marionettes' who died without a 'penny to his name'. He tells Barbara: 'My father had very little when he died. I had neither his skill nor his talent. All I knew was showbusiness. I started as a boxer and now I own a pin-table saloon! But it's been a means to an end. I've made money. And the end is nearly in sight, Barbara.'[51]

Unfortunately, Luigi's overarching ambitions are never fully realised in the film. Luigi flees persecution in order to protect Barbara as he initially believes she is the murderer of his ex-girlfriend Angele after finding Barbara's glove near the site of the murder. However, by collaborating with the police in order to force Limpy's confession, the film allows Luigi to acquire hero status, despite his 'shadowy' background and questionable vocation running a gambling establishment in Soho. Following Limpy's confession, Luigi reunites with Barbara. The film draws to a close as the interlocked pair move out from the shadows and leave behind the saloon *and* Soho. Luigi triumphs by shedding his Soho roots to become a moral (and very soon affluent) member of English society. This unfulfilled ambition adheres to the behaviour of traditional noir hero. Nick Browne states that: 'Characters [in film noir] keep attempting to escape their specific biography or the particulars of history … Earlier crimes, betrayals, failures, and infidelities are desperately hidden and generate new crimes, betrayals, failures, and infidelities.'[52]

Supernatural Noir Spaces

Although largely filmed at Merton Park Studios, several sequences in *Street of Shadows* were shot on location in London's Piccadilly Circus, Trafalgar Square,

Soho, Covent Garden and Fitzrovia. One sequence is a marvellous visual document of 1950s Soho. It is one of two sequences within the film to take place during daylight hours. Following the opening credits, which are superimposed over an aerial shot of a policeman surveying his Soho beat, we cut to a black cat that jumps out from behind a rubbish bin. We then sharply cut to saloon owner Luigi's disabled assistant Danny 'Limpy' Thomas (Victor Maddern), who briskly moves down Charing Cross Road, then travels west on Shaftesbury Avenue and finally ends his journey at the intersection between Brewer Street and Wardour Street. This sequence is accompanied by composer Eric Spear's skipping, defiant harmonica score. The recurring harmonica theme composed by Spear features a solo performed by Tommy Reilly. The theme is played in both major and minor keys throughout the film to reflect Luigi and Limpy's conflicting states of mind. Critics have remarked upon the theme's similarity to the scores found in film noir, which includes Anton Karas' score in *The Third Man* (Carol Reed, 1949). One review from *Monthly Film Bulletin* called the soundtrack to this 'conventional thriller … somewhat enlivened by Tommy Reilly's harmonica solos, particularly "The Limping Man", which seems destined to share the fate of the "Harry Lime Theme"'.[53]

There are also elements of the supernatural in the film. During the opening sequence, Limpy is called upon by name to help an elderly woman named Starry Darrell (Molly Hamley-Clifford) who has suddenly collapsed in the street. Limpy recognises Starry and brings her to Luigi's saloon, where Luigi kindly offers her tea and company. We then learn Starry is a Soho-based clairvoyant who predicts that Limpy will most likely die from the 'love of a good woman'.[54] Her prediction later proves to be correct. Limpy will murder Luigi's ex-girlfriend Angele in a fit of jealousy, framing his employer for the crime. The character of the fortune-teller or psychic medium appears in numerous American noir films, such as *Ministry of Fear* (Fritz Lang, 1944), *Murder My Sweet* (Edward Dmytryk, 1944), *Power of the Whistler* (Lew Landers, 1945), *Fallen Angel* (Otto Preminger, 1945), *Pickup on South Street* (Samuel Fuller, 1953) and *Touch of Evil* (Orson Welles, 1958).[55] Although current scholarship fails to identify the deeper meanings behind the mystic in noir, when positioned in Soho, it reinforces the area's reputation as a supernatural space. It may also signal a threat to modern stability, reinforcing the hero's conflicted state of mind.

Soho Incident

Soho Incident (retitled *Spin a Dark Web* for its US release) was based on Robert Westerby's novel *Wide Boys Never Work*, which was first published in 1937. The story follows Jim Bankley, who, after losing his dead-end job in a Northern motor factory, duly hitches a ride to London in search of better prospects. In the novel, Westerby paints London's hedonistic playground of Soho as full of 'tarts, touts, ponces, louts, bookies, ex-pugs, petty-gangsters, perhaps a stray newspaper reporter'.[56] By the end of his adventures, Bankley has 'tasted blood', but is 'not quite the twist of the criminal', and the author concludes with a grave warning to his readers, a pseudo-public service announcement on the dangers of living in the sprawling metropolis: 'Someone has to keep the boy, whether it is his family, or Society. He's there, a parasite, hanging on with dead weight. So, what are you going to do about it?'[57]

British Columbia Pictures' watered-down version of the novel was directed by Vernon Sewell, who began his career at Nettlefold Studios as a camera assistant in 1929 before directing his first feature *The Medium* (1934) with a script penned by Michael Powell. Sewell would then direct *The Silver Fleet* (1943) for Powell and Pressburger's The Archers Films Productions, which, like *Soho Incident,* was produced by George Maynard, who produced and managed several London-set films such as Herbert Wilcox's *Piccadilly Incident* (1946) and *Maytime in Mayfair* (1949).[58] The script was written by Ian Stuart Black, whose version wholly deviates from the original source material. Northerner Jim from Westerby's novel is transposed for a hapless Canadian ex-serviceman who holds a 'get-rich-quick' mentality. It was shot on location in Soho and at Nettlefold Studios (Walton-on-Thames). *Variety* called it 'sufficient thriller entertainment' and it received varying shrugs of praise upon release, noting its ambitions to conquer the American marketplace.[59]

The film imports American actors Lee Patterson, Faith Domergue and Robert Arden (all of whom appeared steadily in British 'B' films and television programmes during the 1950 and 1960s) in order to bolster its box office appeal and potential distribution in the United States and Europe. Incidentally, Arden would later star in the television crime series *Saber of London*, which was broadcast from 1957 to 1959 on the National Broadcasting Company (NBC) network. The series was produced by the Danziger Brothers, Edward J. Danziger and Harry Lee Danziger, who, since 1952, had produced films for television and later produced the Soho thriller *Striptease Murder* (1961). In the *Saber of London* series, Arden played the role of Bob Page, an assistant to the series protagonist, a police captain named Mark Saber (Donald Gray). The episode entitled 'Incident in Soho', which first aired on US network NBC in 1959, provided real footage of the Soho Fair from that year.

Before filming *Soho Incident*, the actress Faith Domergue had only just emerged from the shadow of Howard Hughes, who had groomed her to be a Hollywood movie star from the age of fifteen. In a similar vein to the *Picturegoer* article on Romero published in 1941, Elizabeth Forrest, writing in the same publication in the year of *Soho Incident*'s release, snidely asked: 'What happened to Faith?' In the piece, Forrest negatively critiqued Domergue's performance in the American noir film *Where Danger Lives* (John Farrow, 1950) and pronounced it both unsellable to audiences and accountable for her adult career performing predominantly in second feature films.[60] In contrast, the Canadian actor Lee Patterson has been dubbed by Chibnall and McFarlane as one of the leading men of the British 'B' films of the 1950s and 1960s. Patterson spent 'most of his career his Britain … most often to be found playing Americans in such bottom-of-the-bill crime films … with his luxuriant quiff and air of virility [he] was a useful presence in such films'.[61]

Femmes Fatales

The narrative of the troubled male villain/anti-hero trapped by his past and whose future is obstructed by a woman he has only recently met is yet another pronounced noir element in these films. American actresses Carole Landis and Faith Domergue in *Noose* and *Soho Incident* provide comparative parallels. In *Noose*, Landis is a sophisticated, intelligent and wise-cracking American who initially poses a superficial threat to Sugiani, but later becomes a key player in a mission to destroy him. Domergue's character Bella, who is also sophisticated, is largely depicted as a black widow-type and is intrinsically aligned with racketeering as the sister of a notorious Soho gang boss Rico Francesi, who procures Jim to work on his grand scheme to engineer a device to rig off-track races. Bella also exploits Jim for her own personal amusement and a sexual relationship. She is an overt example of the archetypal noir femme fatale who has been examined extensively in the work by numerous scholars, including Vincendeau, Browne,

Mary Ann Doane, Dominique Mainon and James Ursini.[62] Bella, who is proudly Sicilian, holds stronger agency than her male counterparts, particularly in her treatment of Jim as a sex object. Although it is hinted by the film that she is in fact the ringleader of the Francesi gang, her virulent anger expressed over Jim's later rejection of her love inevitably turns her into a murderer, shooting Buddy and her brother Rico (Martin Benson) in a fit of rage. Unfortunately, the upper-class Barbara in *Street of Shadows* is grossly underused and is reduced to the status of a bit player in order to lend a sympathetic ear and shoulder to cry on for Romero's character Luigi.

Conclusion

By the mid-1950s, British audiences had enjoyed their fair share of 'B' crime thrillers and Hollywood stars in Soho. The cinematic representation of postwar London filled with uncouth teddy boys, murderous delinquents and amoral American expats as seen in other films like *Night and the City* (Jules Dassin, 1950), *The Gambler and the Lady* (Patrick Jenkins and Sam Newfield, 1952) and *Face the Music/The Black Glove* (Terence Fisher, 1953) had seemingly grown stale. James Chapman argues that the British crime film *The Blue Lamp* (1950) directed by Basil Dearden marked a watershed for the British crime film and the 'end of the cycle of post-war underworld thrillers, signalling a shift of narrative interest from the spiv and the racketeer to the policeman and the detective'.[63]

Noose, *Street of Shadows* and *Soho Incident* are examples of the treatment by postwar cinema to explore the fear of Americanisation by portraying the displacement of the expat. Sugiani, Luigi and Jim attempt to advance their socioeconomic status through their aggressive entrepreneurialism. Because of the film's position in Soho, this strongly recalls social anxieties around mass culture and American consumerism.[64] These films' reliance on Hollywood co-financing and the deliberate casting of American stars for commercial purposes showed that these filmmakers exploited the area's historical association with crime and vice alongside its reputation as an entertainment centre for American soldiers during the war. However, more importantly, these films were amongst the first of the canon to shoot on location in Soho, featuring real-life locations like the House of St Barnabas and Soho Square. *Noose* has been recognised by critics as a film with important aesthetic qualities. I argue that *Street of Shadows* and *Soho Incident* are forgotten films worthy of similar acknowledgement due to their engaging and deft deployment of montage and tracking sequences. These Soho 'B' crime films anticipated the chief techniques utilised by filmmakers from the late 1950s onwards, in turn securing Soho as a cinematically noir space.

Notes

1. Christopher Booker, *The Neophiliacs: Revolution in English Life in the Fifties and Sixties*, 2nd edn (London: Pimlico, 1992), 84–85.
2. Ibid.
3. Ina Zweiniger-Bargielowska discusses the bleak 1940s and the Labour government's maintenance of strict control over civilian consumption. See Ina Zweiniger-Bargielowska, *Austerity in Britain: Rationing, Controls, and Consumption 1939–1955* (Oxford: Oxford University Press, 2000), 9.
4. See Booker, *The Neophiliacs*, 84–86.
5. Booker states that: 'Over the first two years of the Fifties it seemed that only the Economist's blackest prognostications were to be borne out … In the London of that summer, where trams still clanked down the Embankment and only the ragwort and willow-herb provided a touch of colour on mile after mile of dust bomb sites.' See Ibid.
6. In 1946, cinema attendance in Britain rose to 1.6 million, with both Hollywood and British films proving popular, such as *The Seventh Veil* (Compton Bennett, 1945) and *Brighton Rock* (John Boulting, 1948). See Alan Burton and Steve Chibnall, *Historical Dictionary of British Cinema* (Lanham, MD: Scarecrow Press, 2013), 10.
7. Ibid.
8. The rise in production of 'B' films (low-budget, second feature films) stemmed from the exhibition practices of the mid-1930s, postwar austerity and most notably, the visual style and realist tendencies seen in Hollywood and European film noir. The origin of the British 'B' has been discussed by numerous scholars, including Brian McFarlane (1996), Tim Pulleine (1999), Robert Murphy (1998), Peter Wollen (2002), and Andrew Spicer (2005). See Tim Pulleine, 'Spin a dark web,' In *British Crime Cinema* edited by Steve Chibnall and Robert Murphy. 27–36 (London: Routledge, 1999), Peter Wollen, *Paris Hollywood: Writings on Film* (London: Verso, 2002), and Andrew Spicer, *Typical Men: The Representations of Masculinity in Popular British Culture* (London: I.B. Tauris, 2001).
9. See Mark Roodhouse, *Black Market Britain: 1939–1955* (Oxford: Oxford University Press, 2013), 227.
10. See Andrew Spicer, 'Creativity and the "B" Feature': Terence Fisher's Crime Films', *Film Criticism* 30(2) (2005), 25–26.
11. Ibid.
12. American GIs were paid a salary three times more than British servicemen and spent more on leisure and entertainment; in turn, West End theatres, clubs and restaurants thrived during wartime. I discuss their influence on sex industries in Chapters 9 and 10. See Mike Hutton, *The Story of Soho: The Windmill Years 1932–1964* (Stroud: Amberley Publishing, 2012), 79.
13. Ibid., 242.

14. The 'American player' Cesar Romero was born in New York of Cuban descent. He began his career in entertainment as a chorus boy in the Metropolitan Opera and performed in various theatrical productions throughout his school years. His first job, according to a feature article in *Picturegoer* published in 1941, was as a runner at the National City Bank in New York. But it was his dance partnership with socialite Lisbeth Higgins, 'well known in the New York night haunts', which led to his discovery in the early 1930s by American theatrical producer Brock Pemberton, who thought of Romero as a successor to Italian actor Tullio Carminati. Romero then held a steady career on Broadway before a screen test by MGM Studios led to his 'reputation making' role as social-climbing gigolo Chris Jorgenson in *The Thin Man*. Coincidentally, Joseph Calleia also starred in *The Thin Man* series as nightclub proprietor Dancer in the sequel *After the Thin Man* (W.S. van Dyke, 1936). See Malcolm Phillips, 'Romero and Romance', *Picturegoer* 11(534) (1941), 9.
15. See the review in 'No Orchids for Miss Blandish', *Monthly Film Bulletin* 15(169) (1948), 47.
16. James Hadley Chase's novel about the kidnapping, drugging and rape of a wealthy American heiress by gangster Slim Grissom was notorious even before moves to turn it into a film. It was first submitted to the BBFC in 1944, but was deemed objectionable. Further controversy surrounding the film was due to the film's 'A' (adult-only) certificate given by the British censors, which shocked many commentators. James Chapman has suggested that the film's release had 'all the characteristics of a moral panic: a hysterical (over) reaction from critics … fueled by national and local politicians'. See further James Chapman, 'Sordidness, Corruption and Violence Almost Unrelieved: Critics, Censors and the Post-War British Crime Film', *Contemporary British History* 22(2) (2008), 181–201.
17. See Robert Murphy, 'Dark Shadows around Pinewood and Ealing', *Film International* (2004), 30. Judith Walkowitz describes the postwar drinking culture boom in London as 'modelled on American speakeasies'. See also Judith Walkowitz, *Nights out: Life in Cosmopolitan London* (New Haven: Yale University Press, 2012), 216.
18. See Nick Browne, *Reconfiguring American Film Genres: History and Theory* (Berkeley: University of California Press, 1998), 153.
19. Ibid., 155.
20. See Ginette Vincendeau, 'How the French Birthed Film Noir', *Sight and Sound*, 15 November 2016. Retrieved 15 October 2021 from http://www.bfi.org.uk/news-opinion/sight-sound-magazine/features/deep-focus/french-film-noir.
21. See Mark Shiel, *Italian Neorealism: Rebuilding the Cinematic City* (London: Wallflower Press, 2006), 18.
22. Ibid., 18.
23. Although set in London, *Night and the City* (Jules Dassin, 1950) deliberately constructs Hollywood noir spaces, such as the Silver Fox nightclub and the American Bar. These businesses function as antithetical manifestations of its American spiv protagonist Harry Fabian (Richard Widmark) and his desire for social mobility. The American Bar is brightly lit, lavishly furnished and perhaps a tribute to the real-life American Bar located inside the historic Savoy Hotel on the Strand. The Bar signifies Fabian's desire for affluence and foreshadows his downfall. His girlfriend works as a hostess, at The Silver Fox, a subterranean clip joint. The bar features mirrored balls that hang limply from low ceilings and, in turn, reflect shattered splinters of light onto the muddy brick walls, where bloated male patrons are depicted as being swindled by being sold bottles of Champagne at marked-up prices.

24. Diack Hunter, 'Review: Noose', *The Spectator*, 27 June 1947, 749.
25. Ibid.
26. Sugiani is called Luciani and deals exclusively with vice; Medbury is called Dora and is a whore rather than a journalist; Jumbo is called Squeaks and is a bruiser instead of a sportswriter, but the story is virtually the same. In 1937, it had provoked strong words and been decisively rejected, but by 1948, the censors had grown slightly more tolerant and with certain changes, they reluctantly approved it. Murphy deems that Sugiani's 'underworld operation was no pale reflection of Hollywood/Chicago'. See Robert Murphy, *Realism and Tinsel: Cinema and Society in Britain 1939–48* (London: Routledge, 1992), 139.
27. Myro, 'Film Review: Noose', *Variety*, 6 October 1948, 11.
28. Wollen, *Paris Hollywood*, 190–94. See also Pulleine, 'Spin a Dark Web', 36.
29. See Vincent Porter, 'Strangers on the Shore: The Contributions of French Novelists and Directors to British Cinema, 1946–1960', *Framework: The Journal of Cinema and Media* 43(1) (Spring 2002), 115.
30. See Wollen, *Paris Hollywood*, 194.
31. See Bertrand Tavernier, 'Odd Man Out: Edmond T. Gréville', *Film Comment* 34(1) (1998), 54.
32. See Pulleine, 'Spin a Dark Web', 29.
33. See Ian Christie's DVD sleeve notes. Piccadilly (E.A. Dupont, 1929). *British Film Institute*, 2004.
34. Tavernier, 'Odd Man Out', 56.
35. Ibid., 56.
36. The upside-down effect created at the outset by a shot of a reflection in a puddle introduces a recurring motif; later, a sense of disequilibrium is maintained via the inverted reflections of Landis in a cocktail-cabinet mirror and of performers at Sugiani's club in the mirror-like dancefloor. See Pulleine, 'Spin a Dark Web', 29.
37. See the official website of The House of St Barnabas, which today runs cultural, social and private events and is also a members-only club. See https://hosb.org.uk/about-us/#our-story (retrieved 15 October 2021).
38. See 'Soho Square Area: Portland Estate, No. 1 Greek Street, The House of St. Barnabas-in-Soho', in F.H.W. Sheppard (ed.), *Survey of London: Volumes 33 and 34, St Anne Soho* (London Country Council: London, 1966), 88–106.
39. See Andrew Dickos, *Street with No Name: A History of the Classic American Film Noir* (Lexington: University Press of Kentucky, 2002), 10.
40. Ibid., 9–10.
41. Ibid.
42. Ginette Vincendeau, 'French Film noir', in Andrew Spicer (ed.), *European Film Noir* (Manchester: Manchester University Press, 2007), 29.
43. Ibid.
44. Steve Chibnall and Brian McFarlane, *The British 'B' Film* (London: BFI, 2009), 97.
45. Ibid., 98–99.
46. See 'International: Anglo-Amalg., Nassour Deal for Six Pictures', *Variety* 23 July 1952, 13.
47. StudioCanal is a subsidiary of the CANAL+ group. It is one of Europe's leading companies in the market for production, acquisition, distribution and sales of international films and television series. It is the only studio that operates in three European territories: France, the UK and Germany. It also functions as a film library with over 9,000 original titles from 60 countries

including 6,000 films. It is also responsible for film restoration. See 'About StudioCanal', studiocanal.com, accessed September 1, 2017.
48. See L.C., 'Street of Shadows', *Picturegoer* 26(949) (1953), 19.
49. 'There is some selling value in the title and the familiarity of Cesar Romero – only American player in the cast – to U.S. audiences, but aside from these elements the offering is no better nor worse than the average of recent lower-budgeted English whodunits to reach domestic screens.' See 'Feature Reviews: Shadow Man (1953)', *Boxoffice*, 12 December 1953, A11.
50. John Hill, *Sex, Class and Realism: British Cinema 1956–1963* (London: BFI, 1986), 5.
51. *Street of Shadows* (Richard Vernon, 1953).
52. Browne, *Reconfiguring American Film Genres*, 163.
53. See Review, 'Street of Shadows', *Monthly Film Bulletin* 20(228) (1953), 76.
54. Dialogue from *Street of Shadows* (1953).
55. Paul B. Rich is one of the few scholars who identify the female fortune-teller in the *Bicycle Thieves* (Vittorio de Sica, 1948), he though does not elaborate on its meaning. See Paul B. Rich, *Cinema and Unconventional Warfare in the Twentieth Century: Insurgency, Terrorism and Special Operations* (London: Bloomsbury, 2018), 102. For a full catalogue of American film noir, see Michael F. Keaney, *Film Noir Guide: 745 Films of the Classic Era, 1940–1959* (Jefferson, NC: McFarland & Company, 2003).
56. See Robert Westerby, *Wide Boys Never Work: A Novel* (London: Arthur Barker, 1937), 1.
57. Ibid.
58. Brian McFarlane, 'Vernon Sewell (1903–2001)', *BFI Screenonline*. Retrieved 15 October 2021 from http://www.screenonline.org.uk/people/id/460103/index.html.
59. 'There's nary a Yank around in this London racketeering feature, supplying a bit of a twist to the British-lensed melodrama which Columbia is distributing stateside. As a gangster pic, it stirs up sufficient thriller entertainment for lowercase dates in the dual market.' See Brog, 'Spin a Dark Web', *Variety*, 26 September 1956, 15.
60. Elizabeth Forrest, *Picturegoer*, 31 October 1953, 11.
61. Chibnall and McFarlane, *The British 'B' Film*, 175–76.
62. For extensive work on the femme fatale, see Mary Ann Doane, *Femme Fatales: Feminism, Film Theory, and Psychoanalysis* (London: Routledge, 1991). See also Dominique Mainon and James Ursini, *Femme Fatale: Cinema's Most Unforgettable Lethal Ladies* (Milwaukee: Limelight Editions, 2009).
63. I have chosen not to discuss Jules Dassin's *Night and the City* due to the existing and expansive scholarship of the film. The film's protagonist Harry was played by Richard Widmark, who was critically lauded for his performance. Following the film's release, critics raved about it. One critic stated: '*Night and the City* is an exciting, suspenseful melodrama ... Widmark delivers one of his finest portrayals, lending absolute conviction to his role of the hustler.' See Whit, 'Film Review: *Night and the City*', *Variety*, 24 May 1950, 6. See also Chapman, 'Sordidness, Corruption and Violence Almost Unrelieved', 197.
64. See Christine Geraghty, *British Cinema in the Fifties: Gender, Genre and the 'New Look'* (London: Routledge, 2000), 15–16.

CHAPTER 5

Old Perils, New Pleasures
West End Jungle (1961) and the Birth of Commercial Vice

> *The hands of Big Ben point to one minute past midnight. The new Street Offences Act has become law. I am standing in Park Lane, London, and there is not a Street Girl in sight.*
>
> —John Ball, 1959

On 16 August 1959, the *News of the World* British tabloid informed its readers of the implementation of a new law in England and Wales called the Street Offences Act with a sensational exposé written by journalist John Ball. The headline for the article, which covered over half of the newspaper's front page, proclaimed: 'The Clock Strikes Twelve for the Cinderellas of The Streets: THE LAST VICE ROUND-UP.'[1] For the first time in British history, prostitutes would be prohibited from soliciting in a public street and on 'any bridge, road, lane, footway, subway, square, court, alley or passage, whether a thoroughfare or not, which is for the time open to the public'.[2] Under the Act, prostitutes would face a fine not exceeding £25 for soliciting or loitering in public and subsequent offences would result in three months' imprisonment.[3] The law was a direct recommendation by the Wolfenden Report, which was published in September 1957. The Report contained results of a study into homosexuality and prostitution in London and was led by the educationalist John Wolfenden.[4] The Home Office's push towards a new 'form of containment' of vice was driven chiefly by the increase in media-circulated reports of sex crime and prostitution within the nation's capital after the Second World War, particularly in the West End and the city's major termini, including Soho.[5] According to Stefan Anthony Slater, the Act 'formalized the distinction between law and morality, to rationalize the control of prostitution and increase the certainty of conviction, and to remove the visibility of vice from the streets'.[6]

One unique film that cast a 'leering eye at the incredulity and arrogance of the [Wolfenden] report' and provides a social portrait of female prostitution in postwar Soho was the pseudo-documentary *West End Jungle* (1961).[7] Not so coincidentally, the film also includes a superimposed shot of the tabloid's front page during its opening sequence. The film was directed by Arnold Louis Miller and produced by Stanley Long. It was made with a budget of £3,200 with a borrowed camera and ex-government 35 mm film stock. It is notable as an exploitation film that was banned from cinema exhibition in London, but was shown nationally, having been granted an 'X' certificate in cities such as Newcastle, Leeds, Cardiff, Coventry, Glasgow, Liverpool and Manchester.[8] Shot on location in London, the film is organised into a series of staged vignettes and is accompanied by a male voiceover provided by David Gell, who details the 'myriad of prurient forms that off-street prostitution was taking in its wake, relying heavily on images of clip joints and call girls from the 1940s and 1950s'.[9] The film, by aiming to critique and satirise the consequences of the Street Offences Act, claims that the legislation inadvertently, and therefore ironically, turned sex into a mass commercial product. But this social message is obstructed by its unashamedly explicit depictions of the female body as a sex object, which are undoubtedly used to titillate its prudish audiences. This chapter will examine *West End Jungle* and its legacy as an important document of the growing liberal attitudes towards sex work, but also of its hypocritical messages of exploitation, which, in turn, reflects Soho's own transformation in the period and the oscillation of its identity that spans two worlds: cosmopolitan and sexual spaces of consumption.

Tabloid Culture and Representations of Prostitution in British Cinema

The *News of the World* reporter's and, subsequently, the film's association of street prostitution with the Cinderella fairytale echo the wider British media's treatment and preoccupation with prostitutes during and after the immediate postwar years, which included the persistent 'association of prostitution with notions of foreignness'.[10] This directly informed cinematic representations of prostitutes in interwar and postwar British cinema. The prostitute's association with vice is similar to fictional literature's branding of Soho as the 'square mile of vice'.[11] Julia Laite unpicks this long-held association of prostitution with vice, which she suggests is historically rooted in the implementation of public policy: 'Prostitution had been considered a problem of public order, collective morality and individual sin for many centuries … combined with the waning of the moral authority of the church [prostitution] inspired the founding of societies dedicated to tackling vice, and sexual vice in particular'.[12] The figure of the female prostitute and her relationship to the Wolfenden Report and the Street Offences Act appear in most if not all the Soho films. This not only confirms that the legislation was the catalyst for prostitution to become a fixture of Soho films, but also confirms Barry Forshaw's summation that: 'The treatment of prostitution in British films is often fatally compromised by the perceived necessity of taking a dual view of the profession.'[13] However, as Melanie Bell states, the prostitute in British cinema 'conventionally … had been relegated to either cameo roles and afforded a degree of respectability by appearing as a "fallen woman" in literary adaptations such as Nancy in *Oliver Twist* (David Lean, 1948) … as a doxy in Elizabethan taverns *The Wicked Lady* (Leslie Arliss, 1945), or as a "good time girl" in aristocrats' clubs in Victorian London, *Fanny by Gaslight* (Anthony Asquith, 1944)'.[14] From the mid-1950s onwards, the prostitute figure was 'atypically' placed at the heart of underworld crime films such as *The Flesh Is Weak* (Don Chaffey, 1957), a film that proclaimed itself to be a direct social response to the Wolfenden Report. It provides both a sympathetic portrayal of the prostitute and is a terrifying examination of the grooming procedures of vulnerable young women in the same period.[15]

During this period, Britain was entering a televised age, though 'in reality, print media still dominated news communication throughout the 1950s'.[16] The media was unashamed in its promotion of salacious sex scandals in this period to increase readership, chiefly directed by popular newspapers such as the *News of the World* and the *Daily Mirror*. This growing national fascination for sex saw the rise in popularity of 'true crime' novels that brazenly published sensationalist material to exploit this new appetite for sexual intrigue. According to Adrian Bingham, the press played an instrumental role in the public debate and knowledge about sexual behaviour, and in this way we may uncover the relationship between cinema and the media's preoccupation with vice and the urban centre, which reflects the tendency to construct a 'cyclical moral panic about the growth of the underground indoor commercial sex industry'.[17] Not so coincidentally, producer Stanley Long later mused: 'I was a voracious reader of the *News of the World* and that particular tabloid had been extremely kind to me over the years. Sleazy Fleet Street journalists lead the world in dishing the dirt and us Brits have always been obsessed with so-called sex scandals.'[18] Long's choice of tabloid also enthusiastically provided the film with an unrivalled marketing campaign under the guise of a moral crusade that allowed *West End Jungle* to lucratively garner reputation throughout the country as the film that 'London Cannot See!'[19]

The Street Offences Act (1959)

Frank Mort has described the Street Offences Act as a 'dramatic example of localized policy making, where close observation of the central areas of the capital city influenced proposals for important changes to the criminal law'.[20] The effects of the Act were instantaneous. Slater notes that within three months, 'prosecutions within the Metropolitan Police District dropped to just 10 per cent of their level in the responding period of the preceding year'.[21] Laite recounts the sentiments of one policeman, who stated: 'The "professional" prostitute knew the Act was coming into force many months before … She had time, therefore, to make her arrangements accordingly. Police officers stationed in Soho and the West End (C Division) similarly noted that the number of arrests of prostitutes had fallen by ninety per cent.'[22] However, many commentators remained sceptical and questioned whether this new type of 'cautioning system' would result in the growth of an altogether new brand of sexual commerce.[23] *The Spectator* asked: 'The call-girl system will boom, we are told, if the Wolfenden recommendations sweep clean the streets. Has any constructive thought been given to the consequent strain on the space available for small advertisements in the newsagents' windows of Soho?'[24] For British sexploitation filmmaker Stanley Long: 'All the Act did was to brush vice under the carpet, forcing girls to find other ways to solicit business.'[25] From 1959 to 1961, the media persisted in a semi-crusade to show the general public that barring prostitution from the streets had simply created new spaces for prostitution, which included soliciting from windowsills or using hotels, gentlemen-only clubs or under the guise of legitimate massage parlours.

In his examination of prostitution in interwar London from a microhistorical perspective, Slater highlights the term 'organized vice' and its deployment by journalists in order to 'describe the role of people involved in marriages-of-convenience, pimping, and the letting of flats to prostitutes at exorbitant rents'.[26] Slater suggests that the mass-marketed stories of underground vice rings such as those run by the Messina Brothers, the models for the fictional antagonists of *Noose* (1948) and *The Flesh is Weak* (1957), are chiefly responsible for this linking of vice with foreignness. The journalist Duncan Webb, who exposed the gang in the early 1950s, 'made the overthrow of the Messinas into the notorious affair it was ... And the linking of the Messina brothers with "vice" made for good copy, for journalists and "true crime" historians alike'.[27] Furthermore, the media's portrayal of the Messina Brothers as 'other' was largely due to the political argument that 'Britain was being corrupted by unwelcome foreign influences – even if the brothers, as Maltese subjects, held British nationality'.[28] On the propensity of the press for publishing stories on prostitution, Bingham states:

> *Of the sexual vices, it was the easiest for newspapers to 'investigate' and 'expose' – after all, prostitutes needed to be visible enough to attract punters – and editors, especially of Sunday papers, could not for long resist the temptation to do so.*[29]

Similarly, in the opening sequence of *West End Jungle*, we witness a transaction between a politician and a prostitute. This plays upon the audience's pre-existing knowledge and consumption of newspaper investigations or 'true crime' stories, described by Christopher Wilson as '"ripped" from the headlines ... what might best be described as a hybrid literary genre: a pop-culture of modern police departments, combing conventions from autobiography, political expose, and crime news itself'.[30] The popular press and their investigations into criminal activity were overtly leaning towards certain political agendas, purporting their own individual moral crusades.

Arnold L. Miller, Stanley Long and Sexploitation Cinema

Rendering a profit from selling Soho as 'virtual mantrap' to the nation continued to prove lucrative for entrepreneurs and entertainers alike after the Second World War.[31] Long and Miller's prowess in capitalising upon a growing permissive society was already proven by this period. After completing his compulsory two years of National Service in the RAF as a medical orderly, working-class-born Londoner Stanley Long scraped by 'photographing weddings and catalogue merchandise', until he was introduced to Hilary Donaldson, a fifteen-year-old schoolgirl who became the youngest dancer hired by the Windmill Theatre.[32] David McGillivray suggests that Donaldson recommended Long to take her nude photograph for a publication with her new employers at a paper manufacturer. These photographs were then procured by Arnold Louis Miller, whose father's publishing house, L. Miller and Company, reprinted American book titles for British readers. Miller, who also served in the RAF, left the family business and set up a publishing company called the Arnold Book Company. Miller and his wife Sheila set up shop on the fringes of Soho's Golden Square on Lower James Street, with Miller's offices above and a tobacconist, newsagent and greeting cards business below. They published the comics *Space Comics* and *Ace Molloy*. Photographer Long had 'learned in the family business that sex and female nudity sold for above-normal prices even in times of austerity … Being on the fringe of Soho I supplied many of the sex book shops and, thus, got to know the managers quite well'.[33] Through this Soho connection, Miller was introduced to Long's nude photography efforts and began publishing them in his glamour magazine *Photo Studio*. When Long began to record his nude subjects on film, Miller saw a further opportunity for financial profit. He recalls, through 'glamour films … prettily packaged 8mm striptease shorts that proliferated until the mid-Sixties. Each featuring a girl who took approximately two and a half minutes to strip to her panties, the films were almost wholesome in their lack of obscenity, but this did not prevent laboratories refusing to process them, or moral groups of the day expressing their disgust as the little boxes began to turn up in the corner newsagent.'[34]

The pair swiftly set up a new company called Stag Films and marketed the glamour films within the pages of *Photo Studio* and sold by mail order. Bingham has examined the history of the pin-up from the end of the nineteenth century to the proliferation of pin-up culture in the 1950s, led by the *Mirror* newspaper. He states that the deployment of pin-up techniques was largely used in commercial advertising, particularly in marketing films and female film stars, which then became known as sex symbols. In their defence, 'Fleet Street tried to defuse criticism by maintaining and rigorously policing a 'common-sense' distinction between pin-ups and "pornography"'.[35] *West End Jungle* humorously depicts the pornography studio in a vignette featuring a young man and a model-for-hire. In the vignette, the man, sheepishly dressed in a duffle coat, pays for the model, wearing a blonde wig, silk robe and a suspender belt, to remove her clothing whilst he sits and watches. A large spotlight is cast on the model whilst she strips. Her exaggerated, pouty performance to the man within a faux pornography studio setting reflects those manoeuvres by newspapers to legitimise pin-up culture.

Inspired by the box office success of the Charles Saunders nudist film *Nudist Paradise* (1959), the pair swiftly moved into producing feature-length films, generating substantial profits from their spin-offs *Nudist Memories* (1960) and *Nudes of the World* (1961). Both films, despite their explicit content, were passed without any cuts from the British Board of Film Classification (BBFC) and were awarded 'X' certificates. The 'X' rating was first introduced by the BBFC in 1951 as 'a necessary development to reflect the fact that many film-makers were tackling more adult-oriented themes'.[36] The BBFC's secretary John Trevelyan was often criticised throughout his career for his liberal attitudes towards approving 'X' rated films. However, following the Queen's coronation in 1953, there had been a 'downward trend of feature films' with universal certificates and a spike in films produced that were 'X' rated.[37] Trevelyan defended the use of the 'X' certificate in *Variety* that same year: 'There have been a good many really good "X" pictures … Much of the criticism is made by people who have not seen the pictures but have got a bad impression of them from their titles and from sensational publicity.'[38] Trevelyan knew there was more to be gained by lending 'greater respectability to the "X" certificate by supporting quality adult productions'.[39] His attitudes reflect the increasing popularity of the newspaper pin-up photograph, highly sexualised illustrations and photographs of women, used as both 'essential circulation props' and also to function as the 'editorial identity' of popular newspapers.

By 1960, Long and Miller had established another company that specialised in producing feature films called Searchlight Films. They then swiftly began plotting an ambitious feature-length exposé into 'how the law had made hookers, and their weak-willed customers, more vulnerable'.[40] This marked the beginning of pre-production for *West End Jungle.* However, the ironic scarcity of real-life prostitutes on the streets of London following the Street Offences Act, in addition to a small budget, forced the filmmaker to use nonprofessional actors, friends and colleagues. Long even scoured the streets of Soho for his leading ladies:

> *The budget didn't stretch to hiring professional actors for the film, so I visited a coffee house in Soho's Dean Street, which was a famous haunt for continental au pair girls who serviced the rich households of Mayfair and Chelsea. I promised a five-pound note to every girl who turned up to my location in Piccadilly the following evening at 7:00pm.*[41]

Figure 5.1. Director Arnold L. Miller 're-creates' sex work on the streets of London. Still from *West End Jungle* (Arnold L. Miller, 1961). DVD, Strike Force Entertainment, 2009

Long's street casting call paid off. Over forty women accepted his challenge to be filmed stalking a street corner or alleyway in tarty outfits. To complete the transformation, Miller dressed the young women in fishnet stockings purchased from Woolworths and high heels from Dolcis Shoes.[42] The 'West End Jungle' was reborn – on celluloid.

Critical Reception

West End Jungle proved an unadulterated success around the nation.[43] Although the film was passed by Berkshire County Council and in several other cities in England, it was vehemently refused the 'X' certificate from the BBFC and banned from public exhibition in the capital by London County Council. However, it did finally preview, albeit to a private audience in the capital at the British Recording Club, a members-only cinema on Archer Street in Soho and later for a special audience of MPs at the Houses of Parliament.[44] The leader of the campaign to stop the film from being shown in theatres was Lord Morrison of Lambeth, President of the Board of Film Censors, who proclaimed the film a disgrace.[45] Meanwhile, the *News of the World* ran a campaign throughout the film's run nationally with the headline: 'Is London Ashamed?' The film screened across the country, from town halls to Women's Institute meeting rooms. In Yorkshire it ran continuously for eighteen months.[46] Did the film's consistent exhibition outside the capital infer the nation's desire for sensationalism, media-controlled recreation or smug localisation vis-à-vis London? More likely, the frequency of the film screenings by municipal authorities and civic institutions functioned as a form of moral rehabilitation, evaluating the success (or failure) of the Wolfenden Report and its recommendations for new legislation.

Critically, *West End Jungle* received mixed reviews. *Monthly Film Bulletin* called it: 'Undeniably factual and well-organized … The accent throughout on the gullibility and stupidity of men who are induced to part with their money for the sake of tawdry and degrading pleasures.'[47] *Variety* suggested that although the film was original in terms of its subject matter, it was largely 'competent [but] not sufficiently pointed'.[48] *Boxoffice* declared the film to be as 'topical as anything emanating from our British film creative sources in many years; it has the hard-hitting impact of the incisive page one melodrama, and moreover, can ride on the appeal of documentary realism … this should reap sizeable box office response'.[49] The film's combination of the inauthentic, utilising nonprofessionals and re-enacting inspired scenarios of sexual transactions, with the authentic, filming on location and the insertion of current-day statistics is arguably what successfully seduced its large provincial audiences into believing its objective focus. However, the film may act as a 'catalyst for an increase in sexual knowledge', although this docudrama treads carefully within its own boundaries. As one reporter from *The Times* asked: 'Is it [the film] an honest warning or a disguised invitation?'[50]

Conclusion

West End Jungle marked the beginning of a fruitful creative partnership between Long and Miller who became keen researchers in the field of sex, following up *West End Jungle* with another exposé *Primitive London* (1965), which Iain Sinclair deemed 'part tit-show, part satire, part tabloid editorial. *Primitive London* never strayed far from its Soho roots'.[51] Long and Miller's subsequent professional relationship with the notorious Soho film producers Michael Klinger and Tony Tenser of Compton-Cameo Films confirmed their legacy of anthropologically tinged cinematic studies of sexual behaviour and subcultures. The film's political position on commercial vice is tagged on to the finale of the film, where an older prostitute moves gormlessly towards Piccadilly Circus. We hear her lament: 'But why do they take it out on us? If men didn't want prostitutes, we wouldn't be here. It takes two to make a bargain.'[52] Failing to attract an inebriated man who stumbles past, a police officer appears from the shadows, and she is forcibly dragged in the opposite direction, away from the illuminated hustle and bustle, neon signs and potential punters in the West End. The narrator Gell then delivers his final sermon:

> The streets have been swept clean at last, but the sickness has not been cured. The love-for-hire women are still there, plying their trade under a dozen different guises, and while men want their services they will continue to flourish in the shadows and darkness like a noxious weed.[53]

There is an ironic recognition by the film of its own 'sickness', demonstrated by the success of the sensational marketing campaign carried out during the film's release, which was greatly assisted by censor disapproval and promotional hyperbole from tabloids such as the *News of the World*. Alongside the pseudo-authentic performances by its untrained cast, melodramatic narration and superficial representations of male customers, *West End Jungle* is a highly commercial object. It combines the published studies of prostitution by Wolfenden and Wilkinson, the true crime stories that proliferated newspapers during and after the war, and lastly, the flourishing pin-up and pornography culture used by tabloid newspapers and nudie magazines to titillate their growingly less prude readership. As with Wolfenden, the film owes its 'intellectual origins to English utilitarianism [but in practical terms] it was the dramatic encounters with London's sexual subcultures that determined their philosophy'.[54]

Unlike the more sympathetic portrayal of prostitution in Soho films from the late 1950s, which combined melodrama with social issues like *The Flesh Is Weak*, *West End Jungle* undermines its own proposed moral crusade by rendering a tongue-in-cheek portrait of commercialised vice in its attempt to critique the failure of the Street Offences Act to eradicate prostitution in the capital. However, the film is ultimately far less concerned with the origins of the prostitute or society's shifting attitudes to sex than with its relationship to capitalism: 'The implication throughout the film is that post-Wolfenden, there was a somewhat less honest exchange of "pounds for pleasures", and that men themselves became unwittingly exploited through an array of ruses that resulted from the 1959 Act. Men drinking mock-alcoholic drinks at hugely inflated prices in unlicensed near-beer joints.'[55]

As we have seen in all Soho films, instead of 'Landmark', we have the Soho equivalent I deem a 'Postcard London' montage – a frenetic succession of shots depicting neon-lit signs for nightclubs, striptease clubs and clip-joints – which convey the topographical arrangement of its night-time economies. *West End Jungle* utilises the 'Soho Tracking Shot' to great effect, emphasising the speed at which these vice businesses grew after the Street Offences Act came into force, confirming that this cash in advance, underground and exclusive sex industry was born in Soho. Laite is critical of Wolfenden, who once suggested that 'prostitute women were on the streets by pathological choice and laziness rather than because of economic need or coercion, Wolfenden was [then] able to construct the right to public space as relative to respectability'.[56] Similarly, Long and Miller were successful in their construction of eroticised fantasies as relative to tabloid sensationalism, but, through the lens of documentary filmmaking, affix a type of authenticity to their claims. Like the development of Soho's sexual industries post-Wolfenden, *West End Jungle* is a highly commercial product that is marketed under the guise of a social portrait – a perfectly packaged Soho artefact, one that heavily impacted, if not chiefly directed, subsequent renderings of commercial sex on screen.

Notes

1. John Ball, 'The Clock Struck Twelve', *News of the World*, 16 August 1959, 1.
2. See Street Offences Act, 1959. Ch. 57. 7 & 8 Eliz, 1–2.

3. For the purposes of this historical study, I am utilising 'prostitution' and 'prostitute', the designations used by lawmakers, journalists and filmmakers during the postwar period to denote sex work and sex workers. It is of course a complex and highly debatable subject, particularly around the ways in which language stigmatises the sex industry. However, I am using these terms within a specific context in order to emphasise the ways in which the postwar era represented sex workers negatively (attaching it to vice) but also sympathetically on screen and in print.
4. The Street Offences Act followed the Wolfenden Report's recommendation on the public treatment of prostitution: 'The main point was that it was designed to make absolutely sure that anyone apprehended or charged should be genuinely of the "type" whose activities it was desired to check.' See 'Making Vice Less Flagrant', *Manchester Guardian*, 30 January 1959, 2.
5. The investigation was Jack Wolfenden's first major government commission, and he was 'keen to prove his intellectual and administrative credentials ... forty-eight at the time ... intensely ambitious, the product of a lower-middle-class back-ground rooted in Methodism'. See Frank Mort, *Capital Affairs: London and the Making of the Permissive Society* (New Haven: Yale University Press, 2010), 143; and Julia Laite. *Common Prostitutes and Ordinary Citizens: Commercial Sex in London, 1885–1960* (Palgrave Macmillan, 2012), 173.
6. Stefan Anthony Slater, 'Containment: Managing Street Prostitution in London, 1918–1959', *Journal of British Studies* 49 (2010). 356.
7. Ibid., 173.
8. David McGillivray, *Doing Rude Things: The History of the British Sex Film 1957–1981* (London: Sun Tavern Fields, 1992), 32. See also Barney Ashton, 'West End Jungle Viewing Notes', *West End Jungle*, DVD, Strikeforce Entertainment, 2009, 8.
9. Julia Laite, *Common Prostitutes and Ordinary Citizens* (Basingstoke: Palgrave Macmillan, 2012), 205.
10. Ibid.
11. Mort, *Capital Affairs*, 51.
12. William Lecky, *A History of European Morals from Augustus to Charlemagne* (New York: D. Appleton and Company, 1869), 282–83. See also Laite, *Common Prostitutes*, 5.
13. See Barry Forshaw, 'Breaking Taboos: Sex and the Crime Film', in *British Crime Film: Subverting the Social Order* (Basingstoke: Palgrave Macmillan, 2012), 123.
14. See Melanie Bell, *Femininity in the Frame: Women and 1950s British Popular Cinema* (London: I.B. Tauris, 2010), 123.
15. See ibid., 124.
16. See Frank Mort, "Scandalous Events: Metropolitan Culture and Moral Change in Post-Second World War London', *Representations* 93 (2006), 118.
17. Adrian Bingham, *Family Newspapers? Sex, Private Life, and the British Popular Press* (Oxford: Oxford Scholarship Online, 2009), 202.
18. See Stanley Long and Simon Sheridan. *X-Rated: Adventures of an Exploitation Filmmaker* (London: Reynolds & Hearn, 2008), 15.
19. Ibid., 6.
20. The most radical recommendation of the Wolfenden Report was that private sexual acts between men should be partly decriminalised. However, this 'produced a flurry of debate but no immediate legislation'. See Mort, *Capital Affairs*, 142, 195.
21. Slater, 'Containment', 357.

22. Laite states that: 'For those women who were arrested, much heavier fines, the hallmark of the new law, were handed out liberally.' See Laite, *Common Prostitutes*, 202.
23. Ibid., 203.
24. Cyril Ray, 'Pre-Wolfenden', *The Spectator*, 27 September 1957, 389.
25. Long and Sheridan, *X-Rated*, 73; Laite, *Common Prostitutes*, 206.
26. Stefan Slater, 'Prostitutes and Popular History: Notes on the "Underworld", 1918–1939', *Crime, Histoire & Sociétés/Crime, History & Societies* 13(1) (2009), 39.
27. Ibid., 27.
28. Bingham states that: 'Between 1918 and 1978 newspapers were right at the heart of British popular culture, with the vast majority of adults regularly reading at least one national paper: at mid-century, indeed, Britons read more newspapers per capita than any other people.' See Bingham, *Family Newspapers?*, 2, 166.
29. Ibid., 200.
30. Slater, 'Prostitutes and Popular History', 27.
31. McGillivray, *Doing Rude Things*, 32.
32. Ibid., 29.
33. See 'Arnold L. Miller before West End Jungle' in Ashton, '*West End Jungle* Viewing Notes', 10.
34. Ibid., 32.
35. 'Ever since the technology to reproduce half-tone photographs in newspapers was perfected at the end of the nineteenth century, editors had assumed that male and female readers alike would appreciate pictures of attractive women as "brightening up" the news columns. Daily picture papers (the *Mirror* became a picture paper in 1904, the *Daily Sketch* was established as its rival in 1908) brought news photography to a mass audience and were soon being mocked for their penchant for shots of "bathing belles".' See Bingham, *Family Newspapers?*, 203–13.
36. Michael Brooke states that: 'Trevelyan believed that raising the X certificate age limit would give him much more freedom to pass the vast majority of films without requesting cuts.' See 'The X Certificate', *BFI Screenonline*. Retrieved 17 October 2021 from http://www.screenonline.org.uk/film/id/591679.
37. 'Sharp Downward Trend of Feature Films in 1955: Nearly 100 Fewer "U" Certificate Films: More "A" and "X"', *Kine Weekly*, 29 December 1955, 5.
38. John Trevelyan, 'British Film Censorship Today', *Variety*, 26 April 1961, 93.
39. Andrew Spicer and A.T. McKenna, *The Man Who Got Carter: Michael Klinger, Independent Production and the British Film Industry 1960–1980* (London: I.B. Tauris, 2013), 22.
40. Long and Sheridan, *X-Rated*, 73.
41. Ibid.
42. Ibid.
43. Ibid., 75.
44. Ibid., 74.
45. Ibid.
46. Ibid., 76.
47. See Review, '*West End Jungle*', *Monthly Film Bulletin* 28(324) (1961), 134.
48. Rich, 'Film Review: *West End Jungle*', *Variety* 224, 11 November 1961, 6.
49. 'Review: *West End Jungle*', *Boxoffice* 82(5) (1963), A11.
50. See Mort, *Capital Affairs*, 194. See also the review of *West End Jungle* in *The Times*, 13 October 1961, 18.

51. The film *Primitive London* conducted a series of interviews with representatives of the coming youth culture, mods, and rockers. See Iain Sinclair, 'Primal Screen', *The Guardian*, 9 September 2006. Retrieved 17 October 2021 from https://www.theguardian.com/film/2006/sep/09/film.
52. Scripted dialogue from *West End Jungle* (Arnold L. Miller, 1961).
53. Ibid.
54. Mort, *Capital Affairs*, 195.
55. Ashton, '*West End Jungle* Viewing Notes', 3.
56. Laite, *Common Prostitutes*, 198.

CHAPTER 6
'An' I Fort Jews Were Supposed to Be Lucky!'
Jewish Wide Boys, Johnny Jackson and Sammy Lee

> *I'd say he was part Soho, part Jewish.*
>
> —Val Guest, 2001

Johnny Jackson (Laurence Harvey) has just pinched a bundle of entertainment trade magazines from a local Soho newsstand, much to the chagrin of the newsagent who reminds the wide boy that his business is *not* a lending library. Without missing a beat, Johnny wheels around to face him and retorts: 'All right! I'm not paying a subscription!' Defeated by Johnny's false indignation, the newsagent retreats back into his shop. This Jewish male protagonist of Val Guest's *Expresso Bongo* (1960) then moves onto his next entrepreneurial opportunity, weaving through the throngs of teddy boys, small-time bookies, street-corner loungers and shopkeepers who are spilling out from the coffee bars, pubs and penny arcades on a warm summer evening in Soho. In this musical-comedy, Johnny, an aspiring pop music manager, discovers and moulds a new talent, a working-class teenager named Bert Rudge (Cliff Richard), who, under Johnny's tutelage, transforms into an idol called Bongo Herbert. Over the course of his efforts to propel Bongo to stardom and by any means necessary, Johnny must overcome various small hurdles. But it's his own ego that ultimately leads to his darkly comic, though hopeful downfall. Johnny is representative of the postwar wide boy/spiv, but he is also 'part Soho, part Jewish', as dubbed by Guest in his memoir entitled *So You Want to Be in Pictures* published in 2001.[1]

British cinema would depict another Jewish Soho wide boy three years later by *The Small World of Sammy Lee* (Ken Hughes, 1963). However, unlike Johnny, who has aspirations of becoming a pop music mogul before retiring to the south of France, Sammy 'Lee' Leeman is a habitual gambler who works, albeit begrudgingly, as a comic compère in a seedy Soho strip club. Sammy owes a large debt to a Soho

Figure 6.1. Johnny swindles Leon whilst grabbing 'the worst salt beef sandwiches in Soho' at his coffee bar. Still, *Expresso Bongo* (Val Guest, 1960). DVD, BFI Flipside, 2016

bookie, whose violent retributions against unpaid debt are infamous. Sammy only has the afternoon to raise the funds or else 'face the razor'.[2] Film historian Andrew Spicer pronounced the 'ducking-and-diving' Sammy Lee to be the 'sad side of Laurence Harvey's pushy entrepreneur'.[3] The film was an adaptation of Hughes' own stage play *Sammy*, which was originally broadcast on television in 1958 as a one-man play called *Eddie* and starring Mickey Rooney.

There is currently very little to no scholarship on the cinematic representation of the Jewish community in Britain. Kevin Gough-Yates and Nathan Abrams have contributed the few major texts that examine the cultural output of Jews, Jewish émigrés and refugees working in the British film industry. More recently, Gil Toffell's *Jews, Cinema and Public Life in Interwar Britain* (2018) contributes a welcome study on the 'lived expressive cultures of cinemas in Jewish areas and the ethnically specific films', in a period in which cinema became 'cultural centrality in Jewish neighbourhoods as film-going became the nation's pre-eminent urban leisure activity'.[4] Gough-Yates writes: 'There are no figures of the numbers of the proportion of Jews within the [British] film industry.'[5] Abrams has addressed this issue of candidly throughout his work and argues that published scholarship on Jews and Jewishness in British film and television are 'divorced from the British-Jewish context from which they derive'.[6]

This chapter expands on my work regarding migrant Soho communities in films like *Miracle in Soho* but will also addresses the lack of engagement with

British-Jewish cinema by identifying two unique Jewish protagonists. *Expresso Bongo* and *The Small World of Sammy Lee* have only recently re-entered the public imagination due to their re-releases as remastered Blu-Ray and DVD editions by the British Film Institute in 2016. By studying their relationship with the Jewish immigrant community in Soho and the surrounding peripheries, I resituate them as substantially Jewish primarily through their shared British-Jewish wide-boy protagonists, Johnny Jackson and Sammy Lee, played by the actors Laurence Harvey and Anthony Newley, respectively.[7] This will confirm these films are not only British-Jewish films, but are an important part of Soho's on-screen legacy of bohemian-cosmopolitans, which again reflects the type of image reproduction of particular archetypes (in this case, the wide boy) repeated throughout the area's prevalence as a locus during the 1960s.

Satirising Soho: From Stage to Screen

The film's screenwriter Wolf Mankowitz based his original newspaper story 'Expresso Bongo: The Story of the Making of a Modern Idol' on the overnight fame of 'Bermondsey boy', the British pop star Tommy Steele, formerly known as Tommy Hicks. Mankowitz was fascinated by the explosive publicity and legend surrounding Steele's rise to stardom in the mid-1950s. The popular legend goes that Steele was discovered by music publicity manager John Kennedy, who found the young man 'singing for shillings' in the famed 2i's Coffee Bar located at 59 Old Compton Street. This discovery forms the basis of *The Tommy Steele Story* (Gerard Bryant, UK, 1957), a formulaic, if not frustratingly slow musical biopic starring Steele as himself, which became a commercial hit at the box office.[8] John Mundy suggests that this is perhaps 'why, in the film [*Expresso Bongo*], the narrative focus is firmly on the antics of Johnny Jackson, the shifty, aspiring show-business agent'.[9]

    Mankowitz, like Emeric Pressburger, was clearly a Soho regular. He located his Bildungsroman in the Soho coffee bars, Jewish delis and subterranean jazz clubs that were mushrooming in the area during the 1950s. The original story was told from the point of view of an anonymous music agent who guides his client, Bongo Herbert, through the perilous maze of show business. The misspelling of espresso as 'expresso' acts as 'a pun between the new Italian coffee and the commissioning newspaper [that] helped to cement the common error of pronouncing "expresso" instead of "espresso".'[10] The 'foaming, furious, farrago [*sic*] of a tropically powerful' story of Bongo and his manager was published by the *Daily Express* in four parts throughout September of 1957.[11] Mankowitz's decision to satirise the tensions between publicity and fame alludes to the dramatic economic, social and cultural shifts seen in mid-1950s Britain.

Mankowitz's stories were then rewritten as a stage musical in 1957 with help from the writer Julian More and composers David Heneker and Monty Norman. The stage version of *Expresso Bongo* opened at London's Saville Theatre on 23 April 1958, starring Paul Scofield as Johnny Jackson and James Kenney as Bert Rudge/Bongo Herbert. The production was a commercial success and the London Critics' poll voted it the best British musical of the year 1957–58. Despite holding the underpinnings of a classic Hollywood musical, the transformation of teenager Bert Rudge into pop superstar Bongo Herbert, as orchestrated by Jewish wide boy Johnny, is treated as 'cruel parody ... [a] swift clobbering of the [music industry] and of the new teen idol phenomenon'.[12]

British-Jewish film director Val Guest expressed interest in directing a film version after his wife, the American actress Yolande Donlan (who stars in the film as a new character, an ageing American star Dixie Collins, the fierce antagonist for Johnny), convinced him of its potential for the big screen. Describing the preproduction process in his memoir, Guest recounts that their first port of call to secure financing for the film was British-Jewish producer Nat Cohen, who had 'established himself in the pre-war period building a small circuit of cinemas in the 1930s'.[13] In 1945 Cohen had founded Anglo-Amalgamated Pictures, a company that was 'highly successful in spotting the potential of the "B" feature market'.[14] Cohen, who Guest called the 'Lord-High-Panjandrum of Anglo Amalgamated', did not see the potential of adapting *Expresso Bongo* for the screen.[15]

After failing to convince Cohen of the film's commercial potential, one of producer Alexander Korda's ex-associates, the Hungarian-born Steven Pallos, managed to convince British Lion Films, which during this period was managed by the Boulting Brothers, to distribute the film. After confirming the main cast of Harvey, Richard and Sylvia Syms as Johnny's stripper girlfriend Maisie, Guest, armed with a script and a distribution contract, applied for a loan from the National Film Finances Corporation. The application was successful: 'All I had to put up were my last two pictures as collateral. C'est le movies.'[16]

The film was a commercial and critical success, 'despite being given an "X" certificate ... boosted by Richard's presence'.[17] It was nominated for two BAFTA Awards: Best British Actor for Laurence Harvey and Best British Screenplay for

Wolf Mankowitz. Guest's 'favourite and most popular film' would only retain the songs 'Nausea', 'Nothing Is for Nothing', 'I Never Had It So Good' and 'The Shrine on the Second Floor' from the original fifteen numbers from the stage musical.[18] However, the film exploited the rising popularity of Cliff Richard, releasing a tie-in EP record, which sold 150,000 copies, and one track from the film, 'A Voice in the Wilderness', sung in the film by Richard and his band The Shadows, which reached Number 2 the following year on the UK Singles Chart.[19] The film was responsible for launching the music career of Richard and is often lauded as one of Britain's best, if not only, film musicals.[20] According to Mundy, Richard's career often obstructs wider critical readings of the film, which he argues is an example of British realist cinema, particularly in its 'recurrent scenes of Soho strip shows and references to "the vice squad" [that] locate the film within that process of earnest social comment shared by British fiction films such as *Look Back in Anger*'.[21]

Expresso Bongo's Jewish Personnel: Wolf Mankowitz

The film's screenwriter Cyril Wolf Mankowitz was born in Bethnal Green, East London, in 1924, to a family of Russian-Jewish descent. According to Hephzibah Anderson, Mankowitz is most fondly remembered for his 'early fables of life in the Jewish East End of his childhood'.[22] Several of his Jewish-themed works were adapted for the screen. His novel *A Kid for Two Farthings*, published in 1953, was adapted into a film the following year and was directed by Carol Reed. Reed's first colour film, it was shot partly on location in Petticoat Lane, East London. The film follows a young boy named Joe (Jonathan Ashmore), who buys a goat under the belief that it is a magical unicorn and will bring good fortune to his family.[23] Mankowitz's 1953 play *The Bespoke Overcoat* was based on a story by Nikolai Gogol (*The Overcoat*), but was reworked to encompass Jewish themes. It was adapted and produced as a short film in 1955 by Jack Clayton, the director of the critically lauded *Room at the Top* (UK, 1959), which also starred Laurence Harvey in his career-defining role. It won an Academy Award in 1957.

Laurence Harvey

According to Laurence Harvey's biographers, Lithuanian-born Larushka Mischa Skikne came from 'a very traditional family in the Jewish sense ... [He] played football and went to synagogue'.[24] Harvey's Jewish immigrant background provides the role with great verisimilitude, but casting the British-Jewish actor was only partly fortuitous. The role of Johnny was originally played on stage by Paul Scofield (a Roman Catholic), who performed a cruder version of Johnny, described by Mankowitz as 'a sort of suburban cockney with a very faint American tinge ... tough'.[25] Harvey's accent for the film was an 'incredible mixture of Cockney, Yiddish and mid-Atlantic', which later lapses into the 'broad South African of his youth', was modelled on Mankowitz's own accent.[26] The character's evolution from stage to screen was largely dictated by Harvey's friendship with Mankowitz and their shared British-Jewish background:

> In his Shepherd Market days, he [Harvey] had met a young writer Wolf Mankowitz, who thought him at the time an arrogant, post-RADA [Royal Academy of Dramatic Art] punk playing hard at being the Young English Actor. But later, as Harvey grew more confident, they became good friends. Mankowitz, whose family had come from the same area in Lithuania as the Skiknes, believed that Lithuanian Jews shared certain characteristics and that Harvey's humour, like his own, was mordant.[27]

Mankowitz's belief that Jewish identity is 'dependent on far more than religious observance' filters into his characterisation of Johnny in *Expresso Bongo*.[28] Johnny exploits conversative religion to transform his client's youth-in-revolt image into a more digestible, commercial one for the predominantly conservative postwar British audience. This is reinforced when Johnny has the idea to compose a song about his new client Bongo's relationship with his mother, 'The Shrine on the Second Floor', which he describes as a type of 'Oedipus Rock'. Johnny then arranges for Bongo to perform the song live on a television variety show, accompanied by a church choir. Throughout his career, Mankowitz 'maintained a strong sense of origin [and was] proud to have come so far from the crowded two-room home in which he was raised'.[29] Comparatively, Johnny's ambition is also demarcated by his Yiddish roots and his relationship with the music industry in Britain. In one sense, his religion is business. But Johnny is also a character who resists his Jewish immigrant identity, reflecting Harvey's journey to adopt Englishness.

According to Roberts, Harvey believed that 'he was often looked on as a "cocky intruder" by a theatrical establishment all too keen to remind him that he was a Jewish immigrant passing as an English Gentleman'.[30] The actor's childhood emigration from Lithuania to South Africa, his ultimate rise to stardom and his naturalisation as a British citizen reinforce the intermingled relationship of Harvey's immigrant background, his performance of Johnny and his desire to be an Englishman. For Harvey: 'To be Lithuanian was not altogether exotic, but he tried to make it so … If he was not going to be accepted as an Englishman … he was going to rename himself and push his "foreignness" to the utmost limit.'[31]

After serving in the Union Defence Forces Entertainment Unit during World War II, Harvey travelled to London, where he rented an unaffordable room in Chelsea. He took various jobs and survived on a 'diet of stale buns and cups of tea' before being awarded a place to study at RADA.[32] After performing in Oscar Wilde's *A Woman of No Importance,* he was spotted by the Warner Brothers agent Sophie Rosenstein. After a successful screen test at the Warner Brothers offices on Wardour Street, he was offered a seven-year contract. He went straight to Savile Row to purchase a suit in celebration of his triumph and fulfil his ambitions of becoming an English gentleman 'measured by the cut of his clothes'.[33] However, strict rationing on materials continued during this period and Harvey failed to convince the tailoring establishments to make his suit on credit. After acquiring the requisite clothing coupons (the procurement of said coupons remains a mystery) and the promise that he would finance monthly payments, he convinced one tailor to construct his dream garment. He 'sank deeply into debt by [further] purchasing a small used car' and struggled to clear his debt on the suit, but in the words of his on-screen persona Johnny: 'Who cares about a few legalities?'[34]

The deliberate change of the name of Johnny's client Bert Rudge to Bongo Herbert is another 'art imitates life' moment. Hickey and Smith and Anne Sinai have noted that there are several versions of the story about how Larry Skikne changed his name to Laurence Harvey. Sinai notes that during the filming of Harvey's debut film, *House of Darkness* (Oswald Mitchell, 1948), distributors criticised his name, which they deemed 'not commercially attractive, and quite unsuitable for a British movie star'.[35] The other legend goes that the inspiration for his name came during a stroll in Soho. Harvey was 'deep in thought when he suddenly looked up to see a sign outside a liquor store reading "Harvey's Bristol Cream". He liked the sherry and the name and became Laurence Harvey'.[36]

Meier Tzelniker

Mr Mayer is the film's other title Jewish protagonist. This role is played by the Yiddish actor Meier Tzelniker, who was born in Warsaw, the 'son of a yeast manufacture and boy chorister at the city's Great Synagogue'.[37] After serving in the Russian cavalry during World War I, Tzelniker toured Russia and Eastern Europe with a Yiddish theatrical company. He arrived in England in 1927 to play at the Pavilion Theatre, located on 191–93 Whitechapel Road.[38] He then relocated his wife and family to Britain, where they lived in Leeds, Manchester and finally London's East End. Tzelniker was a prolific performer on the Yiddish stage and on screen. Although primarily a character actor, he gave many memorable performances as Jewish émigrés and untrustworthy foreigners. He starred as Solly Hyams in *It Always Rains on Sunday*, the Mayor of Mirave in the British Venice-set thriller *Venetian Bird* (Ralph Thomas, 1952), and as the Jewish antiques dealer Wendl in the Mankowitz-penned *Make Me an Offer* (Cyril Frankel, 1954). In *Expresso Bongo*, his character, Mayer, is the embodiment of the Jewish entrepreneur. His chief concern in life and business is to sell records. Mayer is rarely depicted without a cigar in one hand, and his Yiddish inflections and double-breasted pinstripe suit recall the black-market Jewish trader and Jewish entrepreneur of the West End.

Jewish Themes

In 1984, Wolf Mankowitz confirmed the film's Jewish themes, recalling the insertion of Yiddish humour into the script that he 'secretly smuggled past producers': 'When Laurence Harvey played in "Expresso Bongo" in New York, the cinemas were crowded with Jews delighted to hear a few rude Yiddish words and jokes on the screen.'[39] Alongside its frequent deployment of Yiddishisms and Yiddish humour, the film 'references Jewishness from a "Jewish" insider perspective, not merely by featuring two overtly Jewish characters as its principal music business operators'.[40] This confirms Jonathan Karp's statement that the film represents the music industry as an 'essentially Jewish affair'.[41]

Yiddish humour is even 'smuggled' into the film's opening. After stealing the magazines, Johnny moves inside Leon's Delicatessen on Frith Street, where the proprietor, Leon (Eric Pohlmann), is overseeing the renovation of his basement into an espresso bar, which he intends to call the 'Tom-Tom'.[42] Under the false pretence of ordering coffee and a late-night supper, Johnny ambitiously promises Leon that he will transform the Tom-Tom into the most 'habit-ated' teenage club in Soho. For how can Leon's newly purchased jukebox possibly compete with a 'real live artiste, a top personality, someone the kids will eat up'? Unbeknown to Leon, Johnny represents no such talent:

> JOHNNY: *Look, Leon, I'll book you a top personality and throw in a group to back him. A mere 20 the package. No?*
> LEON: *A mere no.*
> JOHNNY: *All right! All right! So, thank you and good night! Leon Romov, espresso bar schlemiel!*
> He puts cash down on the bar.
> LEON: *Hey! You're actually ... paying?*
> JOHNNY: *I told you, foolish man. I own a fortune in talent. It just so happens I'm a fiver short tonight.*[43]

This passionately delivered business pitch proves the perfect deception for the more traditionalist Leon. He reluctantly advances Johnny the money – in cash. Johnny's earlier indignant evocation of the schlemiel – a Yiddish term for an unlucky or unfortunate person – expresses his aggravation over Leon's tentative business style. Johnny's statement that his family tree is filled with 'small-capital-big-hopers' conveys his clear displeasure over Leon's prudent business strategies, but reinforces the seductive power of his exploitation skills. Leon's familiarity with Johnny acts as the contract and reinforces Johnny's social position within the local Jewish Soho community.

The film score also features not-so-subtle Jewish references. The song 'Nausea' was retained from the original stage musical and is sung for the film as a duet by both Tzelniker and Harvey. The first line of the song, 'When I see this little bleeder and compare him to Aida – Nausea', reinforces Karp's argument in relation to the Americanisation of the British music industry and Jewish entrepreneurs: 'It would indeed be remarkable if … the contemporary British music industry turned out to be a kind of ethnic mirror of the American, with a high degree of Jewish overrepresentation.'[44] The crashing rhythmic quality of the song reflects Jewish klezmer music. The song resembles that of a financial transaction or negotiation. While Johnny and Mayer dodge moving cars, pedestrians and punters at a crowded Soho intersection, they jostle and jest about the historical transformations of traditional and new forms of popular music.[45] Johnny challenges Mayer: 'So try to sell the Meistersingers in Expresso bars!' Mayer finally relents: 'All they want is shyster singers … plucking back on their guitars!' The musical number concludes when Mayer agrees to provide a recording contract for Bongo. This, of course, includes a cash advance for Johnny. The biting repartee of their exchange through song reinforces their Anglo-Jewish connection and their understanding of one another's business practices, including using gimmicks to fabricate publicity and bolster record sales.

The Small World of Sammy Lee (1963)

British director Ken Hughes's one-man play *Sammy*, originally written for the BBC, was first broadcast on US television network NBC as *Eddie* in 1958. The half-hour televised play featured Hollywood star Mickey Rooney as Eddie, a habitual gambler who must raise $1,000 whilst confined to his living room or else risk vicious punishment by an unseen gangster on his way to collect Eddie's debt. Hughes won an Emmy Award for his script, along with writer Alfred Brenner and director Jack Smight.[46]

Hughes' film adaptation of his play, originally entitled 'The Spieler', later 'The Small Sad World of Sammy Lee' though eventually baptised *The Small World of Sammy Lee* follows the similar trials of Sammy 'Lee' Leeman (born Shmuel Leeman), played by Anthony Newley.[47] Unlike Rooney's housebound gambler, Sammy works as a comedy compère for the fictional Peep Show Club in Soho.[48] Although he finds the work repugnant, it pays for his gambling addiction. The chief narrative of the film follows Sammy over the course of five hours as he scrounges around for, in this version, the £300 he owes to Soho gang leader Conner (unseen in the film) or else be faced with the 'razor and ignominy'.[49] Critic Raymond Durgnat called the film 'one of the flock of "New Wave" English films exploring the rich and strange subcultures of London life' and enthusiastically praised its

Figure 6.2. Sammy as MC of the Peep Show Club. Still, *The Small World of Sammy Lee*, the London Collection. DVD, StudioCanal, 2009

'psychological study of a man under stress ... an exposé of a way of living, small worlds of jagged, sleazy lives, of fast-talking loneliness'.[50]

Austrian-born Jewish cinematographer Wolfgang Suschitzky provided the film's key elements of New Wave realism. As a result of his extraordinary work on *The Small World of Sammy Lee*, he was recruited to work on *Get Carter* (Mike Hodges, 1971), the film for which he is best known.[51] His background in documentary filmmaking influenced the use of handheld cameras throughout the film, particularly during moments that demonstrate Sammy's conflicted states of cynicism and morality. Sammy's cynicism is conveyed by his blatant refusal to believe in a conventional future with Patsy (Julia Foster), a young woman from the North who travels to London to be with him. He rejects her, and she accepts employment as a stripper so that she can stay near him. He later refuses her selfless charity because he believes her virtue now to be tainted by working in his club. This is confirmed by the bitter harangue he gives to the strip club's unsuspecting male audience towards the film's conclusion: 'I don't know what you come here for. The girls here, they hate you, you make 'em sick.'[52]

Anthony Newley

Born in Hackney, East London, Newley was described by *Life* magazine in 1963 as 'a skinny, undersized man with crafty eyes and a face that resembles a ferret's ... a most unlikely looking boy wonder. Yet he is versatile enough to supply the talent for a dozen entertainers'.[53] In Bardsley's biography, Newley's illegitimacy and impoverished upbringing in the East End greatly influenced his career choices and work ethic.[54] At the age of fourteen, Newley left home and worked as an office boy for an insurance company before attempting to break into acting. After starring in several children's films, he earned the career-making role as the Artful Dodger in David Lean's *Oliver Twist* (1948). Newley then carved out a prolific career as a singer-songwriter.[55] He once said: 'With my background, an illegitimate cockney kid from the worst end of Clapton, I should have ended up a small-time criminal.'[56] Although Newley was recalling his work on *Oliver Twist*, this biography certainly contributes toward his visceral performance as Sammy, whose ambivalence to his Jewishness constitutes the heart of the film. Newley's Quaker heritage is confirmed by various sources. According to a feature article published by *Picturegoer* magazine in 1959, Newley's biological father, George Kirby, was a 'Jewish tailor'.[57] According to his obituary in *The Guardian*, his maternal grandmother was Jewish.[58] Despite not publicising his Jewish background during his career, it suggests that the development of the character could have been partly influenced by his own personal history.[59]

Monochromatic Racetrack: Sammy's Soho and Jewishness

The film exquisitely treats Soho as a metaphor for Sammy's state of mind. Hughes depicts Soho as a monochromatic racetrack, suggesting that Sammy and Soho exist in 'a temporal space'.[60] This temporality, and indeed, ephemerality of Soho is reinforced by the melancholic opening sequence, which follows a dustbin lorry whilst it travels, in no particular sequential order, through the city, weaving in and out of the labyrinth-like, filth-ridden streets of Soho.[61] This 'world that is waking with the traders on Berwick Street market and simultaneously crawling to bed as the spielers kick out their night's trade onto Old Compton Street' is not the vibrant, titillating pleasure centre of the West End at night depicted and advertised by *Expresso Bongo*.[62] The opening sequence functions as a visual representation of

Sammy's physical and spiritual transformation. It also acts as a pseudo-metaphor for the gradual, commercial sanitisation of Soho and the development of the permissive society in Great Britain. It is accompanied by composer Kenneth Graham's beautifully wistful jazz score. The original recordings were recently rediscovered in 2013.[63]

Andrew Pulver states that Hughes was 'fascinated by Jews and Jewish culture, although he wasn't Jewish himself'.[64] The casting of British-Jewish actors as British-Jewish characters confirms Hughes' desire to convey the authenticity of place and community. But Sammy is also the universal symbol for the anxious embodiment of rootless, postwar austerity. He is unable to choose between the frantic, maladjusted (modern) life of a gambler and an unknown (traditional) future with Patsy, who proposes conventional family life. Sammy *desires* to be punished. The film's didactic quality, evident in the bleak, untitillating portrayal of Soho's commercial sex industry and the loss of its cosmopolitan identity, also suggests that the film is not a criminal-on-the-run story, but in fact the tale of a man on the run from *modernity*. Andrew Spicer has described Sammy as 'uncalculated … laconic, preserving an enigmatic quality that links him to the Byronic male'.[65] He is introduced to us as an enigma, in a smoke-filled underground nightclub. After losing £150 during an all-night poker game, a nearby player (an uncredited Barney Thompson) howls: 'An' I fort Jews were supposed to be lucky!' This stereotypical association of economic prosperity with Jews is employed by Hughes to emphasise Sammy's foreignness within the Soho community. His gambling addiction also appears to be rooted in Jewish Soho history. Summers states that: 'Also hanging around on the street corners were Soho's many unofficial bookie's tipsters. Betting was an obsession, particularly among Jewish men, many of whom saw gambling as the only way out of the poverty gap.'[66] Sammy's attitude towards risk differs from Johnny's comparably tame desire to advance through fabricating publicity. Johnny is a speculator, not a gambler. 'If *Sammy Lee* was pushing towards understanding the type rather than the criminal, contemporaneous films reveal a continued confusion or conservatism'.[67] During an interview with *Films and Filming*, Hughes states that Sammy was a semi-autobiographical character, '[in] conflict with the community … an expression of myself … The fact that Sammy is dealing with criminals and gangsters is only relative: they're symbols of authority or of respectability. And strangely it is very much Tony Newley's own psychology'.[68]

Returning to Sammy's Jewish Roots

If we seek to understand Sammy by examining his journey beyond the peripheries of Soho, thereby placing him in the British-Jewish context, we may uncover his own unique signifier. Sammy's first port of call to recoup the debt is his brother, Lou Leeman (British-Jewish actor Warren Mitchell), who owns and manages a local Jewish delicatessen in Whitechapel. This Whitechapel sequence is arguably the film's most poignant and powerful scene and was shot entirely on location in East London. In the scene, following a short exchange of pleasantries, Lou is at first reluctant to comply with Sammy's request to borrow money, calling him a *mashugana*, the Yiddish term for 'crazy'. Lou views family responsibility as an intrinsic part of life. The brothers' shared childhood is the basis of their relationship. Throughout this pseudo-reunion, they grasp for anecdotes from their childhood in an attempt to reconcile, but this too seems futile. After Sammy's final plea, 'Do it for Mama, God rest her soul', Lou agrees to lend him the money. This foreshadows the sale of their deceased mother's antique chair that Sammy has consistently refused to hock throughout the film. Sammy's own 'deathly sentimentality' is persistently inflicted upon other characters, prophesying his ruin.[69] Sammy is given an opportunity to escape from London to freedom with Patsy, but is obstructed by his own nihilistic attitude. Graham's score in this scene (clearly inspired by klezmer music) also accompanies Sammy's journey to Whitechapel and the concluding sale of Sammy's mother's chair, suggesting that this will be the last time he sees his brother. In Soho, Jewish identity can be hidden within the heterogeneous community. In working-class Whitechapel, it invokes impoverished circumstances and a fractured community.[70]

Miriam Karlin and Warren Mitchell

Despite the brief appearances of Miriam Karlin, who plays Lou's protective wife Milly, and Warren Mitchell in the film, their superb performances should not be overlooked. Both actors had substantial careers in theatre and television following their training at RADA. Karlin was born Miriam Samuels in Hampstead, North London. Her notable credits include Lionel Bart's stage musical comedy *Fings Ain't Wot They Used T'Be*, which premiered at London's Garrick Theatre in 1960. She would later star as the Cat Lady in Stanley Kubrick's *A Clockwork Orange*

(1971). Her obituary states that she was an activist and 'a staunch advocate for her profession as a member of the Equity Council'. She also campaigned for nuclear disarmament and the Anti-Nazi League. She was awarded an MBE in 1975 by Harold Wilson.[71] British-Jewish actor Warren Mitchell is best known for his role as Alf Garnett in the BBC television sitcom *Till Death Us Do Part* (1965–75). Mitchell was born Warren Misell in Stoke Newington, North London. His Russian maternal grandparents immigrated to Britain in 1910 and later 'opened a chip shop in Stoke Newington'.[72] He served in the RAF as a navigator during World War II. At Oxford University, his friendship with the actor Richard Burton influenced his decision to attend RADA for two years, '"learning posh" … and [spending] his evenings unlearning posh by playing at the left-wing Unity Theatre'.[73]

Rediscovering Johnny and Sammy

Johnny and Sammy are superficially representative of the interwar and postwar Jewish black-market racketeer as manufactured and promoted by the popular press. They peddle black market goods and exploit their Soho networks in order to improve their socioeconomic circumstances. However, by positioning them in a space historically shaped by cosmopolitan and entrepreneurial immigrant communities, Johnny and Sammy are transformed into multifaceted characters who must exploit their Jewish roots in order to survive. Both filmmakers have attempted to reinvent the Jewish wide boy for a British audience familiar with Jewish spielers and 'foreign' black-market racketeers who feature exhaustively in postwar crime films. But by the mid-1950s, the crime rate in Britain had fallen, the black market was close to extinction and the wide boy/spiv had become a 'figure of fun'.[74] Furthermore, the figure of the criminal wide boy does not align with the dramatic social, economic and cultural shifts seen in the late postwar period that was gradually transitioning towards a more prosperous, commercial and permissive society under the new Conservative government that came to power in 1957. Perhaps this renders Johnny and Sammy's Jewish background irrelevant to British audiences, suggesting that they are symptomatic of what Gough-Yates claims is British cinema's consistency to be 'officially blind to cultural, racial and religious differences. Being Jewish has mattered little to British institutions; being British has mattered a great deal'.[75]

Together with the cinematic imagining of Jewish Soho by the filmmakers Val Guest and Ken Hughes, along with Harvey and Newley's arresting performances, undoubtedly reinforced by their own personal biographies, these vital and important works provide rare and unique representations of the British-Jewish community in postwar British cinema. These films also promoted Soho's cosmopolitanism through the complex representation of their Jewish protagonists.

Notes

1. Val Guest fondly recalls the period filming *Expresso Bongo* and collaborating with actor Harvey on Johnny's accent, modelling his voice on that of writer Wolf Mankowitz: 'Larry and I arranged a couple of lunches with the unsuspecting Wolf to pay attention to the way he spoke. "I think I have it", said Larry by the time we started shooting, "but you'll have to watch I don't lose it along the way!"' See his memoir, *So You Want to Be in Pictures* (London: Reynolds & Hearn, 2001), 134. See also 'This Week's New Films: Whether You're Still Wet Behind the Ears', *The Daily Express*, 10–11.
2. Barry Forshaw infers that by the early 1960s, 'there was something of a fashion for British films which opened up a variety of subcultures of metropolitan life to cinema audiences'. He discusses Sammy Lee in greater detail in his book *British Crime Film: Subverting the Social Order* (London: Palgrave Macmillan, 2012), 105–6.
3. See Andrew Spicer, *Typical Men: The Representations of Masculinity in Popular British Culture* (London: I.B. Tauris, 2001), 129.
4. See Gil Toffell, *Jews, Cinema and Public Life in Interwar Britain* (London: Palgrave Macmillan, 2018), 2.
5. See Kevin-Gough Yates, 'Jews and Exiles in British Cinema', *Leo Baeck Institute Yearbook* 37(1) (1992), 531.
6. See Nathan Abrams, 'Hidden: Jewish Film in the United Kingdom, Past and Present', *Journal of European Popular Culture* 1 (2010), 54. See also Abrams' edited collection *Hidden in Plain Sight: Jews and Jewishness in British Film, Television, and Popular* Culture (Evanston, IL: Northwestern University Press, 2016), which features essays that address the 'historiographical gap' of Jews and Jewishness in the history of British film and television.
7. Film critic Jason Solomons states that: 'I've loved this [*Expresso Bongo*] for a long, long time. I didn't realise how Jewish this film was.' See Jason Solomons and Robert Elms, 'Interview with Sylvia Syms', *BBC Radio London*, 28 April 2016. In 2016, the 20th UK International Jewish Film Festival screened the film accompanied by the performance of live music inspired by Kenny Graham's original film score. See 'Liner Notes, *The Small World of Sammy Lee*, Original Motion Picture Soundtrack' (P&C Trunk Records, 2013).
8. The 2i's was also the venue where Val Guest was introduced to Cliff Richard, who would be ultimately cast as teen idol Bongo in *Expresso Bongo*. Guest 'took a chance and paid him £2000'; Richard's one request was that his 'mates' would be in the film too – the rock band The Shadows. See the profile of Tommy Steele in *The Observer*, 21 December 1958, 7. Laurie Henshaw confirmed that *The Tommy Steele Story* will be 'just what it says. No trimmings. Just

the unvarnished story of Steele's sensational rise to fame'. See 'Don't Do This to Tommy Steele', *Picturegoer*, 16 February 1957, 5.
9. John Mundy, *The British Musical Film* (Manchester: Manchester University Press, 2007), 178.
10. Stephen Glynn, *The British Pop Music Film: The Beatles and Beyond* (Basingstoke: Palgrave Macmillan, 2013), 25.
11. Wolf Mankowitz's story was published in four parts. See '*Expresso Bongo*: The Story of the Making of a Modern Idol', *Daily Express*, 9–12 September 1957, 5, 10.
12. 'The annual London Critics' poll of "Variety" has voted the Wolf Mankowitz musical "Expresso Bongo", with Paul Scofield and James Kenney, at the Saville, the best British musical from the year 1957-8. Of the eleven critics who voted, six were in favour.' See 'Bongo Top of the Critics' Poll', *The Stage*, 3 July 1958, 1. See also Glynn, *The British Pop Music Film*, 47.
13. Andrew Spicer, 'A British Empire of Their Own? Jewish Entrepreneurs in the British Film Industry', *Journal of European Popular Culture* 3(2) (2012), 126.
14. Ibid.
15. Val Guest recalled, 'Nat listened attentively as I outlined the project, then his smile faded and he shook his head, "Who cares about rock 'n' roll?" to which I replied, "They care about Elvis Presley." Cohen shook his head, "When you get Presley, talk to me".' Incidentally, Cohen also produced Ken Hughes' earlier crime films *Wide Boy* (1952) and later, a short film for the Anglo-Amalgamated *Scotland Yard Series*, a 30-minute film Hughes wrote and directed entitled *The Dark Stairway* (1954), also titled *The Greek Street Murder*. The short film, shot on location in Soho, follows a pair of detectives (Russell Napier and Vincent Ball) as they investigate the murder of a man at a boarding house on Greek Street. See Guest, *So You Want to Be in Pictures*, 135. See also the review of 'The Dark Stairway', *Monthly Film Bulletin* 21(240) (1954), 78.
16. See Guest, *So You Want to Be in Pictures*, 136.
17. John Mundy, *The British Musical Film* (Manchester: Manchester University Press, 2007), 178.
18. Adrian Wright haughtily calls Laurence Harvey's Johnny Jackson 'all at sea'. See his discussion of *Expresso Bongo* in *A Tanner's Worth of Tune: Rediscovering the Post-War British Musical* (Woodbridge: Boydell Press, 2010), 146–48.
19. Today the chart is known as the UK Official Singles Chart, which lists the bestselling singles in the United Kingdom.
20. Glynn, *The British Pop Music Film*, 25, 26, 47. See also Geoff Mayer's sardonic synopsis of *Expresso Bongo* in his *Guide to British Cinema* (Westport, CT: Greenwood Press, 2003), 125.
21. Mundy, *The British Musical Film*, 178.
22. See Hephzibiah Anderson, 'Wolf Mankowitz', in Sorrel Kerbel, Muriel Emanuelm and Laura Phillips (eds), *Jewish Writers of the Twentieth Century* (New York: Fitzroy Dearborn, 2003), 664–68. Interestingly, director Jack Clayton asked Mankowitz to write the screenplay for *Room at the Top*, which starred Harvey in his career-making role, but he refused. Only later did he work with Harvey on *Bongo*, and throughout their lives they remained close friends.
23. See Michael Brooke, 'A Kid for Two Farthings', *BFI Screenonline*. Retrieved 17 October 2021 from http://www.screenonline.org.uk/film/id/1005746/index.html.
24. Des Hickey and Gus Smith, *The Prince: Being the Public and Private Life of Larushka Mischa Skikne, a Jewish Lithuanian Vagabond Player, Otherwise Known as Laurence Harvey* (London: Frewin, 1975), 31.
25. Wolf Mankowitz, David Heneker, Julian More and Monty Norman, *Expresso Bongo*. [A Musical Play.] From an Original Story by W. Mankowitz. Book by W. Mankowitz and J. Lyrics by J. More,

David Heneker, and Monty Norman. [With Production Notes by William Chappell], (London: Evans Bros., 1960), 1.
26. See Guest's memoir, *So You Want to Be in Pictures?*, 134.
27. Hickey and Smith, *The Prince*, 128.
28. See Anderson, 'Wolf Mankowitz', 667.
29. Ibid.
30. Roberts praises Harvey's performance in his extensive discussion of the film upon its re-release in 2016. See Andrew Roberts, 'Expresso Bongo DVD Booklet' (London: BFI, 2016).
31. See Anne Sinai, *Reach for the Top: The Turbulent Life of Laurence Harvey* (Lanham, MD: Oxford Publicity Partnership, 2003), 140–41.
32. Harvey was among 139 of 374 applicants who auditioned for a place at RADA. See ibid., 63.
33. Ibid., 71.
34. See 'Hermione Baddeley', in Brian McFarlane and Anthony Slide (eds), *The Encyclopaedia of British Film*, 4th edn (Manchester: Manchester University Press, 2014), 41.
35. Sinai, *Reach for the Top*, 97.
36. Ibid., 98.
37. See W.D. Rubinstein, Michael Jolles and Hilary L. Rubinstein (eds), 'Meier Tzelniker', in *The Palgrave Dictionary of Anglo-Jewish History* (Basingstoke: Palgrave Macmillan, 2011), 992.
38. Ibid.
39. Wolf Mankowitz expressed that he had overwhelmingly positive thoughts on cinema's depictions of British Jews. However, he noted the contrast between the American and British film industries' treatment of Jewish characters. See his article 'Goy and Dolls', *The Observer*, 28 October 1984, 46.
40. Jonathan Karp appears to be one of the very few academics to discuss Johnny Jackson's Jewish background with respect to the British film industry of the mid-1950s. See Jonathan Karp, 'Brokering a Rock 'n' Roll International: Jewish Record Men in the US and UK', in Rebecca Kobrin and Adam Teller (eds), *Purchasing Power: The Economics of Jewish History* (Philadelphia: University of Pennsylvania Press, 2015), 139.
41. Ibid.
42. Both versions of *Expresso Bongo* were derived from the Mankowitz short story published in the *Daily Express* (1957). As in the film, the Tom-Tom may also be found at the 'back of Frith Street', a 'popular hangout for young people in central Soho' according to Peter Leese in *Britain since 1945: Aspects of Identity* (Basingstoke: Palgrave Macmillan, 2006), 57.
43. Kevin Donnelly states that *Expresso Bongo* 'not only satirizes the new breed of manipulative managers that grew up around the new musical culture but [also] firmly sets the music's origin in coffee bars, situating rock 'n' roller figures as a central component of the cinematic coffee bar'. See Kevin Donnelly, 'The Perpetual Busman's Holiday: Sir Cliff Richard and British Pop Musicals', *Journal of Popular Film and Television* 25(4) (1998), 146–54.
44. Karp, 'Brokering a Rock 'n' Roll International', 139.
45. *The Cambridge Companion to Jewish Music* identifies klezmer as a combination of several genres of vernacular music associated with the Yiddish-speaking Jews of Eastern Europe and their descendants. See Joel Rubin. 'Klezmer Music: A Historical Overview to the Present', in Joshua S. Walden (ed.), *The Cambridge Companion to Jewish Music* (Cambridge: Cambridge University Press, 2015), 119. According to Anthony Dunn, extracts from the stage play, including 'Nausea', were shown on the BBC on 11 December 1958. The film heavily criticises television

for its insular, brainwashing capabilities. 'Mankowitz and Guest, however, also propose Johnny Jackson as a "whirling centre of resistance to the bland conformity of TV. He appears in most scenes and dominated all of them".' See Anthony Dunn, *The Worlds of Wolf Mankowitz: Between Elite and Popular Cultures in Post-War Britain* (Edgware: Vallentine Mitchell, 2013), 103–5.

46. According to Wesley Hyatt, several anti-Semitic slurs were deleted for the revised television script of *Eddie*. Regardless of whether this indicates that the character of Eddie was Jewish, it displays Hughes' concern for realism in relocating his British-Jewish anti-hero to a cosmopolitan space. See Wesley Hyatt, *Emmy Award Winning Night-Time Television Shows, 1948-2004* (Jefferson, NC: McFarland, 2006), 138–39.
47. See Ken Hughes, 'The Spieler', shooting script, 26 April 1962. Seven Arts, Film Finances Archive.
48. Barry Forshaw, *British Crime Film: Subverting the Social Order* (Basingstoke: Palgrave Macmillan, 2012), 105–6.
49. See John Coleman's review, 'East and West: Review Small World of Sammy Lee', *New Statesman*, 4 January 1963, 648.
50. Raymond Durgnat, 'The Small World of Sammy Lee', *Films and Filming*. June 1963, 31–32.
51. Jennifer Szalai, 'Wolfgang Suschitzky, Photographer and Cinematographer, Dies at 104', *New York Times*, 8 October 2016. Retrieved 17 October 2021 from https://www.nytimes.com/2016/10/09/arts/international/wolfgang-suschitzky-dead.html.
52. *The Small World of Sammy Lee* (Ken Hughes, 1963).
53. See Richard Oulahan, 'All-Purpose Cockney', *Life*, 29 November 1963, 58.
54. See Garth Bardsley, *Stop the World: The Biography of Anthony Newley, with a Foreword by Leslie Bricusse* (London: Oberon Books, 2003), 21.
55. He cowrote the hit song 'Feeling Good' and the James Bond theme to *Goldfinger* (Guy Hamilton, 1964) with his songwriting partner Leslie Bricusse in 1964. He was also nominated for an Academy Award for the original score of *Willy Wonka & the Chocolate Factory* (Mel Stuart, 1971).
56. Ibid., 24.
57. See Tom Hutchinson, 'The Secret Life of Anthony Newley', *Picturegoer*, 22 August 1959, 10–11.
58. See Dennis Barker, 'Anthony Newley Obituary: Lost Icon on Parade', *The Guardian*, 16 April 1999. Retrieved 17 October 2021 from https://www.theguardian.com/news/1999/apr/16/guardianobituaries1.
59. Julia Foster recalls that Newley was difficult to work with on set: '[He was] forever pacing like a panther.' She also emphasises the significance of the film for his career: 'He had a lot riding on it, having not been seen on the screen for nearly two years … Now he had a chance to prove his worth as a serious actor.' See 'Interview with Julia Foster, *The Small World of Sammy Lee*: The Striptease and Sleaze of Ken Hughes's Crime Film', *British Film Institute*, 14 October 2016. Retrieved 17 October 2021 from http://www.bfi.org.uk/films-tv-people/581b6fe44e152.
60. See Charlotte Brunsdon, *London in Cinema: The Cinematic City since 1945* (London: BFI, 2007), 122.
61. Cathi Unsworth emphasises the film's imagining of Soho in her 'retro' review from 2014: 'Hitch a time tunnel ride on the back of a dustbin lorry through the Soho of 1963 … Watch mesmerised.' See Cathi Unsworth, 'Saturday Night at the Movies', *3am Magazine*, 27 June

62. The remastering and licensing of the score for wide release took place over five years. The subsequent acclaim for the inaugural release of Graham's soundtrack further stresses the importance for a new appraisal of this film as an example of British 1960s and British Jewish canonical cinema. Ibid.
63. Johnny Trunk, founder of Trunk Records, describes how he discovered Graham's lost score for the film after contacting Graham's daughter: 'I paid her a visit to talk about Kenny's life and work and to my delight she's found a box in her attic full of Kenny's old ¼ inch reels. One had the word "Sammy" written on a tiny sticker on the front. It just had to be the lost score – and indeed once I'd got it transferred, confirmed it was. See 'Liner Notes, *The Small World of Sammy Lee*', 1.
64. *The Small World of Sammy Lee* was screened at the BFI London Film Festival in 2016 in a 2K digital film restoration. See Vic Pratt, 'The Small World of Sammy Lee: Anthony Newley and a Long-Gone Soho', *British Film Institute*, 12 October 2016. Retrieved 17 October 2021 from http://www.bfi.org.uk/news-opinion/news-bfi/features/small-world-sammy-lee-anthony-newley-soho.
65. Ibid., 126.
66. Judith Summers, *Soho: A History of London's Most Colourful Neighbourhood* (London: Bloomsbury, 1991), 173.
67. Spicer, *Typical Men*, 135.
68. 'One is never aware of depth when writing a script. It takes a critic to point out the depth; and that sometimes comes as a surprise.' Ken Hughes discusses his filmmaking process in 'Those Nutty Intellectuals', *Films and Filming* (January 1963), 9–10.
69. See Isabel Quigly's review: 'The Small World of Sammy Lee (Columbia; "X" Certificate)', *The Spectator*, 3 May 1963, 567.
70. Mark Slobin discusses the origins of klezmer music in *Fiddler on the Move: Exploring the Klezmer World* (Oxford: Oxford University Press, 2003), 3.
71. Ned Chaillet, 'Obituaries: Miriam Karlin', *The Stage*, 25 August 2011, 45.
72. Jonathan Margolis, 'Obituary: Warren Mitchell', *The Independent*, 15 November 2015, 48.
73. Ibid.
74. Robert Murphy, *Realism and Tinsel: Cinema and Society in Britain 1939–48* (New York: Routledge, 1992), 167.
75. Kevin Gough-Yates, 'Jews and Exiles in British Cinema', *Leo Baeck Institute Yearbook* 37(1) (1992), 541.

CHAPTER 7
Soho Melodrama
Cinematic Spaces of Sexual Blackmail, *The Flesh Is Weak* (1957) and *The Shakedown* (1960)

> *He was staring at me through the mirror just now as if he wanted to eat me.*
> —*The Shakedown* (John Lemont, 1960)

The overwhelming wave of low-budget 'B' films released in the postwar period that explicitly dealt with the repercussions of the Wolfenden Report shows us the immense impact on the way the report 'formulated a new approach to the regulation on sexual and moral behaviour' that, in turn, intensified the British public's interest in the 'ongoing national debate about sex and morality ... the catalyst for an increase in sexual knowledge and about the urban environments associated with them.'[1] Primarily X-rated productions, these films also reflect the gradual relaxation of censorship in this period that affected cinema's position within the cultural mainstream as markers of shifting morality and growing permissive behaviour in Britain. One common thread between these films was their treatment of blackmail, which included the grooming of victims or the extortion of men who purchased sex illegally.

Whilst blackmail was, by and large, used to extort money from closeted homosexual men, sex scandals and blackmail stories involving the 'shakedown' of men who feared an attack on their reputation by prostitutes' pimps also made the headlines.[2] Soho and other metropolitan-set films from the immediate postwar period onwards would remain unconcerned with homosexuality until the end of the 1950s, with groundbreaking films such as *Victim* (Basil Dearden, 1961) paving the way for more realist films like *A Taste Of Honey* (Tony Richardson, 1961) and *The Leather Boys* (Sidney J. Furie, 1964), which provided sympathetic and more complex portrayals of gay men. Blackmail stories regarding the trials of homosexual men would begin to be circulated by the popular press during the nineteenth century and were 'concerned primarily with the victimization of well-off men'.[3] The publication of these reports that chronicled blackmail scandals increased towards the onset of the twentieth century.

Following the First World War, there was a notable increase in the blackmail of homosexual men onwards, though the reported number of incidents declined during the Second World War. But the return of blackmail stories in the 1950s spurred a moral panic and threatened national stability. However: 'In England, blackmail stories based on newspaper and court reports played a key role in the 1950s and 1960s in convincing both the public and politicians of the need for homosexual law reform.'[4] Richard Hornsey has examined the ways in which homosexuality 'challenged the social stability' of postwar society because of its 'inability – or perhaps its unwillingness – to respect the spatial and temporal orders through which peace and civic harmony were currently being pursued'.[5] He describes Wolfenden's investigation into homosexuality and prostitution as 'phenomena [that] had become popularly perceived as virulent metropolitan threats, stoked by frequent tabloid exposé [articles] and mounting calls for political intervention'.[6]

Two forgotten Soho-set films that feature sexual blackmail narratives, *The Flesh Is Weak* (Don Chaffey, 1957) and *The Shakedown* (John Lemont, 1960), examined the Wolfenden Report and the Street Offences Act of 1959 by placing a distinctive spotlight on the victim and the criminal experience respectively. *The Flesh Is Weak* is told from the perspective of a young, foreign woman (Milly Vitale) who is groomed for prostitution by her Italian/American boyfriend Tony Giani (John Derek). Comparatively, *The Shakedown* portrays a villainous pimp-racketeer named Augie Cortona (Terence Morgan) who, recently released from prison, threatens existing vice rackets in Soho by engineering a pornography studio with the help of a down-on-his-luck alcoholic photographer named Jessel (Donald Pleasence). Together, they establish a modelling school and photography studio that acts as a front for a lucrative sexual blackmail enterprise whereby Augie invites middle-class men to watch prostitutes undress while he secretly photographs them. Interestingly, the pornography studio in *The Shakedown* is comparable to the illicit upstairs pornography studio in Michael Powell's *Peeping Tom* (1960) and the use of photography as a form of blackmail in Basil Dearden's *Victim* (1961).[7]

Although the more sympathetic of the two films, *The Flesh Is Weak* was not produced in response to shifting cultural attitudes to prostitution, but rather a desire to understand it from a sociological and cultural perspective and engage with the Wolfenden Report. Both films were released towards the end of a decade that saw the rise in the popularity of commercial television and a growing public desire for working-class realist films, such as the commercially successful *Room at the Top* (Jack Clayton, 1960) and *Saturday Night and Sunday Morning* (Karel Reisz, 1960). Through their Soho placement, these films create a powerful and critical discourse on the relationship between sexual blackmail and urban space. Melanie Bell-Williams states that the absence of existing literature on these films is due to their 'low prestige status', which is 'part of a consistent body of work from a particular production company [they are] afforded brief mention before critical discussion moves on to more "important" films'.[8] This positions them outside of the mainstream consciousness whose exploration of 'anxieties about cultural vulnerability, commercial reorganization and moral deviation' are 'displaced into genre cinema'.[9] Intriguingly, both films were written by the journalist and screenwriter Leigh Vance, who today remains incorrectly credited as Lee Vance on film databases.[10]

This chapter locates these films within the urban and melodramatic context, arguing that although they failed to depict the diversity of Soho's sexual subcultures, their forensic interest in changing sexual attitudes, female sexuality and victimhood makes them worthy of being rediscovered, both as part of the Soho film canon and as important examples of low-budget British cinema and its celebrated legacy of examining social issues.

Sexual Blackmail in British Cinema

Angus McLaren is one of the few scholars who has provided an expansive history of sexual blackmail in the United States and Britain in order to 'reveal the changing public sentiment' on this form of vice prior to and following the Second World War.[11] The term 'blackmail' was first used in England during the mid- to late sixteenth century in reference to the 'extortion Scottish barons levied on farmers in the north of England'.[12] It swiftly evolved into a term denoting the demand for protection money and, later, the ransoming of Tudor border areas. In 1567 and 1587, legislation was passed to make 'black mayle' a capital crime in England and Scotland.[13] The subsequent evolution of this method of extortion, sending threatening letters or notices to fearful victims, did not occur until the eighteenth century and, as McLaren highlights in his work, peaked during the interwar period in England. During this period, sexual blackmail became intrinsically linked to homosexuality.[14] The rigorous examination of Wolfenden by filmmakers coincided with the rise of British films that examined topical social issues such as sexuality, class and racism. This film canon would be later dubbed the 'social problem film'. According to John Hill, the social problem film epitomised 'the "best" of British filmmaking of the 1950s ... less concerned with a literal reconstruction of wartime community than with the exploration of the conditions necessary to the construction of a new community or consensus appropriate to peacetime'.[15] Hill has identified those filmmakers who distinguished themselves as leaders in the genre, such as the celebrated director Basil Dearden and his trilogy of social problem films that focus on racial tensions, juvenile delinquency and homosexuality: *The Blue Lamp* (1950), *Sapphire* (1959) and *Victim* (1961).

The commercially successful *Victim*, an engrossing and politically daring film set in London and starring Dirk Bogarde, candidly addressed homosexuality, blackmail and the Wolfenden Report through its gay-blackmail narrative that follows a closeted, married barrister Melville Farr (Bogarde) who seeks to destroy a blackmail ring after the suicide of Boy Barrett (Peter McEnery), a young man with whom he shared a passionate emotional affair and is now being blackmailed. The script was written by Janet Green and John McCormick, whose melodrama-thriller provides a uniquely sympathetic portrayal of homosexuality and examines the moral conflicts embodied in part by the pair of police officers investigating the case played by John Barrie and John Cairney (Tom in *Miracle in Soho*, a film which was directed by Julian Amyes and released in 1957). The role of Farr's forgiving wife Laura is played by Sylvia Syms, who, following her role as Maisie in *Expresso Bongo*, had gone on to star in several films that examined contemporary social issues, such as *Flame in the Streets* (Roy Baker, 1961), a film that spotlights interracial relationships in London's West Indian community.

British social problem films have an intrinsic parallel to postwar Hollywood melodrama placed within the metropolitan context. Thomas Elsaesser defines melodrama at its most simplistic level as a 'dramatic narrative in which musical accompaniment marks the emotional effect' and may be described as a 'particular form of dramatic mise-en-scène'.[16] Similar to the constraints placed upon British filmmakers after the war, Hollywood films of the late 1950s used melodrama as a mode to tackle social issues. Films such as *Peyton Place* (Mark Robson, 1957) and *Imitation of Life* (Douglas Sirk, 1959) were dictated by 'commercial necessities, political censorship, and the various morality codes [that] restricted directors in what they could tackle as a subject'.[17] This may also be applied to the American film noir of the previous interwar period 'where the hero is edged on or blackmailed by the femme fatale – the smell of honeysuckle and death in *Double Indemnity* (Billy Wilder, 1944), *Out of the Past* (Jacques Tourneur, 1947) or *Detour* (Edgar G. Ulmer, 1946) – into a course of action that pushes him farther and farther in one direction'.[18] Soho social problem films often imported American and foreign stars in order to bolster commercial appeal abroad, and the aesthetic similarities between Hollywood films and low-budget British melodramas is unmistakable.

The Flesh Is Weak (1957)

The Flesh Is Weak follows the manipulation, abuse and subsequent sexual victimisation of a young, European woman who arrives in London to start a new life. It was directed by Don Chaffey and produced by self-described 'risk-taker' producer Raymond Stross of Eros Films, who, during this period, produced a 'small number of interesting sensationalist dramas … presenting it in a palatable manner for audiences'.[19] Bell-Williams has argued the current lack of critical discourse on *The Flesh Is Weak* is due to director Chaffey's status as a B-picture director who 'cut his teeth at Gainsborough in the 1940s'.[20] She states that Chaffey belonged to a group of British directors who are 'not forgotten *auteurs* but *metteurs-en-scène*'.[21] The film's screenplay was by Leigh Vance, who continues to go incorrectly uncredited for his work on *The Flesh Is Weak*.[22] However, his unrelenting fascination for political upheaval in late 1950s Britain, undoubtedly influenced by his work as a journalist, was embodied by the trio of films he wrote in this period: *The Shakedown* (John Lemont, 1960), *Piccadilly Third Stop* (Wolf Rilla, 1960) and *The Frightened City* (John Lemont, 1961). He based the film's narrative on a story by Deborah Bedford. As Chibnall has shown, Vance's work functions on several levels: 'The films written by Vance are significant, less for their cinematic quality than because they document a key moment of transition in both legal and illegal business culture.'[23]

The Flesh Is Weak stars Italian actress Milly Vitale in the title role of Marissa and American star John Derek as her pimp Tony. Born in Rome, Vitale was the daughter of legendary conductor Riccardo Vitale, an artistic director at the Rome

Opera House. Vitale appeared in over forty-seven Italian, Spanish and Hollywood-produced films, although she was only cast in two British films – *The Flesh Is Weak* and Vernon Sewell's *Battle of the V.1* (1958) – in her long career. Despite her engaging screen presence, particularly as Marissa, a young woman groomed into prostitution in *The Flesh Is Weak*, Vitale 'sadly never managed to scale the same degree of international success as her arch-rival Sophia Loren'.[24] American actor John Derek became a 'favourite film star of teenagers in the early fifties, but never fulfilled the promise as an actor that his early performances in such films as the Academy Award-winning film *All the King's Men* (Robert Rossen, 1949) suggested'.[25] Simon Sheridan states that Derek's decision to accept the role of Tony was largely due to Derek's disillusionment with Hollywood as 'he eagerly accepted the invitation to shoot in London'.[26] The casting of Derek as Soho gang member Giani appears to have been fortuitous, for the actor would become known for his 'love of the nude female ... well illustrated by his desire to photograph his wives naked for *Playboy* magazine'. His career following *The Flesh Is Weak* involved shooting low-budget pornographic feature films.[27] Casting Derek was most likely a choice aimed to appeal to the American market. The casting of the European Vitale of course reflects the popular postwar British film convention of positioning non-British bodies in sexualised and/or vice spaces, demonstrated, as we have seen, in *West End Jungle* (Arnold L. Miller, 1961) or in the case of Jewish wide boys.

The Wolfenden Report and Commercialising Female Sexuality

Bell-Williams provides an extensively alternative critical study to Viv Chadder (1999) on the film's 'engagement with 'deviant' female sexuality' through the figure of the prostitute and opens up a wider discourse 'concerning normal and abnormal femininity that circulated during the decade'.[28] *The Flesh Is Weak* is not simply an important marker of late 1950s British society's changing attitudes to sex, but also of female sexuality:

> Her [the prostitute] emergence in popular film at this time was shaped by three factors: censorship in relaxations which permitted the gradual introduction of more 'adult' fare into mainstream film, the increasing presence of sex in mainstream culture more generally (which ranged from sex education literature

to novels and magazines), and a broader anxiety about female sexuality and the place of marriage within contemporary society.[29]

The film's morals were aligned with the Wolfenden Report, which recommended the criminalisation of prostitution, focusing on the 'visible nuisance of street walking... If women were not street walking, then male demand would diminish'.[30] Chadder and Bell-Williams are both interested in the film's depiction of the 'enslavement of women as passive victims of vast criminal organisations ... dismissed as "popular impression"', which, in turn, problematises these films' vehement claims that they provide authentic depictions of London vice rackets.[31] *Passport to Shame* (Alvin Rakoff, 1958) is a West London-set film that shares the post-Wolfenden exploitation narrative and similarly details the mechanics of grooming foreign young women into prostitution, led by a criminal network also modelled on the notorious Maltese Messina gang with Herbert Lom playing a fictional pimp named Nick Biaggi.[32]

Vance's insertion of a bourgeois hero, an investigative journalist named Lloyd Buxton (William Franklyn), which Chadder argues is a version of Vance himself, signifies a desire to emulate the popular television detective series *Fabian of the Yard* that was broadcast on the BBC from 1954 to 1956.[33] However, Buxton will only succeed by providing first-hand testimony to the authorities from a woman who was groomed and prostituted by the gang. After Tony frames Marissa for assaulting another prostitute that leads to a short stint in Holloway Prison, Buxton ultimately convinces Marissa to testify against him and his associates. Buxton's refusal to believe she is, in his words, not a 'decent girl' from an 'apparently normal background' is consistently posited against Tony's belief that she is only interested in material goods.[34] The inclusion of Buxton provides an ally for Marissa, but is also a way to summarise the legislative framework surrounding sex work in the period for national audiences.

Critics were swift to further underscore the commercial shadow that hung over the film's verisimilitude. *Variety* said the producer 'Stross must be relying optimistically on the film's "X" certificate (which bars under sixteens) as a magnet for box office returns ... As a social document, it makes only the mildest impact and fails lamentably to say anything new or penetrating about an urgent problem'.[35] *Monthly Film Bulletin* identified it as: 'A crudely melodramatic film dealing with, but not one feels very gravely concerned about, the real-life problem of organised prostitution.'[36] The 'X' rating was first used by the British Board of Film

Classification (BBFC) in 1951. The BBFC's application of the rating to a 'mixed bag' of films 'produced some strange bedfellows, and the public soon became uncertain whether it indicated the sober treatment of an adult theme or the exploitative treatment of a commonplace story'.[37] The combination of the film's conflicting function as both a commercially appealing melodrama and a social documentary, with an adult 'X' certificate rating, reflects the landmark changes in censorship, permissiveness and the 'popular understanding of vice' during this period.[38]

Despite a muted response from critics, the film was a commercial success. The unabashedly splashy publicity for the film's sensational subject matter most likely accounted for this triumph. According to Chadder, publicity surrounding the film ranged from the creation of a myth that the scriptwriter Vance conducted his own field research of vice rackets and the producer Stross, who 'insured himself for £20,000 against personal injury' out of fear that the film's unadulterated authenticity would enrage Soho's real-life vice kings.[39] Basil Clavering, director of Cameo Cinemas, published a letter he wrote to Leslie Greenspan, sales manager at Eros Films, declaring that their cinemas were filled over forty times per day, a 'house record'.[40]

Spaces of Blackmail

The film was shot on location in Soho and at Walton Studios. The familiar spaces of Berwick Street Market, Shaftesbury Avenue, Wardour Street and Old Compton Street formulate the physical peripheries of Tony's emotional trap for Marissa that facilitates his blackmail and her downward spiral into prostitution. Uniquely, the film does not adhere strictly to the conventional organisation of the spaces of crime and melodrama. Spaces of blackmail are confined to private and interior spaces such as the bedroom or the nightclub. By featuring public spaces, specifically areas of London that contain historic architecture and landmarks, the film engineers a relationship between sexual naïveté and cultural tourism.

The film is clearly fascinated by the 'metaphoric and metonymic presence' of London, going so far as to include a landmark London sequence. Shortly after Marissa meets Tony, he invites her on a tour of the capital and we are subjected to a montage of shots that dissolve into one another depicting the city's historic landmarks, such as Trafalgar Square, Westminster, Big Ben and the Embankment.[41] Unbeknownst to her, Tony is a member of the Giani gang, which runs a Soho vice ring that operates from a West End coffee bar with his brother Angelo (Martin Benson). The film displays London as both a seductive pleasure centre, but also as a space of community, which in turn acts as an allegory for the naïve young woman who will pay dearly as a result of her (modern) desire for goods and sex.

Crossing the Threshold

Charlotte Brunsdon has argued that the use of recognisable London sites 'refers to the urban imaginary of a specific city and also stages it, contributing to the many images, characters and tales that constitute that urban imaginary'.[42] The inclusion of two sequences whereby Marissa explores the city, one with Tony and the other on her own, functions on two levels. Her tour of the city with Tony acts as a visual signifier for 'popular impressions' of Britain and as a device to intensify its melodramatic elements. In the sequence, they tour the major tourist sites of Big Ben and as Katherine Shonfield has shown, the film's rejection of New Wave realism and the new postwar architecture of Brutalism in favour 'of normality and Britishness' suggests that it is a film that holds a 'postwar preoccupation with the nature of nationality and the need for a popular recognition of nationhood'.[43] There is also a consistent slippage in the film's definition of Marissa as moral/immoral, which I argue reflects Soho's postwar identity as a space of sexual permissiveness and commercial/social mobility:

> Marissa's characterisation is potentially more difficult to fit easily within the Wolfenden between prostitutes and ordinary women. [This] suggests her status as an ambiguous figure … Her character offers a space in which the dangers to the pure and the pleasures of the forbidden sit in a productive tension.[44]

During the opening sequence, the camera tracks Marissa's journey from King's Cross St Pancras Station to the West End and Soho. This foreshadows her torturous victimisation by the hands of the Giani prostitution ring. This sequence is placed prior to the opening credits and is notable for its use of King's Cross Station as an allegory for social mobility, but also as pseudo-promotion for urban and social renewal in mid-1950s Britain.[45] Marissa, who appears bright-eyed and hopeful, emerges from a swarm of commuters on the train platform. Chaffey deliberately locates Marissa's starting place in a recognisably liminal space of

King's Cross, which, as Brunsdon states, along with Soho, functions as 'the low-life site of landmark London. It is King's Cross that desperate provincial parents hasten in search of runaway children, and it is life in the infernal London on the streets around King's Cross that signifies the failure of the runaway's dreams'.[46] Brunsdon argues that there is a historical precedent for cinema's persistent association of the area of King's Cross with 'various types of poverty and street life'.[47] This echoes the heavily criticised gentrification of contemporary Soho that, similar to the redevelopment of King's Cross, 'could easily exemplify the city learning the wrong lessons from the cinema ... the elimination of local places in between landmarks ... in favour of an architecture of spectacle, a material montage'.[48]

Soho Clip-Joints: Spaces of Desire and Danger

The clip-joint and its importance within the development of nightlife culture in London remain unexplored. However, exposés of London nightlife published in the 1920s to the beginning of the Second World War suggest that they were to 'entertain' middle-class, heterosexual men by providing companionship and entertainment in the form of female dance hostesses. Walkowitz states that one of the first clip-joints to be established in Soho was the 43 Club located at 43 Gerrard Street, which was opened by Mrs Meyrick in 1921. According to Walkowitz, the extension of drinking hours in London during this period to 11 PM led to the proliferation of American-style drinking clubs and bars in and around Gerrard Street, encouraging its reputation as a place where cross-gender encounters could occur as opposed to the traditional gentlemen's clubs.[49] In 1941, a reporter recounted the 'blitz-time tempo. The velvet rope is nightly in virtually every late spot in town ... sun-tanned faces again are being spotted against the glaring white tablecloths of every clip-joint in town big enough to crowd another customer into its smoke-filled interior'.[50] The Golden Bucket, where Marissa is first given a job in London, is clearly modelled on the drinking dens that populated the West End during the interwar period as they functioned as short-term solutions to the 'shrinking incomes, new forms of housing ... and the need for men to go to work'.[51]

Mrs Meyrick's training of her female employees, whom she referred to as 'Merry Maids', echoes the film's suggestion that nightclub hostesses were trained to blackmail customers, 'taught to fit themselves into a range of types ... highly stereotyped, erotic codes of whiteness'.[52] Similarly, Marissa is directed by the deadpan proprietor of the bar, Doris Newman (Patricia Plunkett), to work the room and orders her to change into a second-hand, figure-hugging dress found in the cloakroom in order to appeal to the club's male clientele. The Golden Bucket's interior is half-hidden by clouds of cigar smoke, whilst expressionless young women roam around the room for prospects. This also confirms Walkowitz's sentiments on the ambiguity of the clip-joint as a sexual and commercial place of exchange where '[r]isky working conditions and the ambiguous status of dance partners, who were neither ladies nor street girls, but glamorized service workers engaged in cross-class liaisons, partially account for this blurring of sexual boundaries'.[53]

Mrs Meyrick's Soho hostesses were required to attract 'free spending customers' and were encouraged to grift male patrons by persuading them to buy alcohol and other goods at marked-up prices.[54] Marissa's role as a hostess lasts only several hours. After dancing with an affluent, bloated patron who bestows her with a large tip and a patronising remark about her ill-fitting girdle, the camera fixes upon her 'delight at the financial rewards that accrue'.[55] Marissa's innocence is deconstructed by this pseudo-form of sexual liberation, embodied by her acceptance of the position as a hostess and the satisfaction of completing a successful exchange. Elizabeth Grosz's study of the body in urban space also applies to Marissa's body, which 're-inscribes and projects' itself onto the sociocultural environment of the Soho clip-joint. Marissa initially displays great hesitancy towards taking on employment (passive). However, after she has been remunerated for the (public) display of her body, she arrives at an 'understanding of, alignment with, and positioning' of the nightclub space.[56] This reinscribes her body as a functioning site for cultural saturation where it 're-inscribes the urban landscape according to its changing (demographic, economic, and psychological) needs, extending the limits of the city, of the sub-urban, ever towards the countryside which borders it'.[57]

Soho's sexual permissiveness renders Marissa's body malleable in order to be blackmailed by Tony, who stages a fake quarrel and assault in the clip-joint with his employee thug Saradine (Denis Shaw). This signifies the second stage of the grooming process. Tony's 'heroic' action of preserving Marissa's sexual integrity (saving her from Saradine) immediately disassociates her from the nightclub space. The vulnerable and malleable Marissa now trusts Tony. This sequence foreshadows the further degradation of her identity as she will later be tortured for Tony's sadistic pleasure as he grooms her through the exchange of goods and love.

Figure 7.1. The clip-joint where Marissa receives her first payment from a client for entertaining him all evening. Still from *The Flesh Is Weak* (Don Chaffey, 1957). DVD, Odeon Entertainment, 2009

The Soho clip-joint sequence is successful in conveying the film's aim to provide social commentary, but, overall, the film is conflicted in terms of in the way it depicts sexual exploitation. It is muddied by its own use of melodrama, amplified by the extended London montage sequence. It signifies a moment for Marissa's emotional blackmail, but also suggests traditional notions of Britishness and the establishment (including Marissa's desire to assimilate to her new life). As Stephen Barber states, 'the incessantly vanishing city carries an aura of being able to oppose its own portrayal with malicious determination ... On London's flaking, decrepit facades, the hold of images soon appears anachronistic'.[58]

The Shakedown (1960)

The Shakedown was retitled *The Naked Mirror* for its US release and was produced by Norman Williams for Ethiro Productions. It partially examines the repercussions of the Street Offences Act (1959), a law that 'forced prostitutes out from Soho's public spaces and into the world of call-girl rackets and massage parlours'.[59] Screenwriter Vance scrutinises the new government legislation by constructing a world in which the criminal protagonist exploits the law by opening up a photography studio and modelling school that acts as a front for a brothel and a sexual blackmail scheme. Dirk Kirby's biography of SAS Hero Detective Sergeant Harry Challenor, who became known as 'The Scourge of Soho', notes the adverse effects of the Street Offences Act and the potential it offered criminals: 'Following the Street Offences Act … The Gangsters behaved as they pleased, corrupt payments were being made to the police and crime was simply out of control.'[60]

The film opens as Augie is released from prison and discovers that his prostitution ring has crumbled due to the repercussions of the Street Offences Act. His girlfriend Zena (Gene Anderson) is now employed as a broker for the rival criminal gang led by Gollar (Harry H. Corbett). After robbing Gollar in an act of revenge, Augie puts the funds towards opening a studio with a once-heralded portrait photographer Jessel (Donald Pleasence), whose alcohol addiction has led to the ruin of his career. Jessel may be likened to Marissa for his vulnerable, pitying characterisation. He is also blackmailed by Augie once he discovers the studio's true function. This drives Jessel back to alcoholism and for the remainder of the film, he does very little else other than drink himself into a melancholic, drunken stupor. In contrast, the character of Augie is depicted as a slick and self-assured villain who wholly understands the shifting political and social changes regarding sexual commerce in postwar Britain.[61]

The film was shot primarily at Twickenham Studios, with some memorably exterior sequences shot on Old Compton Street. Isabel Quigly called it a 'vicious little British piece' and Dal Vaughan declared it: 'Essentially … a Warners-prohibition-type gangster film set in post-Street Offences Act London, with a theme-show *à la Rififi* thrown in for good measure.'[62] Chibnall similarly noted that 'Vance's attempts to offer an authentic depiction of the Soho underworld are bedeviled by Lemont's unimaginative direction'; however, for Chibnall, the film does succeed in the 'knowingness about its own exploitative relationship with its audience'.[63] It displays an awareness of a society with a booming economy. In the

1960s, 'social transformation roared on ... In London, that new, smart Bohemian *demi-monde* that marked the point where the hereditary attitudes of the upper-middle class young were most obviously crumbling into a new freedom ... was beginning to emerge'.[64] The memorable theme song, also called 'The Shakedown', was performed by Manchester-born singer Sheila Buxton, who also performs it in the film. This signifies the film's awareness of cinema as a commercial product.

This 'tired melodrama' marked scriptwriter Vance's second collaboration with the filmmaker Lemont and producer Williams. Their relationship began with the psychological thriller *Witness in the Dark* (Wolf Rilla, 1959) and concluded with the London-set exploration of criminal racketeers *The Frightened City* (John Lemont, 1961).[65] Vance's dedicated career examining social issues through the criminal-melodrama includes the film *Witness in the Dark* (1959), which was directed by German-born Wolf Rilla, who would later direct the Soho-set film *The World Ten Times Over* in 1963.[66] There were hesitations to guarantee the film's funding before production. Film Finances Inc. (FFI), a company incorporated in 1950 to guarantee film lenders that the 'contracted film would arrive "on-schedule and on-budget"', expressed great hesitation in terms of issuing a bond upon reading both the script and proposed budget, though it particularly had issues regarding the film's depiction of the protagonist as 'sympathetic'.[67] This was clearly a misreading of Augie Cortona, who, although 'well-mannered and handsome to the feminine taste', is generally unlikeable and is ultimately punished. This misreading was most possibly shrouded in Vance's proven talent for constructing scripts that condense the criminal story into a recognisable narrative pattern echoing melodrama.[68] Augie's downfall – his death by police firing squad – through the brave efforts of a woman (a female police officer played by Hazel Court) confirms that the film is aligned with Thomas Elsaesser's definitions of melodrama, which, 'at its most accomplished, seems capable of reproducing more directly than other genres the patterns of domination and exploitation existing in a given society, especially the relation between psychology, morality, and class consciousness'.[69]

The Photography-Pornography Studio

Augie engineers a private space for sexual play by allowing male clients to photograph their nude subjects while he simultaneously shoots them behind a two-way mirror. He uses a space that functions for numerous purposes on a day-to-day basis. The minimalist room, decorated in both a classical and a modern style, comparable to a hotel lobby, contributes towards the legitimacy of his modelling school/studio, but is only privately accessible through a back alleyway behind the studio; he rearranges the geography of the room for his specific illicit purpose. This can be seen in Vance's original script, which meticulously dictates the action of setting up the camera(s) and its subsequent effect upon the staged solicitation of the foreign prostitute Sylvia (Linda Castle) and unsuspecting upper-middle class John Arnold (John Salew):

> *The CAMERA ANGLES so that it shows a CINECAMERA and a REFLEX STILL CAMERA on tripods poised facing what is presumably the wall, and below them a TAPE RECORDER. While AUGIE fits the film the CAMERA ANGLES ROUND and we suddenly see through a sheet of glass right into the STUDIO. We realise that the ORNATE MIRROR is a TWO-WAY MIRROR. In the STUDIO the other side of it, SYLVIA, who has just finished pouring out the drink, suddenly looked up full into CAMERA and gives a long slow wink.*[70]

Augie's decision to engage in blackmail reflects the dramatic changes that sexual commerce in the capital was undergoing during the early 1960s, which included the growing popularity of striptease in London.[71] Augie displays not only entrepreneurialism but also an inherent understanding for the 'significant context and frame for the body'.[72] The film's cinematic representation of blackmail is like a type of postmodern performance. Unlike the majority of the male protagonists of Soho films I have discussed, Augie is emblematic of social mobility, class consciousness and moral anxiety. Perhaps the rationale behind *The Shakedown*'s commercial failure was partly due to its refusal to side with either its villain or society's traditional moral order. However, we cannot ignore Augie's aspirations for social mobility: 'As British society moved from relative stability based on well-understood class modes, sexual customs and economical practices into the permissive and commercially rapacious 1960s, so criminal culture began to reject the shared expectations that circumscribed the underworld, and to aspire to a place above ground'.[73] Augie's immoral entrepreneurialism may then account for audience indifference and refusal to accept a narrative that detailed a criminal's rise to power. But the deliberate positioning in Soho reinforces the film's political motivations, in that the stereotypical representation of the area as a place for vice and criminality further underappreciates its dual identity as a commercial, cultural and sexually permissive centre.[74]

Conclusion

We should view *The Flesh Is Weak* and *The Shakedown* as a 'battle between the traditional forces of public morality and sexual progressives over nude displays', for we will then gain a stronger understanding of the evolution of 'cultural and geopolitical meanings associated with static and kinetic female nudity' in British cinema.[75] The depiction of Marissa's body as an ambiguous and vulnerable space foreshadows the arrival of British New Wave cinema and its more liberated representation of women. Augie's blackmail scenario underpins the tensions found within the public display of nudity in exploitation films produced in the latter half of the 1960s. Both films function as a prologue to the 'entirely new, sexually and socially "frank" and "honest" images' embodied by the working-class realist films of Karel Reisz and Tony Richardson alongside an increasingly permissive society.[76]

Soho functions as a liminal intersection where the moral and immoral may converge together freely. The European Marissa's romantic entanglement with Londoner Tony and her subsequent enslavement through blackmail highlight the commercial/sexual transformation of women who are then corrupted by the cosmopolitan centre of Soho. As in the case of *West End Jungle*, these films suggest that it is not the entrepreneur of vice to blame, but rather the male consumer who causes the blossoming of its underground economies. Of course, they depict the favoured media representation of Soho as a locus of sordid trades and tradesman. However, their concern with topical (albeit London-centric) issues confirms their status as important examples of exploitive and explorative documents of the effects of aggressive postwar legislation on sexual commerce.

Notes

1. Frank Mort, *Capital Affairs: London and the Making of the Permissive Society* (New Haven: Yale University Press, 2010), 140, 194.
2. McLaren references one instance in 1921 where 'a Pall Mall caretaker went to a prostitute and was shaken down by her partner, who claimed to be a police constable'. See Angus McLaren, *Sexual Blackmail: A Modern History* (Cambridge, MA: Harvard University Press, 2002), 4, 76.

3. Ibid., 19.
4. Yet, during the Second World War, sexual blackmail ceased to exist – or so it appeared from the newspapers. In 1939, the index to *The Times* of London listed seventeen references to blackmail; in 1940, it listed two; in 1941, one; and in 1942, none at all. See also ibid., 220, 223.
5. Richard Hornsey, *The Spiv and the Architect: Unruly Life in Postwar London* (Minneapolis: University of Minnesota Press, 2010), 3.
6. Ibid., 1.
7. Unfortunately, the dearth of available archival material on *The Shakedown* means that I am unable to provide as detailed a history of its production and creative personnel. I am wholly grateful to have been granted access to some production, financial and script(s) material through the Film Finances archive, which is managed by Charles Drazin. The British Film Institute (BFI) does not currently hold any scripts or ephemera for either film. The UCLA special collection contains the papers of writer Leigh Vance. After discussions with the curator Peggy Alexander, it appears that no material on either film exists. See UCLA Special Collections, 'The Leigh Vance Papers'. Retrieved 20 October 2021 from https://catalog.library.ucla.edu/vwebv/holdingsInfo?searchId=121&recCount=50&recPointer=0&bibId=4435866.
8. See Melanie Bell-Williams, '"Shop-Soiled" Women: Female Sexuality and the Figure of the Prostitute in 1950s British Cinema', *Journal of British Cinema and Television* 3(2) (2006), 266.
9. See Steve Chibnall, 'Ordinary People: "New Wave" Realism and the British Crime Film 1959–1963', in Steve Chibnall and Robert Murphy (eds), *British Crime Cinema*, 2nd edn (London: Routledge, 2005), 111.
10. Besides his work as a journalist and screenwriter, he was the founding officer of the British Writers' Guild. See 'Obituary, Leigh Vance', *LA Times*, 31 October 1994. Retrieved 20 October 2021 from https://www.latimes.com/archives/la-xpm-1994-10-31-mn-56828-story.html.
11. According to McLaren: 'In 1757 a statute specifically declared that sending a letter threatening to accuse a person of a serious crime with intent to extort money or valuables was a misdemeanour punishable by seven years in a penal colony.' See McLaren, *Sexual Blackmail*, 4.
12. Ibid., 12.
13. 'Mayle' is the Anglo-Saxon word for tribute or rent. Ibid., 12.
14. Ibid.
15. See John Hill, *Sex, Class and Realism: British Cinema 1956–1963* (London: BFI, 1997), 67, 69.
16. See Thomas Elsaesser, 'Tales of Sound and Fury: Observations on the Family Melodrama', in Barry Grant (ed.), *Film Genre Reader III* (Austin: University of Texas Press, 2003), 375.
17. Ibid.
18. Ibid., 380.
19. See Melanie Bell-Williams, *Femininity in the Frame: Women and 1950s British Popular Cinema* (London: I.B. Tauris, 2010), 124
20. Bell-Williams, '"Shop-Soiled" Women', 266.
21. Ibid.
22. I am grateful to Peggy Alexander, Curator at the Performing Arts, UCLA Library Special Collections for assisting me in identifying Vance's work on *The Flesh Is Weak* and *The Shakedown*. Vance died in Los Angeles after an extensive career writing and producing for television. The Leigh Vance papers are kept at the University of California, Los Angeles.
23. Chibnall, 'Ordinary People', 110.

24. See Simon Sheridan, 'Sleeve Notes: *The Flesh Is Weak*', *The Flesh Is Weak*. Odeon Entertainment, DVD, 2009.
25. Tom Vallance, 'Obituary: John Derek', *The Independent*, 24 May 1998. Retrieved 20 October 2021 from http://www.independent.co.uk/news/obituaries/obituary-john-derek-1157309.html.
26. Sheridan, 'Sleeve Notes', 1.
27. Sheridan states that: 'Derek's love of the nude female was also well illustrated by his desire to photograph his wives naked for *Playboy* magazine. In 1980, he even helmed a hardcore porn film entitled *Love You*. His final film 1989 *Ghosts Can't Do It* is about a young woman (played by Bo) who attempts to have sex with the spirit of her dead husband.' See ibid.
28. Bell-Williams, '"Shop-Soiled" Women', 66.
29. Bell-Williams, *Femininity in the Frame*, 123.
30. Ibid., 75.
31. Viv Chadder, 'The Higher Heel, 'The Higher Heel: Women and the Post-War British Crime Film', in *British Crime Cinema*, edited by Steve Chibnall and Robert Murphy (London; New York: Routledge, 1999), 75.
32. After emigrating to London in the 1930s by way of Egypt, the five Messina brothers ran a profitable prostitution syndicate in Soho during the Second World War, trafficking young women from France and Italy and forcing them to solicit as prostitutes in the West End. By the mid-1950s, the Messina gang were 'wiped up, imprisoned, deported' following the conviction of one of the brothers in 1951. Similar to the villain Sugiani in *Noose* (1948), the Messina Brothers were cemented as symbol of vice in London and inspired several crime films. See Dick Kirby's *The Scourge of Soho: The Controversial Career of SAS Hero Detective Sergeant Harry Challenor MM* (Barnsley, Pen & Sword True Crime, 2013), Clive Emsley, *Hard Men: The English and Violence since 1750* (London: Hambledon, 2005), 47.
33. *Fabian of the Yard* was based on the memoirs of Robert Fabian, who also wrote a book on Soho vice rings entitled *London after Dark* (1954). The character of Buxton is a journalist and researcher of vice whose sole mission in the film is to indict the Giani brothers for racketeering and trafficking. According to Viv Chadder: 'Screenwriter Leigh Vance is given fictional representation in the film as Buxton, a middle-aged philanthropist who makes notes.' See Chadder, 'The Higher Heel', 76.
34. Bell-Williams, '"Shop-Soiled" Women', 273.
35. See Rich, 'Pictures: *The Flesh Is Weak*', *Variety*, 14 August 1957, 20.
36. Review, '*The Flesh Is Weak*', *Monthly Film Bulletin* 24(276) (1957), 114.
37. The BBFC awarded the X certificate to seventeen films in 1951, which Harper and Porter describe as a 'mixed bag'. See Sue Harper and Vincent Porter, 'The "X" Certificate', in *British Cinema of the 1950s: The Decline of Deference* (Oxford: Oxford University Press, 2003), 220–21.
38. Ibid., 271.
39. Chadder, 'The Higher Heel', 76.
40. 'My dear Leslie ... It is with pleasure that I enclose my cheque for £100 to settle our wager that "THE FLESH IS WEAK" could not break the house record at the Cameo-Royal ... Still the queues continued and you know from the returns that of 43 houses were filled just over 40 times.' Publicity for the *Flesh Is Weak* included this enthusiastic letter from Cameo Cinemas to Eros Films proclaiming the film's commercial success. See 'Eros Films Wins a Wager', *Variety*, 28 August 1957, 19.
41. Ibid., 13.

42. Ibid., 21.
43. Katherine Shonfield, 'Glossing with Graininess: Cross Occupations in Postwar British Film and Architecture', *Journal of Architecture* 3(4) (1998), 355–75.
44. Ibid.
45. The Great Northern Railway opened King's Cross as a permanent station in 1852, which was designed to be 'simple and functional'. The surrounding area was often described as being a 'mixed neighbourhood', with regard to its immigrant population. During the Second World War, the station was severely damaged, with five bombs falling onto it in 1941. The redevelopment of King's Cross as a commercial and tourist hub followed the arrival of Eurostar in 2007: 'It was about the circulation of Capital – a faster connection, a more iconic station and Europe's longest champagne bar.' See Emma Jackson, 'Railway Lands', in Charlotte Bates and Alex Rhys-Taylor (eds), *Walking through Social Research* (Abingdon: Routledge, 2017), 15.
46. Brunsdon states that: 'I have become preoccupied by the relationship between the constantly transforming city and the traces and fragments of its former lives found on film … but it has been King's Cross that has proved to me the power and poignancy of place on film.' See Charlotte Brunsdon, *London in Cinema: The Cinematic City since 1945* (London: BFI, 2007), 213.
47. Ibid., 218.
48. Brunsdon notes that the crime film *Mona Lisa* (Neil Jordan, 1986), which follows a 'small-time crook' who is 'given a job chauffeuring a prostitute' and 'works the exclusive West End hotels', is a contemporary film that shows us the impact of British cinema's persistent articulation the area of King's Cross and Soho as parallel spaces for deviant and/or foreign personalities. This association of King's Cross with poverty and corruption arguably began with *The Ladykillers* (Alexander Mackendrick, 1955). King's Cross Station marks the threshold that Marissa must cross in order to proceed towards the Soho gateway into hedonism and crime; Brunsdon, *London in Cinema*, 218. See also Gwyn Tophan, 'Five-Year £500m Redevelopment of King's Cross Station Almost Complete', *The Guardian*, 14 March 2012. Retrieved 20 October 2021 from https://www.theguardian.com/business/2012/mar/14/five-year-redevelopment-kings-cross-station.
49. Judith Walkowitz, *Nights out: Life in Cosmopolitan London* (New Haven: Yale University Press, 2012), 216.
50. See George Lait, 'More Night-Time and More Nite Life in London; Plenty of Clip Joints', *Variety*, 8 October 1941, 4.
51. Ibid.
52. Ibid.
53. Ibid., 224.
54. Ibid., 225.
55. Bell-Williams, '"Shop-Soiled" Women', 273.
56. Elizabeth Grosz, 'Bodies-Cities', in Beatriz Colomina (ed.), *Sexuality & Space* (Princeton: Princeton University School of Architecture, 1992), 249.
57. Ibid.
58. See Stephen Barber, *Projected Cities: Cinema and Urban Space* (London: Reaktion Books, 200), 100.
59. See Frank Mort, 'Striptease: The Erotic Female Body and Live Sexual Entertainment in Mid-twentieth-Century London', *Social History* 32 (2007), 45.
60. See Kirby, *The Scourge of Soho*, 49.

61. Despite his role as the supporting character, Donald Pleasence provides a multifaceted performance as Jessel, whose conflicted attitude towards the blackmail scheme is embodied by his return to a destructive addiction to alcohol. According to *The Stage*, Pleasence was only largely known through television before this period. In contrast, born in Lewisham, South London, Terence Morgan 'seemed destined to play romantic leads', for after he attended RADA, he won the role of Laertes in Olivier's *Hamlet* (1948) and was swiftly contracted for four years by the Rank Organisation, starring as a supporting player in over twenty British films. In 1956, his contract with Rank ended. In one interview, Morgan was quoted to have said 'At Last – I'm Free' to *Picturegoer* magazine in an article that reveals his clash with Dirk Bogarde and persistent offers of roles as the villain. It is also alleged that the director Basil Dearden once said to Morgan: 'Let's face it – there is something rather nasty about your screen personality'. One of the primary reasons for leaving Rank was that he 'never really carried a film' for the organization and grew frustrated at having no control over his career. See 'At Last – I'm Free', *Picturegoer*, 18 February 1956, 8.
62. See Isabel Quigly's review of *The Shakedown* in *The Spectator*, 22 January 1960, 112. See also review by Dal Vaughan, 'The Shakedown', *Films and Filming*, March 1960, 25.
63. See Chibnall, 'Ordinary People', 109.
64. See Christopher Booker, *The Neophiliacs: Revolution in English Life in the Fifties and Sixties*. 2nd edn (London: Pimlico, 1992), 147.
65. See Howard Thompson, 'Screen: "The Shakedown"', *New York Times*, 16 March 1961.
66. Both Vance and John Lemont co-adapted their script from the original stage play by James Parish. The film follows a blind woman Jane Pringle (Patricia Dainton), who encounters a murderer as he is fleeing the crime scene and must assist the police with their investigation by drawing upon her subjective memory. *Monthly Film Bulletin* noted its 'stolid performances and routine characterisation'. Actor Conrad Phillips, who plays the Inspector, also starred in Don Chaffey's follow-up to *The Flesh Is Weak* entitled *A Question of Adultery* (1958), a second feature melodrama examining artificial insemination. Vance and Lemont's more triumphant crime film *The Frightened City* stars Sean Connery and Herbert Lom as duelling criminal racketeers in the West End. The film was shot on location in Soho and Fitzrovia, and the theme song, performed by The Shadows, who had previously accompanied Cliff Richard in *Expresso Bongo*, became a popular hit on the British singles charts. Vance would work again with producer Williams and director Rilla on the heist film *Piccadilly Third Stop* (1960), which stars Terence Morgan as a thief who plans to rob an embassy in Mayfair.
67. Notes from the film financing company for the original screenplay read: 'I find this a particularly unpleasant story, concerned with the vice racket of street walking, nude photography … To make matters worse, the "hero" is the principal vice king and operator of the school as well as being the black-mailer, and attempts are made to make him "sympathetic"! … I have a feeling that these papers have been drawn up by someone who is new to films or hasn't been associated with production for a long time." See 'The Shakedown', Letter from John Croydon to R.E.F. Garrett, *Film Finances*, 22 August 1959. See also 'About Film Finances'. Retrieved 20 October 2021 from http://www.filmfinances.com/about.
68. Vaughan, 'The Shakedown', 25.
69. Thomas Elsaesser, 'Tales of Sound and Fury: Observations on the Family Melodrama', in Barry Keith Grant (ed.), *Film Genre Reader III* (Austin: University of Texas Press, 2003), 390.
70. Leigh Vance and John Lemont, Screenplay, 'The Shakedown' (1960), Film Finances Archive.

71. As Mort has discussed extensively with regard to the social, cultural and moral implications of this new mode of performance: 'Striptease became a potent and heavily contested symbol of a rapidly changing sexual culture; it stood alongside pornography, male homosexuality, and the contraceptive pill as one of the icons of the so-called permissive society.' See Mort, 'Striptease', 29.
72. Grosz, 'Bodies-Cities', 243.
73. Chibnall, 'Ordinary People', 110.
74. Booker, *The Neophiliacs,* 149.
75. Mort, 'Striptease', 53.
76. Booker, *The Neophiliacs,* 149.

CHAPTER 8
Subversive Female Sexualities and the Soho Coffee Bar
Beat Girl (1960) and *Rag Doll* (1961)

Like a stick of dynamite, sitting on a coffee bar stool.
—'Made You' by Trevor Peacock and John Barry, 1960

On 20 April 2016, the British Film Institute (BFI) hosted a special screening of Edmond T. Gréville's *Beat Girl* (retitled in the United States as *Wild for Kicks*, 1960) at the Regent Street Cinema in London to commemorate the release of a remastered version of the film from the original negatives for UK dual format (DVD and Blu-Ray), a welcome addition to the growing Soho collection of films encompassed within the BFI Flipside Series, which released remastered editions of *Expresso Bongo* (Val Guest, 1960) and *The Small World of Sammy Lee* (Ken Hughes, 1963) in the same year.[1] Following the screening of the film, Vic Pratt, the BFI National Archive's Fiction Curator, hosted a discussion with the Anglo-French actress Gillian Hills, who made her screen debut aged fifteen as the film's protagonist Jennifer Linden, a teenager who rebels against her absent, architect father Paul (David Farrar) through her association with rock 'n' roll, striptease, coffee bar and coffee club culture.

During the interview, the pair touched on numerous subjects, including Hills' self-confessed 'chaotic' childhood, *Beat Girl* co-star Adam Faith and her subsequent career as a pop star in France. Pratt then about her about the experience of shooting the frenetic dance sequence that opens the film. The sequence sees Hills made up to appear as a pseudo-Brigitte Bardot, descending the staircase into a crowded basement beneath the fictional Off-Beat Café.[2] The space was described by the film's screenwriter Dail Ambler (whose real name was Betty Mabel Lilian Williams) as a 'Soho coffee bar where London's teen-age

'Beatniks', the lost kids of the 'beat' generation, search for self-identity.'[3] The sequence was evocatively described by Trevor Johnston in 2017:

> *As a stream of eager youths pours down a staircase from a Soho milk bar into the club below, the attention's firmly on wild-child Gillian Hills ... a feral glare straight down the camera before she joins the frugging throng and dances to her own tune.*[4]

Despite having no 'official' choreographer for the film, Hills likened the experience of dancing in the underground club to 'swimming', claiming that she drew inspiration for her fluid physical movements – accompanying the more electric dance style favoured by an uncredited Oliver Reed – from the film's rock 'n' roll soundtrack.[5]

The score was written by John Barry, marking his first composition and musical direction credit in cinema.[6] Jennifer's voiceless, physical address to the camera during the opening sequence not only signals her lack of maturity but also foreshadows her contained/uncontained sexuality.[7] The Off-Beat is then a

Figure 8.1. Jennifer dances with an uncredited Oliver Reed in the underground club at the Off-Beat Café. Still from *Beat Girl* (Edmond T. Gréville, 1960). DVD, BFI Flipside, 2016

permissive space where Jennifer may freely express her sexuality and, in Ambler's words, a place where she is given 'permission' to take 'flight into the world of the "beat"'.[8]

Rag Doll, retitled in the United States as *Young, Willing and Eager* (Lance Comfort, 1961), is another forgotten, yet-to-be-remastered Soho set-film that also proposes the coffee bar as a locus for teenage rebellion and transgressive female sexuality. The story follows seventeen-year-old Carol (Christina Gregg), who escapes from living with her abusive, alcoholic stepfather, the proprietor of a roadhouse café, for a new life in metropolitan London. Shortly after her arrival in the capital, she is mentored by Soho denizens, 'Auntie' Sophie (Hermione Baddeley) and entrepreneur Mort Wilson (Kenneth Griffith), who provide her with protection and employment at a local coffee bar. However, the potential for Carol's social and cultural development within this commercial sphere is obstructed by the doomed love affair she embarks upon with a burgeoning pop star and petty criminal Jo Shane, played by real-life pop star Jess Conrad.[9] Over the past decade, there has been an increase in interest in these two films. Janet Fink and Penny Tinkler state that the films projected nascent female sexuality and adolescence in a period 'on the cusp of a sexual revolution'.[10] Both films convey two distinct youth experiences of urban cosmopolitanism and consumer culture through the shared inclusion of a burgeoning musician who acts as the principal romantic and sexual interest in the film, played by real-life pop stars Adam Faith and Jess Conrad. This chapter will build upon Fink and Tinkler's examination of female sexuality in these films. However, by placing a more substantial focus on the lesser-known *Rag Doll*, I have uncovered a more ambiguous cinematic representation of sexual innocence that in turn opens up 'new terrain in the cultural histories of young female sexualities [that] can be exposed and established'.[11]

The Soho Coffee Bar and the Teenage Consumer

According to Dominic Sandbrook, the coffee bar represented 'the trend of increasing affluence and projected the values of elusive sophistication'.[12] The coffee-house's historical function in Britain during the eighteenth century as a privileged and intellectual space further confirms its importance as a social meeting place: 'The coffee-house transformation of manners renders its public space a more private and sentimental arena (the "home" or "neighbourhood").'[13] The 1950s coffee bar, widely accepted by historians such as Ellis to have originated in Soho, exploited the spending habits of teenagers by installing jukeboxes and hiring young, predominantly male musicians to perform in the café. The coffee house's resurgence as an affordable and popular leisure activity for English society followed the removal of coffee price controls in 1952. However, prices 'rose steeply' resulting in a global coffee crisis, repositioning it as a 'luxury commodity'.[14] In 1951, a Milanese dental mechanic named Pino Riservato saw a lucrative gap in the British market for coffee. He established an Italian Caffè that imported the famed Gaggia espresso machine to his Dean Street premises in Soho. His customers grew exponentially and by 1953, he had opened a café in the basement that he baptised the Gaggia Experimental Coffee Bar.[15]

The success of Riservato and his imitators subsequently led to the 'espresso revolution', demonstrated by the accelerated growth of cafés in London and across the country: 'coffee bars were convenient ... In the coffee bar there was little of the formality, ritual and expense ... there were no licensing laws regulating the age of customers and hours of business'.[16] Commentators proclaimed that these were spaces of social revolution, while journalists began to document their relationship with mass culture and other growing forms of popular entertainment – they represented a break from 'working-class culture, with its values of solidarity, home and community [an] empty and vapid expression of mass culture'.[17]

Matthew Partington argues that: 'Writers since the 1950s have tended to refer to the coffee bars as if they were one distinct type of teenage social space. Whilst it was evident by the late 1950s that "the teen scene revolved around coffee bars", they continued to cater for a clientele beyond just the teenager.'[18] However, I argue that social/cultural studies insist on this association because of the significant convergence of modes of consumerism; coffee bar landlords, advertising agencies, the music industry and, lastly, cinema aggressively aligned youth culture with coffee bar culture to capture the public imagination. The rise of the coffee bar coincided with the popularity of imported American rock 'n' roll. The increase in the sales of American pop records was 'based not merely on consumer affluence but also on technological innovation', and the inception of the jukebox directly challenged live musical performances, offering a 'crass American commercialism' as a cheap alternative.[19] Less than a decade later, it was announced that jukeboxes in London cafés would 'each night emit during what was formerly the almost imperceptible pause between records, short commercial announcements of interest to the teenage market'.[20]

From 1956 onwards, teenage consumers became a significant economic contributor during the postwar years, and in turn, a figure of fascination. As we will discover, in most of these youth films, the teenage consumer was both exploited and demonised.[21] Alongside the boom in coffee bars, there was alleged moral panic over teenagers' association with them: 'Throughout the 1950s and early 1960s, the post-war press, social investigators and many politicians presented teenage behaviour as both a cause and a consequence of a generational clash.'[22] However, it would appear that the social problems regarding the 'coffee club menace' were primarily confined to London and cities in the North such as Manchester with sizeable entertainment and commercial centres undergoing extensive postwar redevelopment following the Blitz. The coffee bar's popularity with teenagers meant that these areas were subjected to persistent regulation by police and the local authorities'.[23] The reputation of cities with red-light districts like Manchester and London grew as a concern because of the spatial positioning of youth leisure venues that were near centres of vice.[24]

Throughout the 1950s, café spaces were used as testing grounds for burgeoning pop stars. Val Guest was first introduced to popstar Cliff Richard at the historic 2i's Coffee Bar, located at 59 Old Compton Street, which, in turn, led Richard to be cast in *Expresso Bongo*. The 2i's Coffee Bar was opened in 1955 by Freddie and Sammy Irani and was managed by Tom Littlewood in 1958.[25] It was responsible for launching the careers of Terry Dene, The Beatles, and Tommy Steele. The film is often deemed the 'first British pop film'. Andrew Caine has looked at its origins through the lens of the careers of Steele, Richard and Adam Faith.[26] Other films from this teenager and 1950s coffee bar canon include *The Golden Disc/The In-Between Age* (Don Sharp, 1958), a film set in Soho's coffee bars, and *Serious Charge/A Touch of Hell* (Terence Young, 1959), which takes place in a Northern town called Bellington and was Cliff Richard's first film. The film provided 'discourses of youth, delinquency and rock 'n' roll in a coffee bar … Cliff sings to his own records that are playing on the jukebox'.[27] These examples highlight the ways in which the coffee bar was translated into a 'metonymic icon in British films' and, as I will explore in the next section with regard to *Beat Girl* and *Rag Doll*, a symbol of female desire.[28]

Beat Girl (1960)

Beat Girl marked Gréville's second film set in Soho. Whereas *Noose* (1948) mapped its black-market crime narrative onto a topography of American film noir-inspired nightclubs and industrial Fleet Street publishing houses, in contrast, *Beat Girl* is shot primarily within two spaces, the Off-Beat Café and Les Girls strip club. Soho was reconstructed at MGM British Studios in Borehamwood during the summer of 1959. The sets were designed by Elven Webb, who would later win the Academy Award for Best Art Direction for his work on *Cleopatra* (Joseph Mankiewicz, 1963). During the film's production in August, it shared a studio lot at MGM and a star (Christopher Lee) with *Too Hot to Handle* (Terence Young, 1960) filming next door. It was also shot on location, on the corner of Old Compton Street and Greek Street. The exteriors for Jennifer's father Paul's Chelsea house were shot in Marylebone and the sequence preceding the 'chickee run' drag race where Jennifer and her gang attend a candlelit party were shot in the Chislehurst Caves in Kent.

The film was photographed by Walter Lassally, an émigré cinematographer from Berlin who arrived in Britain in 1939. Following *Beat Girl*, he collaborated with the Free Cinema Movement's leading members Tony Richardson, Lindsay Anderson and Karel Reisz, and later won the Academy Award for Best Cinematography for *Zorba the Greek* (Michael Cacoyannis, 1964). In an interview with Peter Bowen in 2004, Lassally described *Beat Girl* as a 'lost film' and Gréville as a director who 'didn't like straight set-ups. He was always photographing from under the legs of a table, or through somebody's armpit ... he had a strange idea of what makes an interesting composition'.[29] It was executive produced and distributed by George Minter, founder of Renown Pictures in 1938, a film distribution company that released the notorious *No Orchids for Miss Blandish* (St John Legh Clowes, 1948). Minter was also responsible for producing other London-set British 'B' films such as *The Rough and the Smooth* (Robert Siodmak, 1959) and *Tread Softly Stranger* (Gordon Parry, 1958).[30]

The film was given an 'X' rating by the British censors for multiple scenes of violence, sexually suggestive lyrics of several songs performed by Adam Faith and the notorious three-minute strip scene, which Kristopher Spencer has proclaimed 'one of the hottest strip club scenes to appear in a non-pornographic film before, during or after the decency code'.[31] Stephen Glynn has published an extensive history into the public resistance to the film after it was submitted to the British censors in March 1959.[32] According to Hills, the film was banned in France. Vic

Pratt similarly confirms that this 'beautifully, hypnotically, intoxicatingly, ludicrously brilliant film' was banned in 'Italy, Israel, South Africa, Turkey, and Malaysia … in Singapore, the censor wouldn't pass on it because Gillian, as the wayward daughter, was rude to her parents. Dig that, daddy-o!'[33] Although there is no way to substantiate this embargo, it was certainly reviled by commentators. *Variety* described it as a '[c]heap little dualer about a London kid who gets mixed up with beatniks … uninspired. Briefly, a British film in which the local industry can take little pride'.[34] This scathing critique reflected the general mood of the press on teen exploitation films of this period.

Spaces of Rebellion

The story of *Beat Girl* is essentially a bildungsroman, chronicling Jennifer's sexual awakening through her exposure to striptease and the generational divide with her father Paul, who has recently married a young French woman (Noëlle Adam). Paul is a man wholly consumed by his newest architectural project called 'City 2000', in relation to which David Sterritt states: 'A logical progression from the Levittowns of '50s America, this design is presented as social engineering at its most advanced and most intimidating.'[35] Katherine Shonfield has examined the architecture of Paul's modern apartment in depth, suggesting that it critiques the 'politics of pure architecture'.[36] The film, she claims, 'draws a parallel with the architect's denial of the physical interior of their domestic home and his synonymous denial and ignorance of his daughter's *interior* life – what is going on in her head. To express this, the film creates a unique architectural interior.'[37]

Gréville's purposefully juxtaposes the bland, interior of Jennifer's home, which has 'done away with all signs of human inhabitation', with the cramped and communal Off-Beat Café. There is barely an inch of space in which to move and with very little of the walls left bare, which are plastered with posters advertising pop records (including the soundtrack of *Expresso Bongo*). However, Paul's bewilderment for his daughter's choice of lifestyle is less about her independence and more about the drastic differences between them in terms of aesthetic and commercial taste:

> PAUL: And where do you get your kicks from? Sitting around in cafés, listening to gramophone records? Jiving in underground cellars and caves?

> JENNIFER: *You* are *a real square, aren't you?*
> PAUL: *This language, these words, what does it mean?*[38]

Jennifer attends the St Martin's School of Art and Design, which at this time was located on Charing Cross Road, a short stroll from Soho (today, the school is located in a new development called the Granary Building in King's Cross). Jennifer's spatial proximity to Soho allows her to freely hang out in cafés and jive to the latest rock 'n' roll record during her lunch hour. Her pursuit of youth subculture as an antidote to boredom and her histrionic declarations on the futility of life are clear references to the Nicholas Ray's celebrated *Rebel Without a Cause* (1955). According to David Sterritt, Jennifer and her gang are representative of the 'generic adolescent anomie (postwar variety) with alleged Beat Nihilism and despair over the future'.[39] Throughout the film, Jennifer expresses fear over potential nuclear war and the need to live 'in the moment'. During one argument with her father, she cries: 'Next week – boom! The world goes up in smoke and what's the score? Zero!'[40] But the film's association with American 'Beat' culture stops right there. Jennifer and her gang's preference for listening to rock 'n' roll looks more 'ahead to the swinging-England scene of the later '60s rather than back to the Beat-bopping '40s and '50s'.[41] David E. James agrees that 'the film's music is linked to neither the cultural industry nor the wider social world'.[42] The lack of authentic Beat culture in the film means very little, for Jennifer's behaviour is more or less dictated by her peers, who are described in the script as follows: Dodo (Shirley Anne Field), 'Blonde, childlike, in her attempt at world weariness. She's a born follower'; Tony (Peter McEnery), a 'weaker looking, very English public school'; and lastly their ringleader Dave (Adam Faith), a working-class, aspiring singer-songwriter with a 'phoney American accent flavoured with beat "expressions" from mixing with jazz musicians', with whom Jennifer is 'caught in a sadomasochistic relationship fraught with class tensions'.[43]

Pop Music, Class Tensions and Generational Fracture

Composer John Barry and his lyricist Trevor Peacock's pop songs are performed throughout the film as if live (though really they were lip-synced) by Faith in the film. One other song, 'It's Legal', is sung by Dodo before Jennifer's defiant strip, after being provoked by Dave, who calls her 'as phony as an iceberg' during an illicit house party. Besides the commercial implications of hiring pop star Faith to play Jennifer's love interest, the songs are chiefly sexual in connotation. The song 'Made You', which is sung by Dave to Jennifer at the café early in the film, signals Faith's intention to pursue and ultimately take Jennifer's virginity. The lines of the first verse emphasise her sexual inexperience as a 'schoolgirl' and compare her burgeoning sexuality with dynamite. The lyrics by Trevor Peacock read as follows: 'I saw you sitting there so cool, Like you just come home from school, Like a stick of dynamite, sitting on a coffee bar stool, You're a gasser that's a fact and I never can relax until I've *made* you.'[44] By comparing Jennifer's sexual inhibitions to inauthenticity, working-class Dave is also questioning her loyalty to beat culture and her identity as an upper-middle-class metropolitan. Unfortunately, the sexual frisson between Jennifer and Dave goes largely undeveloped in the film in favour of the Jennifer versus Nichole plotline.

Roger Philip Mellor places *Beat Girl* 'firmly in the exploitation genre'.[45] The screenplay, like *West End Jungle* (Arnold L. Miller, 1960), 'takes a typically prurient, "News of the World" approach, allowing the viewer to enjoy the illicit activities of strip clubs and Soho vice but with a perfunctory moral tagged on at the end'.[46] But the end of the film, by which time Jennifer has been rescued by Paul and Nichole after witnessing Greta stab Kenny in his office in the Les Girl club (a narrative that is neither developed nor rationalised in any substantial way other than revenge), remains a conundrum for many, including Stephen Glynn, who states that: 'The unresolved conclusion to *Beat Girl* continues to confuse ... It is a cry to *parental* rather than patriarchal control ... It is again a familiar trope of female melodrama.'[47]

For John Hill, the film represents the domestic life as another source of repression. After Jennifer is rescued by her parents, the 'energy and vitality of the Soho world survives' and there is no other mention of justice or retribution for the Soho characters.[48] The film passes no judgement on spaces of vice, meaning Jennifer's interaction with Soho does not represent a form of rebellion. The space of the coffee bar and the strip club are merely superficial tools used by the film to highlight the fractured nature of her family life. Jennifer escapes from vice by rejecting the Soho coffee bar community and the film ultimately denotes it as an immoral influence on the postwar generation.

Rag Doll (1961)

Rag Doll was described by one critic from the *Monthly Film Bulletin* as a 'meandering picture' that 'tells a nickelodian story against London nightlife backgrounds'.[49] The film was directed by Lance Comfort from a story by Brock Williams, who wrote the screenplay with Derry Quinn, a writer who is most well-known for co-writing the award-winning war film *Operation Crossbow* (Michael Anderson, 1965) with Emeric Pressburger. The story of *Rag Doll* charts the journey of seventeen-year-old Carol, who is played by Christina Gregg, an actress who modelled extensively for the *Daily Mirror* throughout the 1960s.[50] As an actress, she appeared in several low-budget films such as *Don't Talk to Strange Men* (Pat Jackson, 1962), where she plays an innocent country girl who is groomed by an anonymous caller. The year before going into production for *Rag Doll*, she played a small role as the ill-fated beauty queen from Torquay in the Soho-set *Cover Girl Killer* (1959).

Until recently, director Lance Comfort has been a forgotten figure in British cinema history despite a substantial record directing 'A' feature films during the war, followed by an extremely prolific period directing and producing for television. Brian McFarlane proclaims him as one of the most 'unjustly neglected directors' within film scholarship.[51] His frequent collaborators included the cinematographer Basil Emmott, composer Martin Slavin and producer Tom Blakeley of the Mancunian Film Corporation.[52] McFarlane and Chibnall suggest that Comfort's idiosyncratic use of location, together with Emmott's stark photography, reflected the filmmaker's keen interest in juxtaposing urban and pastoral landscapes. Emmott's style greatly benefited *Rag Doll* with 'black-and-white images of urban threat and delusive rural calm'.[53] He also provided 'authentic touch of drab ordinariness … and imbues the pastoral … with an undertow of shabbiness'.[54]

Protagonist Carol works as a waitress for her stepfather Paddy (Patrick Magee) at his roadhouse café on the Great North Road, a highway that once functioned as the main route for mail coaches between London and Edinburgh.[55] After one of the café patrons, a trucker named Harry (Michael Wynne), attempts to rape her (this sexual violation is despicably encouraged by Paddy in exchange for a bottle of gin), Carol is rescued by another driver Wills (Patrick Jordan) and duly hitches a ride with him to London. The film subtly implies that Carol, whi has been known since childhood by the regulars as 'Rag Doll', was molested by her stepfather in the years after her mother's death. This is emphasised throughout the film through her revulsion to being physically touched by adult men.

Carol's Soho

Shortly after Carol's arrival in London, she is given refuge by a Soho local, Princess Sophie (Hermione Baddeley, who also played a prostitute in *Expresso Bongo*), who is nicknamed 'Auntie' by the local community. Auntie is also a retired prostitute who works as a fortune-teller at a West End arcade owned by a middle-aged entrepreneur named Mort Wilson (Kenneth Griffith). Mort owns several Soho nightclubs and cafés, including the Cave Coffee Bar, which is located adjacent to the arcade. He immediately offers Carol a job as a waitress at the coffee bar, justifying this heartfelt act of charity as a type of superstition and belief in spreading his luck. He then proceeds to shower her with gifts and nights out dancing in the West End.

Figure 8.2. Carol (Christina Gregg) arrives in Soho. Still, *Rag Doll* (Lance Comfort, 1961). DVD, Odeon Entertainment, 2009

The film then shifts its focus midway through the film on to Carol's doomed love affair with a teenage pop singer named Jo Shane (Jess Conrad), who previously worked as a pimp for a Soho gang. After engaging in a secretive sexual relationship with him, she falls pregnant. The couple hastily marry at the Paddington Registry Office. In order to finance Joe's plan for them to emigrate to Canada, he burgles Mort's house safe, which contains a substantial amount of his business capital. As Mort discovers Jo escaping with the case of money through his kitchen window, Jo panics and shoots him dead. The film concludes with a frantic police chase through woodland and the film depicts Jo's death as a type of execution.

The film's interior sequences were shot primarily at Walton Studios, Walton-on-Thames. Art director John Earl's construction of interior and public spaces, including a West End arcade and the expansive and modernist Cave Coffee Bar, displays a comprehensive knowledge of the topography of Soho. As with the Off-Beat Café, the Cave Coffee Bar operates a members-only dance club in its basement known as the Spanish Dive. The film also features several sequences shot on location in London, spotlighting several city landmarks such as Tower Bridge and Trafalgar Square. The West End, Oxford Street, Paddington and North End Road Market in Fulham, West London, also feature as key locations in the film. Unlike *Beat Girl*, Comfort also shot considerable amounts of footage around Soho. The tracking shot, a 'Postcard London' introduction to the commercial heartbeat of the city that accompanies Carol being driven into the city at night, is a parallel to Jim Blankley's first late-night ramble through the square mile in *Soho Incident* (Vernon Sewell, 1956).

Like *Beat Girl*, the prologue's kinetic and youthful energy is produced through the use of a rock 'n' roll soundtrack by British jazz composer Martin Slavin. Throughout the film, Slavin's pop motif, which contains a signature fingerstyle technique and a chorus of voices provided by the Michael 'Mike' Sammes Singers, is deployed during moments of rising melodrama. Chibnall and McFarlane have shown that many film distributors employed Slavin and others in order to 'embellish its crime narratives with songs that it hoped might appeal to audiences and might also provide lucrative recording spin-offs'.[56] Slavin later collaborated with Comfort on *Pit of Darkness* (1961) and *The Painted Smile* (1962).

The casting of real-life pop star Jess Conrad as the male lead Jo Shane reflects the closing partition between cinema and popular music in the 1960s demonstrated by the casting of pop stars Tommy Steele, Adam Faith and Cliff Richard in film.

Carol's first encounter with Jo occurs at one of Mort's nightclubs where he performs the song 'Why Am I Living?' to an adoring, largely middle-aged audience. The lyrics were written by Abbe Gail with the Michael Sammes Singers and clearly aimed to raise commercial awareness for the film. The song was reported in several trade magazines to have been recorded for British record label Decca. However, famed British music impresario Jack Good, who discovered Jess Conrad during his ITV television live music series *Wham!* (1960), critiqued the track in *Disc* with a scolding commentary: 'You can see Jess sing it in the film ... I must say I am quite surprised ... I wonder, is popular music the right vehicle for expressing the morbid philosophy of an immoral beatnik?'[57]

Jackson and Bartie's examination of the public anxieties around postwar teenage sexuality provides important context for *Rag Doll*'s warnings on the dangers of promiscuity before marriage. But the film also conveys the fear of commercialisation, embodied by Jo, who, like Dave in *Beat Girl*, is superficially representative of the archetypal teenage beatnik, as demonstrated by the nihilism of his theme song 'Why Am I Living?', where the lyrics of the second verse state: 'You're on your own, to die, I'm gonna take what I can.'[58] John Barron Mays suggests that British teenagers who emulated American teenage subculture are 'almost always no more than pseudo-beats, engaged in self-dramatization, rather than total rejectors [sic] of the social structure who find nothing left to live for'.[59] Carol and Jo's desire to live 'for the moment' leads them to embark on a sexual affair as a form of self-preservation.

Carol and Café Spaces

Carol's precarious life working at the roadhouse coffee bar, a place she later describes as a 'good pull-in for Wolves', does not simply function as a convenient narrative catalyst for her decision to move to London leading to the discovery of metropolitan café culture. The atypical interior of the roadhouse café, which features small tables covered by chequered tablecloths, windows framed by chintz curtains, a jukebox and framed posters on the wall of young women holding bottles of Coca-Cola, highlight the ways in which hardworking Carol has attempted to rearticulate the café as a commercial and feminine space, perhaps in an attempt to retain some position of power within the constricted boundaries of the café, owned her alcoholic stepfather and filled with predominantly male patrons. Carol's rebellion is represented by the jukebox, on which she plays the same song on repeat whilst she does her chores. For her, it is symbolic of a better life and freedom from tyranny.

Carol's strong work ethic at the roadhouse café and, later, working as a waitress for Mort at the Cave Coffee Bar and Club in Soho reinforces the sentiments attached to the coffee bar boom in 1950s Soho by young women working in the area, an area deemed as 'the mecca' by residents. Through the lens of a young dressmaker named Rico Teagno, Judith Summers emphasises the draw of this revolutionary space for young people. In one interview, Rico describes the fervour of excitement she felt over the gradual dissolve of the 'old caffs' to the novel Italian espresso bars in this period. This prompted her to leave her position at a dressmaker in Mayfair in order join her father's catering business in Soho:

> 'It was hard work, but you met interesting people,' she recalls. 'I belonged there. It was my domain. When all the people started to come in, I was very proud, actually. I thought, they're coming into my place.'[60]

Carol's parallel desire to belong to a community as depicted by the admirable immigrant entrepreneurial spirit in *Miracle in Soho* is echoed by her eagerness to 'fit in' with café culture in Soho. When she first enters the café, her likeness is described by Mort as a small, vulnerable 'chick' who looks as if 'she's just dropped out of the nest'.[61] As Fink and Tinkler have shown, 'Carol's hairstyle, clothes and bodily demeanour make her girl-woman status immediately recognisable. In a single glance, the coffee bar owner, Mort, can tell "she's a nice girl"; "nice" being a euphemism for a lack of knowledge and experience of sex'.[62] A waitress approaches Carol after she sits down at a table and enquires: 'Espresso, Cappuccino or Café Doppio?' As Carol has no knowledge of Continental food and drink, she nods ignorantly and asks the waitress to choose for her. She is also brought a plate of spaghetti, a dish she has never tried before. The Cave Coffee Bar is therefore depicted as a neighbourhood space of 'elusive sophistication' upon which these teenagers greatly rely as a space of leisure, away from parental authority.[63] The interior of the Cave Coffee Bar draws from the design of a typical 1950s Italian expresso bar as described by commentators at the time. It features a large dining room surrounded by potted plants and a shiny Gaggi machine sits behind the bar. The Spanish Dive Club below is filled with archetypal iconography of Spanish culture. Lit only by candles, there are antique masks and sombrero hats mounted on the walls. There is also a large dancefloor with space for a live band. It is the antithesis of the coffee bar above, which is more reflective of the 'new kind of playful, hyperbolic Modernist design style. At the time, purists derided it as "Theatrical" and "Fake", arguing that it was more like interior design than architecture'.[64] This notion that the architecture is 'fake' is echoed by Wilson's business ethos. After Carol has settled into her new life working and living (with Auntie in a flat above Berwick Street market) in Soho, Mort begins to woo her romantically by inviting her to dance and dine in his various nightclubs. One evening, after seeing Jo perform for the first time, Mort acknowledges the superficiality of consumerism and the ways in which he exploits teenagers by offering them a return to childhood innocence:

> MORT: They come here to find out what it's all about. Laid up. Full treatment. Soho. Beatniks. That's what these phoney places are for! There's a twist. You know what it is? Shane's genuine. Carol, people want heroes. I mean, what did we play at when we were kids?
> CAROL: You tell me.
> MORT: Billy the Kid. Frontier. When people did as they like. No problems. No complications. Youngsters want to feel that way too. Free. So, they have to have their heroes. Pop singers are only a cowboy once removed. Guitar. Blue jeans. I wouldn't have been so successful if I hadn't understood what the teenagers want. Anything but the hard, simple, truth. That's for later.[65]

Mort's self-reflexive speech is similar to the nihilism expressed by *Beat Girl*'s Dave. Although Mort's role as Carol's guide to engaging in metropolitan pleasures, alongside the subtle indications that he is a criminal, makes him a red herring as well as the mouthpiece for the film, his character highlights the film's message for the hypocrisy of promoting mass consumerism to young people under the guise of independence and liberation.

Fink and Tinkler have argued that *Rag Doll* is a neglected postwar film that offered a unique representation of young womanhood framed within a narrative driven by Carol's 'nascent sexuality and adolescent immaturity'.[66] On a superficial level, *Rag Doll* is 'an unremarkable morality tale about how the big city nearly ruins a provincial girl'.[67] However, the film also provides a 'particularly graphic rendering of the predatory nature of men', as demonstrated by the opening sequence at the roadhouse café.[68] Carol's reciprocated sexual desire for Jo shows that the film adheres to the conventional expectations of a social problem film, offering a sympathetic portrayal of premarital sex from a female perspective. I argue that this is largely due to Carol's newly adopted, *anonymous* urban identity.

Carol's social advancement in London provides a conventional representation of Soho as a gateway to economic and sexual possibility for teenagers. But her advancement is hindered by her role as a sexual commodity. Jane Rendell's work on spatial stories and women as commodities in public spaces allows us to better understand Carol's relationship with the men of the film that is demarcated by public space. Rendell suggests that: 'On the market, in the public realm of commerce ... woman as commodity is visible ... As virgin, woman is on the market ... Once deflowered, woman is relegated to the status of use value, to her entrapment in private property: she is removed from exchange among men'.[69] Carol is first the domestic property of her stepfather, then the virginal protégé of Mort and, finally, the sexual object for Jo. Her identity then drifts between the atypical '"problem girl", the "good time girl", and the "wayward girl"'.[70] Therefore, the potential of the film to advance a different narrative from those contemporaneous teenage problem films concerned with the anxieties surrounding teenage sexuality and the 'decline in Christian values and moral standards' is obstructed.[71]

Conclusion

Beat Girl utilises Soho as a 'location to run together the teen world of coffee bars with the illegitimate sexuality of the strip club', confirming the suggestion made by filmmakers that the coffee bar is a dangerous and subversive gateway to immorality.[72] *Rag Doll* initially suggests that the Soho coffee bar is a sanctuary from those corrupt spaces beyond the peripheries of London. However, Carol is ultimately punished, as she is left destitute without a partner as a single mother. Both films overtly warned audiences of the seduction of London and, in the words of Mort, who warns Carol on pursuing Jo for pleasure: 'He's a bad lot ... A genuine bad lot.'[73] The combined sexual and criminal element of these films clearly signals the approaching women's liberation movement in British cinema. These films were released shortly before the celebrated, award-winning film adaptation of Shelagh Delaney's play *A Taste of Honey* (Tony Richardson, 1961), which spotlighted interracial relationships and premarital sex. Its success stimulated the subsequent production of more and more films that examined the lives of young women, later dubbed the 'Swinging London' film canon. These films follow female characters who relocate from provincial towns and villages to the capital, such as *Billy Liar* (John Schlesinger, 1963), *Darling* (John Schlesinger, 1965), *The Knack* (Richard Lester, 1965) and *Smashing Time* (Desmond Davis, 1967).[74] The mid-1960s film *The Knack* follows the bright-eyed Nancy (Rita Tushingham) to London so that she may encounter new adventures. Luckett suggests that Nancy 'does not simply enter this new space as a tourist: she conquers it'.[75] Instead, she 'trusts in a feminine image of public space and carries this with her into the city'.[76] In contrast, Carol and Jennifer trust in a *masculine* image of the city, as engagement with the liminal space of the coffee bar is operated by male entrepreneurs and exploited by male musicians.[77] Although I argue that Carol's journey is more of a reflection of Julia Gozzi's own struggle to choose between love and emigration in *Miracle in Soho*, both of these films represent the coffee bar as a gateway to hedonism, petty crime and sexual liberation through the initial depiction of idealised forms of femininity that are then dismantled due to the absence of parental control and exposure to Soho's commercialised vice.

Notes

1. Following her acting debut in *Beat Girl*, Hills appeared in the British/European films *Blow up* (Michelangelo Antonioni, 1966) and *A Clockwork Orange* (Stanley Kubrick, 1971). Her French pop hit 'Zou Bisou Bisou' – recorded in 1960 – re-entered the mainstream after it was sung on series five of the hit television show *Mad Men* in 2015. See Trevor Johnston, 'From Beat Girl to Mad Men: The Life of Gillian Hills', *BFI Online*, 11 July 2016. Retrieved 21 October 2021 from http://www.bfi.org.uk/news-opinion/sight-sound-magazine/interviews/gillian-hills-beat-girl.
2. Hills' appearance in the film – bouffant blonde hair, cat-eye eyeliner, slacks and ballet flats – is clearly a reference to the French bombshell, the actress/singer Brigitte Bardot, who, by this time, was a bona fide celebrity. See Roger Philip Mellor, '"Beat" Girl (1959)', *BFI Screenonline*. Retrieved 21 October 2021 from http://www.screenonline.org.uk/film/id/1022053.
3. Dail Ambler, 'The Beat Girl', BFI Book Library, 1959, 1.
4. See Johnston, 'From Beat Girl to Mad Men'.
5. Gillian Hills, 'In Discussion with BFI National Archive Fiction Curator Vic Pratt'. Special screening of *Beat Girl* (1960), Regent Street Cinema, London, 20 April 2016, personal transcript.
6. Ibid.
7. Other films that feature young women who turn to stripping in order to 'make it big' include *Passport to Shame* (Alvin Rakoff, 1958), *The Rough and the Smooth* (Robert Siodmak, 1959) and *Too Hot to Handle* (Terence Young, 1960). See Mellor, '"Beat" Girl'.
8. Ambler, 'The Beat Girl' Screenplay, 1.
9. See review of 'Rag Doll', *Monthly Film Bulletin* 28(324) (1961), 67.

10. Janet Fink and Penny Tinkler, 'Teetering on the Edge: Portraits of Innocence, Risk and Young Female Sexualities in 1950s and 1960s British Cinema', *Women's History Review* 26:1 (2017), 1.
11. Ibid., 2.
12. Dominic Sandbrook, *Never Had It So Good: A History of Britain from Suez to The Beatles* (London: Abacus, 2005), 134.
13. Markman Ellis, 'Coffee-Women, *The Spectator* and the Public Sphere in the Early Eighteenth Century', in *Women, Writing and the Public Sphere 1700–1830* (Cambridge: Cambridge University Press, 2001), 27, 30.
14. Ibid., 226.
15. Nonetheless, the speed of the service and the theatre of its production, amid clouds of steam, found favour with customers all over Europe. In 1946 the Italian engineer Archille Gaggia patented a revision to this system: the water was heated to a temperature below boiling point (approximately 90°C), and then forced through the coffee grounds by pressure supplied by pistons powered by the waiter operating the machine. Ibid., 227.
16. Ibid., 233.
17. Ibid., 234.
18. I spoke to Matthew Partington about his excellent conference paper 'The London Coffee Bar of the 1950s', which highlights the tendency in scholarship to assume that coffee bars are a primarily teenage space. He is currently working on a more extensive study, but he rightly identifies the cosmopolitan identity of the coffee bar that is a component of British youth culture, but still a very distinct form of commercial leisure. See 'The London Coffee Bar of the 1950s: Teenage Occupation of an Amateur Space?', Proceedings of the Occupation: Negotiations with Constructed Space Conference, University of Brighton, 2–4 July 2009, 7. Supplied by Matthew Partington.
19. See 'Teenage Tyranny', *The Stage*, 21 November 1957, 12.
20. 'Commercials on Juke Box', *The Guardian*, 15 June 1963, 1.
21. This was primarily due to their large disposal income, which was unprecedented for young people before this period. In 1959, Mark Abrams conducted a study, *The Teenage Consumer* and *Teenage Consumer Spending*. This seminal research project consisted of consumer surveys conducted throughout the year and ultimately concluded that 'quite [a] large amount of money at the disposal of Britain's average teenager is spent mainly on dressing up in order to impress other teenagers … In other words, this is distinctive teenage spending for distinctive teenage ends in a distinctive teenage world'. See Mark Abrams, *The Teenage Consumer* (London: London Press Exchange Ltd., 1959), 10.
22. Hilary Young and Selina Todd, 'Baby-Boomers to "Beanstalkers"', *Cultural and Social History* 9(3) (2012), 451.
23. Young and Todd state 'It was undoubtedly the case that some vulnerable young women were exploited by adults who they met in the unlicensed music clubs of Soho and Manchester. However, what is notable is that the "moral panics" connected to leisure venues tended to brand each "new" phenomenon as a social "menace" and offered little recognition of young people's agency or ability to make choices.' Ibid., 195.
24. In one history of coffee club culture in Manchester between 1962 and 1968, we find that teenage commercial spaces assisted in creating myths about the city itself that, although assisted in its 'reputation of being a swinging city … the police viewed the club culture associated with it – which they linked to drugs misuse, sexual incontinence and juvenile

delinquency – as a "public scandal"'. See Louise A. Jackson, 'The Coffee Club Menace', *Cultural and Social History* 5(3) (2008), 290.

25. Andrew Roberts suggests that Richard was 'typical of an anti-rock musical that also had to appeal to the teenage market, [as] young audiences were keeping many picture houses open in the face of competition from television'. See Andrew Roberts, *Expresso Bongo*, DVD booklet (London: BFI, 2016), 1.
26. See Andrew Caine, *Interpreting Rock Movies: The Pop Film and Its Critics in Britain* (Manchester: Manchester University Press, 2004), 115.
27. See Kevin Donnelly, *British Film Music and Film Musicals* (Basingstoke: Palgrave Macmillan, 2007), 140.
28. 'Britain imported the figure of the rock 'n' roller directly (lock, stock and barrel) from the United States.' See ibid., 140; and Kevin Donnelly, 'The Perpetual Busman's Holiday: Sir Cliff Richard and British Pop Musicals', *Journal of Popular Film and Television* 25(4), 148.
29. Walter Lassally, 'Interview by Peter Bowen', *Web of Stories*, June 2004. Retrieved 21 October 2021 from https://www.webofstories.com/play/walter.lassally.
30. *Beat Girl* was given a completion guarantee by Film Finances Ltd., a completion bond guarantor that supported British productions such as *Peeping Tom*, *Dr. No* (Terence Young, 1962) and *The Servant* (Joseph Losey, 1964). My own visit to the archive revealed documentation on several Soho films that were guaranteed by Film Finances Ltd., including *The Shakedown* (John Lemont, 1960) and *The Small World of Sammy Lee*. As Sarah Street has shown, the company encouraged independent productions that would become known as British New Wave films, guaranteeing 'the most significant' of the canon such as *Room at the Top* (Jack Clayton, 1959), *A Taste of Honey* and *Billy Liar* (John Schlesinger, 1963). See Sarah Street, 'Film Finances and the British New Wave', *Historical Journal of Film, Radio and Television* 34(1) (2014), 24.
31. Amongst the films that dealt with the themes of young women who attempt to make it in the big city but ultimately suffer at the hands of the sex industry, see *The Good-Time Girl* (David MacDonald, 1948), *Secrets of a Windmill Girl* (Arnold L. Miller, 1966) and *Too Hot to Handle* (Terence Young, 1960). See Kristopher Spencer, *Film and Television Scores, 1950–1979* (Jefferson, NC: McFarland & Company, Inc., 2008), 106.
32. Stephen Glynn, *The British Pop Music Film: The Beatles and Beyond* (Basingstoke: Palgrave Macmillan, 2013).
33. Vic Pratt, 'Beat Girl: Dig That, Daddy-o!', BFI Flipside DVD Booklet, 5–6.
34. See '*Beat Girl* (1959)', *Monthly Film Bulletin* 27(322) (1960), 154; and Rich, 'Film Reviews: "Beat" Girl', *Variety*, 16 November 1960, 6.
35. David Sterritt states that the filmmakers of *Beat Girl* 'don't seem quite sure whether they fear or admire' beat culture. See David Sterritt, *Mad to Be Saved: The Beats, the '50s, and Film* (Carbondale and Edwardsville: Southern Illinois University Press, 1998), 158.
36. Katherine Shonfield, 'Glossing with Graininess: Cross Occupations in Postwar British Film and Architecture', *Journal of Architecture* 3(4) (1998), 370.
37. Ibid.
38. Ambler, 'The Beat Girl' Screenplay, 20.
39. Sterritt, *Mad to Be Saved*, 158.
40. Ibid., 159.
41. Ibid., 158.

42. David E. James, *Rock 'n' Film: Cinema's Dance with Popular Music* (Oxford: Oxford University Press, 2016), 136–37.
43. Dail Ambler describes her protagonists in the final *Beat Girl* script from 1950. See Ambler, 'The Beat Girl' Screenplay, 135.
44. 'Made You', music by John Barry and lyrics by Trevor Peacock from *Beat Girl* (1960).
45. Mellor, '"Beat" Girl'.
46. Ibid.
47. Glynn, *The British Pop Musical Film*, 45.
48. John Hill, *Sex, Class and Realism: British Cinema 1956–1963* (London: BFI, 1997), 119.
49. See review of 'Rag Doll', *Monthly Film Bulletin* 28(324) (1961), 67.
50. 'The three lovelies in swimsuits', the caption reads below a full tabloid-page photograph of Gregg in a bikini. She also appeared in several *Daily Mirror* summer fashion specials. See, for example, *Daily Mirror*, 20 November 1962, 4–5.
51. In 2008, on the centenary of Comfort's birth, the BFI hosted a short season of his work that included his *Temptation Harbour* (1947), an unusual postwar British film full of 'imaginative concentration and moral complexity'. *Temptation Harbour* is now available to rent on the BFI's online streaming service BFI Player. The later film *Daughter of Darkness* (Lance Comfort, 1948) is still unavailable for commercial purchase. For more on this film, see Brian McFarlane, 'Temptation Harbour', *Quarterly Review of Film and Video* 27(5) (2010), 362–64. See also Brian McFarlane, *Lance Comfort* (Manchester: Manchester University Press, 1999).
52. Blakeley also produced Lance Comfort's *The Painted Smile* (1961), *The Break* (1962) and *Tomorrow at Ten* (1962), which starred *Miracle in Soho*'s John Gregson as a detective. Mancunian Films produced over sixty films between 1926 and 1967. However, Lee suggests that it was their comedies that 'regularly outdrew Hollywood movies at the box office'. See C. P. Lee, '"Northern Films for Northern People": The Story of the Mancunian Film Company', in I.Q.Q. Hunter and Laraine Porter (eds), *British Comedy Cinema* (Hoboken, NJ: Taylor & Francis, 2012), 51–65. Cinematographer Emmott also worked with Comfort on *The Painted Smile* (1962), which was released on DVD in 2009 along with *Rag Doll* by Odeon Entertainment, a company that regularly release forgotten postwar, low-budget films, as part of its Best of British Collection.
53. Steve Chibnall and Brian McFarlane, *The British 'B' Film* (London: BFI, 2009), 142.
54. On Basil Emmott (1894 – 1976), 'who has nearly a hundred credits, not all of them for "B" films, see Ibid., 168.
55. In popular culture, the Great North Road is often referred to as the Route 66 of Great Britain. Devised by the Romans, it was later used for mail coaches during the sixteenth century. It was renamed in 1921 as the A1 road, which parallels the original coaching route of the Great North Road. See Charles Harper, *The Great North Road: The Old Mail Road to Scotland*, 2nd edn (London: Cecil Palmer, Bloomsbury, 1922), 2.
56. Ibid., 174.
57. See 'Jack Good: Should This Song Be Put on Wax?', *Disc*, 29 April 1961, 5. See also Jack Good's biography: Tise Vahimagi, 'Jack Good', *BFI Screenonline*. Retrieved 21 October 2021 from http://www.screenonline.org.uk/people/id/574989/index.html.
58. *Rag Doll* (Lance Comfort, 1961).
59. John Barron Mays, 'Teen-Age Culture in Contemporary Britain and Europe', *Annals of the American Academy of Political and Social Science* 338 (1961), 25.

60. Judith Summers, *Soho: A History of London's Most Colourful Neighbourhood* (London: Bloomsbury, 1991), 194–96.
61. *Rag Doll* (Lance Comfort, 1961).
62. Fink and Tinkler, 'Teetering on the Edge', 11.
63. Sandbrook, *Never Had It So Good*, 134.
64. Ellis, *The Coffee-House: A Cultural History* (Weidenfeld & Nicolson, 2004), 231.
65. *Rag Doll* (Lance Comfort, 1961).
66. Fink and Tinkler, 'Teetering on the Edge', 1.
67. Chibnall and McFarlane, *The British 'B' Film*, 168.
68. Fink and Tinkler, 'Teetering on the Edge', 11.
69. Jane Rendell, '"Bazaar Beauties", or "Pleasure Is Our Pursuit": A Spatial Story of Exchange', in Iain Borden, Joe Kerr, Jane Rendall and Alicia Pivaro (eds), *The Unknown City: Contesting Architecture and Social Space* (Cambridge, MA: MIT Press, 2000), 110.
70. Louise Jackson and Angela Bartie, *Policing Youth: Britain, 1945–70* (Manchester: Manchester University Press, 2014), 117.
71. Ibid.
72. Hill, *Sex, Class and Realism*, 19.
73. *Rag Doll* (Lance Comfort, 1961).
74. Jackson and Bartie have suggested that the premiere of Delaney's play on stage in 1958, which depicted 'inter-racial relationships, teenage pregnancy and homosexuality … offered new social realities and important counter-narrative to the voices of experts and officials in church and state'. Jackson and Bartie, *Policing Youth*, 118.
75. Moya Luckett, 'Travel and Mobility: Femininity and National Identity in Swinging London Films', in Andrew Higson and Justine Ashby (eds), *British Cinema: Past and Present* (London: Routledge, 2000), 238.
76. Ibid.
77. Jackson and Bartie, *Policing Youth*, 186.

CHAPTER 9

Soho Strip Clubs (Part One)
The Windmill Theatre and Its Cinematic Legacy

> *The audience is a bit sad. This is 'typically' British. So is the way in which we give the Lord Chamberlain powers of censorship and a law which allows clubs to open in the afternoon, which is why, in Soho at the moment, we can see the uncovering of a multitude of skins.*
>
> —*Soho Striptease Clubs* (John Rhodes, 1958)

In the summer of 1958, Daniel Farson, a journalist, raconteur and later author of *Soho in the Fifties* (1987), paid a visit to the newly opened Panama Theatre Club accompanied by a seasoned camera crew of ITV's *This Week*, a current affairs programme that was broadcast on UK television between 1956 and 1968. The Panama Club was a nonstop revue strip club operated by Len Mitelle and was located on the fringes of Soho and Piccadilly Circus at 69 Great Windmill Street.[1] The club was situated south of the famed Windmill Theatre, a theatre that 'for an age held a surprising monopoly on nudity – but in Van Damm's famous hall the tinselled torsos stood frozenly still'.[2] The Windmill Theatre's reputation was cemented by its unique staging of female nudity in the form of static, nude tableaus from 1932 until it closed in 1964. As Walkowitz has shown in her expansive history of the Windmill Theatre, in order to rationalise the public staging of nudity for the Lord Chamberlain, the official censor for British theatre, an agreement was made between the censors and proprietors, which maintained that nude displays acted as a 'safety valve to contain disorderly male sexuality and would act to enhance London's reputation as an international tourist attraction'.[3]

Farson's documentary is an important example of the ways in which the popular press exploited the commercial sex industry in order to boost readership during this period, whilst maintaining strict moral attitudes on the dangers of metropolitan vice.[4] Similar campaigns were developed by strip club owners such as Paul Raymond, who sought to attract affluent members of society in order to cement a pseudo-image of respectability in the public consciousness. These conflicting strategies were used in *The Small World of Sammy Lee* (1963) in its attempt to convey gritty realism, whilst showcasing explicit striptease. The decision to spotlight the striptease club in documentary form is unsurprising because it proved to be the more popular of the new and aggressive forms of sexual commerce that proliferated in the postwar metropolis. British Pathé produced its own version of *Soho Striptease Clubs* the same year entitled *Clubs Galore!*, which featured an exclusive interview with Paul Raymond.[5] Other documentaries released in the 1960s period, such as *Carousella* (John Irving, 1965), provide more graphic striptease performances, but aimed for authenticity through depicting the lives of three real-life performers in Soho.

Throughout this period, the press entertained its readers with first-hand accounts and interviews conducted within illicit and forbidden strip clubs located in Soho. In one article from the *New Statesman* published in 1959, reporter Tom Baistow provides an evocative account of his visit to one unnamed Soho basement club, where he meets a performer, Miss Janette. Following her striptease act, she 'emerges in a demure black frock. Now she looks like someone's sister. Over a gin and lime, I ask her how she likes the job'.[6] In 1960, the popular press estimated there to be 300 strip clubs in Britain and 200 strip clubs in London. Frank Mort states that the annual turnover of these clubs stood at £2 million a year from 1958.[7] However, 'an accurate figure is elusive because they flit as elusively as the bulbs on a pin-table. But enough of them have opened in the past three years to have caused the Public Morality Council to brand London "the Mecca of the strip-tease industry"'.[8]

The space of the strip club appeared in a plethora of low-budget British crime thrillers from the late 1950s onwards. Chibnall and McFarlane have confirmed that by this period, 'the nightclub [was] increasingly a strip club and songs are supplemented by gyrating tassels and enough wobbling cellulite to cause disquiet among the censors of Soho Square'.[9] Films such as *Night and the City* (Jules Dassin, 1950), *Face the Music* (Terence Fisher, 1954), *Undercover Girl* (Francis Searle, 1958), *Cover Girl Killer* (Terence Bishop, 1959), *Jungle Street* (Charles Saunders, 1961) and *The World Ten Times Over* (Wolf Rilla, 1963) projected archetypal representations of the Soho strip club and clip-joint in London: underground smoke-filled basements where bloated male audience members wearing mackintoshes ogle and whistle at female strippers who peel off articles of clothing whilst shimmying and shaking to syncopated rhythms.[10] The examination of the day-to-day operations and employees of strip clubs were depicted by several Soho-set films, such as *Beat Girl* (Edmond T. Gréville, 1960), *Expresso Bongo* (Val Guest, 1960), *Too Hot to Handle* (Terence Young, 1960), *Strip Tease Murder* (Ernest Morris, 1961) and *The Small World of Sammy Lee*. However, the fictional strip club, the 'In-Time Theatre' from *Expresso Bongo*, *Cover Girl Killer* and *Strip Tease Murder* project a far more tongue-in-cheek, arguably more conservative representation of the Soho strip club, as emphasised by their musical numbers, which were wholly reminiscent of the Windmill Theatre's choreography, which itself was 'reassuringly wholesome and domesticated'.[11]

Drawing on Mort's summation that 'Striptease is a productive point of departure from which to unpack important strands in the cultural meanings [and] consumption associated with the sexual changes to London's post-war commercial culture', this chapter will trace an expansive historiography of striptease from its function as wartime propaganda to a highly commercial product.[12] Through examining cinema's engineering of striptease, we will uncover a deeper appreciation for these low-budget exploitation films, which aimed to expose the world of Soho's vice to the general public. The absence of literature on the way in which cinema ascribes further meaning to striptease/strip clubs renders it a unique and worthy topic for discussion.[13] This chapter forms the first part of my study of Soho striptease clubs. It will focus on the legacy of the first strip club in Soho, the Windmill Theatre, charting its impact upon the evolution of the nonstop revue and its postwar successor, Paul Raymond's Revuebar, whose origins were adapted for the screen in Michael Winterbottom's *The Look of Love* (2013).

The Windmill Theatre

The Windmill Theatre was a national institution, famed for staying open throughout the Blitz during the Second World War.[14] Its motto 'We Never Closed' become synonymous with nationalistic sentiments and was used as a device to boost morale during wartime. According to Walkowitz, these strategies formed part of Blitz propaganda in their pseudo-demonstration of patriotism, which in turn symbolised the developing 'consumer industries of the 1930s', embodying 'suburban values in an urban setting ... transmuting ordinariness into an idealized expression of wartime morale'.[15] The Windmill 'purveyed its borderline erotic material in a border space between the West End and Soho [its] liminal geography was crucial to its commercial success and political survival'.[16] The building originally functioned as the Palais de Luxe cinema when it opened in 1909. Mrs Laura Henderson, the wealthy widow of a jute merchant, who purchased and renovated the theatre in 1930. Over two years, it failed to be profitable as a traditional playhouse and again as a cinema. However, once Henderson recruited British-Jewish *bon vivant* Vivian van Damm, the 'liveliest of go-getters of Wardour Street' who was married to the niece of Joe Lyons of the Lyons food empire, she was then able to reimagine and ultimately renovate the space.[17] Shortly after taking up the post, van Damm was approached by French producer Lucien Samett and together they devised the Windmill's chief theatrical programme entitled *Revudeville*, a show that would run from 2.30 PM until 11 PM and would consist of four performances running for approximately two hours, with seven minutes for each act:

> That genre was 'revue', itself an offshoot of so-called 'variety theatre', the latter-day incarnation of music hall ... Like variety, revue consisted of numerous sketches and other routines ... Where revues diverged from variety shows was in their thematic cohesiveness, often signposted by their titles. Assimilating the words 'revue' and 'nude', Revudeville *hinted at both the show's preoccupation with sex and its star turn – a troupe of attractive young girls, minus their clothes.*[18]

According to Mike Hutton, a striptease variety show produced by an unnamed and unmarked strip club located down a nearby Soho street inspired van Damm's decision to include nudity in the mill's reformulated revue. However, because the Windmill was located in an area historically shaped by cosmopolitanism and sexual commerce, the 'Lord Chamberlain, the theatre censor, could be more easily persuaded to license the performance of stationary nude tableaux at a theatre tucked into a Soho side street'.[19] The Theatre's success was also 'hinged on the savvy marketing strategies' deployed by its owner Mrs Henderson who cast her interest in the transformation of the former cinema into a music and dance variety space.[20]

Soho's long association with female nudity on public display was rooted in the 'product of long-standing genres of static and kinetic female nudity' as performed in its theatre spaces.[21] The establishment of Soho and the West End as Britain's entertainment centre began long before the postwar period. The Windmill Theatre's legacy of displaying the static female nude body intermingled with variety entertainment such as musical comedy pervades postwar British cinema's representation of the Soho strip club. The exotic costumes, gags and other 'corny' elements to striptease and other public displays of nudity originated at the Windmill. Versions of these 'harem maidens, garage mechanics' and 'Salome, Delilah and Jezebel, or Maracas in Caracas' are depicted in many of the more contemporary strip club performances for comic relief.[22] However, unlike the more risqué strip clubs that would be operated by the likes of entrepreneur Paul Raymond in the late 1950s, the Windmill 'represented daring departure for London theatres ... renditions consisted of impersonations of classical art and painting ... Compared to the striptease acts performed in American burlesque they seemed to worldly observers to be passé and sedate'.[23] Mort has shown that van Damm's reshaping of the 'mill' after the war established 'British girlhood' and 'came to exert a cultural influence that extended well beyond its actual presence in Archer Street. Endorsed by official agencies and opinion formers, the theatre's success as a national institution was largely in its offering of a version of English erotica'.[24]

The Windmill Theatre strengthened its international reputation during the war as the 'amusement centre for privates and non-commissioned officers' and also as a 'meeting ground for many people increasingly living their private lives in public who did not want to die alone'.[25] There were some challenges for nearby establishments during wartime, and the popular press reported excitably on the ways in which 'patrons were treated to floor shows of showgirls dancing barebreasted'.[26] This led to a public inquiry in 1940 that was attended by the police, the licensing authorities and members of the entertainment industry. Following this inquiry, the Lord Chamberlain tightened regulations surrounding public displays of nudity, requesting that photographs of the Windmill's nude tableaux be submitted in advance before any new edition of the revue was staged. He maintained that there would be regular visits to the theatre by the Lord Chamberlain's Office (LCO). This 'heavily intensified the micro-inspections of costumes and the staging of nude poses' and during the wartime Blitz, the correspondence between censor and theatre manager were 'comically surreal'.[27]

Both Walkowitz's and Hutton's histories of the Windmill Theatre emphasise the intensity of the commercial impact of American servicemen's on Soho and the West End in 1942. Walkowitz references an American newspaper, which estimated that over one million GIs contributed $200,000 towards the Windmill revenue, where for 'three years and a half, GIs sat in the auditorium, smoking cigars, chomping their jaws, and yelling "Take it off"'.[28] American GIs were paid a salary three times more than British servicemen and spent more on leisure and entertainment; in turn, West End theatres, clubs and restaurants thrived during wartime.[29] The American Red Cross Club that became known as Rainbow Corner, located at 23 Shaftesbury Avenue near Piccadilly Circus, offered 'nothing less than a slice of authentic America dished up in the centre of London'.[30] It was open twenty-four hours a day and contained two large dining rooms, offered accommodation, valet and laundry services, and hosted live music performances from Glenn Miller's Band.

The Rainbow Club had even appeared in cinema, reconstructed at Welwyn Studios for *I Live in Grosvenor Square/A Yank in London* (Herbert Wilcox, 1945), a romance starring Rex Harrison and Anna Neagle, an actress who had incidentally worked at the Windmill Theatre early on in her career.[31] The Rainbow Club's closure was recorded by Pathé in *The Rainbow Ends* (1946). The Windmill's popularity with American GIs during the war shows that van Damm was a keen promoter who understood his target male audience. However, by the late 1950s, the Windmill's customers moved into the more privatised spaces of the home and cinema, where 'sexualized representations of the female body ... [were] increasingly integrated into a wider range of artistic and cultural genres'.[32] The Windmill's successor, the nonstop Revue strip club, offered patrons sexually explicit performances in exclusive surroundings.

The Windmill Theatre in Postwar British Cinema

There are several low-budget postwar films that replicate the space of the Windmill Theatre and two notably forgotten films that were entirely staged and shot inside the establishment. Val Guest's tongue-in-cheek crime-musical *Murder at the Windmill/Mystery at the Burlesque* (1949) featured real-life Windmill performers as themselves who, following the murder of an anonymous audience member in the stalls, must restage the Windmill's *Revudeville* performance in its entirety for the benefit of the detectives investigating the crime.[33] The film acts as a quasi-promotion for the theatre and emphasises its moral and nationalistic identity. During an early scene in which the showgirls are informed they will have to stay at the Theatre for police questioning, a dancer called Anita D'Ray insists her boyfriend be brought inside: 'He'll catch his death of cold. You know how the wind whistles around Archer Street!'[34] The Windmill also appeared briefly in Burt Hyams' *Sunshine in Soho* (1956) as a way to highlight Soho's seedier commercial entertainments. In the late 1960s, *West End Jungle*'s director Arnold L. Miller used the site of the Windmill for his sexploitation film *Secrets of a Windmill Girl* (1966). The film was produced by Michael Klinger and Tony Tenser of Compton Cameo Films, a production house based in Soho that produced largely low-budget exploitation and pornographic films. Klinger and Tenser purchased the Mill after it closed, converting it into the Windmill Cinema Club and casino in 1964.[35] *Secrets of a Windmill Girl* follows 'the rise and fall of a stripper ... something of an afterthought, made cheaply and quickly by Long and miller as the final film of their partnership, using footage they had shot before the Windmill Theatre had closed'.[36]

A celebrated cinematic history of the Windmill would eventually be brought to the screen in 2005 by director Stephen Frears. *Mrs Henderson Presents* stars Judi Dench and Bob Hopkins as Laura Henderson and Vivian van Damm, the 'odd couple who helped to create a market niche for English middlebrow entertainments'.[37] Films that replicated the Windmill Theatre include the US Columbia Pictures musical film *Tonight and Every Night* (Victor Saville, 1945). This film stars Rita Hayworth as a showgirl named Rosalind Bruce who is the headline act at the fictional Music Box theatre in London, which, against the odds, remains open during the Blitz. A later offering, the British independent crime-thriller *Cover Girl Killer* (Terence Bishop, 1959), frames its nameless serial murderer with multiple personalities and his appetite for pornography within a burlesque-revue theatre named the Casbar. The killer is played by Harry H. Corbett, shortly before he would play the role of rival racketeer Gollar to Terence Morgan's Augie Cortona in *The Shakedown* (John Lemont, 1960). One of the film's more memorable murder sequences was shot on location in St Anne's Court and Dean Street in a sequence where Corbett lures an innocent beauty queen named Joy Adams (played by *Rag Doll*'s Christina Gregg) to his photography studio.[38]

The Windmill's Legacy and Paul Raymond

Raymond opened the Revuebar in April 1958 on the first two floors of Maurice House, a building previously occupied by the Doric Ballrooms. According to Judith Walkowitz, the ballrooms first operated as event function rooms and were leased from Jack Isow, the Jewish owner of the 'Shim Sham Club turned restauranteur' with a 'history of unashamed hucksterism even longer than Raymond's'.[39] It was located at 11 Walker's Court, a pedestrian street that runs between Brewer Street and Peter Street in Soho. The building was specifically chosen because it was nestled in-between restaurants and butcher shops that would be later demolished by Raymond as he expanded his business interests into property. It functioned as a members-only club where entry was secured through paid membership. One week after the Revuebar opened, more than one thousand customers signed up as members, generating 'well in excess of £10,000 in fees'.[40] The club was far more appealing to punters than the existing bars and existing strip clubs in the area by offering its customers *mobile* nude female performances as opposed to the traditional, static displays of female sexuality first established by the Windmill Theatre, situated only a few streets south from Walker's Court on Great Windmill Street. Raymond would ultimately purchase the Windmill in 1974. The Theatre's national legacy and reputation and its owner, Mrs Henderson, became the subject of Stephen Frears' *Mrs Henderson Presents* (2005). The film was released (perhaps not so coincidentally) the year after the Revuebar closed permanently and was later adapted into a commercially successful West End musical in 2015.

Following on from the Revuebar's overnight success, during the 1960s, Raymond acquired the freehold of eight out of twelve shop premises located on Walker's Court, transforming them into an array of peep shows, strip clubs and sex shops, their 'signage immersing passers-by in a multicoloured neon light that made them resemble tropical fish'.[41] Bernard, a Soho resident known for his 'Low-Life' column in *The Spectator* magazine that was later adapted into an acclaimed play *Jeffrey Bernard Is Unwell* by Keith Waterhouse, blamed Raymond for the redevelopment of the area's local businesses. Shortly before his death in 1997, Waterhouse stated: 'I have nearly always blamed the decline of Soho on property tycoons like Paul Raymond who has in my street alone turned a baker, a butcher and an Italian delicatessen into dirty bookshops.'[42] Bernard's lamentation over the closure of his neighbourhood shops stemmed from the period shortly after the opening of the Revuebar, where Raymond had publicly promised to preserve Soho's independent businesses and restaurants by purchasing the freehold to 9 Walker's Court that was once the site of Kramer's shoe shop. According to Willets, legend has it that Raymond promised the local community organisation Soho Society that he would allow the shop to remain. However, a few months later, he subsequently forced Kramer's to move premises by increasing the rent in order to lease the site to a Maltese sex shop.[43] This story reinforces Raymond's character as a ruthless businessman who cared little for the preservation of Soho's local businesses. However, it also demonstrates that he made great efforts in terms of rearranging the topography of Soho to suit the rapid expansion of his property and porn empire.

In 1983, Raymond had completely monopolised the commercial sex market in the West End and Soho. He was also perhaps one of the few who saw the lucrative potential of the male homosexual market, or 'the pink pound'. In 1984 he opened 'Raymond's Piano Bar', which was 'among the first openly gay venues to set up in the area … it was soon so profitable that Raymond was bragging about it being "a little goldmine"'.[44] The success of the club prompted him to open a 'much larger gay venue on that section of Brewer Street several years later. This new venue was run by John Wright, better-known as Madame Jojo'.[45] Raymond's significant investment in the area suggests that he personally regarded Soho as a special neighbourhood. The area's bifurcated identity in the public imagination as a space of bohemia and cosmopolitanism assisted with Raymond's aggressive self-promotion as a liberal entrepreneur. The opening sequence of *The Look of Love* highlights this important aspect of Raymond's life, but it is swiftly discarded in Michael Winterbottom's biopic.

The Look of Love (2013)

During the opening credits of Michael Winterbottom's biographical film on Paul Raymond, *The Look of Love* (2013), a technicolour kaleidoscope of female pin-up photographs, neon signage and black-and-white Soho topography dissolve into a shot of a young girl sat in the passenger seat of a moving limousine. She counts the buildings one by one, enquiring after their ownership, whilst an unseen male voice responds with an affirmative 'Yes' for each property. The girl then asks: 'Why do you buy so many houses, Grandpa?' The affectionate voice replies: 'They're not houses. They're shops, restaurants, offices, cafés, clubs.' As the limousine arrives at its destination in Dean Street, Soho, the girl's grandfather is revealed to be Paul Raymond, the real-life strip club entrepreneur and real estate mogul known as the 'Porn King of Clubs'.[46]

The film charts Raymond's life over an expansive period from the mid-1950s to the 1990s and focuses primarily upon his tumultuous relationship with his daughter Debbie (played by Imogen Poots), who died in 1992 after overdosing on heroin. Raymond, who died in 2008 aged eighty-two, is perhaps best known for opening the first members-only strip club in Soho, the Raymond Revuebar in 1958, and later expanding his empire to include the publication of pornographic magazines and commercial real estate. In Winterbottom's film, Raymond is played by the British actor-comedian Steve Coogan, marking his fourth collaboration with the director. According to the sole biography (and source material for the film) of Raymond written by Paul Willetts in 2010, entitled *The Look of Love*, originally published as *Members Only*, Soho's 'perennial association with sex [and] its densely populated network of streets, alleys and squares, sometimes known as "the Black Mile"' fuelled Raymond's decision to locate the Revuebar and his other businesses in Soho, which lent the Revuebar with an 'unexpected glamour'.[47]

The Look of Love was released one year before the closure of Soho institution Madame Jojo's. Located at 8–10 Brewer Street in Soho, the club had played host to an expansive array of entertainment acts, bringing together 'gay culture and burlesque culture with mainstream music and club nights' to audiences for over fifty-years.[48] In 2014, the premises licence for the nightclub was revoked by Westminster City Council, the local authority for Greater London, Shortly after the licence was revoked, the freeholder of the venue, Raymond's own property company Soho Estates, expedited the process for its closure. *City AM* newspaper has estimated that the company, which today is operated by his two granddaughters, is worth £565million.[49] The decision to revoke the licence was reported as the consequence of an incident between members of staff from Madame Jojo's and the adjacent Escape Nightclub at 10a Brewer Street who violently attacked a Somali man, resulting in the injury of an innocent passer-by on 24 October that year.[50] The Council's official statement clarified that its decision was 'determined solely by its lack of faith in the venue's' management and a concern for the safety of the public'.[51] Despite the efforts of supporters of Madame Jojo's to petition against its closure, which included a protest march through the streets of Soho that the *Londonist* described as a 'New Orleans style funeral', the redevelopment of the 5,000 sq m area between Brewer Street and Walker's Court is almost completed. Since its closure, local and celebrity campaigners have protested against mass commercialisation of the area and the nightclub, launching the 'Save Soho' campaign, which today has become a wider symbol for the debates around Soho and London's mass gentrification and eradication of commercial landmarks, spanning two documentary films, *Battle of Soho* (Aro Korol, 2017) and *Soho Is…* (Tim Arnold, 2020).

The Look of Love was universally panned by critics and performed poorly at the box office both in Britain and globally.[52] Critic Stephen Holden of the *New York Times* said: 'Has any movie about swinging London been less glamorous [and] barely mentions the politics of pornography as a freedom-of-speech or feminist issue.'[53] The *New Statesman*'s Ryan Gilbey observed that 'Raymond [was] being remade in Coogan's image'.[54] Trevor Johnston of *Sight and Sound* criticised Winterbottom's direction: 'Winterbottom is too busy breezing through … using the repeated device of faux newsreels, radio and TV docs … It's the insider's view we want, but between myriad music cues and fidgety montages, we never get it.'[55] The film's failure to examine Raymond's life critically or authentically is deeply ironic. Producer Melissa Parmenter stated publicly before shooting the film: 'Our number one priority was to try and shoot in the real places, and in Soho a lot of places haven't changed that much. It's like going back in time, they never seem to change.'[56] Despite these claims, the film's interiors were entirely reconstructed *outside* of Soho. The film's Revuebar was built at the Battersea Mess and Music Hall in Wandsworth.[57] According to Frank Mort, in reality, the Revuebar hosted its guests in a lavish space with 'none of the elaborate physical barriers and management controls designed to separate performers from the audience'.[58] Raymond filled his club with 'foreign bodies' whose erotic performances featured 'sexual parody, quirky humour and light-hearted "foreplay"' he then marketed to both heterosexual couples and homosexual men.[59]

Despite Willetts' engaging social history of Raymond's empire, the book provides a somewhat anecdotal reconstruction of his past. Willetts admits in his author's note prefacing the book that he 'resorted to the type of fraudulent "imaginative reconstructions" favoured by a disconcerting number of contemporary writers of what masquerades as non-fiction'.[60] Winterbottom's career, which spans three decades, features an eclectic array of film genre hybrids. One editorial from *The Guardian* declared his work to be a mixture of 'realism with stylisation'.[61] This combination can be seen explicitly in the cinematic adaptation of Willetts' book, which could account for the widespread criticism for the undeveloped nature of the film and Winterbottom's preference for style over substance. Raymond's mythical status as a leader of permissiveness in British society also largely remains unchallenged in Soho histories detailing the development of sexual subcultures. This was partly due to his aggressive self-promotion in the press and his relentless pursuit to control Soho's property market. The latter remains his most significant impact on the commercial development of Soho today.

Conclusion

The Look of Love was not a unique contemporary British film in terms of its attempt to cinematically historicise the development of the new sexual economies that emerged in the capital during the late 1950s like striptease or youth culture. *Mrs Henderson Presents* (2005), which is one of the rare films to successfully portray the origins of the Windmill Theatre in the 1930s, and earlier in 1997, the film *Mojo*, based on Jez Butterworth's acclaimed play of the same name, re-created 1950s Soho and were extensively shot on location. Perhaps more notable is the 1986 musical film *Absolute Beginners*, which is today considered a cult, camp classic largely due to the casting of David Bowie. It was directed by Julien Temple and adapted from Colin MacInnes' novel of the same name, which was first published in 1959. Temple chose to adapt the book into a musical and cast the late music icon David Bowie in a supporting role. The story followed the life of a burgeoning fashion/music photographer and aimed to expose Soho's 'vice of every kink ... Soho provided MacInnes with a literary opportunity to showcase the area's "un-silent teenage revolution"'.[62] It was also a critical and commercial flop upon its release. In 2015, Temple spoke to *The Guardian* newspaper about the film. According to him, the film attempted to 'mirror' 1950s *and* 1980s society. However, the production went £1 million overbudget before filming and was such a failure for Temple that he was 'forced to leave' Britain for the United States: 'Legend has it that this was the film that destroyed the British film industry ... I had a breakdown and had to leave the country.'[63]

Soho films produced during the latter half of the twentieth century such as *Absolute Beginners*, *Mojo*, *The Look of Love* and the more recent *Adrift in Soho* (Pablo Behrens, 2019), a film that was given a limited release and received middling reviews, have several cinematic antecedents in Soho films from the postwar era, specifically influences from *Murder at the Windmill* (1949), *Too Hot to Handle* (1960) and more overtly *Expresso Bongo* (1960). In *Mojo*, there is a character named Silver Johnny who clearly references Laurence Harvey's wide boy character Johnny. All three films examined Soho's vice industries like striptease, citing Mrs Henderson's rule over the Windmill Theatre and the rise of Raymond. Incredibly, *The Look of Love* even reuses footage from *Expresso Bongo* for a montage sequence. In *Absolute Beginners* and *Mojo*, there are also references to Soho films of the past. The opening tracking shot of *Absolute Beginners* and *Mojo* that follows Colin (Eddie O'Connell) in the former and Baby (Aidan Gillen) in the latter film ramble – or rather parade – down a crowded Soho street at night. There are near-identical sequences in *Soho Incident* (Vernon Sewell, 1956) and *Expresso Bongo*. Finally, these two films' exploration of 1950s youth culture in Soho reflects films such as *Beat Girl* (1960) and *Rag Doll* (Lance Comfort, 1960), two interconnected exploitation films that warned audiences of the sexual dangers for teenage girls and boys in the metropolis and featured a rock 'n' roll 'beatnik' soundtrack performed live on screen by established pop stars.

In the 1950s, Soho entrepreneurs seized upon the opportunities created by barring street prostitution and pornography, by introducing members-only striptease clubs that offered nonstop revue-inspired performances in private though intimate and classless settings. This, in turn, reorganised the commercial topography of Soho and created a series of specific codified representations of the female body and of male desire on screen. In early Renaissance theatre, there was the notion that a building might directly affect the redevelopment/regeneration of its environment. Marvin Carlson has argued that a theatre/space of performance acts as 'a cultural monument, a site of display of dominant social class, an emblem of depravity and vice, a centre of political activism, a haven of retreat from the world of harsh reality'.[64] As we have seen in the case of *The Look of Love*, adapting the stories of these buildings and their mythmakers can prove to be a difficult task. However, these spaces, which reproduced sexuality in diverse forms, were not at all interested in creating worlds of reality.

Notes

1. Farson trained as a journalist at the Central Press Agency and later Cambridge, where he founded *Panorama* magazine. In the 1950s, he appeared on television as an interviewer for *This Week*: 'A larger-than-life figure, usually seen in bohemian bars of London's Soho holding court with the literary and theatrical.' See more of Patrick Newley's highly descriptive obituary of Daniel Farson in *The Stage*, 11 December 1997, 32. See also Farson's autobiography, *Never a Normal Man* (New York: HarperCollins, 1997) and *The Dan Farson Black and White Picture Show* (Monterey, CA: LemonTree Press, 1975). The documentary *Soho Striptease Clubs* (John Rhodes, 1958) was produced by independent British production company Associated Rediffusion, which made many current affairs news programmes for *The Week*, for ITV. See the film's catalogue entry in the BFI Library Archive: http://collections-search.bfi.org.uk/web/Details/ChoiceFilmWorks/150001914 (retrieved 22 October 2021).
2. Kenneth Allsop's article 'Brave New Underworld' is a lengthy and pithy expose into the changing strip culture in London; see *The Spectator*, 12 August 1960, 240.
3. See Judith Walkowitz, *Nights Out: Life in Cosmopolitan London* (New Haven: Yale University Press, 2012), 260.
4. Journalist Francis Newton states: 'Indeed, stripping is an ideologically purer example of private enterprise than most, it produces neither goods, nor services, for the only real service that is in the minds of the men who watch a strip.' See Francis Newton, 'Any Chick Can Do It', *New Statesman*, 6 January 1961, 486.
5. Paul Raymond became the recognisable face of Soho following the opening of his club Raymond Revue Bar in 1958 and when the Windmill closed in 1964, Raymond's expanding businesses into pornography and property changed Soho's urban and commercial arrangement forever. 'His controlling stake in Soho ...meant that he could experiment with a version of the cluster economy': Frank Mort, *Capital Affairs: London and the Making of the Permissive Society* (New Haven: Yale University Press, 2010), 278.
6. Tom Baistow's evocative first-hand report on his visit to a Soho strip club is one amongst numerous articles published in this period reaffirming the British public's desire to learn more. See Tom Baistow, 'Strip and Shake', *New Statesman*, 17 January 1959, 67.
7. According to Mort, 'Journalists identified strip's spectacular rise' (and profit) during the late 1950s, and 'Post-war sexology sought to provide an intellectual explanation for the appeal'. See Mort, *Capital Affairs*, 246.
8. Kenneth Allsop, 'Brave New Underworld', *The Spectator*, 12 August 1960, 240.
9. Although the film *Jungle Street* (Charles Saunders, 1961) takes place in West London, the strip club is a 'fully designed and carpentered set, but many of these films settle for a flimsy plywood bar and a few chromed stools – enough to accommodate a slinky blonde with an extravagantly cantilevered bosom and a cigarette in need of a light'. See Steve Chibnall and Brian McFarlane, *The British 'B' Film* (London: BFI, 2009), 255.
10. The strip club also makes an appearance in critically acclaimed films such as the adaptation of John Le Carré's novel *The Spy Who Came in from the Cold* by director Martin Ritt (1965), which appears to model its luxurious club environment on the successful Raymond Revuebar.
11. Walkowitz, *Nights Out*, 262.
12. Mort, *Capital Affairs*, 248.

13. Historical, social and culture studies that examine both burlesque and the contemporary strip club are primarily situated in the United States from scholars such as Brian McNair, *Striptease Culture Sex, Media and the Democratization of Desire* (New York: Routledge, 2002) and Rachel Shteir, *Striptease: The Untold History of the Girlie Show* (New York: Oxford University Press, 2004).
14. Walkowitz, *Nights Out*, 255–56.
15. Ibid.
16. Ibid.
17. Discussions on the importance and influence of the British-Jewish Lyons on the West End entertainment and food industries were explored in Chapters 3 and 6 on Soho's immigrant communities. See also ibid., 257.
18. Paul Willetts notes that the first recorded shows of female and male nude tableaus were in fact in 1847 at the Walhalla Gallery in Leicester Square: 'Customers could admire Madame Warton's "Tableaux Vivants and Poses Plastiques" … men as well as women – wore body stockings that gave the appearance of full or partial nudity.' See Paul Willetts, *The Look of Love: The Life and Times of Paul Raymond Soho's King of Clubs* (London: Serpent's Tail, 2010), 27. See also Mike Hutton, *The Story of Soho: The Windmill Years 1932–1964* (Stroud: Amberley, 2013), 22–23.
19. Hutton, *The Story of Soho*, 23; Walkowitz, *Nights Out*, 255.
20. Mrs Henderson bought the Great Windmill property in 1931. She refitted the theatre house 'in miniature', 'complete with proscenium stage, lounge, auditorium seating for 320 and dressing rooms in the basement'. She presided over the theatre until her death in 1944. She also 'graced the first page of Windmill souvenir programs surrounded by her troupe of performers who consisted of clothed men and scantily attired women'. See Walkowitz, *Nights Out*, 256–57.
21. Mort, *Capital Affairs*, 247.
22. Walkowitz, *Nights Out*, 262; and Mike Hutton, 'Stripping away the 1950s', in Hutton, *The Story of Soho*, 120–21.
23. Walkowitz's history of the Windmill Theatre and the idea to feature 'static nudity' will be explored later on, but for specific history on *tableaux vivants*, see Walkowitz, *Nights Out*, 259.
24. The Windmill was famous for providing its female performers with a conventional work/life balance, and van Damm's daughter, who took over the theatre in 1955, 'reiterated the theatre's commitment to the moral welfare of the girls'. See Mort, *Capital Affairs*, 262–63.
25. Walkowitz, *Nights Out*, 275, 283.
26. Ibid., 276
27. According to Walkowitz, 'The LCO's surveillance of Windmill entertainments implicated it in the same voyeuristic scrutiny of female bodies as the dirty mackintosh brigade … Memoirs of the war tend to confirm the Lord Chamberlain's suspicions that the Windmill's performers exposed more flesh than what was actually licensed'. See ibid., 277–78.
28. Ibid., 284.
29. Hutton, *The Story of Soho*, 79.
30. Jon Savage, 'Pop at the Pictures: Wartime London Dances to America's Tune', *The Guardian*, 26 October 2011. Retrieved 22 October 2021 from https://www.theguardian.com/music/musicblog/2011/oct/26/1940s-london-rainbow-corner-swing.

31. Mort, *Capital Affairs*, 263.
32. Ibid., 266.
33. According to *The Stage*: 'New British Talent is given a chance by Daniel Angel Films in their musical thriller ... Smaller speaking parts go to seven other Windmill Girls, who thus get their first break on the screen: Anita D'Ray, Margot Holden, June Kennedy, Maureen O'Dea, Pat Hamilton, Tauna Beckham and Linda Gray.' See 'Murder at the Windmill', *The Stage*, 25 November 1948, 3.
34. An unremastered copy of *Murder at the Windmill/Mystery at the Burlesque* (1949) can be purchased online from Sinister Cinema.
35. Michael Ahmed, 'Independent Cinema Exhibition in 1960s Britain: Compton Cinema', *Postscript – Essays in Film and the Humanities* 30(3) (2011), 56–57.
36. Andrew Spicer and A.T. McKenna, *The Man Who Got Carter: Michael Klinger, Production and the British Film Industry 1960–1980* (London: I.B. Tauris, 2013), 29.
37. Mort, *Capital Affairs*, 256.
38. See 'Cover Girl Killer', *Monthly Film Bulletin* 27(312) (1960), 36.
39. Walkowitz, *Nights Out*, 295.
40. 'Raymond observed that many of them asked 'specifically that their membership cards when available should not be sent to their homes'. Instead, Raymond created a direct-debit format, whereby fees would be automatically generated by their banks to his club. See Willetts, *The Look of Love*, 99.
41. Ibid., 364.
42. Based on the writings and life of Bernard, the play *Jeffrey Bernard Is Unwell* was first performed in 1989 as a vehicle for actor Peter O'Toole and is set entirely inside the Coach and Horses pub in Soho that unfortunately closed in 2019. See Jeffrey Bernard, 'So Long, Soho', *The Spectator*, 16 November 1996, 71.
43. Willetts, *The Look of Love*, 364.
44. Ibid., 376.
45. Ibid., 382.
46. Ibid., 1.
47. Ibid., 90.
48. Journalist Hannah Ellis-Peterson evocatively described the club's interior in her 2014 article: 'Push your way through the double doors beneath a seedy flashing neon sign, however, and you encounter a plush world of opulence, red velvet curtains and art deco mirrors.' See 'Madame Jojo's, Legendary Soho Nightclub, Forced to Close', *The Guardian*, 24 November 2014. Retrieved 22 October 2021 from https://www.theguardian.com/uk-news/2014/nov/24/madame-jojos-legendary-soho-nightclub-forced-close.
49. Raymond died aged fifty-six of respiratory failure in March 2008 and left his empire to his granddaughters Fawn and India Rose James. See Kasmira Jefford, 'Soho Property Empire Rises in Value to £565m', *City AM*, 24 August 2015, 8.
50. See 'Review of the Premises Licences for Madame Jo-Jo's, 8–10 Brewer Street'. Minutes of Licensing Sub-Committee. Westminster Council, 20 November 2014: 24–28.
51. Tim Mitchell, 'Statement on Madame Jojo's', City of Westminster, 26 November 2014. Retrieved 22 October 2021 from https://www.westminster.gov.uk/statement-madame-jojos. See also Stuart Love, 'Petition Update from Council', 7 April 2015. Retrieved 22 October 2021 from http://petitions.westminster.gov.uk/savemadamjojos.

52. *The Look of Love* made a box office gross of $710,619 (£549,790) in the United Kingdom, though it performed badly internationally and in the United States, made a total gross profit of $21,252 (£16,442). See 'The Look of Love', *Box Office Mojo*, July 5, 2013, accessed January 1, 2019, https://www.boxofficemojo.com/movies/?page=intl&id=lookoflove.htm.
53. Stephen Holden, 'Smut's Softer Side: Rakish Pornographer as Loving Parent, Review: *The Look of Love*', *New York Times*, 4 July 2013. Retrieved 22 October 2021 from https://www.nytimes.com/2013/07/05/movies/the-look-of-love-stars-steve-coogan-as-a-sex-impresario.html.
54. Ryan Gilbey, 'Mags to Riches', *New Statesman*, 26 April (2013): 50.
55. Trevor Johnston, 'Look of Love – Review', *Sight and Sound* 23(5) (2013), 100.
56. Film London, 'Look of Love', *Film London News*, 24 April 2013. Retrieved 22 October 2021 from http://filmlondon.org.uk/news/2013/april/the_look_of_love.
57. Ibid.
58. Mort, *Capital Affairs*, 269.
59. Ibid., 270.
60. Willetts, 'Author's Note' in Willetts, *The Look of Love*, ii.
61. Editorial, 'In Praise of … Michael Winterbottom', *The Guardian*, 4 November 2019. Retrieved 22 October 2021 from https://www.theguardian.com/commentisfree/2010/nov/04/michael-winterbottom-films.
62. Ibid., 228.
63. See 'How We Made: *Absolute Beginners*', *The Guardian*, 21 September 2015. Retrieved 22 October 2021 from https://www.theguardian.com/culture/2015/sep/21/how-we-made-absolute-beginners-julien-temple-patsy-kensit.
64. Marvin Carlson, *Places of Performance: The Semiotics of Theatre Architecture* (New York: Cornell University Press, 1989), 8.

CHAPTER 10
Soho Strip Clubs (Part Two)
The Stage and the Dressing Room

> *Look kid, this is a strip club, right? For all I know, under all that gear you might be a man or something. I mean, you never know these days.*
> —*The Small World of Sammy Lee* (Ken Hughes, 1963)

Too Hot to Handle (Terence Young, 1960) and *The Small World of Sammy Lee* (1963) were two distinctly different strip club films released during the period that saw the collapse of the Windmill Theatre's wartime product of fan dances, comic revue and static nude tableaus. But how did these new forms of sexual display evolve and how did cinema respond to these changes? In part two of my study of Soho striptease clubs, I look at the new commercial ethos laid out by entrepreneurs in Soho where '[t]he sitting and lay-out of the club testified to the way the glamour market was changing'.[1] The more traditional and arguably democratic theatre venues like the Windmill were being displaced by commercially minded, members-only clubs that catered to its middle-class audiences with cocktail bars and restaurants located inside. This chapter will look at those pioneering entrepreneurs who were responsible for moving the economic, cultural and physical boundaries of sexual permissibility alongside a study of the topographical arrangement of their clubs, before moving on to a close examination of the two aforementioned films in an attempt to discover the reasons behind the conflicted zones of cinematic representations of striptease: both as a humorous but also a cynical commentary on popular consumption, both on and off the stage.

The Nonstop Revue Strip Club

The Irving Club (also known as the Irving Theatre Club) offered continuous, all-day striptease performances and was originally established in 1957 by Dhurjati B. Chaudhuri, a Bengali barrister who is credited by multiple sources as having invented the nonstop striptease club.[2] Located at 17 Irving Street near Leicester Square, the club initially functioned as the Asian Institute of Art and Theatre. The failure of this enterprise led Chaudhuri to transform the space into a club, but one that would require membership and that would offer a first, nonstop, continuous striptease from 2.30 PM to 11 PM. It also circumvented a loophole that allowed the club to stage plays formerly banned by the Lord Chamberlain. According to Hutton, London County Council's refusal to grant strip clubs music and dancing licences meant that he was forced to 'pay the regular £100 fine and cost it into his regular overheads'.[3] This rule similarly applied to other club owners in the area, who would also factor in this cost. Despite the inaugural performances of the Irving Club, described as so 'amateurish as to be embarrassing ... poorly rehearsed', Chaudhuri began to swiftly devise other marketing strategies in order to boost membership, going so far as to take the Irving Theatre's show to the Edinburgh Fringe Festival in 1957, where 'they played to full houses of culture-sodden intellectuals'.[4] The following year, he sold nude photographs with free 3D glasses and began to publish a magazine quarterly entitled *Vues from Revues*, whose cover pages were splashed with large black-and-white nude photographs of Irving's performers framed within a bright yellow backdrop.[5] The 1958 summer edition of the magazine included an article by Wolf Mankowitz. This contributes to my and others' speculation that the Irving was the real-life inspiration behind the In-Time Theatre in *Expresso Bongo* (Val Guest, 1960). The In-Time strip club introduces us to Johnny's girlfriend Maisie, described by *Monthly Film Bulletin* as a striptease soubrette.[6] Maisie leads the In-Time's Windmill-inspired show of risqué static tableaus that stage historical events such as the execution of Mary, Queen of Scots, along with corny song-and-dance numbers choreographed by Kenneth MacMillan, most notably the playful jazz tune called 'You Can Look at the Goods, But Don't Touch!'

According to reports in *Picturegoer* and *The Stage*, membership at the Irving stood at 44,000 members in 1958 and rose to 60,000 in 1959.[7] But this success would soon be challenged by the arrival of the illustrious and controversial figure of Paul Raymond (née Geoffrey Anthony Quinn). Mort describes Raymond as a

Figure 10.1. Maisie (Sylvia Syms) performs at the In-Time Theatre. Still from *Expresso Bongo* (Val Guest, 1960). DVD, BFI Flipside, 2016

provincial entrepreneur who was brought up in Liverpool and during the war worked as a 'self-confessed part-time spiv'.[8] Together with his wife Jean, they opened the Raymond Revue Bar in April of 1958 at 11 Walker's Court, Soho.[9] According to Willetts' biography of Raymond, the Revue Bar was the antithesis of the Panama Club, a strip club owned by Len Mitelle and featured in *Soho Striptease Clubs* (1958), and the Irving Theatre. It contained a 240-seat auditorium with 'cabaret-style' furnishings such as small tables, where 'patrons sat grouped ... where they were serviced by restaurant and bar staff as they watched nude displays'.[10] Willetts also praised Raymond's ingenious decision to remove the building's former entrance from Brewer Street to Walker's Court. Replacing the entrance from a junction to a pedestrianised street proved 'inspired, psychologically astute decision ... not having an entrance on a main street was a potent advantage in those days', as was the deliberate removal of the traditional comedy and variety acts as popularised by the Windmill in favour of 'promoting a sexy atmosphere focused on erotic female display and audience arousal'.[11]

In *The Story of Soho*, Hutton described the ways in which the Panama Club, which featured in Farson's documentary, and its geography in the West End were 'a different form of threat' with regard to Raymond's monolithic expansion of strip clubs in Soho.[12] Both the Panama Club and Raymond's Revue opened within the same year, and Raymond's desire to recruit female performer Julie Mendez, a 'dark-haired beauty doing some very bizarre gyrations with a live snake', was momentarily threatened; however, he ultimately lured her away to work at the Revue.[13] Another entrepreneur named Murray Goldstein would swiftly appear the following year with his club called The Tropicana on Greek Street in 1959, which 'enlarged the existing stage and installed improved lighting and a sound system'.[14] Other rivals included the Casino de Paris, 'which had established a reputation for staging more daring shows'.[15] By the end of the decade, Soho strip clubs allegedly hosted 200,000 members and garnered an annual profit of more than £2.5 million.[16]

The Pink Flamingo: *Too Hot to Handle* (1960)

The postwar press frequently enjoyed dramatising so-called wars between club owners, who they claimed were in fierce competition with one another over who could invent the most risqué routines. This formulates the chief narrative of *Too Hot to Handle/Playgirl After Dark* (1960), which highlights the power of the investigative journalist to promote and/or dissuade the public in relation to strip clubs. The film was described by one critic as a 'flamboyant and overdone' musical-crime film.[17] It stars Jayne Mansfield, Leo Genn, Christopher Lee and Carl Boehm, who transform into recognisable archetypes of stripper, gangster, club owner and journalist who must navigate the sordid Soho clubland, a world that was constructed on a set located at MGM British Studios. Incidentally, Christopher Lee, who plays the Pink Flamingo Club's spivvy American compère Novak, was simultaneously filming Edmond T. Gréville's *Beat Girl* (1960), where he played Kenny, the predatory owner of Les Girls strip club, on the same studio lot. He later recalled: 'I remember that film because I was doing *Too Hot to Handle* at MGM Studios at the same time on another set. And I would actually go from one set to the other, taking off and putting on a moustache.'[18] Shortly before playing serial killer Mark Lewis in Michael Powell's *Peeping Tom* (1960), Carl Boehm played a French journalist named Robert Jouvel who is granted unprecedented backstage access to the fictional Pink Flamingo Club by threatening its proprietor Johnny Solo (Leo Genn) that he will simply 'hop across the road' and publish his tell-all exposé about rival strip club called The Diamond Horsehoe. The Jouvel character initially functions as a passive spectator, but as he swiftly develops a keen fascination for a stripper named Lilliane (Danik Patisson), 'an intelligent foreign girl with a guilty secret', and his position duly changes into that of an unremarkable romantic hero.[19]

The film was directed by Terence Young and photographed in Eastmancolor by Otto Heller, who also worked on *The Ladykillers* (Alexander Mackendrick, 1955), *Peeping Tom* and *Victim* (Basil Dearden, 1961). The film attempts to appeal commercially, importing Hollywood sex symbol Jayne Mansfield as Midnight Franklin, the chief attraction of the Pink Flamingo Club. The character of Midnight, who is nicknamed 'Twelve o'clock', also works as the club's choreographer, membership manager, matriarch and sometime girlfriend of its owner Johnny Solo (Leo Genn), whose misogyny, violent outbursts and fierce rivalry with club owner Diamonds Dinelli (Sheldon Lawrence) ultimately lead to his downfall. Unbeknownst to Solo, his confidante and club compère Novak (Christopher Lee) is secretly working for Dinelli in order to gain a more powerful foothold in the industry independently. Solo also makes the mistake of employing underage dancer 'Pony-Tail' Swanson (played by Barbara Windsor), who he later prostitutes to an affluent, though anonymous associate named Mr Arpels (Martin Boddey), a plump Cockney gangster who never removes his thick-rimmed sunglasses. After their arranged date, Arpels takes Pony-Tail back to his flat, where, after she resists his sexual advances, she is murdered. The parallel narrative of journalist Jouvel (Carl Boehm) who discovers that Lilliane, one of the club's striptease artists, is a Jewish exile is largely sacrificed in favour of these criminal elements and highly theatrical performance sequences where Midnight, favouring pink and sequined cowboy-inspired chaps, feathers and little else, struts onto the stage, eliminating the barriers between her body and the Pink Flamingo's middle-class audience, much to their shock and delight.

The club was constructed on a set at MGM British studios. Its extravagant stage, bar and dining room was designed by Alan Withy, who, according to Laurie N. Ede entered the film industry working as a draughtsman and engineer, and whose early work includes Michael Powell and Emeric Pressburger's *The Red Shoes* (1948). The Pink Flamingo's set was dressed by Freda Pearson who worked on several James Bond films, including *Dr. No* (Terence Young, 1962) and *From Russia with Love* (Terence Young, 1963).[20] This film is an interesting example of one that purposefully constructed and marketed lurid images of its bombshell star Mansfield. Like Ken Hughes, Terence Young was clearly interested in the social, cultural and moral markers of the strip club, a liminal space, one that blurs the boundaries between the roles of spectator and performer. According to Tom Johnson and Mark Miller, cinematographer Heller's 'garish lighting in *Too Hot to Handle* accentuates the sleazy lifestyle of many of the film's characters and paints the strippers' musical numbers in tawdry brushstrokes. The overall effect is memorable chromatic noir'.[21] However, critics of the period were less impressed with the 'average' striptease acts. *Variety* declared: 'The nightclub settings are flamboyant and overdone. Some of the production numbers come over reasonably well on the screen, though it is doubtful if they could be staged (even allowing for expense) in the average stripteasery.'[22]

The Peep Show Club: *The Small World of Sammy Lee* (1963)

Although *Too Hot to Handle* provides a first-hand look inside the organisation of a strip club, the Peep Show Club in *Sammy Lee* is a less glamorous representation of the seedier, more isolated clubs of Soho. The club is first introduced in the film following the mesmerising opening tracking sequence where Hughes' camera, fixed behind a rubbish van, moves through Soho and the West End in the early hours of the morning. After we arrive outside the club, where mounds of rubbish are piled up in front of it, a young woman named Patsy (Julia Foster) enters the frame carrying a suitcase. As we track her pass the laminated posters depicting the club's nude female performers on the club's exterior, the camera stops in front of a large, framed photograph of Sammy. Patsy then smiles sheepishly before making her way inside, where two women are scrubbing the floor. The domestic atmosphere is punctured after Patsy enquires after Sammy, who has yet to arrive for work. As Patsy exits, her head turns to smile again at Sammy's photograph. We then cut to Sammy in a basement gambling club (the exterior of the club was shot on Gerrard Street), where he continues to lose. The next time we are at the Peep Show Club, its proprietor Gerry Sullivan (Robert Stephens) is arguing with an unruly stripper who continues to forget her dance routine. Patsy enters, enquiring again after Sammy, who she wrongly believes operates the club, as she has been promised a job in London. Gerry then invites her into his office for a preliminary interview and then directly asks her to strip off in front of him:

> GERRY: What's your name then?
> PATSY: Patsy.
> GERRY: Oh, Patsy. Come on, let's have a look at you. Well, come on.
> PATSY: What do you want me to do?

GERRY: *Look kid, this is a strip club, right? For all I know, under all that gear you might be a man or something. I mean, you never know these days.*[23]

Hughes makes no effort to hide Patsy's humiliation during this job interview, and this scene is reflective of *Soho Striptease Clubs*, in that Farson humorously poses questions to the Panama Club's Mitelle on what type of employee 'fits the bill'. The Peep Show Club's live offerings are also clearly inspired by the Panama Club and the Irving Club, and in the words of the film's protagonist Sammy Lee, the Peep Show Club offers the 'most second rate, nasty, small-minded, dirty little show in the West End'.[24] The Club's exterior design is similarly unsophisticated; its candy-striped marquee, which covers the entire building, provides shades of framed, titillating photographs of the club's female strippers. At the beginning of the twentieth century, a transitional period when the names of theatres and those of productions received almost equal emphasis on the typical façade, the theatre's name was commonly placed on the two sides of the marquee, built permanently into it, with a changing production name beneath. 'This practice, now rarely seen in live theatres, has been much more consistently followed in film theatres ... the more common practice today is to display the name of the theatre on a protruding sign in this same area, which has greater visibility from the street'.[25] As Willetts has stated, Paul Raymond was responsible for intensifying publicity on the exterior of the building, 'words such as "sexational" and "sexciting", devised in collaboration with his employees' blazoned across posters on the walls. This is confirmed by a 1960 account of the area chronicled by *The Spectator*:

> *Around the alleyway doorways and the Aladdin's cave lobbies the neon flickers, the lamps flare in the haloes around the curves and contortions, and the superlatives contest shrilly: 'SEXIEST', 'SAUCIEST', 'NAUGHTIEST', 'MOST EXCITING' 'MOST GLAMOROUS', 'MOST INTIMATE'. In fact, there proves to be what is, I suppose, unavoidable sameness about the actual fare.*[26]

The interior and exterior design, alternating historical modes of striptease performances and the marketing of the nonstop revue club also features in *The Small World of Sammy Lee*. The Peep Show Club's revue, described by Sammy as a 'hysterical [and] historical tableaux', which includes acts named the 'Garden of

Allah' where strippers dress as slaves in a harem-style setting, and 'Evette', which involves a stripper wading into a bubble bath nude on stage. It is revealed for comic effect backstage that the bath is filled only with icy cold water, much to the chagrin of the showgirl, who must endure it for the club clientele. This is clearly a signal to the Panama Club, the Irving Club and Raymond's Revue Bar. However, the inclusion of comic performances led by Sammy as compère, exhibits more traditional forms of nude revue, as successfully cemented in the public consciousness by the Windmill Theatre.

Hughes also grants us access to several backstage spaces, including the Peep Show Club owner Gerry Sullivan's office, Sammy's dressing room, the striptease performers' dressing rooms and the wings of the theatre. A pair of telephones, one located in the wings and one located below the main dressing room, transform into Sammy's personal office shortly after Soho gangster Conner's men visit his workplace to threaten him. He swiftly begins cold calling potential clients, convincing them to purchase stolen goods so that he can raise money to pay back his debt. Hughes consistently and effectively maintains the tension between the live strip tease shows by keeping Sammy and the striptease in frame simultaneously. Sammy's growing fear while he converses with black market racketeers on the telephone and female nude performers prance around in the background contributes towards the film's authenticity, as it facilitates our interaction with the space as active participants. We too become complicit in these morally questionable activities and, in turn, develop sympathy for Sammy's plight.

Staging Morality

The penultimate sequence in the film delineates the strip club space as a metaphor for Sammy's shifting morals after his visit to Whitechapel and his brother Lou. After returning to his flat, a close friend and prostitute named Joan (Toni Palmer) offers to lend him the money. Sammy replies indignantly: 'What do you think I am, a ponce or summit?' He then storms out of the room and he is then called by his dresser Harry (Wilfrid Brambell), who reports that stage manager Jimmy (Harry Locke) is desperately awaiting Sammy's return to perform. We then cut back to the club as Sammy enters and makes a beeline directly to the bar. He offers a deal on purchasing bottles of whisky wholesale to the barman, while the club's owner Gerry looks on suspiciously. After sealing the liquor deal, Gerry informs Sammy that he can work the week out until his contract ends. This exchange is overheard by Patsy, who is now working as a barmaid at the club.

The next striptease act is a repeat of the morning's revue named 'The Garden of Allah'. Patsy, having learnt about Sammy's debt, volunteers to perform the revue on her first day of work in exchange for Sammy's extended employment there. Sammy discovers her sacrifice only after she has taken to the stage and the veil is removed from her face. The sequence that follows this is used to convey Sammy's conscience and guilt of allowing Patsy to work at the club. A tracking shot snakes across the white male audience, who are, rather interestingly, diverse in terms of age and social class. They appear unimpressed at first as Patsy makes her way down the catwalk. This emphasises the alienation and fear she feels during her first performance. We then cut back to Sammy, who appears deeply concerned, but his expression changes to anger, and he blames Gerry, who whispers cruelly: 'Any girl who takes her clothes off is a whore.'[27] We then cut to a close-up of a male audience member, where the camera lens focuses upon a single bead of sweat running from his brow. This emphasises the sexual anticipation for Patsy to remove all of her clothing. Hughes employs a sharp cut to a midshot as she unhooks the front clasp of her bra, and as her hands move to her G-string, there is another cut to a high angle of an audience club member. In one smooth motion, she strips off entirely. She then moves off stage, where we observe her face, which is now filled with shame and embarrassment. Sammy gently covers her in a bathrobe. He tells her that she's been a fool before ordering her to go to his flat, a space that transforms from a bachelor pad into a place of sanctuary for Patsy.

Following Patsy's forced removal from the club, we learn that Sammy has successfully raised the £300 debt he owes to Conner. He duly celebrates in the pub across the road before his evening performance at the Peep Show Club. However, we feel his trepidation as his dresser Harry abruptly informs him that he has the cheque from the purchase of his mother's antique chair. The cheque, of course, Conner will not accept. The onset of the striptease performance on stage builds the intensity of Sammy's loss. He begins to harangue Harry for his mistake, but when Sammy is called to the stage, the strength is drained from his body and he gives Harry some cash from the day's swindle after all. Sammy moves towards the centre of the stage as Conner's men Fred (Kenneth J. Warren) and his partner Johnny (Clive Colin Bowler) enter the club. The low angle shot which frames Sammy on stage, lit by one spotlight, makes him appear ethereal and briefly removes us from the performance space entirely. Gerry then calls to Sammy from the bar, which sharply cuts this rare moment of reflection. Sammy then proceeds to give his final monologue, a muscular harangue that reinforces my previous argument for his postwar anxiety. It is also a reflection of his genuine moral stance on the commercial sex industry:

> *In a few moments' time, this bunch of slags we got back here will remove their clothing before your very eyes. Now don't get the wrong idea, this isn't a sexual invitation. This is what is known as a striptease club Gentlemen, with an emphasis on the word 'tease'… Should I tell you something? These birds back here, they hate you. Right? They hate you, believe me, they hate you. You make them sick. There's no love in this place fellas! God forbid that's what you came here for. There's not even any sex.*[28]

Sammy's virulent sermon to the club audience and, without doubt, the film's audience symbolises the traditional theatre's function as a platform for vernacular drama. Marvin Carlson and Juliet Rufford have both examined the urban arrangement of the traditional and nontraditional theatre. Rufford argues that: 'Theatre *is* a temporal art, but it is also one that signifies spatially… choreography is concerned not only with bodies and movement but with inscribing dance moves *across space.*'[29] If we apply this sentiment to Sammy's speech, the striptease club is stripped of its meaning as a space that functions as a 'cultural emblem for the enhancement of surrounding commercial property'.[30] The film is not only a marker of Sammy's journey from entertainer to failed entrepreneur to moraliser, but is also a historiography of cinematic Soho. The space of the Peep Show Club and striptease choreography combined the nationalism and conservatism of the Windmill Theatre with the titillating, British colonial-inspired fare of the late 1950s offered by immigrant entrepreneurs such as Mitelle, Chaudhuri and Raymond. There is also a cosmopolitan connection through Sammy's Jewish immigrant identity and finally, the criminal element that is demonstrated by his gambling addiction, and the subsequent physical and emotional pain inflicted on him both by Conner's thugs and by the loss of love interest Patsy. The watershed year of the film's release in 1963, a year that will be discussed in my conclusion, further reinforces the importance of this film as a powerful document that foreshadows the transition of Britain and its capital into the 'Swinging Sixties'.

Conclusion

In this chapter I have examined the history and cinematic representation of the striptease club, a space that was sensationalised and aggressively promoted by artists, entrepreneurs and journalists during the postwar period. This discussion has widened my own understanding of the cultural meanings of this new form of sexual commerce, which included its dramatic impact upon growing permissive attitudes in London and in cinema. Furthermore, commercial television offered these evolving forms of sexual display to national audiences, as in the case of Daniel Farson's popular documentary TV series *This Week*. Farson would later be dubbed a Soho bohemian both for his penchant for Soho's drinking clubs and for his friendship with the artist Francis Bacon. Farson's career as a television host began in 1956 with production company Associated Rediffusion and the live debate show *Seconds Out*, which led to his role as a host on *This Week*, where he worked as both a scriptwriter and interviewer. Farson swiftly became a 'household face, one of a new kind of celebrity (which also included Gilbert Harding, John Freeman and Robin Day) made entirely by television'.[31] Farson's reputation as one of Soho's popular *demi-mondes* during the late 1950s and 1960s is often overshadowed in literature by other bohemian figures such as Francis Bacon. Farson's close, yet exploitative personal relationship with Bacon resulted in a well-received biography entitled *The Gilded Gutter Life of Francis Bacon*, which was published in 1993. Farson even made a cameo appearance as himself in John Maybury's *Love is the Devil: Study for a Portrait of Francis Bacon* (1998).

Documentaries of the period such as Farson's *Soho Striptease Clubs* attempted to 'uncover' the realities of striptease and its labourers, influence filmmakers, thereby exploiting the relaxation of censorship. It is clear that the cinematic strip club, its operators, audiences and victims functioned as the seemingly perfect backdrop to explore these social transformations. However, this attempt was too often obscured by the filmmakers' preoccupation with exploiting the relaxation of film censorship laws in order to attract and titillate audiences with liberal projections of nudity. This is particularly evident in *Expresso Bongo* and *Too Hot to Handle*, two films that failed to highlight the 'gendered dynamics of a modern sexual economy' and the 'expanding regime of eroticised consumer freedoms' by adhering to strict rules of genre filmmaking, underlining their musical-comedy and criminal elements respectively.[32] Unlike the Windmill, which became symbolic of wartime patriotism, the 'underground', more intimate strip clubs guaranteed a far more intense and aggressive 'collective sexual release', reinforced by Soho's dense and 'localised cultural geography'.[33] Whereas the Windmill promoted femininity, 'Paul Raymond promoted his artists as sexually and culturally cosmopolitan'.[34] This demonstrates that Raymond successfully, and perhaps immorally, bridged the relationship gap between Soho's cosmopolitanism past with new forms of bohemian commerce through the illusion of foreignness. This reality was inextricably linked to the rebranding of postwar London as a global city. Striptease could therefore be branded commercially as another convergence of Soho's cosmopolitan and bohemian identities.

Notes

1. Frank Mort, *Capital Affairs: London and the Making of the Permissive Society* (New Haven: Yale University Press, 2010), 269.
2. See Mike Hutton, *The Story of Soho: The Windmill Years 1932–1964* (Stroud: Amberley, 2013), 120.
3. Despite the fact that Chaudhuri's art gallery and theatre patrons included figures such as Sir Laurence Olivier and Sir Jacob Epstein, it continued to haemorrhage money. See ibid., 120.
4. Derek Hill, 'Glamour in a G-String – Part II: Nude Shows, the Real Dangers', *Picturegoer*, 16 August 1958, 16.
5. Ibid.
6. B.D., 'Expresso Bongo', *Monthly Film Bulletin* 27(312) (1960), 2.
7. Derek Hill, 'Glamour in a G-String – Part I', 8.
8. Mort, *Capital Affairs*, 256–65.
9. Paul Willetts' definitive biography of Raymond describes him as 'the second child of socially and temperamentally mismatched parents'. His father, Francis 'Frank' Joseph had 'grown up in poverty amid the slums of the West Derby area of Liverpool … Defying the handicaps of this impecunious background, the future strip-club maestro's father had ended up running his own Liverpool-based "forwarding agency"'. See Paul Willetts, 'Educating Geoffrey', in *The Look of Love: The Life and Times of Paul Raymond, Soho's King of Clubs* (London: Serpent's Tail, 2010), 7–15.
10. Critics were largely unimpressed with *The Look of Love*. Peter Bradshaw of *The Guardian* said: 'This is a shallow but watchable movie' (*The Guardian*, 25 April 2013; retrieved 24 October 2021 from https://www.theguardian.com/film/2013/apr/25/the-look-of-love-review). Tim Robey of the *Daily Telegraph* said: 'This one, smirkily flaunting the tackiness and sheer non-movie-ness of its subject, is a bit on the flaccid side' (*Daily Telegraph*, 25 April 2013; retrieved 24 October 2021 from https://www.telegraph.co.uk/culture/film/filmreviews/10018223/Steve-Coogan-in-The-Look-of-Love-review.html). Winterbottom's film made $21,252 at the US domestic box office, though it did substantially better in the United Kingdom, with a total box office of $710,619, and in Australia, with a total box office of $189,880. See 'The Look of Love', *Box Office Mojo*. Retrieved 24 October 2021 from http://www.boxofficemojo.com/movies/?id=lookoflove.htm.

11. Willetts, *The Look of Love*, 95; Frank Mort, 'Striptease: The Erotic Female Body and Live Sexual Entertainment in Mid-twentieth-Century London', *Social History* 32(1) (2007), 270.
12. Hutton, *The Story of Soho*, 125.
13. Ibid., 126.
14. Ibid.
15. Willetts, *The Look of Love*, 117.
16. Ibid., 127.
17. Rich, 'Pictures: *Too Hot to Handle*', *Variety*, 28 September 1960, 26.
18. Robert W. Pohle, Douglas C. Hart and Rita Pohle Baldwin, *The Christopher Lee Film Encyclopaedia* (London: Rowman & Littlefield, 2017), 14.
19. The character Lilliane, who we learn trained as a ballerina, does have a secret, but not a sensational one. It is revealed towards the conclusion of the film that she escaped to London from Nazi Germany. See P.J.R., 'Too Hot to Handle', *Monthly Film Bulletin* 27(312) (1960), 153.
20. Laurie N. Ede, *British Film Design: A History* (London: I.B. Tauris, 2010), 108.
21. Tom Johnson, Tom and Mark Miller, *The Christopher Lee Filmography: All Theatrical Releases, 1948-2003* (London: McFarland & Company, Inc., 2004), 84.
22. See Rich, 'Pictures: *Too Hot to Handle*', 26.
23. See Ken Hughes, release script. 'The Small World of Sammy Lee', donated by BAFTA.
24. Ibid.
25. See Marvin Carlson, *Places of Performance: The Semiotics of Theatre Architecture* (New York: Cornell University Press, 1989), 122.
26. Kenneth Allsop, 'Brave New Underworld', *The Spectator*, 12 August 1960, 240.
27. Ibid.
28. Ibid.
29. See Juliet Rufford, *Theatre & Architecture* (London: Palgrave Macmillan, 2015), 8.
30. Carlson, *Places of Performance*, 97.
31. See Dick Fiddy, 'Daniel Farson (1927–1997)', *BFI Screenonline*. Retrieved 24 October 2021 from http://www.screenonline.org.uk/people/id/745404/index.html.
32. Mort, *Capital Affairs*, 29.
33. Ibid., 30.
34. Ibid., 48.

CONCLUSION

'Warm-Hearted Tarts' and the Year 'Old Soho' Died
Campaigns, Rebirth and *The World Ten Times Over* (1963)

> *A whole new lot of people ... are discovering Soho now or think they are, but they are also misunderstanding it. Soho is dead, so long, Soho.*
>
> —Jeffrey Bernard, 1996

Soho and the Swinging Sixties

In 1963, British society was undergoing intense transformations morally, culturally and politically. One of the most explosive events of that year was the widely publicised Profumo affair, whereby John Profumo, the Secretary of State for War, admitted to having an affair with a young model named Christine Keeler. This became the subject of several films and theatrical adaptations, such as the banned film *The Christine Keeler Story* (Robert Spafford, 1963), starring Keeler as herself, *Scandal* (Michael Caton-Jones, 1989) with John Hurt, a stage musical *Stephen Ward* with music by Andrew Lloyd Webber, and, more recently, a BBC television series entitled *The Trial of Christine Keeler* (2019). As Mort's work in *Capital Affairs* has extensively revealed: 'The Profumo affair also had a double plot that coupled sex with the geopolitics of the Cold War, and it therefore needs to be seen in relation to the other genre of public scandal dominating the post war years: the high-profile cases of spying that characteristically twinned homosexuality and espionage.'[1] The Profumo affair was the catalyst for the destruction of the Conservative government and 'unlocked the outrage about declining moral standards that had built up during the 1950s'.[2] Christopher Booker has described the considerable cultural and political developments during 1963, that he also deemed the 'year "Old England" died':

In December a special edition of the Evening Standard *summed up 1963 as having been simply 'The Year of the Beatles'. Niagara had been shot, 'Old England' was dead. The following year 'Swinging London' was being hailed as 'the most exciting city in the world'. Bringing an end to '13 years of Tory rule', the 'dynamic' little poseur Harold Wilson – a proto-Blair – strode proudly into No. 10. The new world we have lived in ever since had been born.*[3]

London secured a new title in the global sphere as the 'Swinging City', a mere three years on from the Profumo affair. The phrase 'Swinging London' is often credited to the American journalist Piri Halasz, who wrote a cover story for *Time* magazine entitled 'Great Britain: You Can Walk across It on the Grass', first published in 1966.[4] Steve Chibnall has suggested that the cover story was 'timed to appear for the start of the American tourist exodus, and took inspiration from a stream of celebratory reports in international media about the delights of London ... Short skirts, Beat groups, "groovy" clubs, and the diligent efforts of the new London Tourist Board all helped to double the number of foreign visitors to the capital in the first half of the 1960s'.[5] The capital simultaneously recalibrated itself to suit the needs of an exponential increase in international tourism. Paul Willetts describes the commercial expansion of Carnaby Street in the same period: 'Hithero an urban backwater ... [it] had, since 1960 become the teenage Savile Row ... Now its pavements were aflutter with fashionably dressed young people.'[6] In the West End and Soho, the metropolitan police intensified their measures to crack down on organised crime syndicates. This was allegedly successful, for reports at the time suggested there were fewer crimes committed in London than in previous years. The local authority, London County Council, began to aggressively monitor and regulate establishments offering popular entertainments such as music or dancing clubs located in the Soho district. This also included clubs that were 'sometimes not ostensibly run as places of entertainment but about which something should be done in the good name of London and all Britain'.[7] However, underground sexual economics continued to blossom throughout this decade. Gangsters such as Bernie Silver and 'Big Frank' Mifsud formed alliances to control twenty-four of Soho's strip clubs and other premises they operated as brothels and dirty bookshops. Calling themselves the 'Syndicate', they were 'able to operate with impunity thanks to corrupt links to senior Scotland Yard detectives'.[8] In comparison, Paul Raymond's property empire continued to grow extensively and in 1964 his pornographic magazines 'infused with a flavour of hedonistic consumerism' defined the decade as sexually permissive.[9]

Soho, 1966 to 1999

Soho through the decades was recently remembered in a series entitled 'Soho Stories' published in *The Observer*. The series featured personal histories about the area from various figures such as Colin Vaines and John Maybury. Tailor John Pearse said: 'When *Time* magazine ran its London: The Swinging City issue in 1966, Carnaby Street was gone up in smoke for us. It had become vastly overpopulated and commercialised by then ... a lot of the indigenous little shops had gone.'[10] In the 1970s, strip clubs were offering more sexually explicit performances that Mort suggests led to Raymond becoming a target for the contemporary women's movement.[11] This included the proliferation of porn cinemas and sex shops that peaked in the area around this period and were involved in other types of criminality like money laundering and hard drug dealing.[12] Live music clubs also blossomed all over Soho, 'playing soul, funk, reggae, African music, goth, punk, mod, electro, Latin and jazz, and the area was jumping again'.[13] By the 1980s, Soho had become a metropolitan locus for gay culture. Filmmaker John Maybury, who directed and produced a biographical film about Francis Bacon entitled *Love Is the Devil* in 1998, said: 'Soho is always mutating. Back then, people moaned about the influx of gay clubs, saying that was a kind of gentrification. Old Compton Street turned into something they didn't recognise in the 1990s. A lot of the old Colony Room crowd resented the imposition of gay culture, because they saw themselves as queers, not gays. They existed at a time when being gay was illegal and they found the gay scene contrary to their code of being.'[14] In 1999, Soho saw a devastating attack on its main intersection: three people were killed and seventy-nine were injured in a nail-bomb attack near the Admiral Duncan on Old Compton Street, a pub that is often described as the heart of the gay community. In 2019, there was a vigil to mark two decades since the attack on Soho's gay community.[15]

Has Soho's reputation as a haven for drugs and sex shops that was earned during the 1970s and 1980s overshadowed postwar conceptions of it? Christopher Howse's *Soho in the Eighties* describes the cultural dregs of the 1950s and 1960s, which include the chroniclers, movers and shakers of those bohemian years like

Bernard and Bacon, arguing they remained very much part of the Soho fabric. However, novelist Will Self wryly states in his review of Howse's biography that these figures were becoming a fading backdrop to the newer forms of subculture emerging from the 1970s onwards: 'But then all bohemian milieus are really the creation of their minor not their major figures – the big beasts cruise through, ships in the night, en route for more exalted destinations, leaving bobbing in their wake parasitic poetasters, ready to cash in.' Indeed, Self even suggests that Howse imagines himself as one of those figures, who 'seems to have been blinded – perhaps by his spiritual inclinations – to the truly dark side of Soho'.[16] It is impossible to assume that postwar British cinema's imagining of Soho will continue to sustain the next generation's understanding of its contemporary character. However, it is irrefutable, as demonstrated by the tensions found in Self's critique of Howse's lived experience, that Soho's past will continue to be reimagined not on the street, but on celluloid, cemented in the popular cultural memory as an aesthetic artefact that is habitually reawakened.

Soho on Screen

In this book I have attempted to underscore the significance of a British film canon that positioned their shared narratives of crime, prostitution, immigrant communities and subcultures in Soho, an area whose global reputation as a bohemian, cosmopolitan and commercial district in the nation's capital rendered it wholly unique within the context of postwar British filmmaking. Unlike the British New Wave, a celebrated group of films emerging during the same period, whose important aesthetic and technical innovations continue to be recognised by the media, cinema scholars and new generations, there remains little acknowledgement for these low-budget Soho films that were comparably responding to the political, social and cultural transformations of postwar British society. Furthermore, these Soho films highlighted the ongoing battle facing British filmmakers in terms of developing new strategies in order to attract a dwindling cinema-going audience due to the meteoric rise in popularity of commercial television. One strategy was to import American actors for 'B' productions in order to bolster box office revenues and appeal to the international marketplace. In Chapter 4, I discussed the ways in which these films' promotion of archetypal representations of American criminals and their milieu was inevitably rejected by 1950s audiences in an increasingly consumer-led society. Soho films were also responsible for the promotion of the area's cosmopolitan and moral identity. *Miracle in Soho* (1957) was a film that was clearly a passion project for Emeric Pressburger. It admirably portrayed the ways in which modern life could lead to the disintegration of the family unit and loss of community ties through the perspective of an Italian immigrant and her love for an outsider. Although the film was a critical and commercial failure, it promoted Soho's cosmopolitanism and was in tune with developments put forward by local Soho entrepreneurs to reinvent the area as a post-imperial spectacle. In many ways, Soho functioned as a cultural petri dish, reflecting the decisions made by government and local lawmakers after the war who painstakingly put in place commercial redevelopment to reinvent the metropolis on a global scale.

For a large number of these Soho filmmakers, budgetary constraints impacted the types of topical issues they chose to explore. In parallel to the tabloid press, filmmakers took advantage of the Wolfenden Report and the implementation of the Street Offences Act (1959), producing salacious films about their impact on prostitution and the evolution of underground striptease and nightclub culture, which they alleged led the moral denigration of British society. This was the chief concern of pseudo-documentary *West End Jungle* (Arnold L. Miller, 1961) and crime-melodramas *The Flesh Is Weak* (Don Chaffey, 1957) and *The Shakedown* (John Lemont,1960). These films dramatised the relationship between society, sex and urban vice. Soho films were also concerned with the impact of this legislation on the postwar generation. *Beat Girl* (Edmond T. Gréville, 1960) and *Rag Doll* (Lance Comfort, 1961) used the spaces of the 1960s coffee bar, strip club and nightclub as a way to comment on growing permissive attitudes and new forms of commercial leisure. They also functioned as 'warnings' for younger audiences on the dangers of metropolitan life that could lead to being groomed into prostitution or other forms of vice. In Chapter 9 and 10 I explored the ways the mushrooming of striptease clubs and the legacy of the area highlighted these transformations further, focusing on Paul Raymond, who reinforced this message with a larger-than-life persona, rendering it palatable for the British public. In the films *Too Hot to Handle* (Terence Young, 1960) and *The Small World of Sammy Lee* (Ken Hughes, 1963), we see a more streamlined denotation of Soho as a sleazy underbelly, a cinematic articulation that would continue to permeate films from the 1970s and beyond. The sheer volume of films released following 1963 that depicted second-dimensional striptease centred narratives, known as 'sexploitation films' in one sense devalued the efforts of the Soho Fair in its attempt to promote both sides of Soho's character.

One Soho film that marked the end of the postwar Soho film canon, *The World Ten Times Over* (Wolf Rilla, 1963), integrated the themes I have examined throughout this book seamlessly – sexual liberation, hedonism, generational fracture and social mobility are woven together, arguably successfully, though perhaps in the wrong decade. The film also signalled the end of the British New Wave canon in 1963 and the onset of the Swinging Sixties and permissive society.[17] This little-recognised film, whose position within this transitory period echoed the beginning of a lost interest for filmmakers to depict Soho's real-life cosmopolitan diversity, is worth examining in this context. The film starred two well-known British actresses in the main roles, Sylvia Syms and June Ritchie. However, like most Soho films, the critical/commercial failure represented the catalyst for their hedonistic behaviour on multiple, if not ambiguous levels, which included the displacement within metropolitan life, fear of romantic entanglement and, lastly, control by male archetypes (father/lover/client). Nevertheless, the film makes a lasting impression, through its loose editing, beautiful cinematography, on-location shooting and naturalistic performances.

The World Ten Times Over (1963)

During the penultimate sequence of *The World Ten Times Over*, first released in the United Kingdom in 1963 and retitled *Pussycat Alley* for its US release in 1965, a prudish schoolmaster (William Hartnell) wanders the labyrinth of Soho as he wrestles with his conscience over whether to reconcile with his twentysomething daughter Billa (Sylvia Syms). A largely absent father who lives outside of the metropole, he has just learned of Billa's engagement as a nightclub hostess in the fictional 'Ecstasy' club in Soho, where she barters sex to exploit clients for petty cash and gifts. The truth is revealed during a heated exchange between them at her bedsit in Marylebone that she shares with colleague and best friend Ginnie (June Ritchie), and Syms plays the confession to her father in this scene beautifully as both bitter and cathartic. In a trance-like state, her father leaves her home and moves towards Soho, then down Old Compton Street, past the clip-joints, brothels and strip clubs, where he is heckled by doormen and teenagers, and solicited by beggars and buskers. In an attempt to represent Soho wholly from the father's perspective, Rilla follows him with a handheld camera that seemingly blurs together the casinos, coffee bars and restaurants. Billa's father even passes by the Compton-Cameo Cinema club that is currently screening *West End Jungle* for its members. This sequence recalls the tracking shots through Soho at night similarly deployed by the films *Soho Incident* (Vernon Sewell, 1956), *Expresso Bongo* (Val Guest, 1960) and *Rag Doll* (Lance Comfort, 1961). Tonally, however, it is very unlike Jim, Johnny and Carol's bright-eyed discovery of Soho's winding topography, discarding the depiction of their subsequent ownership of its commercial spaces. Instead, Billa's father is lost in his partly liberal attempt to conduct a moral ethnography of the bohemians, hedonists and tourists. Stopping off for a drink in a smoke-filled pub, a man nearby (played by television comedian John Junkin, who went uncredited for his role) philosophises over the state of the nation. His nihilist monologue, much like Dave and Jess' sorrowful pop ballads in *Beat Girl* and *Rag Doll*, touches upon delinquency, violence, immigration, infidelity and the threat of nuclear war: 'Beardless boys beating up old ladies with bicycle chains. Hooligans with flick knives going around slashing people and sitting down in Trafalgar Square … talk about the Bomb … People coming and going … When's it going to end?'[18] After the man finishes his speech, the schoolmaster finishes his beer, and the camera closes in on a pamphlet crumpled in his palm for a lecture on juvenile delinquency.

Billa's father eventually finds her place of employment in Soho and apprehensively enters. Billa feigns embracing him into her world as he is jostled back and forth between her inebriated male clients. The Ecstasy club is representative of those clip-joint and strip clubs reinvented as more exclusive spaces of consumption by Paul Raymond that appear in films like *Beat Girl* (Edmond T. Gréville, 1960) and *Striptease Murder* (Ernest Morris, 1961). Similar to *The Small World of Sammy Lee* (Ken Hughes, 1963) the club's compère (Davy Kaye) entertains the male clientele with lewd jokes and predictions of future infidelity with the female employees. Although Billa's father initially asks her to leave with him, Billa and Ginnie humiliate him in front of their clients and push other hostesses-for-hire onto him, 'compliments of the house'.[19] After plying him with champagne and insipid company, Billa then orders him to leave. He stays until the club closes in the early hours of the morning and confronting her on his exit, he tells her dryly and without emotion: 'You're just trash.'[20] Prior to this sequence, Ginnie, the more juvenile of the two women, has been engaged in a similarly virulent discussion with her boyfriend, a married businessman named Bob (Edward Judd).[21] After abandoning his wife in favour of marrying Ginnie, he goes to her apartment, where she hides from him, demanding Billa keep him occupied. Ginnie ultimately dismisses him and a potential future together. Her dreams of leaving behind Soho and Billa are further obstructed by her unplanned pregnancy with Bob's child. However, throughout the film, she expresses a desire to return to the autonomy of her youth: 'When I was a child, I used to dig holes in the sand. Oh, nothing was impossible then. I was "Queen of the World", ten times over.'[22] This sentiment could be read as a scathing discourse on 1960s female sexuality. Despite Ginnie's seemingly 'liberated' promiscuous behaviour, she understands her function within society as a male object of desire, reflecting Carol's pregnancy and subsequent isolation at the end of Rag Doll.

The World Ten Times Over was shot on location in London and at Elstree Studios in Hertfordshire. It was produced on a modest budget of £350,000.[23] However, despite the commercial draw of its two young stars Syms and Ritchie, and its metropolitan setting, it was a commercial and critical flop. One review in Monthly Film Bulletin highlighted its 'crudely' conceived premise, where 'the old "warm-hearted tart" cliché is turned inside out, to unpleasant and implausible effect'.[24] My research failed to uncover why the film was released two years later in the United States, though it was most likely due to budgetary restrictions regarding the promotion of the film. Boxoffice called the film a 'strikingly effective dramatic study of London life, circa these Soaring Sixties', but Variety noted that it held 'scant marquee value for U.S. release'.[25] According to Robert Murphy, The World Ten Times Over marked the end of Rilla's career: 'Rilla, son of the German actor Walter Rilla, was a competent director... But in 1963 he switched from solid, mainstream entertainment (Village of the Damned and Piccadilly Third Stop, 1960) [and] The World Ten Times Over seems to have damaged Rilla's career even more effectively than Peeping Tom did Powell's.'[26] Several years after the failure of The World Ten Times Over, Rilla and his wife retired to run a hotel in Provence.[27] Stephen Bourne believes that Rilla failed to fully explore the first instance of a Lesbian relationship in postwar British cinema. Interviewing Syms in 1989, the actress confirms this fact: 'As far as I was concerned my character was in love with June Ritchie and I wanted to play it that way, but in those days one could only suggest lesbianism.'[28] Bourne suggests that the film 'desperately tried to imitate the French New Wave [but] failed to create a British entry'.[29] The film may draw upon European cinemas and the clichés of traditional melodrama, but it also fits neatly into the 'girl problem' films of the mid-1950s, echoed by its themes of generational divide and female sexuality:

> *The cycle's major narrative structures hinge on women – for example, the story of a young girl who is lured to the glitter of the city and is corrupted by it – though the films are very unclear as to how much is the corruption of the city and how much is perversity in the girl.*[30]

The film also echoes the ways in which British cinema was changing, 'as in the culture at large, the stifling censorship apparatus quickly crumbled, and sexual themes became a commonplace in mainstream films and in the now more visible pornography industry'.[31] The film's staccato-like 'terrible' dialogue, crisp and atmospheric cinematography by Larry Pizer, and Rilla's sharp, jarring, experimental editing style suggest that it cannot be simply categorised as a pseudo-New Wave film.[32] The British New Wave consisted of a group of films produced between 1959 and 1963 led by documentary filmmakers such as Tony Richardson and Karel Reisz who broke 'into the closed shop of the British film industry'.[33] As Gavin Lambert notes, the 'key movies of the British "New Wave" of the 1960s are set in the bleak, industrial north'.[34] But by 1963, the movement had 'failed to sustain a renaissance' and came to a conclusion with the films *This Sporting Life* (Lindsay Anderson, 1963) and *Billy Liar* (John Schlesinger, 1963). These films 'remained firmly on the autonomy and integrity of the individual versus social forces [and] the insidious, stultifying consumer and television culture that threatened the spirit and soul running through almost all the films'.[35] Both *The Small World of Sammy Lee* and *The World Ten Times Over* expressed a 'moral and cultural critique than an overtly political one' like their New Wave equivalents, particularly in their shared, negative representation of Soho's sexual economies and its subsequent impact upon the morality of its labourers.[36] But it is worth noting that the year prior to the film's release, the James Bond franchise was launched successfully with *Dr. No* (Terence Young), but cinema attendance continued to wane in its battle with commercial television. At the end of 1963, cinema admissions in Britain declined another 8%, and a further 7% of national cinemas closed.[37] The return of the 'warm-hearted tart' cliché positioned in Soho would not be seen until the low-budget sexploitation film *Secrets of a Windmill Girl* (Arnold Louis Miller, 1966). This film charts the 'rise and fall of a stripper' and was shot inside the Windmill Theatre, which by this time was owned by British-Jewish entrepreneurs Michael Klinger and Tony Tenser of Compton-Cameo Films. The film was shown to a limited audience in select pornographic cinemas. Klinger and Tenser had purchased the Windmill Theatre in 1961 and converted it into a casino and cinema called the Windmill Cinema

Club.[38] Andrew Spicer has suggested that Klinger's dedication to supporting burgeoning, independent directors showed the 'complexity' of his ability to straddle several modes of production, 'exploitation, middle-brow and art-house'.[39] Both Klinger and Tenser went on to produce other pornographic films that marketed and exploited Soho's sex industry in the mid-1960s such as *London in the Raw* and *Primitive London*, two films from 1965, which aimed to show 'how depraved London was'.[40]

Perhaps *The World Ten Times Over* failed to land with critics and audiences precisely because it entangled itself within the moral/cultural debates of the period, but due to its limited scope and isolated metropolitan setting, it could not hope to compete with the more lavish, escapist films that established cinema's status quo, like *Dr. No*. Ultimately, the film's decision to spotlight two female protagonists in an urban setting highlights its double significance as a feminist film and, as such, it should be included within the British New Wave and Swinging Sixties canon. It is in one sense an abstract imagining of Soho's past, but also foreshadows its decline in the public sphere as a cosmopolitan space, a reputation driven by the mass proliferation of sex shops and strip clubs during the 1970s.

Campaigns and Rebirth

In Chapter 9, I briefly touched on the forced closure of beloved Madame Jojo's nightclub in 2014. Was its closure simply a draconian move by Westminster City Council to facilitate the expansion of private, globalised neoliberal capitalist forces? One promoter of the club told *The Guardian*: 'In my opinion, it seems that the council just used the incident as a good excuse to take away the licence. If you look at the way the area is changing, they clearly don't want a late-night drinking presence anywhere in Soho anymore.'[41] The press later revealed that Soho Estates had already been scheduled to demolish Madame Jojo's in 2013 and that those plans to redevelop the premises by Matt Architecture had already been approved by the Council.[42] Matt Architecture is a design firm located in nearby Leicester Square. The firm conveyed its promise online to 'revitalise one of Soho's seediest alleyways' and to restore the 'globally recognised icon of Soho, the neon "Raymond Revuebar" sign, to prominence in the West End's night-time panorama'.[43] In May 2019, Raymond's granddaughter began construction of a new theatre, The

Boulevard, on the old site of the bar, an intimate 165-seat venue that opened in autumn of 2019 with a showcase of new and existing British plays.[44]

In 2014, the British press swiftly churned out stories detailing the impact of Madame Jojo's closure on employees, patrons, tourists, celebrities and local Soho residents. Over the next few years, national newspapers, television personalities and popular commentators were largely unanimous in agreement that the closure of the club was 'the last nail in Soho's coffin'.[45] Today, Madame Jojo's has evolved into a cultural symbol for the wider debates surrounding the commercial gentrification of Soho and the City of London. It has generated high-profile movements of political and social activism, first led by Tim Arnold, a musician and resident of Soho who founded the 'Save Soho' group shortly after the closure of Madame Jojo's. The group's chairman is British actor Stephen Fry. Its motto is 'Keeping Soho inclusive, not exclusive'.[46] The group is currently endorsed by numerous actors, musicians and celebrities such as Benedict Cumberbatch, and actively leads and supports campaigns against the closure of public spaces, restaurants, pubs and entertainment venues in the area. It newest documentary film, *Soho Is...*, was released online in April 2020. The film chronicled the journey of Save Soho by assembling various clips of interviews with Arnold, Fry and other campaigners. This includes the Curzon Soho cinema on Shaftesbury Avenue, which has been threatened with demolition for the Crossrail 2 route since 2015. Another example is the Coach and Horses Pub at 29 Greek Street, which was made infamous by its landlord Norman Balon, who was given moniker of the 'rudest landlord in London' by Jeffrey Bernard. Despite its association with bohemia and British journalism, in early 2019, the Coach and Horses embarked on a public campaign to convince Fuller's, a regional pub company, to renew its lease on the pub to save the famed institution from closure. In order to raise awareness for the petition, the pub collaborated with a theatre company to revive *Jeffrey Bernard Is Unwell* in May 2019 as an immersive production performed inside the pub.[47] In 2019, the pub's existing landlord was permanently removed by Fuller's, though the original exteriors and interiors remain.

Madame Jojo's closure did not simply re-ignite the public interest in the gentrification of Soho; it was also responsible for refocusing the spotlight on the historical significance of London's urban village. The Soho Society, a volunteer-led organisation founded by local residents in 1972 that officially consults with Westminster Council on planning, licensing, traffic and environmental matters, launched a substantial project in collaboration with the Photographer's Gallery on a series of podcasts accompanied by archival photographs entitled *Soho Then* and produced by Soho resident and producer Clare Lynch.[48] The Museum of Soho, founded in 1991, was recently digitised by Tony Shrimplin, who continues to update his fascinating repository of Soho histories online. It is no coincidence that Christopher Howse's *Soho in the Eighties* and Peter Speiser's history for the British Library entitled *Soho: The Heart of Bohemian London* were published in 2018. This was followed by Dan Cruickshank's *Soho: A Street Guide to Soho's History, Architecture and People*, which was published in August 2019.[49]

The closure of Madame Jojo's also formed the foundation for the documentary film *Battle of Soho* (Aro Korol, 2016), which aimed to highlight Soho's function as a site for the development of subculture. The film was poorly received by mainstream critics, who thought that its sentimentalism and lack of social context failed to contribute any further understanding of Soho's significance. Rowan Pelling's review of the film in the *Daily Telegraph* suggests that its director Korol believes that 'unless we act now, the joyful, smutty, anarchic underbelly of London will be lost forever'.[50] But it would appear that Soho has indeed returned as a chief location for filmmakers: the queer film *Postcards from London* (Steve McLean) in 2018 closed the BFI's Flare Festival and was followed by *Adrift in Soho* (Pablo Behrens, 2019), an adaptation of Colin Wilson's novel published in 1961, and Edgar Wright's *Last Night in Soho*, which was released in October of 2021.[51]

The Future of Soho

In 2016, three researchers from Middlesex University conducted a sociological study of Soho's commercial redevelopment. In their study, they described the differentiation of the currently gentrifying areas within London as the 'interplay between social, cultural and economic capital'.[52] They then embarked on an ethnography of Soho over a period of fifteen months. Drawing on Shoreditch, East London as an example for comparison, they concluded that the increasing number of middle-class professionals, alongside creative and tech businesses that moved to Shoreditch from 2005 onwards, is what subsequently caused a 'hipsterfication' of the area.[53] This, alongside the regeneration project of the East End as part of the 2012 London Olympics, caused a dramatic social and culture shifts in local communities, which saw low-income residents and migrant populations displaced from their homes. However, in the case of Soho, they argued that its rapid development was predominantly driven by private companies facilitated by Westminster City Council, which has, in turn, resulted in a hegemonic gentrification and sanitisation of Soho's independent businesses.[54] This echoes Mort's summation that historically 'Soho's status as the city's most influential cosmopolitan quarter was transformed many times ... Subsequent versions of bohemian Soho were driven by businesses marketing a wide variety of goods and sexual services to successive generations of customers and fashionable cognoscenti'.[55]

The 'Real' Soho

The aim of this book has been to spotlight a particular group of unique films that located their stories within the dense, geographical locality of Soho, an area whose global reputation as a bohemian and cosmopolitan district rendered them distinctive objects within the context of postwar British filmmaking. But it was also partly driven by my own desire to examine the reproduction of cosmopolitanism on screen, and the relationship between film and the social, industrial and commercial context in which they were produced. This includes the ongoing battle for British filmmakers to develop new strategies in order to combat the decline of cinema-going. During this project, my interest grew in relation to the new forms of legislation regarding prostitution in the postwar period, which led to the growth of underground sexual economies, resulting in the birth of sexploitation cinema. My chief concern has been with how these films arranged the urban topography of Soho in order to uncover their intrinsic relationship with local entrepreneurs, lawmakers and the popular press who were similarly working to rebrand the area of Soho to suit Britain's global objectives after the war. Ultimately, I have discovered that although these films privileged a particular (masculine) representation of Soho, they did not simply 'reflect' the shifting national ideologies and culture(s), but were also responsible for shaping them, particularly in the case of teenage cultures, striptease and sexual permissiveness.

Soho is elusive. Dramatic social, cultural and political change over the centuries have made this commercial square mile in the heart of London a type of chameleon. Like an animal in the wild, shades of its character have adapted in accordance with its environment, inextricably linked to the city's migrant community and aggressive commercial development by its business and political leaders. Regarding isolated geographical areas with a rich cultural history and multifarious reputation, we are often bombarded with the vociferous cries of those who claim they truly 'possess' it. However, the urban and commercial topography of Soho, along with the living, breathing community of the area, continues to weave itself into the very fabric of London before swiftly moving on, making room for the next group of hopeful denizens and expatriates. The reasons behind these consumer migrations are complex and it is too easy to simply blame rising property prices, though there is an intimate correlation between them. Despite the Soho chameleon's war with an impending cultural homogeneity that is currently enveloping London society, in the public imagination, Soho's essence, spirit or, to put it in a more aptly contemporary vein, 'vibe' continues to offer us a consistency of underlying representations that include a definition of this urban village as a subcultural, nonconformist, multicultural hub of activity. However, ultimately, Soho belongs to no one and everyone. Perhaps the reason behind Soho's absence today as a mainstream cinematic setting is due to its historical function as a liminal space of consumption. My relationship with Soho can be best described by Marcel Proust: 'Desire makes everything blossom; possession makes everything wither and fade.'[56] Ergo, Soho's enduring allure is because of its ephemerality. As cultural historians have argued throughout the decades, Soho survives because of its commercial adaptability. We must remember that film can only ever evoke the spirit of a place, never truth. In essence, these films are like the Soho they occupy: unpredictable, indefinable, human.

Notes

1. Frank Mort, 'Scandalous Events: Metropolitan Culture and Moral Change in Post-Second World War London', *Representations* 93 (2006), 107.
2. Ibid.
3. Christopher Booker, 'Profumo. Chatterley. The Beatles. 1963 was the Year "Old England" Died', *The Spectator*, 23 November 2013. Retrieved 24 October 2021 from https://www.spectator.co.uk/2013/11/it-all-began-in-1963.
4. Piri Halasz's cover story included a kaleidoscopic cover emphasising London's landmarks such as Big Ben and flower power designed by Geoffrey Dickinson. See Piri Halasz, 'Great Britain: You Can Walk across It on the Grass', *Time*, 15 April 1966, 30–34.
5. See Steve Chibnall, 'Standing in the Shadow: Peter Whitehead, Swinging London's Insider/Outsider', *Framework* 52(1) (2011), 257–58.
6. Paul Willetts, *The Look of Love: The Life and Times of Paul Raymond, Soho's King of Clubs* (London: Serpent's Tail, 2010), 182.

7. Dick Kirby states that in C Division, the area which makes up the West End, 'Comparing the statistics of the first six months of 1963 to the same period in 1962 580 fewer crimes were committed, 256 more were cleared up and there was an increase of 287 arrests. Dick Kirby, *The Scourge of Soho: The Controversial Career of SAS Hero Detective Sergeant Harry Challenor MM* (Barnsley: Pen & Sword True Crime, 2013) 70. See also 'Attack on "Sleazier Soho Joints": Inquiry into Law Promised', *The Guardian*, 29 May 1963, 2.
8. Paul Willetts, *The Look of Love: The Life and Times of Paul Raymond, Soho's King of Clubs* (London: Serpent's Tail, 2010), 182.
9. Ibid., 188.
10. 'Soho Stories: Celebrating Six Decades of Sex, Drugs and Rock 'n' Roll', *The Guardian*, 17 May 2015. Retrieved 1 May 2016 from https://www.theguardian.com/culture/2015/may/17/london-soho-stories-sex-drugs-rock-and-roll.
11. Frank Mort, 'Striptease: The Erotic Female Body and Live Sexual Entertainment in Mid-twentieth-Century London', *Social History* 32(1) (2007), 42.
12. See Robin de Peyer and Gareth Richman, 'Soho through the Ages', *Evening Standard*, 3 April 2015, https://www.standard.co.uk/news/london/soho-through-the-ages-fascinating-pictures-show-changing-face-of-iconic-london-district-10152182.html.
13. Mort, 'Striptease', 42.
14. Ibid.
15. See '1999: Dozens Injured in Soho Nail Bomb', *BBC News*, 30 April 1999. Retrieved 24 October 2021 from http://news.bbc.co.uk/onthisday/hi/dates/stories/april/30/newsid_2499000/2499249.stm.
16. Will Self, 'Soho in the Eighties', *The Guardian*, 6 September 2018. Retrieved 24 October 2021 from https://www.theguardian.com/books/2018/sep/06/soho-in-the-eighties-by-christopher-howse-review.
17. A substantial reconsideration of the 1960s and British cinema in that decade has recently been produced by scholars from the University of York and University of East Anglia, whose research project was published in May 2019: see Richard Farmer, Laura Mayne, Duncan Petrie and Melanie Williams, *Transformation and Tradition in 1960s British Cinema* (Edinburgh: Edinburgh University Press, 2019).
18. *The World Ten Times Over* (Wolf Rilla, 1963).
19. Ibid.
20. Ibid.
21. One critic said: 'Edward Judd as one of the male pawns in the game of passing-out-the-favours, is convincing in the moments of personal truth'. See 'Pussycat Alley', *Boxoffice*, 7 February 1966, a11.
22. Robert Murphy, *Sixties British Cinema* (London: British Film Institute, 1992), 83.
23. Ibid., 82.
24. See 'The World Ten Times Over', *Monthly Film Bulletin* 30(348) (1963), 156.
25. See Rich, 'Film Reviews: The World 10 Times Over', *Variety*, 13 November (1963), 6.
26. Murphy, *Sixties British Cinema*, 82.
27. Frederic Raphael, *Going up: To Cambridge and Beyond, a Writer's Memoir* (London: Robson Press, 2015), 22.
28. Stephen Bourne, *Brief Encounters: Lesbians and Gays in British Cinema 1930–1971* (London: Cassell, 1996), 181.

29. Ibid., 179.
30. Richard Dyer, *The Matter of Images: Essays on Representation* (London: Routledge, 2002), 79.
31. Jim Leach, *British Film* (Cambridge: Cambridge University Press, 2006), 127.
32. John Coleman of the *New Statesman* said: 'Only Miss Syms, under a *Golden Marie* kind of hairstyle, brings a moment of pathos to the lesbian finale. The dialogue is terrible.' See John Coleman, 'Reviving', *New Statesman*, 1 July 1963, 674. Born in London, Pizer started his film career at the Alexander Korda Studios at Denham, first working as an office boy on Michael Powell's *49th Parallel* (1941) and *Major Barbara* (1941), and then joining the camera department on Leslie Howard's *First of the Few* (1942) and *Gentle Sex* (1942). See 'Cinematographer Larry Pizer Dies', *Variety*, 8 April 2008. Retrieved 24 October 2021 from https://variety.com/2008/film/news/cinematographer-larry-pizer-dies-1117983697.
33. Woodfall Films was formed by Richardson in order to bring Osborne's groundbreaking kitchen-sink play *Look Back in Anger* to the screen in 1959. See Gavin Lambert, 'New Wave, Old Problem', *The Guardian*, 3 October 2002, 14.
34. June Ritchie had achieved acclaim for her performance in *A Kind of Loving* (1962) opposite Alan Bates, a film that shares the concern for the same issues as the New Wave, such as class and premarital sex. See Gavin Lambert, 'New Wave, Old Problem', *The Guardian*, 3 October 2002, 14.
35. Richardson relocated to the United States in 1970, and his colleagues, Karel Reisz and John Schlesinger, divided their time between the two. See Leonard Quart, 'The Religion of the Market: Thatcherite Politics and the British Film of the 1980s', in Lester Friedman (ed.), *Fires Were Started: British Cinema and Thatcherism* (New York: Wallflower Press, 2006), 16.
36. Ibid.
37. Mark Duguid says: 'Of the studios that had dominated the post-war period, only Rank at Pinewood and Associated British at Elstree survived, both Michael Balcon's Ealing and Alexander Korda's London Films having collapsed by 1958.' See Mark Duguid, 'British Film in the 1960s', *BFI Screenonline*. Retrieved 24 October 2021 from http://www.screenonline.org.uk/film/id/1291628. See also '"Crisis in Confidence" in Film Industry', *The Guardian*, 10 December 1963, 3.
38. See Andrew Spicer and A.T. McKenna, *The Man Who Got Carter: Michael Klinger, Production and the British Film Industry 1960–198* (London: I.B. Tauris, 2013), 11.
39. Andrew Spicer, 'Creativity and Commerce: Michael Klinger and New Film History', *New Review of Film and Television Studies* 8(3) (2010), 302.
40. 'Soho was a formative influence on Michael Klinger … Not only was Soho bohemian, multi-ethnic, cosmopolitan and entrepreneurial with a variety of small businesses huddled conveniently together, it was the centre of the film and sex industries whose interconnections moulded his early career.' See ibid., 17, 22.
41. Pete Clark, 'The Slow Death of Soho: Farewell to London's Sleazy Heartland', *The Guardian*, 25 November 2014. Retrieved 24 October 2021 from https://www.theguardian.com/music/2014/nov/25/the-slow-death-of-soho-farewell-to-londons-sleazy-heartland.
42. Today, Soho Estates owns more than 60 acres across Soho and Leicester Square, and is one of London's largest landowners. See 'Kings of Soho: James and Norris's Soho Transformation', *Property Week*, 22 June 2012, 30.
43. Matt Architecture. 'Walker's Court'. Retrieved 24 October 2021 from https://mattarchitecture.com/Walker-s-Court-London-SW1.

44. I was fortunate enough to have been given a tour of the venue being built in May 2019. The building is shared with the notorious club venue The Box, which took ownership of the original Revuebar site. See also Robert Dex, 'Boulevard Theatre: King of Soho's Legacy Takes Centre Stage at London's Newest Art Venue', *Evening Standard*, 19 March 2019. Retrieved 24 October 2021 from https://www.standard.co.uk/go/london/theatre/boulevard-theatre-king-of-soho-london-arts-venue-a4095321.html.
45. Clark, 'The Slow Death of Soho'.
46. The Save Soho group also lobbied against the use of Soho Square as a work depot for Crossrail, meaning that the area would not be accessible for ten years. See http://savesoho.com/about (retrieved 24 October 2021).
47. Bernard did not quite invent Norman Balon, the cantankerous but golden-hearted landlord of the Coach and Horses, who figured in his column. Balon was a Frankenstein's monster. See Christopher Howse, 'Obituary: Jeffrey Bernard', *The Independent*, 6 September 1997. Retrieved 24 October 2021 from https://www.independent.co.uk/news/people/obituary-jeffrey-bernard-1237687.html. See also Jonathan Romney, 'The Battle to Save the Curzon Soho', *The Guardian*, 17 April 2016. Retrieved 24 October 2021 from https://www.theguardian.com/film/2016/apr/17/fight-to-save-curzon-soho-cinema-landmark-london. See also Tim Arnold, 'The Coach and Horses: A Soho Jewel', *Tim Arnold Official Website*. Retrieved 24 October 2021 from https://www.timarnold.co.uk/the-coach-and-horses-a-soho-jewel.
48. See 'Soho Then', producer: Clare Lynch, The Photographer's Gallery. Retrieved 24 October 2021 from https://thephotographersgallery.org.uk/content/new-podcast-series-soho-then.
49. Peter Speiser, *Soho: The Heart of Bohemian London* (London: British Library Publishing, 2017); Christopher Howse, *Soho in the Eighties* (London: Bloomsbury Continuum, 2018); and the Dan Cruickshank, *Soho: A Street Guide to Soho's History, Architecture and People* (London: Orion Publishing, 2019).
50. Rowan Pelling, 'The Battle of Soho: Meet the Maverick Fighting to Save London's Anarchic Underbelly', *Daily Telegraph*, 26 October 2017. Retrieved 24 October 2021 from https://www.telegraph.co.uk/films/0/battle-soho-meet-mavericks-fighting-save-londons-anarchic-underbelly.
51. The author interviewed Wright for Soho Radio in October of 2021 where Wright highlighted the great influence of Soho B films in *Last Night in Soho*. See 'Interview: Edgar Wright on the Museum of Soho,' Soho Radio Podcast, 24 October 2021, https://podcasts.apple.com/gb/podcast/edgar-wright-on-the-museum-of-soho. See also Jingan Young's accompanying article which ties to the release of Wright's film, 'Soho Striptease Clubs, Exploitation and the British B Film,' *Sight and Sound*, Vol. 31, No. 9, November 2021, 48–49.
52. See Erin Sanders-McDonagh, Magali Peyrefitte and Matt Ryalls, 'Sanitising the City: Exploring Hegemonic Gentrification in London" Soho', *Sociological Research Online* 21(3) (2016), 2.
53. Ibid.
54. Ibid., 1.
55. Mort, *Capital Affairs*, 365.
56. The original Proust quotation reads: 'L'ambition enivre plus que la gloire; le désir fleurit, la possession flétrit toutes choses.' See Chapter 6 of Marcel Proust's *Les Plaisirs et les Jours* (Paris: Calmann Lévy, 1896).

Filmography

Piccadilly (E.A. Dupont, 1929)
Greek Street (Sinclair Lewis, 1930)
Strip! Strip! Hooray!!! (Norman Lee, 1932)
The Thin Man (W.S. van Dyke, 1934)
A Yank at Oxford (Jack Conway, 1938)
Murder in Soho/Murder in the Night (Norman Lee, 1939)
They Drive by Night (Arthur Woods, 1939)
East of Piccadilly (Harold Huth, 1941)
This Happy Breed (David Lean, 1944)
Gilda (Charles Vidor, 1946)
Piccadilly Incident (Herbert Wilcox, 1946)
Nightbeat (Harold Huth, 1947)
They Made Me a Fugitive (Alberto Cavalcanti, 1947)
The Good-Time Girl (David Macdonald, 1948)
Hamlet (Laurence Olivier, 1948)
Oliver Twist (David Lean, 1948)
The Red Shoes (Michael Powell, 1948)
It Happened in Soho (Frank Chisnell, 1948)
The Flamingo Affair/Blonde for Danger (Horace Shepherd, 1948)
Noose/The Silk Noose (Edmond T. Gréville, 1948)
The Noose Hangs High (Charles Barton, 1948)
The Blue Lamp (Basil Dearden, 1949)
Boys in Brown (Montgomery Tully, 1949)
Murder at the Windmill/Mystery at the Burlesque (Val Guest, 1949)
The Blue Lamp (Basil Dearden, 1950)
Night and the City (Jules Dassin, 1950)
Soho Conspiracy (Cecil H. Williamson, 1950)
An American in Paris (Vincente Minnelli, 1951)
The Gambler and the Lady (Patrick Jenkins and Sam Newfield, 1952)
I Believe in You (Basil Dearden and Michael Relph, 1952)
Moulin Rouge (Jean Huston, 1952)
Wide Boy (Ken Hughes, 1952)
The Blue Parrot (John Harlow, 1953)

Cosh Boy/The Slasher (Lewis Gilbert, 1953)
Mantrap/Man in Hiding (Terence Fisher, 1953)
Street of Shadows/Shadowman (Richard Vernon, 1953)
Turn the Key Softly (Jack Lee, 1953)
The Wild One (László Benedek, 1953)
The Dark Stairway/The Greek Street Murder (Ken Hughes, 1954)
Cell 2445, Death Row (Fred F. Sears, 1955)
Wicked Woman (Russell Rouse, 1953)
36 Hours/Terror Street (Montgomery Tully, 1953)
Operation Manhunt (Jack Alexander, 1954)
Cry Vengeance (Mark Stevens, 1954)
Face the Music/The Black Glove (Terence Fisher, 1954)
Five Days/Paid to Kill (Montgomery Tully, 1954)
Murder by Proxy/Blackout (Terence Fisher, 1954)
Touchez pas au grisbi (Jacques Becker, 1954)
Youth Club (Norman Prouting, 1954)
44 Soho Square/Soho Incident/Spin a Dark Web (Vernon Sewell, 1955)
Coffee House (British Pathé, 1955)
Timeslip/The Atomic Man (Ken Hughes, 1955)
Value for Money (Ken Annakin, 1955)
Film Fanfare – No 26 – Section 2 (British Pathé, 1956)
Gelignite Gang/The Dynamiters (Terence Fisher, 1956)
Stars at the Fair (British Pathé, 1956)
Blonde in Bondage (Robert Brandt, 1957)
The Flesh Is Weak (Don Chaffey, 1957)
Mademoiselle Striptease/The Fast Set/Striptease du Paris (Pierre Foucaud, 1957)
The Man from Tangier/Thunder over Tangier (Lance Comfort, 1957)
Miracle in Soho (Julian Amyes, 1957)
Nice Time (Claude Goretta, Alain Tanner, 1957)
Rafles sur la ville (Pierre Chenal, 1957)
Rock You Sinners (Denis Kavanagh, 1957)
These Dangerous Years/Dangerous Youth (Herbert Wilcox, 1957)
The Tommy Steele Story/Rock Around the World (Gerard Bryant, 1957)
Clubs Galore! (British Pathé, 1958)
The Duke Wore Jeans (Gerald Thomas, 1958)
The Golden Disc/The In-Between Age (Don Sharp, 1958)
It's the Age of The Teenager (British Pathé, 1958)
Party Girl (Nicholas Ray, 1958)
Passport to Shame/Room 43 (Alvin Rakoff, 1958)
Sapphire (Basil Dearden, 1958)
Soho Striptease Clubs (John Rhodes, 1958)

Touch of Evil (Orson Welles, 1958)
Oh Boy! (Rita Gillespie, television series, 1958–59)
Blue Denim (Philip Dunne, 1959)
The Lady Is a Square (Herbert Wilcox, 1959)
Look at Life: Coffee Bar (Rank Organisation, 1959)
Saber of London (1957–60). 'Incident in Soho'. Season 6, Episode 6. American Broadcasting Company (Godfrey Grayson, 1959)
Serious Charge/A Touch of Hell (Terence Young, 1959)
We Are the Lambeth Boys (Karel Reisz, 1959)
Beat Girl/Wild for Kicks (Edmond T. Gréville, 1960)
Beatnik Wedding (British Pathé, 1960)
Can-Can (Walter Lang, 1960)
The Challenge/It Takes a Thief (John Gilling, 1960)
The Entertainer (Tony Richardson, 1960)
Expresso Bongo (Val Guest, 1960)
The Gentle Trap (Charles Saunders, 1960)
Hell Is a City (Val Guest, 1960)
Living for Kicks (Rollo Gamble, 1960)
Peeping Tom (Michael Powell, 1960)
Piccadilly Third Stop (Wolf Rilla, 1960)
Rag Doll/Young, Willing and Eager (Lance Comfort, 1960)
Saturday Night and Sunday Morning (Karel Reisz, 1960)
The Shakedown/The Naked Mirror (John Lemont, 1960)
Too Hot to Handle/Playgirl After Dark (Terence Young, 1960)
The Frightened City (John Lemont, 1961)
Jungle Street/Jungle Street Girls (Charles Saunders, 1961)
The Rebel/Call Me Genius (Robert Day, 1961)
Striptease Murder (Ernest Morris, 1961)
A Taste of Honey (Tony Richardson, 1961)
Victim (Basil Dearden, 1961)
West End Jungle (Arnold Miller, 1961)
The Young Ones/It's Wonderful to Be Young! (Sidney J. Furie, 1961)
Danger by My Side (Charles Saunders, 1962)
Down at The Two I's (British Pathé, 1962)
Gypsy (Mervyn LeRoy, 1962)
A Kind of Loving (John Schlesinger, 1962)
The Painted Smile/Murder Can Be Deadly (Lance Comfort, 1962)
Play It Cool (Michael Winner, 1962)
She Knows Y'Know (Montgomery Tully, 1962)
Some People (Clive Donner, 1962)
Billy Liar (John Schlesinger, 1963)

Impact (Peter Maxwell, 1963)
It's All Over Town (Douglas Hickox, 1963)
Live It Up!/Sing and Swing (Lance Comfort, 1963)
Palm Springs Weekend (Norman Taurog, 1963)
Saturday Night Out (Robert Hartford-Davis, 1963)
The Small World of Sammy Lee (Ken Hughes, 1963)
Strictly for the Birds (Vernon Sewell, 1963)
Summer Holiday (Peter Yates, 1963)
What a Crazy World (Michael Carreras, 1963)
The World Ten Times Over/Pussycat Alley (Wolf Rilla, 1963)
Yesterday, Today and Tomorrow (Vittorio de Sica, 1963)
Goldfinger (Guy Hamilton, 1964)
London in the Raw (Arnold L. Miller, 1964)
Primitive London (Arnold L. Miller, 1964)
Rattle of a Simple Man (Muriel Box, 1964)
The System/The Girl-Getters (Michael Winner, 1964)
Where Has Poor Mickey Gone…? (Gerry Levy, 1964)
Carousella (John Erwin, 1965)
The Spy Who Came in from the Cold (Martin Ritt, 1965)
Alfie (Lewis Gilbert, 1966)
The Hunchback of Soho/Der Bucklige von Soho (Alfred Vohrer, 1966)
Secrets of a Windmill Girl (Arnold Louis Miller, 1966)
Strip (Don Defina, Peter Davis, Staffan Lamm, 1966)
Bronco Bullfrog (Barney Platts-Mills, 1969)
A Clockwork Orange (Stanley Kubrick, 1971)
Villain (Michael Tuchner, 1971)
The Naked Civil Servant (Jack Gold, 1975)
Just Another Day – Soho (John Pitman, BBC, 1985)
Absolute Beginners (Julien Temple, 1986)
A Day in the Life of Jeffrey Bernard (Gerry Pomeroy, BBC Arena, 1987)
Mojo (Jez Butterworth, 1997)
Mrs Henderson Presents (Stephen Frears, 2005)
An Englishman in New York (Richard Laxton, 2009)
The Look of Love (Michael Winterbottom, 2013)
8 Things Made Inside 103 Wardour St (British Pathé, 2017)
Battle of Soho (Aro Korol, 2017)
Adrift in Soho (Pablo Behrens, 2018)
Postcards from London (Steve McLean, 2018)

Bibliography

Abercrombie, Patrick, Great Britain. Ministry of Town Country Planning and Standing Conference on London Regional Planning. *Greater London Plan, 1944: A Report Prepared on Behalf of the Standing Conference on London Regional Planning at the Request of the Minister of Town and Country Planning*. London: HMSO, 1945.
Abel, Richard (ed.). *Encyclopaedia of Early Cinema*. New York: Routledge, 2005.
Abrams, Mark. *The Teenage Consumer*. London: Press Exchange Ltd., 1959.
Acton, William, Charles Planck, St Thomas's Hospital, Medical School Library and Royal College of Physicians of London. *Prostitution: Considered in Its Moral, Social, and Sanitary Aspects, in London and Other Large Cities and Garrison Towns: With Proposals for the Control and Prevention of Its Attendant Evils*, 2nd edn. London: John Churchill and Sons, 1870.
Abrams, Nathan. 'Hidden: Jewish Film in the United Kingdom, Past and Present'. *Journal of European Popular Culture* 1 (2010): 53–68.
Abravanel, Genevieve. *Americanizing Britain: The Rise of Modernism in the Age of the Entertainment Empire*. Oxford: Oxford University Press, 2012.
Aldgate, Anthony. 'I Am a Camera: Film and Theatre Censorship in 1950s Britain'. *Contemporary European History* 8(3) (1999): 425–38.
———. *Censorship and the Permissive Society: British Cinema and Theatre 1955–1965*. Oxford: Clarendon Press, 1995.
Ahmed, Michael. 'Independent Cinema Exhibition in 1960s Britain: Compton Cinema'. *Postscript: Essays in Film and the Humanities* 30(3) (2011): 52–63.
Aldgate, Anthony, and Jeffrey Richards. *Britain Can Take It: British Cinema in the Second World War*. London: I.B. Tauris, 2007.
Allsop, Kenneth. 'Brave New Underworld'. *The Spectator*, 12 August 1960, 240.
Ambler, Dail. 'The Beat Girl' (1959). Screenplay. London: BFI Book Library.
Anderson, Hephzibiah. 'Wolf Mankowitz', in Sorrel Kerbel, Muriel Emanuel and Laura Phillips (eds), *The Routledge Encyclopaedia of Jewish Writers of the Twentieth Century*. New York, London: Fitzroy Dearborn, 2003, 664–68.
Arnold, Tim. 'The Coach and Horses: A Soho Jewel'. *Tim Arnold Official Website*. Retrieved 28 October 2021 from https://www.timarnold.co.uk/the-coach-and-horses-a-soho-jewel.
Ashby, Justine, and Andrew Higson. *British Cinema, Past and Present*. London: Routledge, 2000.

Ashton, Barney. 'West End Jungle Viewing Notes'. *West End Jungle* DVD, Strikeforce Entertainment, 2009.
Attallah, Naim. *A Scribbler in Soho: A Celebration of Auberon Waugh.* London: Quartet Books, 2019.
Baillieu, Bill, and John Goodchild. *The British Film Business.* Chichester: John Wiley & Sons, Ltd., 2002.
Baistow, Tom. 'Strip and Shake'. *New Statesman*, 17 January 1959: 67.
Baker, Howard. *Espresso Jungle.* London: Fleetway Publications, 1959.
'Balance Sheet of Hollywood's British Productions'. *Picturegoer*, 16 September 1950, 12.
Ball, John. 'The Clock Struck Twelve'. *News of the World*, 16 August 1959, 1.
Barber, Stephen. *Projected Cities: Cinema and Urban Space.* London: Reaktion Books, 2002.
Bardsley, Garth. *Stop the World: The Biography of Anthony Newley.* London: Oberon Books, 2003.
Bates, Charlotte and Alex Rhys-Taylor (eds). *Walking through Social Research.* Abingdon: Routledge, 2017.
BBC News. 'Dozens Injured in Soho Nail Bomb', 30 April 1999. Retrieved 28 October 2021 from http://news.bbc.co.uk/onthisday/hi/dates/stories/april/30/newsid_2499000/2499249.stm.
B.D. 'Expresso Bongo'. *Monthly Film Bulletin* 27(312) (1960): 2.
'Beat Girl Press Book' (1959). London: BFI Book Library.
'Beat Girl: Statement of Production Cost and Balance Sheet', 27 February 1960, Film Finances Archive, London.
Bell, Melanie. *Femininity in the Frame: Women and 1950s British Popular Cinema.* London: I.B. Tauris, 2010.
Bell-Williams, Melanie. '"Shop-Soiled" Women: Female Sexuality and the Figure of the Prostitute in 1950s British Cinema'. *Journal of British Cinema and Television* 3(2) (2006): 266–83.
Bendixson, Terence. 'New Ways to Soho'. *The Spectator*, 29 November 1963.
Benjamin, Walter. 'The Work of Art in the Age of Mechanical Reproduction', in *Illuminations. Essays and Reflections*, translated by Harry Zohn. New York: Schocken Books, 2007, 217–52.
Bergan, Ronald. 'Obituary: Terence Morgan'. *The Guardian*, 1 September 2005. Retrieved 28 October 2021 from https://www.theguardian.com/news/2005/sep/01/guardianobituaries.artsobituaries1.
Bergfelder, Tim, and Christian Cargnelli (eds). *Destination London: German-Speaking Emigres and British Cinema, 1925–1950.* Oxford: Berghahn Books, 2008.
Bergfelder, Tim, Sue Harris and Sarah Street. *Film Architecture and the Transnational Imagination: Set Design in 1930s European Cinema.* Amsterdam: Amsterdam University Press, 2007.
Bernard, Jeffrey. 'So Long, Soho'. *The Spectator*, 16 November 1996, 71.
——. 'Obituary'. *The Guardian*, 5 September 1997, A11.

Bill, Peter. 'The Great Estates, Part Five: Soho'. *The London Magazine*, 24 October 2016. Retrieved 28 October 2021 from http://www.thelondonmagazine.co.uk/people-places/area-guides/the-great-estates-part-five.html.
Bingham, Adrian. *Family Newspapers? Sex, Private Life, and the British Popular Press 1918–1978*. Oxford: Oxford Scholarship Online, 2009.
Black, Gerry. *Living up West: Jewish Life in London's West End*. London: London Museum of Jewish Life, 1994.
Blottner, Gene. *Columbia Noir: A Complete Filmography, 1940–1962*. Jefferson; NC: McFarland & Company, 2015.
Bollerey, Franziska, and Christoph Grafe (eds). *Cafés and Bars: The Architecture of Public Display*. London: Routledge, 2007.
Booker, Christopher. *The Neophiliacs: Revolution in English Life in the Fifties and Sixties*, 2nd edn. London: Pimlico, 1992.
——. 'Profumo. Chatterley. The Beatles. 1963 Was the Year "Old England" Died'. *The Spectator*, 23 November 2013. Retrieved 28 October 2021 fromhttps://www.spectator.co.uk/2013/11/it-all-began-in-1963.
Borde, Raymond and Étienne Chaumeton. *A Panorama of American Film Noir, 1941–1953*. San Francisco: City Lights Books, 2002.
Borden, Iain (ed.). *The Unknown City: Contesting Architecture and Social Space*. Cambridge, MA: MIT Press, 2000.
Bordwell, David. *Narration in the Fiction Film*. Hoboken, NJ: Taylor & Francis, 2013.
Botting, Jo. 'Edmond T Gréville (1906–1966)'. BFI Flipside DVD Booklet, 2016, 12–13.
Bourne, Stephen. *Brief Encounters: Lesbians and Gays in British Cinema 1930–1971*. London: Cassell, 1996.
Boyd, Francis. 'An End to Clip Joint Fleecing?' *The Guardian*, 11 June 1964, 7.
Bradley, Dick. *Understanding Rock 'n' Roll: Popular Music in Britain 1955–64*. Buckingham: Open University Press, 1992.
Bradshaw, Peter. 'Review: *Postcards from London*'. *The Guardian*, 22 November 2018. Retrieved 28 October 2021 from https://www.theguardian.com/film/2018/nov/22/postcards-from-london-review-steve-mclean-harris-dickinson.
——. 'Soho and *Night and the City* (1950)'. Interview by Jingan Young. Soho Bites Podcast, 28 February 2019. Retrieved 28 October 2021 from itunes.apple.com/au/podcast/sohoonscreen/id1444212180.
Brandon, John. *A Scream in Soho*. London: Wright & Brown, 1940.
Brewer. 'Foreigners in London'. *The Sunday at Home: A Family Magazine for Sabbath Reading* (July 1893): 612–15.
Bridge, Gary, and Sophie Watson (eds). *The New Blackwell Companion to the City*. Oxford: Blackwell Publishing, 2011.
The British Film Industry: A Report on Its History and Present Organisation, with Special Reference to the Economic Problems of British Feature Film Production. London: Political & Economic Planning, 1952.

'British Feature Directors: An Index to their Work'. *Sight and Sound* 27(6) (Autumn 1958): 289.
Brog. 'Spin a Dark Web'. *Variety*, 26 September 1956, 15.
Brooke, Michael. 'A Kid for Two Farthings'. *BFI Screenonline*. Retrieved 28 October 2021 from http://www.screenonline.org.uk/film/id/1005746/index.html.
Brown, Gavin, and Kath Browne (eds). *The Routledge Research Companion to Geographies of Sex and Sexualities*. London: Routledge, 2016.
Brown, Geoff, and Bryony Dixon. 'Edmond T Gréville (1906–66)'. *BFI Screenonline*. Retrieved 28 October 2021 from http://www.screenonline.org.uk/people/id/1114980/index.html.
Brown, Simon. 'Flicker Alley: Cecil Court and the Emergence of the British Film Industry'. *Film Studies* (Spring 2007): 21–33. Retrieved 28 October 2021 from http://www.screenonline.org.uk/people/id/1114980/index.html.
Browne, Nick. *Reconfiguring American Film Genres: History and Theory*. Berkeley: University of California Press, 1998.
Brunsdon, Charlotte. 'The Poignancy of Place: London and the Cinema'. *Visual Culture in Britain* 5 (2004): 59–73.
———. *London in Cinema: The Cinematic City since 1945*. London: BFI, 2007.
———. 'Towards a History of Empty Spaces'. *Journal of British Cinema and Television* 4(2) (2007): 219–34.
Bryden, Ronald. 'Adrift in Soho by Colin Wilson (Book Review)'. *The Spectator*, 8 September 1961, 329.
Buchwald, Art. 'Homey Clubs in London's Soho'. *Los Angeles Times*, 18 August 1960, 1.
Burke, John. *The World Ten Times Over: From the Screenplay by Wolf Rilla*. London: Pan Books, 1963.
Burns, Lucy. 'The Windmill Theatre'. *BBC World Service*, 15 November 2017. Retrieved 28 October 2021 from http://www.bbc.co.uk/programmes/w3csvtxx.
Burton, Alan, and Steve Chibnall. *Historical Dictionary of British Cinema*. Lanham, MD: Scarecrow Press, 2013.
Butler, Rupert. 'Miracle in Soho'. *Films and Filming* (1957): 27–28.
Butterworth, Jez. *Mojo*. London: Nick Hern Books, 1995.
Caine, Andrew. *Interpreting Rock Movies: The Pop Film and Its Critics in Britain*. Manchester: Manchester University Press, 2004.
Calder, John. 'Obituary: Wolf Mankowitz'. *The Independent*, 22 May 1998.
Campbell, Peter. 'In Soho'. *London Review of Books* 23(10) (2001): 37.
Campbell, Russell. *Marked Women: Prostitutes and Prostitution in the Cinema*. Wisconsin: University of Wisconsin Press, 2006.
Carlson, Marvin. *Places of Performance: The Semiotics of Theatre Architecture*. New York: Cornell University Press, 1989.
'Carole Landis Is Dead'. *Boxoffice*, 10 July 1948, 14.
Castle, Hugh. 'The Battle of Wardour Street'. *Close Up* 3(3) (1929): 10–17.

Cave, Dylan. 'Miracle in Soho (1957)'. *BFI Screenonline*. Retrieved 28 October 2021 from http://www.screenonline.org.uk/film/id/712912.
Chadder, Viv. 'The Higher Heel: Women and the Post-War British Crime Film', in British Crime Cinema, edited by Steve Chibnall and Robert Murphy. London' New York: Routledge, 1999, 66–80.
Chapain, Caroline, and Tadeusz Stryjakiewicz (eds). *Creative Industries in Europe: Drivers of New Sectoral and Spatial Dynamics*. Dordrecht: Springer International Publishing, 2017.
Chapman, James. 'Sordidness, Corruption and Violence Almost Unrelieved: Critics, Censors and the Post-War British Crime Film'. *Contemporary British History* 22(2) (2008): 181–201.
Chapuis, Amandine, Phil Hubbard, Alan Collins and Andrew Gorman-Murray. 'Touring the Immoral: Affective Geographies of Visitors to the Amsterdam Red-Light District'. *Urban Studies* 54(3) (2017): 616–32.
Chatterton, Paul, and Robert Hollands. *Urban Nightscapes: Youth Cultures, Pleasure Spaces and Corporate Power*. London: Routledge, 2003.
Chibnall, Steve. 'Juke Box Fury'. *New Society*, 20 September 1985, 414–16.
———. 'Ordinary People: "New Wave" Realism and the British Crime Film 1959–1963', in Steve Chibnall and Robert Murphy (eds), *British Crime Cinema*, 2nd edn. London: Routledge, 2005, 97–112.
———. 'Standing in the Shadow: Peter Whitehead, Swinging London's Insider/Outsider'. *Framework* 52(1) (2011): 244–77.
———. 'Banging the Gong: The Promotional Strategies of Britain's J. Arthur Rank Organisation in the 1950s'. *Historical Journal of Film, Radio and Television* 37 (2016): 242–71.
Chibnall, Steve, and McFarlane, Brian. *The British 'B' Film*. London: BFI, 2009.
Chibnall, Steve, and Murphy, Robert (eds). *British Crime Cinema*. London: Routledge, 1999.
Chibnall, Steve, and Julian Petley. 'Introduction'. *Journal of British Cinema and Television* 4(2) (2007): 213–18.
'Chinatown Pagoda Is Demolished as Part of Regeneration Scheme'. *West End Extra*, 28 November 2016. Retrieved 28 October 2021 from http://westendextra.com/article/chinatown-pagoda-is-demolished-as-part-of-regeneration-scheme.
'Chit Chat'. *The Stage and Television Today*, 24 September 1959, 8.
Christie, Ian. *Powell, Pressburger and Others*. London: BFI, 1978.
———. 'Alienation Effects: Emeric Pressburger and British Cinema'. *Monthly Film Bulletin* 51(600) (1984): 318–20.
'Cinematographer Larry Pizer Dies'. *Variety*, 8 April 2008. Retrieved 28 October 2021 from https://variety.com/2008/film/news/cinematographer-larry-pizer-dies-1117983697.
Clapson, Mark and Peter J. Larkham. *The Blitz and Its Legacy: Wartime Destruction to Post-War Reconstruction*. Farnham: Ashgate, 2013.

Clark, Anthony. 'Jew Suss (1934)'. *BFI Screenonline*. Retrieved 28 October 2021 from http://www.screenonline.org.uk/film/id/570808/index.html.
——. 'Oh Boy! (1958–59)'. *BFI Screenonline*. Retrieved 28 October 2021 fromhttp://www.screenonline.org.uk/tv/id/561801.
Clarke, David (ed.). *The Cinematic City*. London: Routledge, 1997.
Clark, Peter. 'The Slow Death of Soho: Farewell to London's Sleazy Heartland', *The Guardian*, 25 November 2014. Retrieved 24 October 2021 from https://www.theguardian.com/music/2014/nov/25/the-slow-death-of-soho-farewell-to-londons-sleazy-heartland.
Clark, Peter, D.M. Palliser and M.J. Daunton. *The Cambridge Urban History of Britain*. Cambridge: Cambridge University Press, 2008.
Clarke, Cath. 'Adrift in Soho Review: Tedious Times in London's Louchest Locale'. *The Guardian*, 14 November 2018. Retrieved 28 October 2021 from https://www.theguardian.com/film/2018/nov/14/adrift-in-soho-review-pablo-behrens-owen-drake.
Clayton, Antony. *London's Coffee Houses: A Stimulating Story*. Whitstable: Historical Publications, 2004.
Clem. 'Pictures: Miracle in Soho'. *Variety*. 24 July 1957, 26.
Clunn, Harold Philip. *The Face of London: The Record of a Century's Changes and Development*. New York: E.P. Dutton & Company, 1937.
Coleman, John. 'East and West: Review Small World of Sammy Lee'. *New Statesman*, 4 January 1963, 648.
——. 'Reviving'. *New Statesman*, 1 July 1963, 674.
Collins, Alan (ed.). *Cities of Pleasure: Sex and the Urban Socialscape*. New York: Routledge, 2006.
Colomina, Beatriz (ed.). *Sexuality & Space*. Princeton: Princeton University School of Architecture, 1992.
Conrad, Joseph. *The Secret Agent: A Simple Tale*. Oxford: Oxford University Press, 2004.
Cook, Pam. *Screening the Past: Memory and Nostalgia in Cinema*. Abingdon: Taylor & Francis, 2004.
Coton, A.V. 'Review: *Women of the Streets: A Sociological Study of the Common Prostitute*. Edited by C. H. Rolph'. *The Spectator* (8 April 1955): 446.
'Cover Girl Killer'. *Monthly Film Bulletin* 27(312) (1960): 36.
Cowan, Margaret. 'No Trouble Selling this to the States'. *The Stage and Television Today*, 3 September 1959, 13.
Crowther, Bosley. 'The Screen in Review: "Oliver Twist", Rank Film Based on Charles Dickens Novel, at Park Avenue Theatre'. *New York Times*, 31 July 1951, 17.
——. 'Screen: A Look at Sammy's World. Soho Gambler Played by Anthony Newley'. *New York Times*, 14 August 1963, 28.
Croydon, John. 'Letter to Mr. R.E.F. Garrett, Esquire, Guarantee of Completion. RE: Willoughby Film Prods. Ltd. "The Beat Girl"', 9 July 1959, Film Finances Archive, London.

Daniels, Stephen, and Catherine Nash. 'Lifepaths: Geography and Biography'. *Journal of Historical Geography* 30(3) (2004): 449–58.
'The Dark Stairway'. *Monthly Film Bulletin* 21(240) (1954): 78.
De Certeau, Michel. *The Practice of Everyday Life*, translated by Steven Rendall. Berkeley: University of California Press, 1988.
Dillon, Carmen. 'Building Soho at Pinewood'. *Kinematograph Weekly*, 28 March 1957, ix.
———. Interview by Sidney Cole. BECTU History Project. Interview No. 288. Side 1 and 2 recorded on 22 June 1993. Sides 3 and 4 recorded on 6 May 1994. Side 5 recorded on 30 September 1994. Retrieved 28 October 2021 fromhttps://historyproject.org.uk/interview/carmen-dillon.
Dimendberg, Edward, and American Council of Learned Societies. *Film Noir and the Spaces of Modernity*. Cambridge, MA: Harvard University Press, 2004.
Doane, Mary Ann. *Femme Fatales: Feminism, Film Theory, and Psychoanalysis*. London: Routledge, 1991.
Doncaster, Patrick. 'On the Record: He's O.K. For Sound'. *Daily Mirror*, 11 February 1960, 19.
Donnelly, Kevin. 'The Perpetual Busman's Holiday: Sir Cliff Richard and British Pop Musicals'. *Journal of Popular Film and Television* 25(4) (1998): 146–54.
Donnelly, Mark. *Sixties Britain: Culture, Society and Politics*. London: Routledge, 2013.
Doubles, Malcolm C. *The Seduction of the Church: How the Concern to Create Gender-Neutral Language in Bible and Song Is Being Misused to Betray Members' Faith*. Eugene, OR: Wipf & Stock, 2010.
Dryhurst, Edward. 'Obituary'. *Variety*, 15 March 1989, 68.
Duguid, Mark. 'British Film in the 1960s'. *BFI Screenonline*. Retrieved 28 October 2021 from http://www.screenonline.org.uk/film/id/1291628.
Dunbavan, Peter. *An Avid's Guide to Sixties Songwriters*. Bloomington: AuthorHouse, 2017.
Dunn, Anthony J. *The Worlds of Wolf Mankowitz: Between Elite and Popular Cultures in Post-War Britain*. Edgware: Vallentine Mitchell, 2013.
Dunn, Nell. 'The Clip Joint'. *New Statesman*, 6 July 1962, 925.
Durgnat, Raymond. 'The Small World of Sammy Lee'. *Films and Filming* (1963): 31–32.
———. 'The Powell and Pressburger Mystery'. *Cineaste* 23(2) (1997): 16–19.
Durmaz, S. Bahar. 'Analyzing the Quality of Place: Creative Clusters in Soho and Beyoğlu'. *Journal of Urban Design*, 20(1) (2015): 93–124.
Dyer, Peter John. 'Expresso Bongo'. *Sight and Sound* 29(1) (1959): 40.
Dyer, Richard. *The Matter of Images: Essays on Representation*. London: Routledge, 2002.
Dyhouse, Carol. *Girl Trouble: Panic and Progress in the History of Young Women*. London: Zed Books, 2013.
Eade, John. *Placing London: From Imperial Capital to Global City*. Oxford: Berghahn Books, 2000.
Ede, Laurie N. *British Film Design: A History*. London: I.B. Tauris, 2010.

Editorial. 'In Praise of … Michael Winterbottom'. *The Guardian*, 4 November 2019. Retrieved 28 October 2021 from https://www.theguardian.com/commentisfree/2010/nov/04/michael-winterbottom-films.

Edgell, Wyatt. 'Moral Statistics of the Parishes of St. James, St. George, and St. Anne Soho, in the City of Westminster. Supplementary to the Third Report of the Education Committee of the Statistical Society of London'. *Journal of the Statistical Society of London* 1(8) (1838): 478–92.

Eisinger, Jo. 'Night and the City'. Original story: based on the novel by Gerald Kersh. Script type: combination title script and trailer script. Script date: June 1950. BFI Special Collections.

Eldridge, David. 'Britain Finds Andy Hardy: British Cinema Audiences and the American Way of Life in the Second World War'. *Historical Journal of Film, Radio and Television* 31(4) (2011): 499–521.

Ellis, David A. *Conversations with Cinematographers*. London: Scarecrow Press, 2012.

Ellis, Markman. *The Coffee-House: A Cultural History*. London: Weidenfeld & Nicolson, 2004.

Ellis-Peterson, Hannah. 'Madame Jojo's, Legendary Soho Nightclub, Forced to Close'. *The Guardian*, 24 November 2014. Retrieved 28 October 2021 fromhttps://www.theguardian.com/uk-news/2014/nov/24/madame-jojos-legendary-soho-nightclub-forced-close.

Emsley, Clive. *Hard Men: The English and Violence since 1750*. London: Hambledon, 2005.

'Eros Films Wins a Wager'. *Variety*, 28 August 1957, 19.

Eyles, Allen. 'Cinemas & Cinemagoing: WWII and Beyond'. *BFI Screenonline*. Retrieved 28 October 2021 from http://www.screenonline.org.uk/film/cinemas/sect4.html.

Commentary with Yolande Donlan and Val Guest. Recorded December 2005. 1962 re-issue version. London: BFI, 2016.

Fairclough, Pauline (ed.). *Twentieth-Century Music and Politics: Essays in Memory of Neil Edmunds*. Abingdon: Routledge, 2016.

Farag, Maryse. 'Where There's Muck, There's Brass: Porn King's Granddaughters Reportedly TRIPLE Their Inheritance with a £482m Property Empire'. *The Sun* 25 April 2016. Retrieved 28 October 2021 from https://www.thesun.co.uk/archives/news/1143941/where-theres-muck-theres-brass-porn-kings-granddaughters-reportedly-triple-their-inheritance-with-a-482m-property-empire.

Farmer, Richard, Laura Mayne, Duncan Petrie and Melanie Williams. *Transformation and Tradition in 1960s British Cinema*. Edinburgh: Edinburgh University Press, 2019.

Farson, Daniel. *Soho in the Fifties*. London: Michael Joseph, 1988.

Feldman, Christine Jacqueline. *We Are the Mods: A Transnational History of Youth Culture*. New York: Peter Lang, 2009.

Figg, Cynthia. 'The Coffee-Bar Sensation'. *Picturegoer*, 1 December 1956, 18–19.

'Film Companies and Studios'. *Sight and Sound* 19(10) (1951): 69.

Film London. 'Look of Love'. *Film London News*, 24 April 2013. Retrieved 28 October 2021 from http://filmlondon.org.uk/news/2013/april/the_look_of_love.
Fitzmaurice, Tony, and Shiel, Mark. *Screening the City*. London: Verso, 2003.
Fleming, E.J. *Carole Landis: A Tragic Life in Hollywood*. Jefferson, NC: McFarland & Company, 2011.
Fink, Janet, and Penny Tinkler. 'Teetering on the Edge: Portraits of Innocence, Risk and Young Female Sexualities in 1950s' and 1960s' British Cinema'. *Women's History Review* 26(1) (2017): 1–17.
Flannery, Seamus. 'Letter to Film Finances: Art Director of "The Small World of Sammy Lee" to Film Finances, The Spieler', 26 June 1962, Film Finances Archive, London.
'The Flesh Is Weak'. *Monthly Film Bulletin* 24(276) (1957): 114.
'The Flesh Is Weak'. *Picturegoer*, 21 September 1957, 17.
'"The Flesh Is Weak" at the Rialto', *New York Times*, 9 November 1957, 26.
Flory, Dan. *Philosophy, Black Film, Film Noir*. University Park: Pennsylvania State University Press, 2009.
Forrest, Elizabeth. 'The Hughes Girl Comes Back'. *Picturegoer*, 31 October 1953, 11.
Forshaw, Barry. *British Crime Film: Subverting the Social Order*. Basingstoke: Palgrave Macmillan, 2012.
——. *Sex and Film: The Erotic in British, American and World Cinema*. Basingstoke: Palgrave Macmillan, 2015.
Foster, Julia. 'Interview by Jo Botting'. *British Film Institute*, 14 October 2016. Retrieved 28 October 2021 from https://www.youtube.com/watch?v=n5Npo9mP5Uw.
Fowler, David. *Youth Culture in Modern Britain, c.1920–c.1970*. Basingstoke: Palgrave Macmillan, 2008.
French, Philip. 'Newley in the Underworld'. *The Observer*, 21 April 1963. 27.
Gabler, Neal. *An Empire of Their Own: How the Jews Invented Hollywood*. London: W.H. Allen, 1989.
Gans, Eric Lawrence. *Carole Landis: A Most Beautiful Girl*. Jackson: University Press of Mississippi, 2008.
Garland, Jon et al. 'Youth Culture, Popular Music and the End of "Consensus" in Post-War Britain'. *Contemporary British History* 26(3) (2012): 265–71.
Geraghty, Christine. *British Cinema in the Fifties: Gender, Genre and the 'New Look'*. London: Routledge, 2000.
Gifford, Denis. *The British Film Catalogue: Volume 1. Fiction Film, 1895–1994*, 3rd edn. London: Routledge, 2001.
Gilbert, Pamela K., and Chris Hamnett. *Imagined Londons*. Albany: State University of New York Press, 2002.
Gildart, Keith. *Images of England through Popular Music: Class, Youth and Rock 'n' Roll, 1955–1976*. Basingstoke: Palgrave Macmillan, 2013.
Gilby, Ryan. 'Mags to Riches'. *New Statesman*, 26 April (2013): 50.
Gillett, Charlie. *The Sound of the City: The Rise of Rock 'n' Roll*. London: Souvenir, 1983.

Gillett, Philip. *The British Working Class in Postwar Film*. Manchester: Manchester University Press, 2003.
Girling, Brian. *Soho & Theatreland through Time*. Stroud: Amberley Publishing, 2012.
Girelli, Elisabetta. *Beauty and the Beast: Italianness in British Cinema*. Bristol: Intellect Books, 2009.
Glancy, Mark. *When Hollywood Loved Britain: The Hollywood 'British' Film, 1939–1945*. Manchester: Manchester University Press, 1999.
———. *Hollywood and the Americanization of Britain: From the 1920s to the Present*. London: I.B. Tauris, 2014.
Glynn, Stephen. *A Hard Day's Night*. London: I.B. Tauris, 2005.
———. *The British Pop Musical Film: The Beatles and Beyond*. Basingstoke: Palgrave Macmillan, 2013.
'The Golden Disc'. *Monthly Film Bulletin* 25 (1 January 1958): 46.
Goldstein, Murray. *Naked Jungle: Soho Stripped Bare*. London: Silverback Press, 2005.
Good, Jack. '"Expresso Bongo": It Aims at a Target That Doesn't Exist'. *Disc*, 24 May 1958, 12.
———. 'Jack Good: Should This Song Be Put on Wax?' *Disc*, 29 April 1961, 5.
Goodhead, Paul. *Success Story: Anthony Newley*. Worcester: Stagedoor Productions Ltd., 2010.
Gosling, John and Douglas Warner. *The Shame of a City: An Inquiry into the Vice of London*. London: W.H. Allen, 1960.
Glynn, Stephen. *The British Pop Music Film: The Beatles and Beyond*. Basingstoke: Palgrave Macmillan, 2013.
Gough-Yates, Kevin. 'Jews and Exiles in British Cinema'. *Leo Baeck Institute Yearbook* 37(1) (1992): 517–41.
———. 'Pressburger: England and Exile'. *Sight and Sound* 5(12) (1995): 30–35.
———. 'Letters: Separating Powell from Pressburger'. *Cineaste: America's Leading Magazine on the Art and Politics of the Cinema* 23(3) (1998): 61.
Gow, Gordon. 'Miracle in Soho'. *Films and Filming* (August 1957): 27–28.
Grafe, Christoph, and Franziska Bollery. *Cafes and Bars: The Architecture of Public Display*. London: Routledge, 2007.
Grant, Barry Keith (ed.). *Film Genre Reader III*. Austin: University of Texas Press, 2003.
Grant, Linda. 'Nostalgia Doesn't Come More Joyous Than This'. *The Guardian*, 27 October 2018. Retrieved 28 October 2021 from https://www.theguardian.com/commentisfree/2018/oct/27/nostalgia-doesnt-come-much-more-joyous-than-this.
Grosz, Elizabeth. 'Bodies-Cities', in Beatriz Colomina (ed.), *Sexuality & Space*. Princeton, NJ: Princeton University School of Architecture, 1992, 241–54.
Guest, Val, *So You Want to Be in Pictures*. London: Reynolds & Hearn, 2001.
Guha, Malini. *From Empire to the World: Migrant London and Paris in Cinema*. Edinburgh: Edinburgh University Press, 2015.

Habermas, Jurgen. *The Structural Transformation of the Public Sphere: An Inquiry into a Category of Bourgeois Society*, translated by Thomas Burger, with the assistance of Frederick Lawrence. Cambridge, MA: MIT Press, 1991 [1962].
Halasz, Piri. 'Great Britain: You Can Walk across It on the Grass'. *Time*, 15 April 1966, 30–34.
Halden, Bill. 'The King of Teenage Music'. *Picturegoer* 35(1199 (April 1958): 6–7.
Hall, Jean Graham. 'The Prostitute and the Law'. *British Journal of Delinquency* 9(3) (1959): 174–81.
Hall, Lesley A. *Sex, Gender and Social Change in Britain since 1880*. Basingstoke: Palgrave Macmillan, 2013.
Hall Williams, J.E. 'The Street Offences Act, 1959'. *Modern Law Review* 23(2) (1960): 173–79.
Hallam, Julia. 'Film, Space and Place: Researching a City in Film'. *New Review of Film and Television Studies* 8(3) (2010): 277–96.
——. 'Mapping City Space: Independent Filmmakers as Urban Gazetteers'. *Journal of British Cinema and Television* 4(2) (2007): 272–84.
Hamilton, Ian. 'The Comic Strip'. *London Review of Books* 3(16) (1981): 20.
Hamilton, Margaret. 'Opposition to the Contagious Diseases Acts, 1864–1886'. *Albion: A Quarterly Journal Concerned with British Studies* 10(1 (1978): 14–27.
Harper, Sue. 'The Representation of Women in British Feature Film, 1945–1950'. *Historical Journal of Film, Radio and Television* 12(3) (1992): 217–30.
——. *Women in British Cinema: Mad, Bad and Dangerous to Know*. London: Continuum, 2000.
Harper, Sue, and Vincent Porter. 'Throbbing Hearts and Smart Repartee: The Reception of American Films in 1950s Britain'. *Media History* 4(2) (1998): 175–93.
——. *British Cinema of the 1950s: The Decline of Deference*. Oxford: Oxford University Press, 2003.
Hasted, Nick. 'DVD: Miracle Soho'. *The Arts Desk*. Retrieved 28 October 2021 from http://theartsdesk.com/film/dvd-miracle-soho.
Hatziprokopiou, Panos, and Nicola Montagna, 'Contested Chinatown: Chinese Migrants' Incorporation and the Urban Space in London and Milan'. *Ethnicities* 12(6) (2012): 706–29.
Head, Dominic. *The Cambridge Introduction to Modern British Fiction, 1950–2000*. Cambridge: Cambridge University Press, 2002.
Heindel, Richard. 'The United States in the British Press'. *Public Opinion Quarterly* 3(2) (1939): 320–26.
Henry, Michael. 'Edmond T. Gréville, Cinema Retrouve, e Mal d'Amour Au Feminin Greville Outre Manche'. *Positif–Revue Mensuelle de Cinéma* (2006): 83–87.
Henry, Paul. 'The Death of a Spiv'. *BBC Radio 4*, 22 February 2014. Retrieved 28 October 2021 from http://www.bbc.co.uk/programmes/b03vthkv.
Hickey, Des, and Gus Smith. *The Prince: Being the Public and Private Life of Larushka Mischa*

Skikne, a Jewish Lithuanian Vagabond Player, Otherwise Known as Laurence Harvey. London: Frewin, 1975.

Hill, Derek. 'Glamour in a G-String'. *Picturegoer*, 9 August 1958, 12–13.

——. 'Glamour in a G-String – Part II: Nude Shows'. *Picturegoer*, 16 August 1958, 16–17.

Hills, Gillian. 'Gillian Hills Remembers Beat Girl'. BFI Flipside DVD Booket. London: BFI, 2016, 1–2.

——. Interview by BFI. *Beat Girl* DVD/Blu-Ray, BFI Flipside. London: BFI, 2016.

——. 'In Discussion with BFI National Archive Fiction Curator Vic Pratt'. Special screening of *Beat Girl*, Regent Street Cinema, London, 20 April 2016. Personal transcript.

Hill, John. *Sex, Class and Realism: British Cinema 1956–1963*. London: BFI, 1997.

Hinxman, Margaret. 'Stepping out Tonight?' *Picturegoer*, 28 September 1957, 5.

Hirsch, Pam, and Chris O'Rourke (eds). *London on Film*. London: Palgrave Macmillan, 2017.

Holden, H.M. 'A Note on "Alienated" Youth the Functions of the District of Soho, London'. *Journal of Child Psychology and Psychiatry* 13(4) (1972): 289–97.

Holden, Stephen. 'Smut's Softer Side: Rakish Pornographer as Loving Parent, Review: *The Look of Love*'. *New York Times*, 4 July 2013. Retrieved 28 October 2021 from https://www.nytimes.com/2013/07/05/movies/the-look-of-love-stars-steve-coogan-as-a-sex-impresario.html.

Holmes, Su. *British Television and Film Culture in the 1950s: 'Coming to a TV Near You!'* Bristol: Intellect Books, 2009.

——. *Entertaining Television: The BBC and Popular Television Culture in the 1950s*. Manchester: Manchester University Press, 2008.

Home Office and Scottish Home Department. *Report of the Committee on Homosexual Offences and Prostitution*, Cmnd. 247. London: HMSO, 1957.

Hornsey, Richard. *The Spiv and the Architect Unruly Life in Postwar London*. Minneapolis: University of Minnesota Press, 2010.

Houlbrook, Matt. *Queer London: Perils and Pleasures in the Sexual Metropolis, 1918–1957*. Chicago: University of Chicago Press, 2006.

Howse, Christopher. *Soho in the Eighties*. London: Bloomsbury/Continuum, 2018.

——. 'Obituary: Jeffrey Bernard'. *The Independent*, 6 September 1997. Retrieved 28 October 2021 from https://www.independent.co.uk/news/people/obituary-jeffrey-bernard-1237687.html.

Hubbard, Phil. 'Sex and the City: Social and Economic Explorations in Urban Sexuality'. *Urban Studies* 41(9) (2004): 1631–856.

——. 'Afterword: Exiting Amsterdam's Red Light District'. *City* 16(1–2) (2012): 195–201.

——. *Cities and Sexualities*. London: Routledge, 2012.

Hughes, Ken. 'The Small World of Sammy Lee Release Script'. Donated by BAFTA, 1963. London: BFI Special Collections.

Hunter, Diack. 'Review: Noose. Contemporary Arts'. *The Spectator*, 27 June 1947, 749.

Hunter, I.Q.Q., and Laraine Porter. *British Comedy Cinema*. Hoboken, NJ: Taylor & Francis, 2012.
Huntley, John. *British Film Music*. London: Skelton Robinson, 1947.
Hutton, Mike. *The Story of Soho: The Windmill Years 1932-1964*. Stroud: Amberley Publishing, 2012.
Hyams, Edward. 'Pretending to Be Soho'. *The New Statesman and Nation*, 16 July 1955, 65–66.
Hyatt, Wesley. *Emmy Award Winning Night-Time Television Shows, 1948-2004*. Jefferson, NC: McFarland & Company, 2006.
'In Darkest Soho'. *Manchester Guardian*, 23 June 1947.
'Inside of the Week: Soho Fair'. *Church Times*, 19 July 1957, 6–7.
'International: British Teenagers Pay 28% of Cinema Take'. *Variety*, 8 February 1961, 59.
'International: 20th-Fox Uses Gimmicks at British Soho Fair'. *Variety*. 211(9) (30 July 1958): 12.
Irigaray, Luce. *This Sex Which Is Not One*, translated by Catherine Porter, with Caroline Burke. New York: Cornell University Press, 1985.
Jacobson, Howard. 'The Last Bohemia'. *BBC Radio 4*, 7 January 2018. Retrieved 28 October 2021 from https://www.bbc.co.uk/sounds/play/b09kx83w.
Jackson, Emma. 'Railway Lands', in Charlotte Bates and Alex Rhys-Taylor (eds), *Walking through Social Research*, London: Routledge, 2017, 12–19.
Jackson, Louise A. 'The Coffee Club Menace'. *Cultural and Social History* 5(3) (2008): 289–308.
Jackson, Louise A., and Angela Bartie. *Policing Youth: Britain, 1945-70*. Manchester: Manchester University Press, 2014.
James, David. E. *Rock 'n' Film: Cinema's Dance with Popular Music*. Oxford: Oxford University Press, 2016.
Jefford, Kasmira. 'Soho Property Empire Rises in Value to £565m'. *City AM*, 24 August 2015, 8.
The Jewish Encyclopaedia. http://www.jewishencyclopedia.com.
Johnston, Trevor. 'Look of Love, Review'. *Sight and Sound* 23(5) (2013): 99–100.
——. 'From Beat Girl to Mad Men: The Life of Gillian Hills'. *BFI Online*, 11 July 2016. Retrieved 28 October 2021 from http://www.bfi.org.uk/news-opinion/sight-sound-magazine/interviews/gillian-hills-beat-girl.
Jones, Lewis. 'Spiv on a Grand Scale'. *The Spectator*, 11 September 2010. Retrieved 28 October 2021 from https://www.spectator.co.uk/2010/09/spiv-on-a-grand-scale.
Julius, Anthony. *T.S. Eliot, Anti-Semitism and Literary Form*. Cambridge: Cambridge University Press, 1995.
——. *Trials of the Diaspora: A History of Anti-Semitism in England*. Oxford: Oxford University Press, 2012.
Karp, Jonathan. 'Brokering a Rock 'n' Roll International: Jewish Record Men in the US and

UK', in Rebecca Kobrin and Adam Teller (eds), *Purchasing Power: The Economics of Jewish History*. Philadelphia: University of Pennsylvania Press, 2015, 125–52.

Keaney, Michael F. *Film Noir Guide: 745 Films of the Classic Era, 1940–1959*. Jefferson, NC: McFarland & Company, 2003.

———. *British Film Noir Guide*. Jefferson, NC: McFarland & Company, 2008.

Kerridge, Roy. 'Voice of the Yob'. *New Statesman*, 30 April 1960, 618.

———. 'A Teenage Who's Who'. *New Statesman*, 2 July 1960, 422.

Kersh, Gerald. *Night and the City*. London: London Books, 2007 [1938].

Kine Weekly. 'Sharp Downward Trend of Feature Films in 1955: Nearly 100 Fewer "U" Certificate Films: More "A" and "X"'. *Kine Weekly*, 29 December 1955, 5.

Kinsey, Alfred. 'Departmental Committee on Homosexual Offences and Prostitution Notes of a Meeting', 29 October 1955, PRO HO 345/8, 12–13.

Kingsford, Charles Lethbridge. *The Earth History of Piccadilly, Leicester Square, Soho & Their Neighbourhood: Based on a Plan Drawn in 1585 and Published by the London Topographical Society in 1925*. Cambridge: Cambridge University Press, 1925.

Kirby, Dick. *The Scourge of Soho: The Controversial Career of SAS Hero Detective Sergeant Harry Challenor MM*. Barnsley: Pen & Sword True Crime, 2013.

Kochberg, Searle. 'On Dunn's "The Worlds of Wolf Mankowitz: Between Elite and Popular Cultures in Post-War Britain"'. *Jewish Film & New Media* 1(2) (2013): 223–25.

Koeck, Richard, and Roberts, Les. *The City and the Moving Image: Urban Projections*. Basingstoke: Palgrave Macmillan, 2010.

Kracauer, Siegfried. 'The Hotel Lobby'. *Postcolonial Studies* 2(3) (1999): 289–97.

———. 'Hollywood's Terror Films: Do They Reflect an American State of Mind?', in Kristy Rawson, and Johannes von Moltke (eds), *Siegfried Kracauer's American Writings: Essays on Film and Popular Culture*. Berkeley: University of California Press, 2012, 45–49.

Kretzmer, Herbert. 'Too Hot to Handle'. First draft script, 14 April 1959, Film Finances Archive, London.

Kynaston, David. *Austerity Britain: 1945–51*. London: Bloomsbury, 2008.

Lack, Roland-François. 'Expresso Bongo'. *The Cine-Tourist*. Retrieved 28 October 2021 from http://www.locationlondon.net/london-streets-on-screen/hanway-street-w1-expresso-bongo-val-guest-1959.

Lait, George. 'More Night-Time and More Nite Life in London; Plenty of Clip Joints'. *Variety*, 8 October 1941, 4.

Laite, Julia. *Common Prostitutes and Ordinary Citizens*. Basingstoke: Palgrave Macmillan, 2012.

Lambert, Gavin. 'New Wave, Old Problem'. *The Guardian*, 3 October 2002, 14–15.

Landy, Marcia. *British Genres: Cinema and Society, 1930–1960*. Princeton: Princeton University Press, 1991.

Langhamer, Claire. 'Love, Selfhood and Authenticity in Post-War Britain'. *Cultural and Social History* 9(2) (2012): 277–97.

Larkham, Peter J., and David Adams. 'The Postwar Reconstruction of Planning of London: A Wider Perspective'. Centre for Environment and Society Research Working Paper Series No. 8. Birmingham: Birmingham City University, 2011.

Lassally, Walter. 'Interview by Peter Bowen'. June 2004. *Web of Stories*, Retrieved 24 January 2008. https://www.webofstories.com/play/walter.lassally.

Latimer, Hugh. 'Good, Bad and Indifferent'. *The Observer*, 2 October 1955.

———. 'Coffee Bar Skiffles'. *The Observer*, 21 October 1956. 13.

Lay, Samantha. *British Social Realism: From Documentary to Brit-Grit*. London: Wallflower Press, 2002.

L.C. 'Street of Shadows'. *Picturegoer*, 11 July 1953, 19.

Leach, Jim. *British Film*. Cambridge: Cambridge University Press, 2006.

Leacroft, Richard, and Helen Leacroft. *Theatre and Playhouse: An Illustrated Survey of Theatre Building from Ancient Greece to the Presence Day*. London: Methuen, 1984.

Lecky, William. *A History of European Morals from Augustus to Charlemagne*. New York: D. Appleton and Company, 1869.

Leese, Peter. *Britain since 1945: Aspects of Identity*. Basingstoke: Palgrave Macmillan, 2006.

Leggott, James. 'Dead Ends and Private Roads: The 1970s Films of Barney Platts-Mills', in Paul Newland (ed.), *Don't Look Now: British Cinema in the 1970s*. Bristol: Intellect Books, 2010, 229–40.

'Leigh Vance: Obituary'. *LA Times*, 31 October 1994. Retrieved 28 October 2021 from https://www.latimes.com/archives/la-xpm-1994-10-31-mn-56828-story.html.

'Letter from Willoughby Film Productions to John Trevelyan, British Board of Film Classification', 6 December 1959. BBFC Archive, London.

'Letters'. *Cinéaste* 23(3) (1998): 61.

Lewis, Chaim. *From Soho to Jerusalem*. Hexam: Flambard Press, 2000.

Ling-Wan, Pak. 'Ping Pong (1986)'. *BFI Screenonline*. Retrieved 28 October 2021 from http://www.screenonline.org.uk/film/id/475922/index.html.

'Live It up'. *Monthly Film Bulletin* 31(360) (1964): 10.

Llewellyn, Richard. 'Noose/The Silk Noose'. Dialogue sheets, 1948. BFI Special Collections. BFI: London.

'The London Blitz during 7th October 1940 to 6th June 1941'. *The Bomb Sight*, version 1.0. Retrieved 28 October 2021 from http://bombsight.org.

Love, Stuart. 'Petition Update from Council'. *Westminster City Council*, 7 April 2015. Retrieved 28 October 2021 from http://petitions.westminster.gov.uk/savemadamjojos.

Lovell, Alan. 'The Unknown Cinema of Britain'. *Cinema Journal* 11(2) (1972): 1–8.

Low, Rachel. *Film Making in 1930s Britain*. London: George Allen & Unwin, 1985.

Luckett, Moya. 'Travel and Mobility: Femininity and National Identity in Swinging London Films', in Andrew Higson and Justine Ashby (eds), *British Cinema: Past and Present*. London: Routledge, 2000, 233–46.

Lyman, Eric. 'Italian Actress Vitale Dies at 74'. *Hollywood Reporter*, 3 November 2006. Retrieved 28 October 2021 from https://www.hollywoodreporter.com/news/italian-actress-vitale-dies-at-141784.
Lynch, Clare. 'Soho Then'. *The Photographer's Gallery*. Retrieved 28 October 2021 from https://thephotographersgallery.org.uk/content/new-podcast-series-soho-then.
Lynch, Kevin. *The Image of the City*. Cambridge MA: MIT Press, 1960.
Lyons, John F. *America in the British Imagination: 1945 to the Present*. New York: Palgrave Macmillan, 2013.
Macdonald, Kevin. *Emeric Pressburger: Life and Death of a Screenwriter*. London: Faber & Faber, 1996.
MacInnes, Colin. *Absolute Beginners*. London: MacGibbon & Kee, 1959.
MacKenzie, S.P. *British War Films 1939–1945: The Cinema and the Services*. London: Hambledon, 2001.
MacKillop, Ian, and Neil Sinyard (eds). *British Cinema of the 1950s: A Celebration*. Manchester: Manchester University Press, 2003.
Maclaren-Ross, Julian. *The Nine Men of Soho*. London: Metcalfe and Cooper Ltd., 1946.
———. 'The Polestar Neighbour'. *London Magazine*, 1 November 1964, 102.
———. *Memoirs of the Forties*. London: Alan Ross, 1965.
Macnab, Geoffrey. *J. Arthur Rank and the British Film Industry*. London: Routledge, 1993.
———. 'The Seductive Streets of Soho on Film'. *The Independent*, 5 April 2013. Retrieved 28 October 2021 from http://www.independent.co.uk/arts-entertainment/films/features/the-seductive-streets-of-soho-on-film-8560238.html.
MacPherson, Kerrie L. *A Wilderness of Marshes: The Origins of Public Health in Shanghai, 1843–1893*. Oxford: Oxford University Press, 1987. Reprint. Oxford: Lexington Books, 2002.
Maginn, Paul J., and Christine Steinmetz. *(Sub)Urban Sexscapes: Geographies and Regulation of the Sex Industry*. London: Routledge, 2015.
Mainon, Dominique, and Ursini, James. *Femme Fatale: Cinema's Most Unforgettable Lethal Ladies*. Milwaukee: Limelight Editions, 2009.
Malchow, H.L. *Special Relations: The Americanization of Britain?* Stanford: Stanford University Press, 2011.
Malcolm, Derek. 'Perfect Partner'. *The Guardian*, 6 February 1988.
Mankowitz, Wolf. 'Expresso Bongo: The Story of the Making of a Modern Idol', *Daily Express*, 9 September 1957, 10.
———. 'Expresso Bongo Part Two'. *Daily Express*, 10 September 1957, 5.
———. 'Expresso Bongo Part Three'. *Daily Express*, 11 September 1957, 10.
———. 'Expresso Bongo Part Four'. *Daily Express*, 12 September 1957, 10.
———. 'Expresso Bongo Shooting Script', 23 April 1959. London: BFI Special Collections.
———. *Expresso Bongo*. From an original story by Wolf Mankowitz/book by Wolf Mankowitz and Julian More, music by David Heneker and Monty Norman, lyrics by Julian More, David Heneker and Monty Norman. Evans Plays. London: Evans Bros, 1960.

———. *Make Me an Offer, Expresso Bongo, and Other Stories: Illustrations by Gaynor Chapman.* London: Hutchinson Educational, 1961.
———. 'Goy and Dolls'. *The Observer,* 28 October 1984, 46.
Marber, Patrick. *Don Juan in Soho: After Moliere.* London: Faber & Faber, 2017.
Mayer, Geoff *Guide to British Cinema.* Westport, CT: Greenwood Press, 2003.
Mays, John Barron. 'Teen-Age Culture in Contemporary Britain and Europe'. *Annals of the American Academy of Political and Social Science* 338 (1961): 22–32.
McCallum, Ronald Buchanan, and Alison Violet Readman. *The British General Election of 1945.* Abingdon: Cass, 1964.
McFarlane, Brian. 'The British B Film and the Field of Cultural Production'. *Film Criticism* 21(1) (1996): 48–70.
———. *Lance Comfort.* Manchester: Manchester University Press, 1999.
———. 'Pulp Fictions: The British B Film and the Field of Cultural Production'. *Film Criticism* 21(1) (1996): 48–70.
———. 'Vernon Sewell (1903–2001)'. *BFI Screenonline.* Retrieved 28 October 2021 from http://www.screenonline.org.uk/people/id/460103/index.html.
McFarlane, Brian, and Anthony Slide (eds). *The Encyclopaedia of British Film,* 4th edn. Manchester: Manchester University Press, 2014.
McGillivray, David. *Doing Rude Things: The History of the British Sex Film 1957–1981.* London: Sun Tavern Fields, 1992.
McKernan, Luke. 'Charles Urban (1867–1942)'. *BFI Screenonline.* Retrieved 28 October 2021 from http://www.screenonline.org.uk/people/id/514893.
McLaren, Angus. *Sexual Blackmail: A Modern History.* Cambridge, MA: Harvard University Press, 2002.
McNair, Brian. *Striptease Culture: Sex, Media and the Democratization of Desire.* London: Routledge, 2002.
Meynell, Laurence. *The Creaking Chair.* London: Orion Books, 2014 [1941].
Melly, G. *Revolt into Style: The Pop Arts in Britain.* London: Penguin, 1970.
Mellor, Roger Philip. 'Noose (1948)'. *BFI Screenonline.* Retrieved 28 October 2021 from http://www.screenonline.org.uk/film/id/1259696.
Mercer, John, and Martin Shingler. *Melodrama: Genre, Style, Sensibility.* London: Wallflower Press, 2004.
Michael, Chris. 'Rupert Everett: "We've Lost Our London – and Soho Is the Last Victim"'. *The Guardian,* 28 April 2014. Retrieved 28 October 2021 from http://www.theguardian.com/cities/2014/apr/28/rupert-everett-london-soho-prostitution.html.
Milazzo, Franco. 'In Pictures: Madame Jojo's Protest March'. *Londonist,* 30 November 2014. Retrieved 28 October 2021 from https://londonist.com/2014/11/in-pictures-madame-jojos-protest-march.
Mills, Helena, 'Using the Personal to Critique the Popular: Women's Memories of 1960s Youth'. *Contemporary British History* 30(4) (2016): 463–83.

Mills, Sarah. 'Desire, Disorder and Design: Metropolitan Threats and Urban Sexual Citizenship in Post-War London'. *City* 15(6) (2011): 754–56.

'Miracle in Soho'. *Monthly Film Bulletin* 24(276) (1957): 104.

'Miracle in Soho'. *What's on in London*, 12 July 1957, n.p. Pamphlet scan courtesy of Steve Crook.

'Miracle in Soho'. *Picturegoer*, 3 August 1957, 14.

Mitchell, Gillian. 'A Very "British" Introduction to Rock 'n' Roll: Tommy Steele and the Advent of Rock 'n' Roll Music in Britain, 1956–1960'. *Contemporary British History* 25(2) (2011): 205–25.

Mitchell, Neil. '10 Great Films Set in Soho'. *BFI*, 28 April 2016. Retrieved 28 October 2021 from http://www.bfi.org.uk/news-opinion/news-bfi/lists/10-great-films-set-soho.html.

Mitchell, Tim. 'Statement on Madame Jojo's'. *City of Westminster*, 26 November 2014. Retrieved 28 October 2021 from https://www.westminster.gov.uk/statement-madame-jojos.

Moor, Andrew. *Powell & Pressburger: A Cinema of Magic Spaces. Cinema and Society*. London: I.B. Tauris, 2005.

Moran, Leslie. *The Homosexual(ity) of the Law*. London: Routledge, 1996.

Mort, Frank. 'Cityscapes: Consumption, Masculinities and the Mapping of London since 1950'. *Urban Studies* 35(5/6) (1998): 889–907.

———. 'Scandalous Events: Metropolitan Culture and Moral Change in Post-Second World War London'. *Representations* 93 (2006): 106–37.

———. 'Striptease: The Erotic Female Body and Live Sexual Entertainment in Mid-twentieth-Century London'. *Social History* 32(1) (2007): 27–53.

———. *Capital Affairs: London and the Making of the Permissive Society*. New Haven: Yale University Press, 2010.

Mort, Frank, Becky Conekin and Chris Waters. *Moments of Modernity: Reconstructing Britain: 1945–1964*. New York: Rivers Oram, 1999.

Morton, James. *Gangland Soho*. London: Piatkus, 2008.

Mosley, Leonard. 'This Week's New Films: Whether You're Still Wet behind the Ears or Well-Aware Like Me You'll Go Bundle on This Kind of Bongo!' *Daily Express*, 27 November 1959, 10–11.

Moss, Norman. 'London's "Foreign Quarter" Plans a Week of Special Festivity'. *New York Times*, 15 May 1955.

Mundy, John. *The British Musical Film*. Manchester: Manchester University Press, 2007.

'Murder at the Windmill'. *The Stage*, 25 November 1948, 3.

'Murder at the Windmill'. *Monthly Film Bulletin* 16(181) (1949): 115.

Murphy, Robert. *Realism and Tinsel: Cinema and Society in Britain 1939–48*. London: Routledge, 1992.

———. *Sixties British Cinema*. London: British Film Institute, 1992.

———. *Smash and Grab: Gangsters in the London Underworld 1920–1960*. London: Faber & Faber, 1993.
———. *British Cinema and the Second World War*. London: Continuum, 2000.
———. 'Dark Shadows around Pinewood and Ealing'. *Film International* 7 (2004): 28–35.
Myers, Harold. 'Wardour St. Back When'. *Variety* 20 January 1988, 126.
Myro. 'Film Review: *Noose*'. *Variety*, 6 October 1948, 11.
Napper, Lawrence. *British Cinema and Middlebrow Culture in the Interwar Years*. Exeter: University of Exeter Press, 2009.
Naughton, Bill. 'Meet the Spiv'. *News Chronicle*, 13 September 1945, 2.
Nava, Mica. *Visceral Cosmopolitanism: Gender, Culture and the Normalisation of Difference*. Oxford: Berg, 2007.
Nead, Lynda. *The Tiger in the Smoke: Art and Culture in Post-War Britain*. New Haven: Yale University Press, 2017.
Nead, Lynda, and Frank Mort. 'Introduction'. *Sexual Geographies: A Journal of/culture/theory/politics. New Formations* 37 (1999): 1–6.
Neale, Stephen, and Murray Smith. *Contemporary Hollywood Cinema*. London: Routledge, 1998.
'New Film for Jess'. *Disc*, 21 January 1961, 1.
Newley, Patrick. 'Obituaries: Daniel Farson'. *The Stage*, 11 December 1997, 32.
News on Screen, 'Look at Life'. Retrieved 28 October 2021 from http://bufvc.ac.uk/newsonscreen/search/index.php/series/147.
Newton, Francis. 'Any Chick Can Do It'. *New Statesman*, 6 January 1961, 486.
Nicholls, James. *The Politics of Alcohol: A History of the Drink Question in England*. Manchester: Manchester University Press, 2009.
'Noose'. *Monthly Film Bulletin* 15(169) (1 January 1948): 125.
Obscene Publications Act, 1959. 7 & 8 Eliz. 2, Ch. 66. London: Her Majesty's Stationary Office, 1959.
Ogidi, Ann. 'Black British Film'. *BFI Screenonline*. Retrieved 28 October 2021 from http://www.screenonline.org.uk/film/id/1144245/index.html.
Ostrer, Nigel. *The Ostrers & Gaumont British*. Self-Published by Author. United Kingdom: Nigel Ostrer, 2010.
O'Rourke, Chris. 'Soho's Silent Cinemas'. *Soho Clarion*, 17 February 2016.
Oulahan, Richard. 'All-Purpose Cockney'. *LIFE Magazine*, 29 November 1963, 58.
Our Dramatic Critic. 'All My Sons'. *Musical Express*, 25 June 1948, 4.
Our Labour Correspondent. 'Better to Ignore the Spiv?' *Manchester Guardian*, 11 August 1947, 3.
Our London Correspondent. 'Coffee Comes to Town'. *Manchester Guardian*, 6 April 1956, 13.
Our Own Reporter. 'Street Offences Act: A Success So Far'. *The Guardian*, 28 July 1960, 1.
———. 'Attack on 'Sleazier Soho Joints': Inquiry into Law Promised'. *The Guardian*, 29 May 1963, 2.

———. '"Crisis in Confidence" in Film Industry'. *The Guardian*, 10 December 1963, 3.
Padva, Gilad, and Nurit Buchweitz (eds). *Sensational Pleasures in Cinema, Literature and Visual Culture: The Phallic Eye*. Basingstoke: Palgrave Macmillan, 2014.
Palmer, Tim. 'Soho: On the Front Line of London Gentrification, But Would You Live There?' *The Times*, 21 May 2017. Retrieved 28 October 2021 fromhttps://www.thetimes.co.uk/article/soho-property-market-london-gentrification-vttd3d66v.
Partington, Matthew. 'The London Coffee Bar of the 1950s: Teenage Occupation of an Amateur Space?', in *Occupation: Negotiations with Constructed Space* (Interior Architecture Conference), University of Brighton, Grand Parade, Brighton, 2–3 July 2009. Document courtesy of Partington.
Pelling, Henry. *Britain and the Marshall Plan*. Basingstoke: Palgrave Macmillan, 1988.
Pelling, Rowan. 'The Battle of Soho: Meet the Maverick Fighting to Save London's Anarchic Underbelly'. *Daily Telegraph*, 26 October 2017. Retrieved 28 October 2021 from https://www.telegraph.co.uk/films/0/battle-soho-meet-mavericks-fighting-save-londons-anarchic-underbelly.
Penz, François. 'The Architectural Promenade as Narrative Device: Practice-Based Research in Architecture and the Moving Image'. *Digital Creativity* 15(1) (2004): 39–51.
———. 'Towards an Urban Narrative Layers Approach to Decipher the Language of City Films'. *CLCWeb: Comparative Literature and Culture* 14(3) (2012). DOI: https://doi.org/10.7771/1481-4374.2041.
Penz, François, and Andong Lu (eds). *Urban Cinematics: Understanding Urban Phenomena through the Moving Image*. Bristol: Intellect Books, 2011.
Penz, François, Maureen Thomas and Symposium on Cinema Architecture. *Cinema & Architecture, Méliès, Mallet-Stevens, Multimedia*. London: BFI Publishing, 1997.
Petrie, Duncan James. 'Bryanston Films: An Experiment in Cooperative Independent Production and Distribution'. *Historical Journal of Film, Radio and Television* 38(1) (2017): 95–115.
Phelps, Guy. 'Censorship and the Press'. *Sight and Sound* 42(3) (1973): 138.
'Pictures: "World of Sammy Lee Gets Legion's C-Rate"'. *Variety*, 4 September 1963, 7.
Pim, Keiron. *Jumpin' Jack Flash: David Litvinoff and the Rock 'n' Roll Underworld*. London: Jonathan Cape, 2016.
Porter, Michael. E. *The Competitive Advantage of Nations*. New York: Free Press, 1990.
———. 'Clusters and the New Economics of Competition'. *Harvard Business Review* (November–December 1998): 77–90.
Porter, Roy. *London: A Social History*. Cambridge, MA: Harvard University Press, 1994.
Porter, Vincent. 'Strangers on the Shore: The Contributions of French Novelists and Directors to British Cinema, 1946–1960'. *Framework: The Journal of Cinema and Media* 43(1) (2002): 105–26.
Pratt, Andy C., and Paul Jeffcutt (eds). *Creativity, Innovation and the Cultural Economy*. New York: Routledge, 2009.

Pratt, Vic. 'Beat Girl: Dig That, Daddy-o!' *Beat Girl*, BFI Flipside DVD Booklet. London: BFI, 2016: 3–6.
——. 'Beauty in Brief (Pin-Up Productions, 1955)'. *Beat Girl*, BFI Flipside DVD. London: BFI, 2016: 16.
——. 'Goodnight with Sabrina'. *Beat Girl*, BFI Flipside Booklet. London: BFI, 2016: 16–17.
——. 'The Small World of Sammy Lee: Anthony Newley and a Long-Gone Soho'. *British Film Institute*, 12 October 2016. Retrieved 28 October 2021 from http://www.bfi.org.uk/news-opinion/news-bfi/features/small-world-sammy-lee-anthony-newley-soho.
'Pre-production: Calleia Gets "Noose"'. *Variety*, 28 January 1948. 9.
Pressburger, Emeric. 'Miracle in Soho Script. EP's Original Hand-Written Notes in Pencil'. 1937. EPR/1/37/3. BFI National Archive, London.
——. *Miracle in Soho* final script, 28 November 1956. Annotated. Emeric Pressburger BFI National Archive, London.
——. *Miracle in Soho* script revisions, 10 January 1957. BFI National Archive, London.
——. *Miracle in Soho* post-production script. Domestic version, 27 June 1957. J. Arthur Rank Productions Ltd. Donated by BAFTA. BFI National Archive, London.
——. Handwritten Treatment of *Miracle in Soho*. Special permission from the Michael Powell Estate, n.d. London: BFI National Archive.
——. *Miracle in St. Anthony's Lane*. An original story by Emeric Pressburger. Script written by Emeric Pressburger in collaboration with Michael Powell. With special permission by the Michael Powell Estate, n.d.
——. *Miracle in Soho* Breakdown Script. Production no. R.O.F.P. 307. n.d. Emeric Pressburger Collection. BFI National Archive, London.
Priestman, Martin (ed.). *The Cambridge Companion to Crime Fiction*. Cambridge: Cambridge University Press, 2003.
Proust, Marcel. *Les Plaisirs et les Jours*. Paris: Calmann Lévy, 1896.
Pryors, Thomas M. 'Film Studios Get British Warning: U.S. Movies Accenting Crime, Passion and Violence Face Distribution Ban'. *New York Times*, 29 April 1955, 28.
Psarra, Sophia. *Architecture and Narrative: The Formation of Space and Cultural Meaning*. London: Routledge, 2009.
Pudney, John. 'The Coffee-House Graze Returns to England'. *New York Times*, 8 April 1956, 27.
Pulver, Andrew. 'The Great Lost London Beat Thriller: Why to Watch *The Small World of Sammy Lee*'. *The Guardian*, 8 November 2016. Retrieved 28 October 2021 from https://www.theguardian.com/film/2016/nov/08/the-great-lost-london-beat-thriller-why-to-watch-the-small-world-of-sammy-lee.
Pulleine, Tim. 'Spin a Dark Web', in Steve Chibnall and Robert Murphy (eds), *British Crime Cinema*. London: Routledge, 1999, 27–36.
'Pussycat Alley'. *Boxoffice*, 7 February 1966, a11.
Quart, Leonard. 'The Religion of the Market: Thatcherite Politics and the British Film of

the 1980s', in Lester Friedman (ed.), *Fires Were Started: British Cinema and Thatcherism*. London: Wallflower Press, 2006, 16–29.
Quigly, Isabel. 'Review: The Shakedown'. *The Spectator*, 22 January 1960, 112.
——. 'Two Daughters. (Academy Late-Night Show; "U" Certificate), *The Small World of Sammy Lee* (Columbia; "X" Certificate)'. *The Spectator*, 3 May 1963, 56.
'Rag Doll'. *Monthly Film Bulletin* 28(324) (1961): 67.
Ransome, Arthur. *Bohemia in London*. New York: Dodd, Mead & Company, 1907.
Raphael, Frederic. *Going up: To Cambridge and Beyond, a Writer's Memoir*. London: Robson Press, 2015.
Rasmussen, Steen Eiler. *London: The Unique City*. Cambridge, MA: MIT Press, 1982.
Ray, Cyril. 'Pre-Wolfenden'. *The Spectator*, 27 September 1957, 389.
R.B.M. 'Week in the Theatre: Lunchtime with Sammy at the New Arts'. *The Stage and Television Today*, 3 November 1966, 13.
Readers Report. 'Beat Girl', 1 April 1959. British Board of Film Classification Archive, London.
Reel Streets. 'Expresso Bongo', 'The Small World of Sammy Lee'. Accessed 10 March 2017. https://www.reelstreets.com/films/small-world-of-sammy-lee-the/.
Reid Burnett, T. 'Make Soho Fair a Great International Festival!' *The Stage*, 29 May 1958, 13.
Rendell, Jane, 'The Clubs of St. James's: Places of Public Patriarchy – Exclusivity, Domesticity and Secrecy'. *Journal of Architecture* 4(2) (1999): 167–89.
——. '"Bazaar Beauties", or "Pleasure Is Our Pursuit": A Spatial Story of Exchange', in Iain Borden, Joe Kerr, Jane Rendall and Alicia Pivaro (eds), *The Unknown City: Contesting Architecture and Social Space*. Cambridge, MA: MIT Press, 2000, 104–21.
——. 'Architecture-Writing'. *Journal of Architecture* 10(3) (2005): 255–64.
'Review: Beat Girl'. *Monthly Film Bulletin* 27(322) (1960): 154.
Rhode, Eric. 'A Kind of Loving'. *Sight and Sound* 31(3) (1962): 143.
Rich, Paul. B. *Cinema and Unconventional Warfare in the Twentieth Century: Insurgency, Terrorism and Special Operations*. London: Bloomsbury, 2018.
Rich. 'Pictures: *The Flesh Is Weak*'. *Variety*, 14 August 1957, 20.
——. 'Film Reviews: *The Golden Disk*'. *Variety*, 12 March 1958, 5.
——. 'Film Review: *Expresso Bongo*'. *Variety*, 2 December 1959, 6.
——. 'Film Review: *West End Jungle*'. *Variety*, 11 November 1961, 6.
——. 'Film Reviews: 'Beat' Girl'. *Variety*, 16 November 1960, 6.
——. 'Film Reviews: *The World 10 Times Over*'. *Variety*, 13 November, 1963, 6.
Richards, Dick. 'Vaudeville: Soho's Shoddy Stripperies'. *Variety*, 4 January 1961, 256.
Richards, Jeffrey (ed.). *The Unknown 1930s: An Alternative History of British Cinema, 1929–1939*. London: I.B. Tauris, 2000.
Richardson, Maurice. 'The Crime Ration'. *The Observer*, 13 April 1941.
Richardson, Nigel. *Dog Days in Soho: One Man's Adventures in 1950s Bohemia*. London: Phoenix, 2000.

Roberts, Andrew. 'Laurence Harvey: A Dandy in Aspic'. *Sight and Sound* 16(4) (2006): 36–39.
——. 'Expresso Bongo DVD Booklet'. London: BFI, 2016.
Robertson, James. C. *Hidden Cinema: British Film Censorship in Action 1913–1975*. New York: Routledge, 1993.
Robinson, David. 'United Kingdom' in Alan Lovell (ed.), *Art of the Cinema in Ten European Countries*. Strasbourg: Council for Cultural Co-operation of the Council of Europe, 1967.
Rolph, C.H., and British Social Biology Council (eds). *Women of the Streets: A Sociological Study of the Common Prostitute*. London: Secker & Warburg, 1955.
Romney, Jonathan. 'The Battle to Save the Curzon Soho'. *The Guardian*, 17 April 2016. Retrieved 28 October 2021 from https://www.theguardian.com/film/2016/apr/17/fight-to-save-curzon-soho-cinema-landmark-london.
Roodhouse, Mark. *Black Market Britain:1939–1955*. Oxford: Oxford University Press, 2013.
——. 'In Racket Town: Gangster Chic in Austerity Britain, 1939–1953'. *Historical Journal of Film, Radio and Television* 31(4) (2011): 523–41.
Ross, Ellen. 'Missionaries and Jews in Soho: "Strangers within Our Gates"'. *Journal of Victorian Culture* 15(2) (2010): 226–38.
Rosselli, John. 'Space-Time and Sine Curves in the Coffee House'. *The Guardian*, 29 December 1959, 5.
Rufford, Juliet. *Theatre & Architecture*. London: Palgrave Macmillan, 2015.
Rubin, Joel. 'Klezmer Music: A Historical Overview to the Present', in Joshua S. Walden (ed.), *The Cambridge Companion to Jewish Music*. Cambridge: Cambridge University Press, 2015, 119–42.
Rubinstein, W.D., Michael, Jolles and Hilary L. Rubinstein (eds). *The Palgrave Dictionary of Anglo-Jewish History*. Basingstoke: Palgrave Macmillan, 2011.
Sandbrook, Dominic. *Never Had It So Good: A History of Britain from Suez to The Beatles*. London: Abacus, 2005.
Sanders-Mcdonagh, Erin, Magali Peyrefitte and Matt Ryalls. 'Sanitising the City: Exploring Hegemonic Gentrification in London's Soho'. *Sociological Research Online* 21(3) (2016): 1–6.
Sandher, Hardeep. 'Kings of Soho: James and Norris's Soho Transformation'. *Property Week*, 22 June 2012, 30.
'The Saville'. *The Stage*, 17 April 1947. 1.
Schaefer, Eric, and American Council of Learned Societies. 'The Obscene Seen: Spectacle and Transgression in Postwar Burlesque Films'. *Cinema Journal* 36(2) (1997): 41–66.
——. *Bold! Daring! Shocking! True! A History of Exploitation Films, 1919–1959*. Durham, NC: Duke University Press, 1999.
Schleier, Merrill. 'The Griffith Observatory in Ray's *Rebel Without a Cause* (1955): Mystical Temple and Scientific Monument'. *Journal of Architecture* 16(3) (2011): 365–85.

——. *Skyscraper Cinema: Architecture and Gender in American Film*. Minneapolis: University of Minnesota Press, 2009.
Selwood, Jacob. *Diversity and Difference in Early Modern London*. Farnham: Ashgate, 2010.
Sennett, Richard (ed.). *Classic Essays on the Culture of Cities*. Englewood Cliffs, NJ: Prentice Hall, 1969.
——. *Flesh and Stone: The Body and the City in Western Civilization*. New York: W.W. Norton, 1994.
'Sensational? No – Just Realistic'. *Picturegoer*, 1 February 1958, 8.
'Shadow Man'. *American Film Institute Catalogue*. Retrieved 1 January 2017 from https://catalog.afi.com/Catalog/moviedetails/51020.
'Shadow Man'. *Boxoffice*, 12 December 1953, a11, a12.
Shail, Robert. *British Film Directors: A Critical Guide*. Edinburgh: University of Edinburgh Press, 2007.
'The Shakedown'. Letter from John Croydon to R.E.F. Garrett. Film Finances, 22 August 1959.
'The Shakedown, Pictures: Hollywood Production Pulse'. *Variety*, 7 October 1959, 22.
'The Shakedown'. *Monthly Film Bulletin* 27(312) (1960): 26.
Shapiro, Jill. 'There Was Something Special about the Windmill Girls'. *Daily Telegraph*, 15 March 2016. Retrieved 28 October 2021 from http://www.telegraph.co.uk/women/life/jill-shapiro-there-was-something-special-about-the-windmill-girl.html.
Sharf, Zach. 'Edgar Wright Horror Film'. *Indiewire*, 21 February 2019. Retrieved 28 October 2021 from https://www.indiewire.com/2019/02/edgar-wright-last-night-in-soho-cast-thomasin-mckenzie-matt-smith-1202045774.
Shearer, Martha. *New York City and the Hollywood Musical: Dancing in the Streets*. Basingstoke: Palgrave Macmillan, 2016.
Sheridan, Simon. 'The Flesh Is Weak'. Sleeve notes, Odeon Entertainment DVD, 2009.
Sheridan, Simon, and Stanley Long. *X-Rated: Adventures of an Exploitation Filmmaker*. London: Reynolds & Hearn, 2008.
Shiel, Mark. 'Cityscapes and Cinematic Spaces', in Peter Bondanella (ed.), *The Italian Cinema Book*. London: BFI, 2014, 84–91.
——. *Italian Neorealism: Rebuilding the Cinematic City*. London: Wallflower Press, 2006.
Shiel, Mark, and Tony Fitzmaurice. *Screening the City*. London: Verso, 2003.
——. *Cinema and the City Film and Urban Societies in a Global Context*. Chichester: John Wiley & Sons, 2008.
Shonfield, Katherine. 'Glossing with Graininess: Cross Occupations in Postwar British Film and Architecture'. *Journal of Architecture* 3(4) (1998): 355–75.
——. *Walls Have Feelings: Architecture, Film and the City*. London: Routledge, 2000.
Shteir, Rachel. *Striptease: The Untold History of the Girlie Show*. New York: Oxford University Press, 2004.
'The Silk Noose'. *Boxoffice*, 9 December 1950.

Simmel, Georg, 'The Metropolis and Mental Life', in *The Sociology of Georg Simmel*, edited and translated by K.H. Wolff. New York: Free Press, 1950, 409–24.
Sims, George R. 'Trips about Town'. *Strand Magazine: An Illustrated Monthly* 29 (1905): 273–80.
Sinclair, Iain. 'The Last London'. *London Review of Books*. Vol.39. No.7. March 30, 2017. 7–11.
Sinai, Anne. *Reach for the Top: The Turbulent Life of Laurence Harvey*. Lanham, MD/Oxford: Scarecrow Press/Oxford Publicity Partnership, 2003.
Slater, Stefan Anthony. 'Pimps, Police and Filles de Joie: Foreign Prostitution in Interwar London'. *London Journal* 32(1) (2007): 53–74.
——. 'Containment: Managing Street Prostitution in London, 1918–1959'. *Journal of British Studies* 49 (2010): 332–57.
Slide, Anthony. *A Special Relationship: Britain Comes to Hollywood and Hollywood Comes to Britain*. Mississippi: University Press of Mississippi, 2015.
Slobin, Mark. *Fiddler on the Move: Exploring the Klezmer World*. Oxford: Oxford University Press, 2003.
'The Small World of Sammy Lee: In Review: Alcoa Theatre'. *Broadcasting*, 24 November 1958, 15.
'The Small World of Sammy Lee'. *Monthly Film Bulletin* 30(348) (1 January 1963): 348.
'The Small World of Sammy Lee'. *Boxoffice* 83, 26 August 1963, a23, a24.
Smith, Earl. 'Louis Wirth and the Chicago School of Urban Sociology: An Assessment and Critique'. *Humanity and Society* 9 (1985): 1–12.
Smurthwaite, Nick. 'One Man and His Wobbly Dog', *The Guardian*, 20 April 2001. Retrieved 28 October 2021 from https://www.theguardian.com/film/2001/apr/20/culture.features2.
Soanes, Catherine, Angus Stevenson, Judy Pearsall and Patrick Hanks. *Oxford Dictionary of English*. Oxford: Oxford University Press, 2005.
'Soho Incident'. *Monthly Film Bulletin* 23(264) (1956): 49.
'Soho Stories: Celebrating Six Decades of Sex, Drugs and Rock 'N' Roll'. *The Observer*, 17 May 2015. Retrieved 28 October 2021 from http://www.theguardian.com/culture/2015/may/17/london-soho-stories-sex-drugs-rock-and-roll.html.
'Sohonet'. Retrieved 28 October 2021 from http://www.sohonet.com.
'So Long, Soho: Inner-City Gentrification'. *The Economist* (8919) (2015): 43.
'Soursweet'. *Variety*, 31 December 1988. Retrieved 28 October 2021 from https://variety.com/1988/film/reviews/soursweet-1200427837.
Spicer, Andrew. *Typical Men: The Representations of Masculinity in Popular British Culture*. London: I.B. Tauris, 2001.
——. 'Creativity and the "B" Feature: Terence Fisher's Crime Films'. *Film Criticism* 30(2) (2005): 24–42.
——. *Historical Dictionary of Film Noir*. Lanham, MD: Scarecrow Press, 2010.
——. 'A British Empire of Their Own? Jewish Entrepreneurs in the British Film Industry'. *Journal of European Popular Culture* 3(2) (2012): 117–29.

———. 'On Émigrés and British Cinema'. *Jewish Film & New Media* 1(1) (2013): 100–7.
Spicer, Andrew, and A.T. McKenna. *The Man Who Got Carter: Michael Klinger, Production and the British Film Industry 1960–1980*. London: I.B. Tauris, 2013.
'Spin a Dark Web'. *UCLA Library Catalogue*. *Film & Television Archive*. Retrieved 28 October 2021 from http://cinema.library.ucla.edu/vwebv/holdingsInfo?bibId=174139.
Speiser, Peter. *Soho: The Heart of Bohemian London*. London: British Library Publishing, 2017.
Springhall, John. 'Censoring Hollywood: Youth, Moral Panic and Crime-Gangster Movies of the 1930s'. *Journal of Popular Culture* 32 (1998): 135–54.
S.S. 'The Shakedown'. *Picturegoer*, 30 January 1960, 12.
Staff Reporter. 'A Fair Week's Run for the Real Soho'. *The Observer*, 10 July 1955, 9.
Stanley, Barry. 'Soho Is Not So Bad, Says a "Club-Watcher"'. *Daily Mirror*, 12 April 1961, 6.
Sterritt, David. *Mad to Be Saved: The Beats, the '50s, and Film*. Carbondale: Southern Ilinois University Press, 1998.
Stewart, Jez. 'Bob Godfrey'. *BFI Online*. Retrieved 28 October 2021 from https://www.bfi.org.uk/news/bob-godfrey-1921-2013.
Stoddart, Sarah, and John Williams. 'But These Nudes Are Marked Sexport Only'. *Picturegoer*, 26 September 1959, 8–9.
Stokes, Melvyn. *Gilda*. Basingstoke: Palgrave Macmillan, 2010.
Storey, David. *Flight into Camden*. London: Penguin, 1960.
Storper, Michael. *Keys to the City: How Economics, Institutions, Social Interaction, and Politics Shape Development*. Princeton: Princeton University Press, 2013.
Stranger-Ross, Jordan. *Staying Italian: Urban Change and Ethnic Life in Postwar Toronto and Philadelphia*. Chicago: University of Chicago Press, 2009.
Street, Sarah. *British National Cinema*, 2nd edn. London: Routledge, 2009.
———. *Colour Films in Britain: The Negotiation of Innovation 1900–1955*. London: BFI/Palgrave Macmillan, 2012.
———. 'Film Finances and the British New Wave'. *Historical Journal of Film, Radio and Television* 34(1) (2014): 23–42.
———. 'Colour and the Critics', *The Eastmancolor Revolution and British Cinema, 1955–85 Project Blog*, 22 June 2017. Retrieved 28 October 2021 from https://eastmancolor.info/2017/06/22/colour-and-the-critics.
———. 'The Colour of Social Realism'. *Journal of British Cinema and Television* 15(4) (2018): 469–90.
'Street of Shadows'. *Monthly Film Bulletin* 20(228) (1953): 76.
'Strip Tease Murder'. *Monthly Film Bulletin* 30(348) (1963): 174.
Sullivan, John. London Report. *Boxoffice*, 21 August 1948, 30.
Summers, Judith. *Soho: A History of London's Most Colourful Neighbourhood*. London: Bloomsbury, 1991.
'Sunset over Soho for Clip Joints'. *Variety*, 24 June 1964, 1.
'Sunshine in Soho'. *Monthly Film Bulletin* 23(264) (1956): 110.

Survey of London. *Volumes 33 and 34, St Anne Soho*. London: London County Council, 1966.
Swann, Paul. 'The British Culture Industries and the Mythology of the American Market: Cultural Policy and Cultural Exports in the 1940s and 1990s'. *Cinema Journal* 39(4) (2000): 27–42.
Sweet, Matthew. 'Snakes, Slaves and Seduction'. *The Guardian*, 6 February 2008. Retrieved 28 October 2021 from https://www.theguardian.com/film/2008/feb/06/china.world.
Symanski, Richard. *The Immoral Landscape: Female Prostitution in Western Societies*. Toronto: Butterworths, 1981.
Syms, Sylvia. 'Interview by Jason Solomons'. *BBC Radio London*, 28 April 2016.
Szalai, Jennifer. 'Wolfgang Suschitzky, Photographer and Cinematographer, Dies at 104'. *New York Times*, 8 October 2016. Retrieved 28 October 2021 from https://www.nytimes.com/2016/10/09/arts/international/wolfgang-suschitzky-dead.html.
Tames, Richard. *London: A Cultural History*. Oxford: Oxford University Press, 2006.
Tavernier, Bertrand. 'Odd Man out: Edmond T. Gréville'. *Film Comment* 34(1) (1998): 55–62.
Taylor, Laurie. 'Bohemian Soho'. *BBC Radio Four*, 16 September 2013. Retrieved 28 October 2021 from https://www.bbc.co.uk/programmes/b039q5f7.
'Teenage Tyranny'. *The Stage*, 21 November 1957, 12.
Temple, Julien. 'How We Made Absolute Beginners'. *The Guardian*, 21 September 21, 2015. Retrieved 28 October 2021 from https://www.theguardian.com/culture/2015/sep/21/how-we-made-absolute-beginners-julien-temple-patsy-kensit.
'There Are Many Absurdities at the Soho Fair'. *The Spectator*, 15 July 1955, 85–86.
Thomas, Nicola J., Harriet Hawkins and David C. Harvey. 'The Geographies of the Creative Industries: Scale, Clusters and Connectivity'. *Geography* 95(1) (2010): 14–21.
Thompson, Howard. 'Screen: "The Shakedown"'. *New York Times*, 16 March 1961.
Thorpe, Vanessa. 'How a Soho Coffee House Gave Birth to the New Left'. *The Observer*, 23 April 2017. Retrieved 28 October 2021 from https://www.theguardian.com/politics/2017/apr/22/cafe-cnd-new-left.
'Those Nutty Intellectuals'. *Films and Filming* Magazine (January 1963): 9–10.
Tinkler, Penny. *Constructing Girlhood: Popular Magazines for Girls Growing up in England 1920–1950*. London: Taylor & Francis, 1995.
———. 'Cause for Concern: Young Women and Leisure, 1930–1950'. *Women's History Review* 12(2) (2003): 233–60.
———. '"Are You Really Living?" If Not, "Get with It!"' *Cultural and Social History* 11(4) (2014): 597–619.
Toffell, Gil. *Jews, Cinema and Public Life in Interwar Britain*. London: Palgrave Macmillan, 2018.
'Tommy Steele'. *The Observer*, 21 December 1958.

Tophan, Gwyn. 'Five-Year £500m Redevelopment of King's Cross Station Almost Complete'. *The Guardian*, 14 March 2012. Retrieved 28 October 2021 from https://www.theguardian.com/business/2012/mar/14/five-year-redevelopment-kings-cross-station.

Travlou, Penny. 'Teenagers and Public Space Literature Review'. OPENspace Research Centre, Edinburgh College of Art/Heriot Watt University, July 2003.

Trevelyan, John. 'Letter to Dick Patterson, Esq., Seven Arts Productions', 19 July 1962. Courtesy of the British Board of Film Classification Archives.

——. 'British Film Censorship Today'. *Variety*, 26 April 1961, 93.

Trunk, Johnny, 'John Barry and Beat Girl'. *Beat Girl*, BFI Flipside Booklet. London: BFI, 2016: 8–9.

——. Notes. *The Small World of Sammy Lee*. Original Motion Picture Soundtrack. P&C Trunk Records, 2013.

Turner, Steve. *Cliff Richard: The Biography*. Oxford: Lion, 1993.

Turnock, Rob. *Television and Consumer Culture: Britain and the Transformation of Modernity*. London: I.B. Tauris, 2007.

Unsworth, Cathi. 'Saturday Night at the Movies'. *3am Magazine*, 27 June 2009. Retrieved 28 October 2021 from https://www.3ammagazine.com/3am/saturday-night-at-the-movies-2.

Vallance, Tom. 'Obituary: John Derek'. *The Independent*, 24 May 1998. Retrieved 28 October 2021 from http://www.independent.co.uk/news/obituaries/obituary-john-derek-1157309.html.

——. 'Obituary: Anthony Newley'. *The Independent*, 15 April 1999. Retrieved 28 October 2021 from http://www.independent.co.uk/arts-entertainment/obituary-anthony-newley-1087464.html.

Vallance, T. 'Soundtrack'. *Film: The Magazine of the Federation of Film Societies* 32 (1962).

Vance, Leigh, and John Lemont. 'The Shakedown'. Original Screenplay. Film Finances, n.d.

Vaughan, Dal. 'The Shakedown'. *Films and Filming* (March 1960): 25.

Vernon, Richard. 'Street of Shadows'. Export Script. 1953. BFI Book Library. BFI National Archive, London.

Vincendeau, Ginette. 'French Film Noir', in Andrew Spicer (ed.), *European Film Noir*. Manchester: Manchester University Press, 2007, 23–54.

——. 'Deep Focus: How the French Birthed Film Noir'. *BFI*, 15 November 2016. Retrieved 28 October 2021 from http://www.bfi.org.uk/news-opinion/sight-sound-magazine/features/deep-focus/french-film-noir.

Vitapointe of Paris. 'Just 1-Minute Brushing – and My Hair is Shining! By Belinda Lee'. *Daily Express*, 26 September 1957, 13.

Waligórska, Magdalena. *Klezmer's Afterlife: An Ethnography of the Jewish Music Revival in Poland and Germany*. 2013.

Walker, Derek. 'Belinda Lee Covers up Her Past'. *Picturegoer*, 16 March 1967, 5.

——. 'Lee: A Star by Friendly Persuasion'. *Picturegoer*, 11 May 1957, 13.
——. 'A Star by Friendly Persuasion – Part II: Why She's Not a Blonde Bombshell'. *Picturegoer*, 18 May 1957, 14–15.
Walkowitz, Judith. *Prostitution and Victorian Society Women, Class, and the State*. Cambridge: Cambridge University Press, 1980.
——. 'Cosmopolitanism, Feminism, and the Moving Body'. *Victorian Literature and Culture* 38(2) (2010): 427–49.
——. *Nights out: Life in Cosmopolitan London*. New Haven: Yale University Press, 2012.
'Wardour Street Area: Pulteney Estate', in F.H.W. Sheppard (ed.), *Survey of London: Volumes 33 and 34, St Anne Soho*. London: London County Council, 1966, 288–96.
Warren, Patricia. *British Film Studios: An Illustrated History*. London: Batsford, 2001.
Waterhouse, Keith. *Soho or Alex in Wonderland*. London: Hodder & Stoughton, 2001.
——. *Jeffrey Bernard Is Unwell*. London: Samuel French, 2015.
Watts, Stephens. 'Observations on the London Screen Scene'. *New York Times*, 16 March 1952, 5.
Webb, Lawrence. *The Cinema of Urban Crisis: Seventies Film and the Reinvention of the City*. Amsterdam: Amsterdam University Press, 2014.
Webster, Wendy. *Englishness and Empire 1939–1965*. Oxford: Oxford University Press, 2005.
Weiler, A.H. 'A True Chip off the Old Maltese Block'. *New York Times*, 21 November 1943.
Wells, Paul. 'John Halas and Joy Batchelor'. *BFI Screenonline*. Retrieved 28 October 2021 from http://www.screenonline.org.uk/people/id/581849/index.html.
Review: West End Jungle. *Monthly Film Bulletin* 28(324) (1961): 134.
Review: West End Jungle. *Boxoffice* 82, 11 February 1963: A11.
Westerby, Robert. *Wide Boys Never Work: A Novel*. London: Arthur Barker, 1937.
Westminster Council. 'Review of the Premises Licenses for Madame Jo-Jo's, 8–10 Brewer Street'. Minutes of Licensing Sub-Committee. Westminster Council, 20 November 2014: 24–28.
White, Jerry. *London in the Twentieth Century: A City and Its People*. London: Vintage Books, 2008.
White, Maxine, and Michael Lutwyche. *Clipped: Inside Soho's Clip Joints*. Birmingham: VHC Publishing, 2009.
Whitehand, J.W.R. 'Architecture of Commercial Redevelopment in Post-War Britain'. *Journal of Cultural Geography* 4(2) (1984): 41–55.
Williams, Linda Ruth. 'The Pornographic Subject: Feminism and Censorship in the 1990s', in Sally Ledger, Josephine McDonagh and Jane Spencer (eds), *Political Gender: Texts and Context*. London: Routledge, 2014, 189–203.
Williams, Melanie. *Female Stars of British Cinema: The Women in Question*. Edinburgh: Edinburgh University Press, 2017.
Williams, Melanie, and Melanie Bell. *British Women's Cinema*. Abingdon: Routledge, 2010.

Willetts, Paul. *North Soho 999: A True Story of Gangs & Gun-Crime in 1940s London.* Stockport: Dewi Lewis Publishing, 2007.
——. *The Look of Love: The Life and Times of Paul Raymond, Soho's King of Clubs.* London: Serpent's Tail, 2010.
Wilson, Colin. *Adrift in Soho: Beatniks, Bums and Bohemians.* London: Victor Gollancz Ltd., 1961.
Wilson, Elizabeth. *Only Halfway to Paradise: Women in Postwar Britain: 1945–1968.* London: Tavistock, 1980.
——. *The Sphinx in the City: Urban Life, and the Control of Disorder, and Women.* Berkeley: University of California Press, 1991.
——. *Bohemians: The Glamorous Outcasts.* New York: Tauris Parke Paperbacks, 2003.
Wilton, G.C. *The Story of Soho.* Gloucester: British Publishing, 1925.
Wirth, Louis. 'Urbanism as a Way of Life'. *American Journal of Sociology* 44(1) (1938): 1–24.
Wollen, Peter. *Paris Hollywood: Writings on Film.* London: Verso, 2002.
Wood, Linda. 'Lance Comfort (1908–1966), Reference Guide to British and Irish Film Directors'. *BFI Screenonline.* Retrieved 28 October 2021 from http://www.screenonline.org.uk/people/id/552314/index.html.
'The World Ten Times Over'. *Monthly Film Bulletin* 30(348) (1963): 156.
Wright, Adrian. *A Tanner's Worth of Tune: Rediscovering the Post-War British Musical.* Woodbridge: Boydell Press, 2010.
Xue, Charlie Q.L. *Hong Kong Architecture 1945–2015: From Colonial to Global.* Singapore: Springer Nature, 2016.
Young, Hilary and Todd, Selina. "Baby-Boomers" to "Beanstalkers"'. *Cultural and Social History* 9(3) (2012): 451–67.
Young, Jingan. 'Where the Kids Get Their Kicks, The Soho Coffee Bar in Expresso Bongo and Beat Girl (1960)'. *Soho Clarion Magazine,* Summer 2016, 25.
——. 'Noose: A Soho on Screen Video Essay'. *YouTube,* 5 November 2018. Retrieved 28 October 2021 from https://www.youtube.com/watch?v=zLxXHrZwY3g.
——. 'Interview: Edgar Wright on the Museum of Soho,' Soho Radio Podcast, 24 October 2021, https://podcasts.apple.com/gb/podcast/edgar-wright-on-the-museum-of-soho.
——. 'Soho Striptease Clubs, Exploitation and the British B Film,' *Sight and Sound* 31(9) (November 2021): 48–49.
Zec, Donald. 'A "Bardot" from Britain – Aged 14'. *Daily Mirror,* 11 December 1958, 11.
——. 'Keeping Faith – By Keeping Cool'. *Daily Mirror,* 1 February 1960, 9.
Zweiniger-Bargielowska, Ina. 'Bread Rationing in Britain, July 1946–July 1948'. *Twentieth Century British History* 4(1) (1993): 57–85.
——. *Austerity in Britain: Rationing, Controls, and Consumption, 1939–1955.* Oxford: Oxford University Press, 2000.

Index

Abercrombie, Patrick, 7–8n, 30–31
Abrams, Nathan, 103–4
Absolute Beginners, 6, 175–76
Ackroyd, Peter, 38
Ambler, Dail, 143
Americanisation, 83, 110, 145, 155–56. *See also* Rock 'n' Roll
American GIs, 71, 169
Amyes, Julian, 6, 46–49, 55–57, 69, 125
anti-vice campaigns, 11, 32–33, 83, 88–92, 98
The Archers, 51, 59, 81
Arden, Robert, 72, 81

Baddeley, Hermione, 145, 153
Barry, John, 143–44, 150
Beat Girl, 20, 143–45, 148–51. *See also* Youthquake
Beatniks, 20, 144, 149, 155, 157, 176. *See also Beat Girl*
Bell-Williams, Melanie, 124, 126, 127–28
Bernard, Jeffrey, 171, 196, 204
Black, Gerry, 34
blackmail, 20, 122–25, 132–34, 136–37
Blitz, the, 15, 33, 36, 131, 147, 166, 168, 170
Bohemianism, 1, 5, 6, 7, 11, 15, 25–27, 31–32, 37, 39, 191–92, 196–97, 206. *See also* homosexuality
Booker, Christopher, 58, 70, 194
Bradshaw, Peter, 9, 38
British Columbia Pictures, 16, 26, 72, 81
British Film Industry
  box office strategies, 15, 70, 72, 196
  impresarios, 14, 52
  production offices in Soho, 10, 16–18 (*see also* Wardour Street)
  wartime, 70–71

British Film Studios
  Merton Park, 78–79
  MGM British, 148, 183, 185
  Nettlefold, 81
  Pinewood, 17, 59, 61
  Twentieth Century Fox, 10
  Twickenham, 134
  Walton, 81, 129, 154
  Warner Brothers First National, 77
British New Wave, 111–12, 130, 137, 197, 202–3
Brunsdon, Charlotte, 3, 18, 63, 130–31
Brutalism, 130
Butcher's Film Service, 16

Calleja, Joseph, 72 –73
Carousella, 165
censorship, 71, 78 122, 126–27, 129, 164, 191, 202
Chadder, Viv, 127–29
Chaffey, Don, 6, 90, 123, 126, 130, 133, 198
Chapman, James, 83, 85
Chibnall, Steve, 40, 59, 61, 195
Chinatown, 35–37
churches
  House of St. Barnabas, 77
  St. Anne's Church, 2, 13
  St. Patrick's Catholic Church, 10, 12
clip-joint, 131–33. *See also* nightclubs
Coffee Bars, 10, 15, 20, 27, 38, 41, 102–4, 143, 145–46, 158
  interior design, 149, 154, 157
  roadside cafés, 153, 155
  rock 'n' roll, 41, 107, 147, 150, 156
Comfort, Lance, 6, 145, 152–54, 200
commercial television, 49, 58–59, 61, 65
Commonwealth, 4, 18, 32, 70. *See also* Imperialism

Conrad, Jess, 145, 154–55
consumer culture, 9, 11, 13, 31, 53–54
Corbett, Harry. H., 134
cosmopolitanism
   entrepreneurs, 25
   markets, 20, 26, 28, 34
   migration, 31 (*see also* Jewish Soho)
   pubs, 29, 32, 46, 56, 63, 73, 204
County of London Plan, 30–31, 182. *See also* Abercombie, Sir Patrick
Creative Industries, 10, 17–18 *See also* British Film Industry
crime
   gangsters, 39, 41, 45, 70, 72–73, 81, 92, 128
   Black-Market, 39–41, 116
   Spivs; Wide Boys, 38–40, 70–71
Crisp, Quentin, 39
Cusack, Cyril, 7, 46

Danziger Brothers, the, 81
Dearden, Basil, 38, 83, 122, 123, 125
Derek, John, 21, 123, 126–27
Dillon, Carmen, 49, 59–60
documentary, 19, 21, 30, 68, 89, 96, 98, 112, 164–65, 187, 191, 202, 204–5
Domergue, Faith, 72, 81–82
Donlan, Yolande, 105
Durgnat, Raymond, 64, 111

Eade, John, 32, 43
East End, 34–35. *See also* Jewish Soho
Eastmancolor film stock, 27, 59, 68, 185
editing, 18–20
   montage effect on topography, 11, 18–21
   tracking shot, 12, 18–19
Elizabeth II (queen), 10, 26, 37
Elsaesser, Thomas, 125, 135
Empire, 4, 32, 70. *See also* Commonwealth
erotic performance, 131, 167–68, 174, 183, 189. *See also* striptease
Expresso Bongo, 6, 11, 16, 19, 20, 40, 102–6, 143, 147, 166, 176, 182–83, 191

Faith, Adam, 143, 145, 157, 148, 150, 154
Farrar, David, 143

Farson, Daniel, 29, 31, 42, 164, 191
female sexuality, 124, 127–28, 145, 151, 155, 171, 176, 201
Festival of Britain, 10, 26
Film Finances, 135
Film Noir
   European, 74, 77, 78
   Hollywood, 73, 79–80, 82, 126, 148
Fifties Britain
   post-war re-development, 54, 79
   rationing, 70, 79 180
Fink, Janet, 145, 160
The Flesh Is Weak, 11, 20–21, 41, 90, 92, 98, 122–23, 126–27, 133, 137
Forshaw, Barry, 90
Foster, Julia, 112, 120, 186
Frightened City, The, 126, 135

generational conflict, 5, 147, 149, 150–51, 199, 201
Geraghty, Christine, 38
Give us the Moon, 33
Globalisation, 4, 6, 17, 25, 32–33, 37, 50
   film marketplace, 71–72
   promotion, 192, 195, 197
The Golden Disc, 147
Greater London Plan, 30. *See also* County of London plan
Great Windmill Street, 165, 171. *See also* Windmill Theatre
Gregg, Christina, 145, 152–53, 170
Gregson, John, 29, 46
Gréville, Edmond T. 5–6, 41, 71, 74–78, 143–44, 148–49, 184, 198, 200
Griffith, Kenneth, 145, 153
Grosz, Elizabeth, 132
Guest, Val, 16, 33, 102–3, 105, 147

Habermas, Jurgen, 4
Harding, Gilbert, 191
Harvey, Laurence, 102–3, 104–9, 176
Hill, John, 4, 79, 125, 151
Hills, Gillian, 20, 143–44
homosexuality. *See also* Wolfenden Report
   blackmail, 122–23
   culture, 32, 38

on film, 37, 125
legalization of, 39
Hong Kong, 2, 7–8n
Houlbrook, Matt, 38
Hughes, Ken, 20, 40, 102–3, 111, 114, 181, 198
Hutton, Mike, 167, 168, 182–83
Hyams, Burt, 26–28, 42, 57, 170

Imperialism, spectacle of, 18, 31, 198
Italians in London
　community, 27, 53, 65n
　fascists, 54, 63
　trades, 29, 53, 57, 146 (see also Coffee Bars)

Jewish Soho
　migration, 34–5
　trades, 34–35 (see also Regent's Street)
　Yiddish culture, 34, 40, 110, 115

Karlin Miriam, 115–16
Karp, Jonathan, 110
King's Cross St Pancras, 130–31
Kinsey, Alfred, 11
Klinger, Michael, 97, 170, 202–3
Kracauer, Siegfried, 4

Landis, Carole, 74–75, 82
Lee, Belinda, 29, 46, 49, 54, 61
lesbianism, 37, 201. See also homosexuality
Llewellyn, Richard, 74–75
London County Council (LCC), 30, 95, 182, 195
Long, Stanley, 89–92
The Look of Love, 6, 172–76

Madame Jojo's, 172–73, 203–5
Mankowitz, Wolf, 60, 104–7, 109, 182
McFarlane, Brian, 78, 82, 152, 154, 165
McLaren, Angus, 124–25
Mellor, Roger Philip, 151
Members Only Clubs, 10, 33, 77, 96, 154, 171, 173, 181–82. See also Raymond Revuebar, the
Messina Brothers, 92, 128
Miller, Arnold L. 89, 92, 93, 95, 151
Miracle in Soho (Julian Amyes 1957)
Mitchell, Warren, 115–16

Mort, Frank, 2, 7, 22–23, 30, 91, 165, 174
Mrs Henderson Presents, 170, 171, 175
Murphy, Robert, 40, 75, 201
myth making, 29, 36, 71, 175–76

Newley, Anthony, 20, 41, 104, 113–14
New York (city), 2–3, 32, 72, 109
Night and the City, 9, 83, 85, 165
nightclubs. See also Members Only Clubs
　jazz clubs, 10, 15, 41, 73, 195
　Mrs Meyrick's, 131–32
Noose, 74–78
North Soho (Fitzrovia), 17, 51

Old Compton Street, 18–20, 97, 104, 113, 129, 134, 147–48, 170, 196, 199

Passport to Shame, 128
Patterson, Lee, 11, 72, 81–82, 242
Patrick, Nigel, 75, 77
Peacock, Trevor, 143, 150–51
Peeping Tom, 51, 123, 184–85, 201
permissive society, the, 92–93, 116, 136, 175, 199–200
Piccadilly (E.A. Dupont, 1920) 35–36. See also Chinatown
Pigalle (Paris quarter), 32
Ping Pong, 35–36
Pleasence, Donald, 123, 134, 141n
pop music, 102, 104–5
popular press, the, 11, 29, 39, 88, 90, 92, 104
pornography, 93, 136–37, 171, 195
Powell, Michael, 51, 59, 62–65, 81, 123, 184
Pressburger, Emeric, 46, 49, 50–52, 62–65
Primitive London, 97
Profumo affair, the, 37, 194, 195
propaganda, wartime, 166–67
prostitution. See also Street Offences Act (1959)
　grooming, 90, 122, 128, 132
　legislation, 88, 91
Proust, Marcel, 207
Pulleine, Tim, 76

queer London, 32, 38–39, 196–97, 205. See also Homosexuality

Rag Doll, 5–6, 11, 20, 41, 143, 145, 147, 152–58
Rank, J. Arthur, 14, 22, 40, 46, 52, 59, 61, 65, 70
Raymond, Paul, 6, 165–66, 168, 171–79, 182–83, 187–88, 192, 196, 200, 203
Regent's Street, ix, 2, 9, 31, 35, 143
Renown Pictures, 16, 76, 148
Richard, Cliff, 102, 106, 147, 154
Rilla, Wolf, 38, 126, 135, 165, 199, 200–2
Ritchie, June, 199, 201
Romero, Cesar, 72–73, 78, 82–83
Roodhouse, Mark, 39, 45, 71

Sandbrook, Dominic, 145–46
Save Soho campaign, 36, 174, 204
Scourge of Soho, 134
Secrets of a Windmill Girl, 170, 202
Sewell, Vernon, 6, 9, 12, 71, 81, 127, 176, 200
sexploitation cinema, 91–93, 170, 199, 202, 208
The Shakedown, 6, 12, 122–23, 134–37, 170, 198
Shonfield, Katherine, 130, 149
shooting in studio, preference of, 5, 11, 49, 59–61, 63, 71
Simmel, Georg, 4
The Small World of Sammy Lee, 6, 11, 19, 20, 41, 102, 104, 111–13, 165–66, 181, 186–90, 198
Social Problem Film, 125–26, 158
Soho
 boundaries, 2, 9–10, 13 –14
 commercial sex, 11, 89–92, 98
 creative industries, 10, 15–16
 cultural and ethnic diversity, 2, 31, 33–36 (*see also* cosmopolitanism)
 post-war re-development, 10–11, 18, 30, 147, 198, 205–6
Soho Conspiracy, 33
Soho Fair, 9–13, 25–30
Soho Incident, 6, 9, 11–12, 16, 19, 71–2, 81–83, 154, 200
Soho Striptease Clubs, 164–65, 183, 187, 191 (*see also* strip clubs)
Soursweet, 35, 36
Spicer, Andrew, 40, 103, 114
Spiv cycle, 39, 76–77, 83 (*see also* Wide Boys)
Steele, Tommy, 104, 117–18, 147, 154

Street Offences Act 1959, 5–6, 88, 89, 90–91, 94, 98, 99, 123, 134, 198
Street of Shadows, 6, 11, 14, 21, 71–73, 78–80, 83
strip clubs, 163–72, 182–83
 entrepreneurs, 164, 182–83, 188, 190 (*see also* Paul Raymond)
striptease
 choreography, 166, 182, 185, 189–90
Summers, Judith, 2, 34, 114, 156
Sunshine in Soho, 26–28, 57, 170
Swinging London, 194–95, 207
Syms, Sylvia, 38, 105, 125, 183, 199

Tenser, Tony, 97, 170, 202–3
Tinkler, Penny, 145, 156–57
Too Hot to Handle, 6, 166, 181, 184–86
Tourism, 2, 21, 27, 32, 35, 58, 129–30, 159, 164, 195
Trevelyan, John, 100
2i's Coffee Bar, 104, 117n, 147
Tzelniker, Meier, 40, 109–10

Van Damm, Vivian, 167, 170
Vance, Leigh, 123–24, 138n, 141n
Victim, 38, 122–23, 125, 185
victimisation, representation of, 74, 122–24, 126, 128, 130
Vincendeau, Ginette, 74, 77, 78, 82
Vitale, Milly, 21, 123, 126–27

Walker's Court, 171–74, 183
Walkowitz, Judith, 1–2, 23, 34, 53–54, 72, 131–32, 164, 166, 168, 171
Wardour Street, 13–16
Westminster Council, 3, 36, 203–6
West End, 2–4, 9–13, 30–32, 35–37, 54, 91, 153–54, 167–69, 195
West End Jungle, 19, 21, 88, 89, 91–101, 127, 137, 151, 170, 198, 200
Wide Boys, 39–41, 45n, 72, 81, 102, 104–6, 127, 176 (*see also* Spiv)
Windmill Theatre
 on film, 16, 165–66
 during wartime, 164, 165–69

Wolfenden Report, 11, 38, 88–91, 96–98, 122–25, 127–28, 198. *See also* Street Offences Act (1959)
Wong, Anna May, 76
World War II
　cinema-going, 70–71
　rationing, 54, 70, 79, 108

The World Ten Times Over, 19, 38, 135, 165, 194–95, 199, 201–3

Yates, Kevin-Gough, 40, 51, 63, 103, 121
Young, Terence, 6, 123, 147–48, 166, 181, 185, 198, 202
Youthquake, 5, 145–46, 155

www.ingramcontent.com/pod-product-compliance
Ingram Content Group UK Ltd.
Pitfield, Milton Keynes, MK11 3LW, UK
UKHW021920060225
454771UK00026B/687